한국 인권문제

유엔 반응 및 동향 2

한국 인권문제

유엔 반응 및 동향 2

한국학술정보

| 머리말

일제 강점기 독립운동과 병행되었던 한국의 인권운동은 해방이 되었음에도 큰 결실을 보지 못했다. 1950년대 반공을 앞세운 이승만 정부와 한국전쟁, 역시 경제발전과 반공을 내세우다 유신 체제에 이르렀던 박정희 정권, 쿠데타로 집권한 1980년대 전두환 정권까지, 한국의 인권은 이를 보장해야 할 국가와 정부에 의해 도리어 억압받고 침해되었다. 이런 배경상 근대 한국의 인권운동은 반독재, 민주화운동과 결을 같이했고, 대체로 국외에 본부를 둔 인권 단체나 정치로부터 상대적으로 자유로운 종교 단체에 의해 주도되곤 했다. 이는 1980년 5·18광주민주화운동을 계기로 보다 근적인 변혁을 요구하는 형태로 조직화되었고, 그 활동 영역도 정치를 넘어 노동자, 농민, 빈민 등으로 확대되었다. 이들이 없었다면 한국은 1987년 군부 독재 종식하고 절차적 민주주의를 도입할 수 없었을 것이다. 민주화 이후에도 수많은 어려움이 있었지만, 한국의 인권운동은 점차 전문적이고 독립된 운동으로 분화되며 더 많은 이들의 참여를 이끌어냈고, 지금까지 많은 결실을 맺을 수 있었다.

본 총서는 1980년대 중반부터 1990년대 초반까지, 외교부에서 작성하여 30여 년간 유지했던 한국 인권문제와 관련한 국내외 자료를 담고 있다. 6월 항쟁이 일어나고 민주화 선언이 이뤄지는 등 한국 인권운동에 많은 변화가 있었던 시기다. 당시 인권문제와 관련한 국내외 사안들, 각종 사건에 대한 미국과 우방국, 유엔의 반응, 최초의 한국 인권보고서 제출과 아동의 권리에 관한 협약 과정, 유엔인권위원회 활동, 기타 민주화 관련 자료 등 총 18권으로 구성되었다. 전체 분량은 약 9천여 쪽에 이른다.

2024년 3월

한국학술정보(주)

일러두기

· 본 총서에 실린 자료는 2022년 4월과 2023년 4월에 각각 공개한 외교문서 4,827권, 76만 여 쪽 가운데 일부를 발췌한 것이다.

· 각 권의 제목과 순서는 공개된 원본을 최대한 반영하였으나, 주제에 따라 일부는 적절히 변경하였다.

· 원본 자료는 A4 판형에 맞게 축소하거나 원본 비율을 유지한 채 A4 페이지 안에 삽입 하였다. 또한 현재 시점에선 공개되지 않아 '공란'이란 표기만 있는 페이지 역시 그대로 실었다.

· 외교부가 공개한 문서 각 권의 첫 페이지에는 '정리 보존 문서 목록'이란 이름으로 기록물 종류, 일자, 명칭, 간단한 내용 등의 정보가 수록되어 있으며, 이를 기준으로 0001번부터 번호가 매겨져 있다. 이는 삭제하지 않고 총서에 그대로 수록하였다.

· 보고서 내용에 관한 더 자세한 정보가 필요하다면, 외교부가 온라인상에 제공하는 『대한 민국 외교사료요약집』 1991년과 1992년 자료를 참조할 수 있다.

| 차례

정 리 보 존 문 서 목 록

기록물종류	일반공문서철	등록번호	2020020016	등록일자	2020-02-04
분류번호	734.21	국가코드		보존기간	영구
명 칭	유엔 인권사무국 접수 한국관련 진정서, 1991				
생 산 과	국제연합과	생산년도	1991~1991	담당그룹	
내용목차					

0001

주 제 네 바 대 표 부

제네(정) 2031-3   1991. 1. 4

수신 : 장관

참조 : 국제기구조약국장

제목 : 유엔인권 사무국 접수 아국관련 진정서 (90-1)

대 : 국연 2031-518(90. 4.17)

1. 당지 유엔인권 사무국은 90. 12.14자 당관앞 공한을 통해 임수경 사건과 관련,
    미국소재 NGO인 Committee for International Human Rights Inguiry 명의
    진정서가 1503 절차에 의거, 접수되었음을 알려온바, 이를 별첨 송부합니다.

2. 상기 진정 내용은 90. 8월 제 42차 인권소위 진정서 실무위원회에서 이미
    기각된 사항이므로 현재로서는 추가 답변자료를 제출할 필요는 없으며, 다만
    동건과 관련된 대호 자료를 인권사무국에 이미 제출한바 있다는 내용의 당관명의
    공한을 91. 2월말경 제출하는 것으로 대처하는 것이 바람직할 것으로 사료
    되는바, 별도 지침 있으면 회시하여 주시기 바랍니다.

첨부 : 동 진정서 1부. 끝.

검토 필(1991. 6. 30.)

일반문서로재분류(1991. 12. 31.)

예고 : 91. 12. 31. 일반

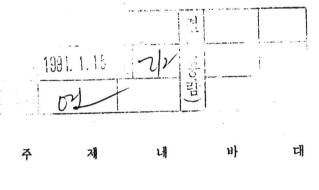

주   제   네   바   대

0002

OFFICE DES NATIONS UNIES A GENÈVE

CENTRE POUR LES DROITS DE L'HOMME

Téléfax: (022) 733 98 79
Télégrammes: UNATIONS, GENÈVE
Télex: 28 96 96
Téléphone: 734 60 11   731 02 11

RÉF. Nº: G/SO 215/1 KOREA REP
(à rappeler dans la reponse)

UNITED NATIONS OFFICE AT GENEVA

CENTRE FOR HUMAN RIGHTS

Palais des Nations
CH-1211 GENÈVE 10

The Secretariat of the United Nations (Centre for Human Rights) presents its compliments to the Office of the Permanent Observer of the Republic of Korea to the United Nations Office at Geneva and with reference to its note No. G/SO 215/1 KOREA REP, dated 7 July 1980, has the honour to transmit herewith copies of one communication dated 3 November 1990, concerning human rights, which refers to the Republic of Korea.

A brief indication of the substance of the communications will be included in a confidential list of communications which is to be submitted to the Commission on Human Rights and the Sub-Commission on Prevention of Discrimination and Protection of Minorities under Economic and Social Council resolutions 728 F (XXVIII) and 1503 (XLVIII).

Any reply which the Permanent Observer may wish to transmit on behalf of its Government under the above-mentioned resolutions should be forwarded to the Centre for Human Rights, United Nations Office at Geneva, with an indication as to whether the reply is to be presented to the Commission and the Sub-Commission in summary form or in full.

14 December 1990

0003

COMMITTEE FOR INTERNATIONAL HUMAN RIGHTS INQUIRY

(Successor to the Committee For Chilean Inquiry)

West Coast Affiliate
204 Avenue B
Redondo Beach, California 90277

East Coast Affiliate
New York City Chapter
National Association of Social Workers
545 8th Avenue (6th Floor)
New York, New York 10018

Reply to:

RUTH WILSON
Secretary
415 Grand Street, Apt. E 1905
New York, New York 10002
(212) 674 - 3762

DAN PILOWSKY
Treasurer

CLYTIE CAUSING
Ass't. Sec'y.
....

SPONSORS:
Mimi Abramowitz
Frederick L. Ahearn
Chauncey A. Alexander
Bernice Augenbraun
Marti Bombyk
Minette Bauer
Carol Brill
Marcus Busch, Canada
Cathy Casriel
Alejandro Duhalde
Stanley Faulkner
Lorraine Foner
Aida Garcia
Gayle Gilchrist James, Canada
Sol Gorelick
Jaime Inclan
Tom Jelfers
Inderjit Jaipaul
Susarn K. Kinoy
Judith Lacerte
Esther M. Lentschner
Harold Lewis
Maryann Mahaffey
Jose Maria
Georgia L. McMurray
Eli C. Messinger
Ruth Messinger
Terry Mizrahi
Marilynn Moch
Marilyn Montenegro
Fred Newdom
Winifred L. Norman
Joan Ohlson
Hank Orenstein
Dan Pilowsky
Arline Prigoff
Bobbie Rabinowitz
Amy & Michael Reisch
Glen Remer-Thamert
Carmen Rohland
Debra W. Rosen
Paulette C. Rothenberg
Mary Russak
Ethel M. Sanjines
Robert Schachter
SEIU, Local 535
Burt Shachter
Nancy Schulz
Ruth & Victor Sidel
T. George Silcott
Beth Silverman
Herbert Sohn
Holbrook Teter
Dorothy Van Soest
Anthony Vera
Ken Walters
Bertram Allan Weinert
Celia B. Weisman

SOL GORELICK
Co-Chair
11-3-90

30/121

PHYLLIS GRUNAUER
Co-Chair

Mr. Javier Perez De Cuellar
Secretary General
The United Nations
New York, NY 10017

Dear Mr. Perez De Cuellar:

On August 15, 1989, Im Su Kyung and Father Moun Kyu Hyun crossed the demarcation line at the DMZ in Panmunjom, Korea as they returned home to their family and friends in the south. This was the first time since 1945 that south Koreans returned home by crossing the DMZ. This peaceful and historic act was countered by the south Korean government's arrest and imprisonment of Ms. Im and Father Moon.

It is the U.N. Command that is stationed in the Demilitarized Zone perpetuating the artificial division of Korea. It is the U.N. that has political and moral responsibility for the suffering and tragedy caused by the division. The present role of the U.N. is in direct contradiction to the wishes of the 70 million Korean people for peace and reunification of their homeland as well as to the principle of world peace.

The south Korean government has accused Ms. Im and Fr. Moon of the "crime" of travelling to the northern part of their own country. Ms. Im participated in the 13th World Youth Festival as a representative of south Korean student organization, Chundachyop. Fr. Moon is a Catholic priest from south Korea who volunteered to accompany Ms. Im on her return.

Now that the two Koreas have taken the courageous step toward peace and reunification of their homeland, the international community must act to support such peaceful initiatives.

At this critical juncture, we call on the U.N. to do everything in its power not to allow any harm to come to Ms. Im and Fr. Moon and to press for their IMMEDIATE RELEASE.

Sincerely,

Ruth H. Wilson, Secy.   Phyllis Grunauer & Sol Gorelick, Co-Chairs

Cooperating Groups:
American Orthopsychiatric Association
Alliance of Hispanic Social Workers
Bertha Capen Reynolds Society
Local #535, Social Services Union, SEIU, Cal.

National Ass'n. of Social Workers, N.Y.C. Chapter
N.Y.C. Social Workers for Peace & Nuclear Disarmament
Social Service Committee, Local 1199, Hospital & Health Care Employees
Social Service Employees Union, Local 371, AFSCME, AFL - CIO

Printing donated by SSEU, Local 371, AFSCME, AFL - CIO

0004

분류번호	보존기간

발 신 전 보

번 호 : WGV-0094   910118 1525   FC   종 별 :

수 신 : 주 제네바   대사·총영사

발 신 : 장 관   (국연)

제 목 : 아국관련 진정서

대 : 제네(정) 2031-3

대호. 귀견대로 조치바람.   끝.

(국제기구조약국장   문동석)

1991. 6.30 에 예고문에
의거 일반문서로 재분됨

앙고재	91년 1월 8일 과	기안자 훙영옥		과 장	국 장 전결	차 관	장관	보안통제	외신과통제

0005

주 제 네 바 대 표 부

제네(정) 2031-10   1991. 2. 8

수신 : 장관

참조 : 국제기구조약국장

제목 : 유엔인권사무국 접수 아국관련 진정서(91-1)

1. 당지 유엔인권 사무국은 91.1.23자 당관앞 공한을 통해 1503 절차에 의거 아국
    인권상황 관련 진정서 1건이 접수되었음을 알려온바 이를 별첨 송부합니다.

2. 상기 진정서는 "남한의 민주 및 인권을 위한 국제 법률가 위원회" 명의로서
    아국내 시국관련 재소자에 대한 교도소내 처우와 관련한 사항입니다.

3. 동 진정서가 일사건에 관한 사항이 아니며, 아국의 교도행정에   대한
    광범위한 내용임을 고려, 진정서내 거명인물에 대한 설명등을 포함하여
    가급적 자세한 답변자료(영문)를 관계부처와 협의 작성하여 91. 4월중순까지
    인권사무국에 제출토록 조치하여 주시기 바랍니다.

첨부 : 1. 상기공한 1부.   일반문서로 재분류(1991. 12.31.)

       2. 진정서 영문번역문 1부. 끝.

                          검토필(1991. 6. 30)

예고 : 91. 12. 31. 일반

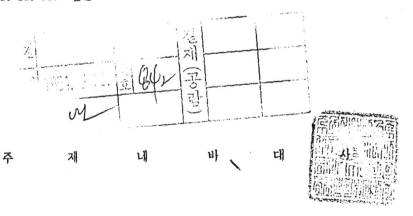

              주   제   네   바   대

0006

CENTRE POUR LES DROITS DE L'HOMME

CENTRE FOR HUMAN RIGHTS

Téléfax: (022) 733 98 79
Télégrammes: UNATIONS, GENÈVE
Télex: 28 96 96
Téléphone: 734 60 11   731 02 11

RÉF. N°:   G/SO 215/1 KOREA REP
(à rappeler dans la reponse)

Palais des Nations
CH-1211 GENÈVE 10

The Secretariat of the United Nations (Centre for Human Rights) presents its compliments to the Office of the Permanent Observer of the Republic of Korea to the United Nations Office at Geneva and with reference to its note No. G/SO 215/1 KOREA REP, dated 7 July 1980, has the honour to transmit herewith copies of one communication dated 3 January 1991, concerning human rights, which refer to the Republic of Korea.

A brief indication of the substance of the communications will be included in a confidential list of communications which is to be submitted to the Commission on Human Rights and the Sub-Commission on Prevention of Discrimination and Protection of Minorities under Economic and Social Council resolutions 728 F (XXVIII) and 1503 (XLVIII).

Any reply which the Permanent Observer may wish to transmit on behalf of its Government under the above-mentioned resolutions should be forwarded to the Centre for Human Rights, United Nations Office at Geneva, with an indication as to whether the reply is to be presented to the Commission and the Sub-Commission in summary form or in full.

23 January 1991

0007

COMITÉ INTERNATIONAL DE JURISTES
POUR LA
DÉMOCRATIE ET LES DROITS DE L'HOMME
EN CORÉE DU SUD

Présidence :
Mᵉ Amar BEN TOUMI (Algérie)
Maréchal Francisco Da COSTA GOMES (Portugal)
Mᵉ Nicole DREYFUS (France)
M. Robert PARRY, Député (Grande-Bretagne)
Prof. Paulette PIERSON-MATHY (Belgique)
Prof. Derek ROEBUCK (Australie)
Mᵉ Kazuyoshi SAITO (Japon)
Prof. Jean SALMON (Belgique)
Mᵉ Doris Brin WALKER (Etats Unis)
Prof. Jean ZIEGLER (Suisse)

Secrétaire Général :

Prof. Robert CHARVIN (France)
Université de Nice
U.E.R. Droit et Sciences Economiques
34, Av. Robert Schuman - 06000 NICE
Téléphone : 93.97.08.00

Mᵉ Luis DE AZEVEDO (...)
M. le Ministre Hans KLECATSKY (Autriche)
M. J.-L. RAMANDRAIARISOA (Madagascar)
Prof. Paul YAO-N'DRE (Côte d'Ivoire)

Le 3 Janvier 1990.

6/80 21511 FOR REP

Nous nous permettons d'attirer votre attention aux fins d'information et d'intervention sur la situation qui règne dans les prisons sud-coréennes et en particulier celles de MOKPO et de SEOUL, où se trouvent incarcérés de nombreux prisonniers politiques (plus de 1200 personnes sont arrêtées pour motifs politiques et incarcérées pour des peines plus ou moins longues chaque année). Or, ces détenus - comme ceux de droit commun - subissent systématiquement violence et arbitraire de la part du personnel pénitentiaire sud-coréen. Des témoignages provenant d'étudiants récemment libérés (reproduits notamment dans le Journal Korea News Letters, organe de "l'Alliance Nationale pour la démocratie et la réunification" (Hanminryeun), indiquent que les prisonniers sont régulièrement : frappés à coup de poings et de pieds; ligotés par les mains et les jambes et attachés à une corde; privés de boisson et de nourriture et sans traitement médical, dans certaines cellules spéciales; nourris de force avec brutalité lorsqu'ils tentent des grèves de la faim.

Par décision du 7.7.1990, le Ministre de la Justice sud-coréen a interdit toute visite aux prisonniers politiques émanant d' amis "politiquement engagés".

A l'issue d'une visite médicale pratiquée par six médecins extérieurs à la prison, le 19 septembre dernier, il a été constaté

0008

à la prison de Séoul, que dans 36 cas, un traitement d'urgence devait être assuré pour blessure grave. Par exemple, RI MYEUNG HOUK, âgé de 23 ans, doit subir une opération pour blessure au poumon. RI SEUNG OU, âgé de 33 ans, éditeur, est même en danger de mort en raison de multiples fractures osseuses et atteint d'une paralysie du visage.

Lors de leur arrestation, un certain nombre d'ouvriers et d'étudiants ont été violemment frappés, étant deshabillés, sur toutes les parties du corps et se sont vus empêchés de dormir durant 2 à 3 jours selon les cas, afin qu'ils acceptent de signer des aveux dans l'affaire dite de l'"Union des ouvriers socialistes". (Cas de HYEUN YEUN DEUK, arrêté en septembre, RI SOUNG SOU, NAM BO HYEUN, DJEUN MI HWA, etc...[informations retransmises par leurs avocats]).

Avec nos remerciements anticipés pour l'action qu'il vous sera possible de mener, nous vous prions de croire à l'assurance de nos sentiments les meilleurs.

Professeur R.CHARVIN
Secrétaire Général

0009

Selon Kim Dae-Jung, le leader de l'opposition parlementaire, les arrestations sont plus nombreuses que sous le régime précédent (3,6 personnes/jour contre 1,6). Les prisonniers d'opinion actuellement en détention sont plus de 1.400 (dont la jeune étudiante Rim Sou Kyeung, condamnée à 5 ans de prison pour s'être rendue au Nord), selon 46 membres de la Chambre des Représentants du Congrès des Etats-Unis, qui ont émis une protestation auprès de Séoul le 5 novembre 1990.

La vieille "Loi sur la sécurité nationale", de plus en plus considérée comme inutile en raison des contacts officiels entre le Nord et le Sud, puisqu'elle pénalise ces contacts, est toujours en vigueur :
- le 6 novembre, les responsables d'une "Union des Ouvriers Socialistes" sont arrêtés ;
- le 7 novembre, l'étudiant Park Djaï Beum de l'Université de Hanyang est emprisonné ;
- une cinquantaine de personnes sont détenues pour violation et le 10 novembre 1990, les autorités de Séoul l'ont encore utilisée contre le "Conseil National des Sud-coréens pour l'indépendance, la démocratie et la réunification", qualifié d'organisation "anti-étatique" (9 arrestations dont l'étudiant Tchoé Ki Yeung , secrétaire général du Conseil National des représentants des Etudiants).

Selon la police, il s'agit d'un vaste complot visant à renverser le régime en..... 1995 !
Il s'agit en réalité de sanctionner toute diffusion d'information sur le Nord ou - ou toute critique radicale du système.

Cette répression et ces manoeuvres politiciennes de diversion n'empêchent pas le développement des oppositions : création le 10 novembre du nouveau parti "Parti pour le Peuple", dont le Président est Ri Ou Djaï, dont l'objectif est "d'instaurer un gouvernement démocratique après avoir chassé les forces étrangères et la dictature militaire" ; de nouveaux comités étudiants ont été fondés à l'Université de Séoul le 19 novembre (pour l'abolition de la Loi sur la sécurité nationale, pour la libération des personnes emprisonnées pour avoir lutté pour la réunification, etc...) ; manifestations à Séoul, Kwangdjou, Daidjeun, etc....contre la police politique et les services de renseignements qui surveillent la population.

Les juristes ne peuvent abandonner le terrain de la lutte pour les Droits de l'Homme sous prétexte que la tension Est-Ouest n'existe pratiquement plus. La Corée du Sud est toujours une fausse démocratie dont les victimes doivent bénéficier de l'aide de chacun : une intervention auprès des Ambassades s'impose.

0010

International Jurists Committee
for Democracy and Human Rights in South Korea

                                        3 January 1991

    We wish to draw your attention to the following facts with
regard to the present situation in South Korean prisons and in
particular the prisons of MOKPO and SEOUL, where a number of
political prisoners are imprisoned (more than 1200 persons are
arrested for political reasons and imprisoned with sentences
ranging from short to long terms each year). However, these
prisoners - like those of common law - are subjected to arbitrary
and systematic violence by the South Korean prison staff.
Evidence given by recently released students (mainly cited in the
Korea News Letters newspaper, organ of the "National Alliance for
Democracy and Reunification" Hanminryeun), indicate that
prisoners are frequently : beaten and kicked; with their hands
and feet tied together with rope; deprived of food and drink, and
do not receive medical treatment, and in certain cells, are
brutally force-fed when they go on hunger strike.

    On 7.7.1990, the South Korean Minister of Justice forbid all
visits to political prisoners from friends with political
tendencies.

    After a medical check-up by six outside doctors to the
prison on 19 September 1990, it was established that in 36 cases,
emergency treatment was required for serious injuries. For
example, RI MYEUNG HOUK, 23 years old, had to have an operation
for an injured lung. RI SEUNG OU, 33 years old, Editor, is even
in danger of dying due to multiple broken bones and is facially
paralysed.

    At the time of their arrest, some workers and students were
badly beaten, undressed, and not allowed to sleep over a period
of 2 to three days, in order that they accept to sign their
confession in the so-called "Socialist workers Union" affair.
(This was the case for HYEUN YEUN DEUK, arrested in September,
RI SOUNG SOU, NAM BO HYEUN, DJEUN MI HWA, etc....(information
given by their lawyers).

    Thanking you in advance for the action that may be taken in
this regard,

    Sincerely yours,

                                                    0011

<u>Annex</u>

<u>According to KIM Dae-Jung, Parliamentary Opposition leader,</u>
<u>arrests are more frequent now than under the previous régime (3.6</u>
<u>per day, against 1.6)</u> Political prisoners are at present more
than 1,400 in detention (one of them being Rim Sou Kyeung,
sentenced to 5 years because he went to North Korea), according
to 46 members of the House of Representatives of Congress in US
who registered a protest to Seoul on 5 November 1990.

The old "National Security Law", is more and more considered
as of being no use, because of the official contacts between
South and North, as it penalizes these contacts, but is still in
vigor :

- 6 November, persons in charge of the "Socialist Workers'
  Union" were arrested;
- 7 November, Park Djai Beum a student at Hanyang University
  was imprisoned;
- 50 persons were detained for violation and on 10 November
  1990, Seoul authorities again used this law against the
  "National Council of South Koreans for Independence,
  Democracy and Reunification", qualifying this organisation
  as being "anti-state" (19 arrests, one of them Tchoé Ki
  Yeung, student, Secretary-General of the National Council
  of Student Representatives).

According to the police, it concerned a vast conspiracy to
overthrow the régime in 1995.

In reality it was to sanction information given about North
Korea or radical criticism of the system.

This repression and political manoeuvers have not stopped
opposition groups developping: 10 November the creation of a new
Pary "People's Party", its President is Ri Ou Djai, with an
objective to "install a democratic government, after expelling
foreign forces and the military dictatorship"; new student
committees have been founded at the Seoul University on 19
November (in order to abolish the National Security Law, and to
liberate prisoners who fought for reunification etc.);
demonstrations in Seoul, Kwangdjou, Daidjeun, etc. against the
political police and the information service who control the
population.

The Jurists cannot abandon the fight for human rights under
the pretext that East-West tensions are pratically non-existant
now. South Korea is still a false democracy, and its victims
should benefit from help by all, with interventions being made
to its Embassies.

0012

기안용지

분류기호 문서번호	국연 2031 - 187	(전화:)	시 행 상 특별취급

보존기간	영구·준영구· 10. 5. 3. 1
수신처 보존기간	
시행일자	1991. 2. 18.

장 관

보조 기관	국 장	전 결	협 조 기 관		문서통제
	과 장				겸열 1991. 2. 18 통 제 관
기안책임자		송영완			발송인
경 유			발 신 명 의		발신 1991. 2. 18 외무부
수 신		법무부장관			
참 조		법무실장			
제 목		유엔인권사무국 접수 아국관련 진정서 (19-1)			

　　1. 제네바소재 유엔인권 사무국은 91.1.23자

주제네바대표부앞 공한을 통해 1503 절차에 의거 아국

인권상황 관련 진정서 1건이 접수되었음을 알려 왔는 바,

동 진정서는 "남한의 민주 및 인권을 위한 국제 법률가

위원회" 명의로서 아국내 시국관련 재소자에 대한 교도소내

처우와 관련한 사항입니다.

　　　　　　　　　　　　　　　0013 //계속...

2. 동 진정서가 특정개인에 관한 사항이 아니며,

아국의 교도행정에 대한 광범위한 내용임을 고려, 진정서내

거명인물에 대한 설명등을 포함하여 가급적 자세한 답변자료

(영문)를 작성, 91.3.20한 당부로 회보하여 주시기 바랍니다.

첨 부 : 상기공한(불.영문) 1부. 끝.

예고 : 91.12.31. 일반

검 토 필(1991. 6. 30.)

일반문서로재분류(1991. 12. 31.)

0014

공   란

공   란

공 란

공   란

법   무   부

인권 2031-ᄼ   503-7045   1991. 3. 12.

수신   외무부장관

참조   국제기구조약국장

제목   유엔 인권사무국 접수 아국관련 진정서 설명자료 송부

1. 국연 2031-187 ('91.2.18)과 관련입니다.

2. 귀부에서 요청한 유엔 인권사무국 접수 아국관련 진정서에 대한

설명자료를 송부하오니 적의 활용하시기 바랍니다.

첨부 : 설명자료 1부. 끝.

예고 : '91.12.31 일반

전 결			결재 종합	
접수일시	1991. 3 13	1380		
처리과	여	무 부 장		

0019

재소자 인권과 관련, 유엔에 진정한 내용에 대한 답변자료
= =

가. 목포교도소 및 서울구치소에 수용된 재소자들을 일부 교도관이 고의적

이고 자의적으로 폭행하고 포승으로 결박하였으며,

재소자 이성우는 심한 복합골절과 안면마비로 죽을위험에 빠졌고,

재소자 이명학은 폐의 타격으로 수술을 받아야 했으며,

6명의 외부의사가 서울구치소 재소자들을 진찰한 결과, 심한 부상을

입고 응급치료를 필요로 하는 재소자가 36명이었고,

의사치료도 없고 음료수도 먹을것도 주지 않았다는 주장에 대하여

o 우리나라에는 우리나라의 국시를 부정하고 자유민주주의 체제를 부인하며
경찰관서나 공공시설을 방화 또는 파괴하는 등 실정법을 위반하여 구속
되거나 형을 받고 수용중인 재소자들이 다수 있음

이들은 수용시설인 구치소나 교도소를 그들의 끝없는 투쟁의 장소로 삼고
구치소나 교도소측의 적법한 처우에 대하여 대부분의 일반재소자들이 만족
하고 있는 사항에 대하여도 사사건건 불만을 토로하며, 직원들과의 시비를
유발하거나 수용시설을 파괴 또는 직원에 대한 폭행, 집단소란등 규율위반
행위를 자행하고 있음

이러한 불법행위에 대하여 구치소, 교도소측의 적법절차에 의한 수갑과
포승의 사용을 재소자들은 물론 그 가족들과 각종 재야단체들은 재소자에
대한 가혹행위라고 허위, 왜곡 주장하며 국·내외에 유포하고 여론화하려는
기도를 버리지 않고 있음

0020

r<1

o 90·7·24 목포교도소에 수용중인 재소자 3명이 규정상 허가할 수 없는
   공범자들과의 합방수용, 접견의 무제한적인 허가, 1일 1시간씩 실시
   하고 있는 운동시간의 연장등을 요구하며 불식한 사실은 있으나 이들을
   포승과 수갑으로 결박하거나 구타한 사실은 전혀 없었음

o 90·8·27 서울구치소에서 재소자들이 읽어서는 아니되는 공산주의 관계
   서적을 읽지 못하게 하자 재소자 김용기등 3명이 수용된 방을 무단으로
   나와 도서담당 교도관에게 완강히 항의하면서 교도관의 얼굴에 신문철을
   던지는 등 소란을 부리므로 이들을 설득하여 방으로 돌려 보냈으나 이들은
   방에 들어가지 않고 다른 재소자들에게 허위로 교도관으로부터 폭행을
   당하였다고 선동하여 많은 재소자들이 때마침 배식을 하기위해 거실문을
   여는 틈을 이용하여 수십명이 집단으로 구치소 교무과에 집결하여 기물을
   파괴하고 장시간 소란을 부리다가 끝까지 자진해산을 하지 않고 각목등을
   휘둘러 많은 교도관과 같은 재소자끼리 상처를 입히고 구치소내의 질서를
   파괴하였으므로 다른 재소자들의 안정과 수용질서 유지를 위하여 부득이
   법절차에 따라 손에 수갑을 채우고 포승으로 팔을 묶어 진압한 사실이
   있음

   · 진압과정에서 교도관들의 구타행위는 일체 없었으며 반대로 재소자들이
      무차별 휘두른 각목에 교도관 8명이 머리등을 맞아 2-10일간을 외부
      병원에 입원하여 치료를 받았으며, 재소자 10명도 소란의 와중에서
      진압에 극렬히 항거하다가 바닥에 넘어지거나 시설물에 부딛쳐 상처를
      입었으나 모두 교도소 의무실에서 즉시 치료하여 완치 되었음

0021

7-2

· 그중 재소자 이성우는 이와같은 진압과정에서 안면에 부상을 입어
사회전문병원에 이송진료한바 약 3주간의 치료를 요하는 비골골절상을
입었으며 그이외에 안면마비등 특이한 증상은 없었으며 3일간의 통원
치료를 하고 구치소내에서 자체 가료를 하면 완치될 것이라는 전문의의
소견이 있었음

서울구치소에서는 이와같은 외부 전문의사의 소견에 따라 3회에 걸쳐
외부전문병원에 통원치료를 하는 한면 , 구치소 의무실에 입원시켜
전문의의 처방에 의한 투약등 자체 치료를 하여 완치되어 건강하게
수용생활을 하다가 90.9.24 형집행유에로 석방하였는 바 안면마비나
죽을위험에 빠졌었다는 주장은 사실과 다름

· 재소자 이명학은 90.8.27 재소자 집단소란에 가담 하였으나 당시는
아무런 부상을 입지 않았으며 동년 9.1 이명학의 모 주영숙이 외부
의사의 진료를 신청하여 인천소재 평화의원 원장 김정범이 내소 ,
검진한 결과에도 특이한 증상을 발견할 수 없었음

그후 이명학은 운동등 일상적인 수용생활을 정상적으로 하여 오다가
집단소란사건 10일후인 동년 9.7 운동을 하면서 근무직원에게 가슴이
답답하다고 호소하여 자체 의무실로 데려다가 검진한 결과 폐기흉의
의심이 있어 즉시 사회전문 병원으로 이송하여 정밀검진한 결과
폐기흉증으로 판명되어 안양성모병원에 입원치료 하다가 수술을 받기
위하여 강남성모병원으로 다시 이송하여 수술을 받고 완치되어 건강
하게 정상적인 수용생활을 하다가 91.3.3 형기종료로 출소 하였음

0022

1-3

수술을 담당한 강남성모병원 전문의의 설명에 따르면 폐기흉의 발생
원인은 다양하나 자연발생적으로 생기는 경우가 가장 많고 가끔
질병에 의한 합병증이나 과로한 운동등이 원인이 될 수 있으나
이명학의 경우는 자연발생적인 경우로 진단하여 이를 본인과 가족에게
설명한바 있으므로 동인의 폐기흉증은 집단소란 사건과는 무관한 것임

· 동년 9·19 집단소란에 가담한 재소자 전원에 대하여 변호인과
가족등이 신청한 외래의사 6명이 교도소를 방문, 재소자 36명을
진찰한 결과 비골골절상을 입은 이성우등 경미한 부상을 입은 재소자
10명을 확인한바 있음에도 변호인과 가족등은 진찰을 받은 36명의
재소자 모두가 치료를 받아야 되는양 주장하며 이들 재소자들과
같은 성향을 지닌 6명의 의사들은 치료를 요하지 않는 재소자들에게
까지 치료를 요하는 것 처럼   진단서를 발부 하였음

서울구치소 의무관들도 집단소란자 모두를 정밀진찰하였으나 위의
10명이외에는 치료를 요하는 사람이 없음을 확인 하였으며 약간의
부상을 입은자들은 즉시 자체 치료를 하여 모두 완치 되었으며 비골
골절상을 입은 이성우도 3회에 걸쳐 외부병원에 이송치료하는 등
적극적인 치료를 하여 완치 하였으나 당시 심한 부상으로 응급처치를
받아야 했던 재소자는 없었음

· 집단소란을 주동한 일부 재소자들을 일시적으로 독거실에 수용한 것은
사실이나 어떠한 경우라도 우리나라의 교도소에서는 이들 재소자에게
의사의 치료를 해 주지 않는다든가 재소자들에게 음료수와 먹을 것을
주지 않는일은 없으며 그것은 재소자의 기본적 생존권이며 교도소의
책무인 것임

0023

7-4

- 우리나라의 모든 교도소에는 재소자들이 충분히 진료 받을수 있는 전문 의사와 의료진을 확보하고 있어 질병에 이환된 재소자는 지체없이 자체 의무관의 진료를 받고 있을 뿐 아니라 교도소내에서 치료가 어려운 환자는 즉시 외부사회병원에 이송진료 할 수 있도록 교도소 소재지의 종합병원과 계약되어 있으므로 재소자에 대한 의료시혜는 완전하게 보장되고 있음

- 또한 급식은 영양관계 전문교수들로 구성되는 급식관리위원회가 결정한 식단에 따라 국제식량농업기구가 권장하고 있는 1일 2,500킬로카로리 를 훨씬 넘는 3,150킬로카로리를 급여하고 있음.

0024

2-5

나. 재소자들이 단식투쟁을 하려면 비참하게 강제급식을 받는다는
　　주장에 대하여

○　90.7.24 목포교도소에 수용된 재소자 이창섭등 3명이 접견의 무제한
　　허가등을 요구하며 7일간 불식하다가 교도관들이 계속 취식을 권유하자
　　영양제주사를 맞고 미음을 먹은 사실은 있으나 강제급식을 한 사실은
　　없음

·　교도소는 재소자의 건강을 보호할 책임이 있으므로 불식자에 대하여는
　　최대한의 설득과 권유로 자진취식을 유도하고 있을뿐 재소자의 의사에
　　반하여 강제로 밥을 먹이는 것은 사실상 불가능할뿐 아니라 인도적 견지
　　에서도 절대로 있을 수 없는 일이며 우리나라의 교도소에서는 어떠한
　　강제급식의 방법도 사용하고 있지 않음

0025

ㄱ-ㅣ

다. 정치적 경향이 있는 재소자들에게 모든 접견을 금지시켰다는
주장에 대하여

○ 우리나라의 행형법에는 재소자의 접견은 친족에 대하여 허가하는 것을
원칙으로 하고   그 이외의 사람에 대하여는 교화상 필요한 용무가
있을때에 한하여 허가 할 수 있도록 규정되어 있으나 재소자들의 편익과
처우의 향상을 위하여   친족이외의 사람이더라도
교화상 극히 부적당한 경우를 제외하고는 모든 사람에 대하여 접견을
허가하고 있음.

· 이와같은 접견은 모든 재소자에게 동일하게 실시되고 있으며 정치적
경향이 있는 재소자라는 이유로 차별하거나 접견을 금지하는 일은 없을
뿐 아니라 접견을 요청하는 사람의 신분이나 직업등에 따라 접견을 제한
하는 사례는 없음

· 다만, 동일 범죄사건의 공범관계에 있거나 재소자가 규율을 위반하여
적법절차에 따라 징벌 (교도소의 질서를 유지하기 위하여 규율위반자
에게 과하는 행정질서벌)을 받았을 때에는 징벌집행기간 동안 교도소
장이 접견을 허가하지 않는 경우가 있음

0026

ㄱ-ㄱ

공   란

공　　　란

발 신 전 보

분류번호	보존기간

번 호 : WGV-0544　910424 1924 FL　종별 : 암 호

수 신 : 주제네바　　　대사.//총영사　(김종훈 서기관님)

발 신 : 장 관　(유엔과 송영완 배)

제 목 : 업 연

대 : 제네(정) 2031-10 (91.2.8)

대호, 답변서는 5월초순경 송부할 예정이오니 양지바람. 건승기원.

끝.

보안통제					
앙고재	91년 4월 24일	기안자성명 송영완	과장	국장	차관 장관

0029

공 란

공   란

공   란

공 란

공   란

공   란

공　　　란

통 화 요 록

91.4.19.

1. 발   신 : 법무부 인권과 박의수

2. 수   신 : 외무부 유엔과 송영완

3. 통화일시 : 91.4.19(금) 14:15

4. 통화내용

   ○ 90.7.7. 법무부는 재소자의 교도소내 규율준수를 지도
      하기 위하여 동일사건 공범자, 폭력행위 및 규율문란행위
      선동자들의 재소자 접견은 신중을 기하여 허가하라는
      공문을 시달한 바는 있으나 재소자들의 친지, 친구, 정치적
      경향이 있는 모든 사람들의 접견을 시달한 적은 없음. 끝.

0037

0038

[illegible]

◦ 서울구치소 : 직원 701명, 재소자 3,665명 (91.3.22 현재)

◦ [illegible] : 직원 229명 재소자 963명 ( )

RECEIVED FROM 5037083 1991.03.22 17:22 P. 2

Reply of the Republic of Korea

6 May 1991.

I. Introduction

The Government of the Republic of Korea is fully committed to a free and open society. It is widely recognized that democratic processes and practices have been steadily promoted in Korea.

Over the last three years since the inauguration of the Sixth Republic, the Government has taken a series of clemency measures including amnesties and restoration of civil rights for prisoners including those convicted for politically-motivated offenses. The National Assembly has also contributed to the enhancement of human rights by amending the laws which were considered to have certain undemocratic elements.

On 10 April 1990, the Republic of Korea acceded to the International Covenant on Economic, Social and Cultural Rights, the International Covenant on Civil and Political Rights and its Optional Protocol. This will certainly contribute to strengthening the protection of human rights and fundamental freedoms and promoting public awareness of them.

0040

I. Political Prisoners

In the Republic of Korea, the freedom of thoughts, conscience and religion is guaranteed by the Constitution and other relevant laws. No one is punished by his belief or opinion. However, the freedom to express one's belief or opinion is subject to certain basic limitations as prescribed by law, such as the need to maintain public safety, order, health and morals or to protect the fundamental rights and freedoms of other people.

People in certain segments of our society insist that "political prisoners" must be released. Those whom they refer to as "political prisoners", in reality, include a broad range of criminals such as radical activists who set fire to public offices and facilities and injure or even cause the death of policemen ; radical college students who destroyed their school facilities ; workers who vandalized their work place and confined, or assaulted their fellow workers and employers ; and even espionage agents.

It is absolutely unacceptable that they should be immediately released on the ground that they were politically motivated or acted for certain political aims, completely neglecting the violent nature of their acts, motivations and purposes.

0041

II. Human Rights in the Correctional Institutions

A. Laws Related to the Protection of the Human Rights in the Correctional Institutions

In the Republic of Korea, every person who is detained, either awaiting trial, or serving a prison term, is protected according to the provisions of the Penal Administration Act and the enforcement regulations thereof. Anyone who mistreats a detained person is liable not only to administrative sanctions but also to criminal prosecution. The Penal Administration Act and its enforcement regulations further provide for the adequate treatment of prisoners, covering their meals, hygiene, cells, and the like so that prisoners may be treated with humanity.

The relevant rules and regulations also provide that inmates be placed under safe custody and that an inmate be punished when he breaches prison disciplines. Censorship of inmates' correspondence, reading materials and supervision of visiting is allowed at a minimum level only for the security of the correctional institutions and for the process of inmate rehabilitation. The housing condition for inmates and the administration of the correctional institutions are under strict supervision of the Ministry of Justice and the Board of Audit and Inspection.

B. Cases

There have been incidents of violent actions of prison inmates disturbing the peace and order inside the correctional institutions.

0042

When prison authorities take steps to control unruly inmates, physical clashes occasionally occur, causing injury to both inmates and prison guards and damage to the facilities of the correctional institutions. Radical prisoners tend to use these clashes as evidence of the infringement of human rights and cruel treatment in prisons and detention centers.

The Government has conducted thorough investigations into the cases cited by the International Jurists Committee for Democracy and Human Rights in South Korea, and the results are as follows :

1. Mr. Ri Seung Ou

On 27 August 1990, three inmates of Seoul Detention Center made a forcible entry into the library at the Center and protested against a prison officer in charge of the library, arguing that they should be allowed to read pro-North Korean books which were banned for instigating communist revolution and social disorder. These inmates turned violent and threw a bunch of newspapers on the prison officer's face. The officer told them to go back to their cells and after a while they complied. However, on their way back, the inmates shouted that they had been beaten. Upon hearing it, several scores of inmates in the ward came out of their cells (doors were open carelessly by prison officers who were distributing food to inmates), and gathered at the administration office at the Center. These inmates screamed, destroyed furniture and violently resisted against prison officers. During the ensuing physical clashes, 8 prison guards and 10 inmates were injured, and all of them received immediate medical treatment.

0043

Mr. Ri Seung Ou, 33 years of age, had his fibula fractured during the clash, which required three weeks' treatment. He was immediately brought to a general hospital outside the penitentiary where he was given treatment for three days. Then, he was moved to the infirmary of the Detention Center and attended by medical doctors.

He was given a stay of execution and released in good health on 24 September 1990.

The allegation of the International Jurists Committee for Democracy and Human Rights in South Korea that he was in mortal danger due to multiple broken bones and was facially paralysed is not true.

2. Ri Myeung Houk

Mr. Ri Myeung Houk, 23 years of age, also took part in the violent struggle at Seoul Detention Center on 27 August 1990. He was not injured and found healthy five days after the incident by a medical doctor who was brought into the penitentiary to examine him at the request of Mr. Ri's mother.

Ten days after the incident, however, Mr. Ri appealed pain in the lung. A infirmary doctor who checked him up advised the prison authority to bring him to a general hospital outside the Center for a thorough examination. He was found to be affected by pleurisy and had an operation in the hospital. After the

0044

operation, he recovered fast and then returned to the Center. According to the lung specialist in the general hospital who operated on him, the pleurisy of Mr. Ri developed from natural causes and did not seem to be linked to the incident of 27 August 1990.

Mr. Ri was released after the termination of his prison term on 3 March 1991.

3. Other Cases involving 36 inmates

After the violent incident on 27 August 1990, all 96 inmates involved received medical attention from the medical team of the Detention Center and 10 of them were found injured and were provided with proper treatment.

Meanwhile, six outside doctors were brought in at the request of either inmates' families or their lawyers and they issued opinion that all 36 inmates whom they checked needed more than one week treatment.

However, the prison medical staff believed that outside doctors overrated the injury of some inmates solely on the basis of their complaints. As a matter of fact, 26 out of 36 inmates suffered only light external wounds, such as bruise or scratch.

0045

4. Instruction of the Ministry of Justice on 7 July 1990

On 7 July 1990, the Ministry of Justice instructed the correctional institutions to pay attention to the visits of an accomplice to a detainee. However, it is not true that the Ministry has forbidden visits of friends to prisoners imprisoned for politically motivated criminal acts.

The basic rights of inmates can not be restricted or infringed upon by the instructions of the Ministry of Justice or prison authority. The visits of family members and lawyers have never been forbidden to any inmates, but visits of friends can be placed under supervision or restricted in some cases where it is considered necessary for the security of the correctional institutions and for the process of inmate rehabilitation.

0046

III. Torture and Cruel Treatments

A. ROK Government's Commitment to Eliminate Torture and Cruel Treatments

In the Republic of Korea, torture and cruel treatments are strictly prohibited by the Constitution, the Criminal Code and the Criminal Procedure Act.

The Government has been doing its utmost to uproot torture through legal and institutional reform. The prosecution has issued strict instructions to police officers and investigators to faithfully adhere to lawful means and procedures in performing their duties. Frequent on-site inspections are made of the detention rooms at police stations and the correctional institutions.

In this connection, significant change has taken place since the inauguration of the Sixth Republic. Severe criminal punishments have been imposed on those investigation officers involved with cruel acts during investigations and lawsuits have been made to have them take civil responsibilities as well. The old practices of employing all possible means, fair or foul, to reap fast results are no longer tolerated. All those who work in law-enforcement agencies are now required to strictly follow lawful procedures.

As a result of the determined effors of the Government, 37 policemen and prison officers were indicted for committing torture or harsh treatment during the last 5 years.

0047

The Government of the Republic of Korea will continue to endeavor to have lawful means and procedures respected by all police officers and investigators in performing their duties.

B. Case (Socialist Worker's Union)

One of the obstacles that has hampered the process of democratization undertaken since the birth of Korea's Sixth Republic has been the dwindling, but increasingly violent radical groups advocating a violent revolution.

Socialist Worker's Union(SWU) is an illegal anti-Government organization which aims at overthrowing the Government through an armed uprising of workers. Investigations found that the behind-the-scene maneuverings and instigation of SWU were responsible for many violent labor movements and attacks on police stations and other public facilities.

On 12 October 1990, the Union published "Special Declaration "which urged the subversion of the Government through armed struggle. Furthermore, it distributed a number of subversive leftist booklets such as "Guide to the Maneuverings and Instigation " and "Instructions to Attack Aggressors " which are still used by radical activists to educate themselves and their sympathizers how to fight against policemen, investigators when arrested, against jurists at the trial and against prison guards when imprisoned.

The following are the results of the thorough investigation conducted by the Government concerning the cases involving 4 core members of SWU.

0048

1. Nam Jin Hyeun (misspelled as Nam Bo Hyeun in the communication)

   Mr. Nam was a member of the Central Committee, the decision-making organ of SWU and indicted for instigating attacks on police stations and distributing subversive leftist publications. He was also involved in several violent demonstrations.

   When he was arrested on 1 October 1990, he resisted violently and tried to run away. Law enforcement officers, however, went through normal arrest procedure and never used excessive force.

   Mr. Nam himself told his mother at a detention center on 16 October 1990 that, while there was a physical clash at the time of arrest, he was never tortured in custody.

   Mr. Nam was sentenced to 12 years in prison on 22 March 1991 and is now awaiting the second trial.

2. Hyeun Jung Deuk (misspelled as Hyeun Yeun Deuk in the communication)

   Mr. Hyeun was a chief liason officer of SWU and indicted for instigating arson on public facilites and distributing subversive leftist leaflets. He was also charged with having thrown fire bombs during many violent demonstrations.

   At the time of his arrest on 18 September 1990, a physical clash occured when he violently resisted against the investigators.

0049

During the interrogation, he exercised the right to be silent for two days, but he subsequently made confession after facing with various pieces of evidence.

On 6 October 1990, he told his mother at a detention center that he had never been harshly treated.

Mr. Hyun was sentenced to 8 years in prison on 15 March 1991 and is awaiting for the second trial.

3. Mr. Ri Soung Sou

Mr. Ri was one of the core members of SWU and actively involved in the indoctrination of students and workers with communist beliefs in favor of an armed revolution. He master-minded many operations with a view to expanding the illegal organization.

At the time of his arrest on 5 October 1990 he violently resisted against the law enforcement officers. He was never forced awake or tortured during the interrogation. As a matter of fact, his confession was not necessary because investigators already secured enough pieces of evidence for the indictment.

He told his sister and father-in-law at a detention center in October 1990 that he was being treated well by the investigators.

Mr. Ri was sentenced to 3 years' imprisonment on 2 April 1991 and is now awaiting the second trial.

0050

4. Ms. Jung Mi Hwa (misspelled as Djeun Mi Hwa in the communication)

Ms. Jung was arrested in October 1990 in connection with SWU. She told her mother on 11 October 1990 that she was never been mistreated upon arrest or during the investigation.

She was sentenced to 1 year in prison but released on probation afterwards.

0051

06002

분류기호 문서번호	국연 2031-	기 안 용 지 (전화 :　　　)	시 행 상 특별취급	
보존기간	영구·준영구. 10.5.3.1.	장　　　관		
수 신 처 보존기간				
시행일자	1991. 5. 6.			

보 조 기 관	국 장	전 결	협 조 기 관		문 서 통 제 (1991. 5. 06)
	과 장				
					발 송 인
기안책임자	송 영 완				

경 유 수 신 참 조	주제네바대사	발 신 명 의		1991. 6. 00
제 목	아국 인권관련 진정서(91-1)			

　　　　1. 대호, 정부 답변서를 별첨 송부하니 인권사무국에 제출

하고 결과 보고바랍니다.

　　　　2. 동 답변서는 법무부(재소자 인권문제등) 및 안기부

(사로맹사건) 자료를 기초로하여 작성한 것인 바, 필요시 동 관련

부처 자료를 참고하시어 답변서 내용을 첨삭하시기 바랍니다.

　　　　첨 부 : 1. 답변서 1부.(영문)

　　　　　　　　2. 법무부 설명자료 1부.(국문)

　　　　　　　　3. 안기부 설명자료 1부(국문).　　　끝.　　　0052

1505-25(2-1) 일(1)갑　　　　　　　　　　　　　　　190mm×268mm 인쇄용지 2급 60g/㎡
85. 9. 9. 승인　　"내가아낀 종이 한장 늘어나는 나라살림"　　가 40-41 1989. 6. 8

법   무   부

인권 2031- 6043   503-7045   1991. 5. 7.

수신 외무부장관

참조 국제연합과장

제목 유엔인권위원회 청원사실 통보

　　　우리부에서 천수만 서산 AB지구 간척공사로 인한 피해상황에 대하여

전정서를 접수하여 대검에 처리 지시하였으나 동 진정서중 상기 피해상황에

대하여 유엔 인권위원회에 청원서를 제출하였다는 내용이 있어 동 청원서

사본을 송부하오니 업무에 참고하시기 바랍니다.

첨부 : 청원서 사본 1부. 끝.

법   무   부   장

M 13131

0053

                    448 Joongjang 5 ku,
                    Anmyon-eup, Taean-kun
                    Chungchongnam-do, Korea

            Korean Committee for Obtaining the Right to
              Live for the Fishermen of Seo San A·B
                              District
              President Sang – keun, Lee

                    His Excellency
                    Abysayed Chowdhury
                    President
                    Center for Human Rights
                    United National Office
                    CH-1211 Geneve 10
                    Switzerland

     May God bless the Committee of the UN Human Rights who
serve for the maintenance of world peace and preserve the humane
lives.·

     We are 12,000 fishermen who live in the sea area of Tae An
Kun, Hong Sung Kun, Bo Ryung Kun, and Chun Su Bay of the Chung
Chong Nam Do Province in South Korea. We are send the following
requests to you, the Committee of the U.N. Human Rights, which
we hope you give a careful attention to if and give us the help
we need.

     It is the truth in the history of the mankind that the
rights to eat and live, and the right to live as human are the
natural rights of man that the God has given. Therefore any
acts or reasons which infringe on the natural rights on man,
the rights to eat and live and the right to live as human, and
any political and administrative acts should not be tolerated
regardless of anyone. If is the teachings of human history and
they are listed on the International Humane the United Nation
Charter and the Constitutions of the world nations.

                                                   0054

1. But unfortunately, denying the natural rights on man, the
   common consciousness of mankind, Korean government exercised
   its government power to run the land reclamation project and
   did not practice the necessary conditions of Korean Environment
   Preservation Law Article 5 and same article Enforcement Ordi-
   nance Article 5 following pre-evaluation of ecological effect.
   Furthermore, clearly unlawful land reclamation project covering
   50 million pyong, which violates the U.N. Human Environmental
   Declaration, is being committed. This desolated completely
   the only source of income for the 12,000 fishermen around the
   sea area of Chun Su Bay, the fishing ground. This caused
   starvation of 12,000 fishermen in the Chun Su bay area, and
   on top of that, many suicides are committed because of hunger
   and the hardships of life. Though the 12,000 fishermen are
   on the verge of starvation, government administration have
   left it alone. This is denying the rights to eat and live
   that God has given to mankind as the natural rights to man,
   and internationally this has reached the worst condition in
   the history of mankind. It is also true that this is violating
   the International Regulation Articles 11 and 12 on the economic,
   social and the cultural rights. Therefore, as the right to
   pursue a life as human and the right to eat are acknowledged
   commonly by the entire human race, it is the popular opinion
   of the Koreans that this kind of action should be condemned
   rogardless of nationality and race by the entire mankind.

2. Especially as the above facts were checked and proved by the
   Korean National Assembly three times, and the facts were revealed
   after thorough research by the National Assembly 7 times a year,
   the unlawful land reclamation project without the constitution
   government done through the exercise of government power has
   reached its worst condition. As this human infringement
   condition is recognized by the Korean governemtn, the National
   Assembly and politicians, it is clearly dereliction of the
   government and National Assembly's duty and infringing political

0055

administration that denies the natural rights of mankind to
eat and live. This is a true fact that cannot be denied by any
human who live on this earth.

3. Therefore detailed explanations are not necessary. Please
   give a careful attention to the comic box that was printed on
   the wide-read Korean newspaper Han and articles of that newspaper. They describe the reality of 12,000 fishermen of Chun
   Su bay for the past 6 years which was extremely miserable and
   full of hardships of life.
   In our free-democratic, constitutional government where preserving the rights of the people, the livelihood of the people, the
   will of the people are thought to be the main goal of the political administration and where humanism and the constitutionalism
   are practiced, how can such denial of human rights and brutal
   human infringement be committed? And how can the government,
   National Assembly, politicians who are responsible for running
   the free country unnotice such brutal and cruel human infringement? They cannot be so unresponsible, unsensible and remain
   quiet.
   We believe, in the face of such cruel human infringement, the
   U.N. Human Rights Committee who proposed the human hignity and
   the guarantee of human rights, will not accept such cruel acts
   which denies the human rights by intentionally killing people
   by starvation. If the U.N. accept such cruel human infringement,
   human society cannot be maintained and go on, not to mention
   the individual nations.
   Therefore, the U.N. must enforce drastic measures as a discipline.

4. Under such circumstances where politics and administration are
   done without responsibility and mercilessly, us fishermen who
   do not have any power, must turn to all the people of the
   world for help. That is the reason why, though we feel ashamed,
   we request the U.N. Human Rights Committee to take necessary
   measures, in hope for change of political administration.

0056

We hope that under the denunciation and discipline of the world, the government will be warned about their action which deny the natural human rights. In addition, we hope you can help us preserve the right to live, which has been lost for the past 6 years, during which the fishermen of Chun Su Bay faced the hardships of life and were on the verge of starvation.

We hope that the above requesting issues will be fully understood by the U.N. Human Rights Committee. We also believe that the people of the world who dignify the lives of the people and pursue a better life help us together in denounce the above issue.

Apr. 30 , 1990

Korean Committee for Obtaining the
Right to Live for the Fishermen of
Seo San A·B District
President   Sang-keun, Lee

Translated by

0057

대한민국 충청남도 태안군 안면읍 중장5구 448

한국 서산A.B지구 어민생존권 쟁취위원회
　　　　　위원장 이　상　근
스위스국 제네바 10 CH-1211
유엔인권위원회
유엔인권위원회 위원장 각하.

　세계평화 유지와 인간다운 삶을 보장하기 위한 인류들
의 인권옹호에 헌신분투 하시는 유엔인권위원회 위원님 제
위의 옥체에 신의가호가 있으시길 기원드리나이다.
불초 소생등은 대한민국 충청남도 태안군, 홍성군, 보령군
천수만해역권 내에서 거주하는 1만2천여 어민들로서 유
엔인권위원회 위원님 제위께 아래와 같은 청원 사항을 올
리는 바이오니 엄밀히 심의하시여서 구조하여 주시기 바
라나이다.
자고로 인간이 먹고사는 권리와 인간다운삶의 권리는 하
나님이 내리신 천부인권이 되여있다는 것이 인류사의 진
리란것입니다.
때문에 이와 같이 하나님이 내리신 천부인권의 인간이 먹
고 사는 권리와 인간다운 삶의 권리를 침해하거나 부정
하는 정치, 행정이나 행위에 대해서는 전 인류에 공적으
로 단정하고 어떠한 이유나 명분이나 어느 누구를 막론
하고 결코 용인해서는 안된다는 것이 인류사의 교훈이되
여 있고 국제연합헌장이나 국제인권장전이나 세계각국 헌
법에는 명시되여 있다는 것입니다.

－ 1 －

0058

1. 그런데 불행하게도 이와같은 인류사의진리요, 인류들의 공통이념인 인간삶의 권리인 천부인권을 부정한채 대한민국 정부가 공권력을 구사하여 법치가 배제된 간척개발사업에 필수전제 조건인 생태학적 사전 영향평가에 따른 대한민국 환경보전법 제 5 조 동법시행령 제 4 조를 이행치 안했을뿐만 아니라, 유엔인간 환경선언문에도 위배되는 5,000 만평에 달하는 명백한 불법 간척 개발사업을 자행하여 대한민국 천수만 해역권내 1 만 2 천여 어민들의 유일한 생활의 터전인 어장터를 전멸 황폐화 시켜놓으므로서 1 만 2 천여 천수만 영세어민들은 생존권을 박탈당한채 어언 6 년간에 걸쳐 기아선상에서 헤메며 생활고에 신음하다 심지어 수많은 어민들이 자살까지 하는 인간비극의 참상이 속출하는가 하면 생존권을 박탈당한 1 만 2 천여 영세어민들이 이제는 속수무책 굶어 죽을지경에 까지 이르렇는데도 방치시켜놓고 있는 정치행정 상황은 하나님이 내리신 천부인권의 인간이 먹고 살 수 있는 인간삶의 권리를 침해 부정하는 국제적으로도 유례없는 최악의 상태에 이른 경제적, 사회적, 문화적권리에 관한 국제규약 제 11 조, 제 12 조를 위반한 인권유린 현상이란것은 인간다운 삶의권리를 추구하고 먹어야만 살수있는, 다같은 인간조건인 전 인류가 공인하는 사실이란데서, 이는 국경과 민족을 초월한 전인류들의 규탄 제재조치를 받아야 마땅하다는 것이 우리국민들의 한결같은

— 2 —

0059

중론이 되여 있다는 것입니다.

2. 특히나 위와 같은 사실은 대한민국 국회가 3차에 걸쳐 현지답사 조사 확인하였고 국회에서 1년간 7차에 걸친 엄밀한 심의 끝에 그진상이 명백히 밝혀졌다고 보면, 공권력을 구사한 법치가 배제된 불법간척개발 사업으로 인하여 1만 2천여 어민들의 생존권을 박탈시켜 어언 6년간 기아선상에서 헤메다 굶어죽게 방치하는 국제적으로도 유례없는 최악의 상태에 이른 인권유린 현상은 대한민국, 정부, 국회, 정치인 다같이 공인하고 있다는데서 이는 정부, 국회의 명백한 직무유기요, 천부인권의 인간이 먹고 사는 인간삶의 권리를 부정하는 국제적으로도 유례 없는 최악의 상태에 이른 인권유린 정치행정 상황이란것은 먹어야만 살 수 있는 인류들로서는 누구나도 부인할 수 없는 사실이라 하겠습니다.

3. 따라서 구구한 설명들이 필요 없이 그간 6년간에 걸쳐 생존권을 박탈당한 1만 2천여 천수만어민들의 처절한 민생고의 참상을 그대로 묘사한 대한민국 국내 굴지의 언론계 한겨레신문의 그림판이나 지상보도를 유엔인권위원회 위원님 제위께서는 명확히 관찰해 보시라는 것입니다.

민권 민생 민의 보장을 정치행정의 최우선 과제로 삼고 인도주의와 법치주의를 실현해 나가는 우리의 주권재민 자유민주 헌정국가 사회속에서 과연 이와 같

-3-

0060

은 인간삶의 권리를 부정하는 국제적으로도·유례없는 최악의 상태에 이른 야만적인 참혹한 인권유린의 만행이 자행되여 질수 있겠으며, 자유국가 국정을 담당한 정부, 국회, 정치인이 이와같은 참혹한 인권유린 현상 앞에서도 구태의연 무감각, 무분별, 무책임 상태속에서 묵과 방치할수 있겠는가요?

이와 같은 참혹한 인권유린 현상앞에서 인간의 존엄성과 인류들의 인권보장을 제창한 유엔인권위원회로서는 의도적으로 인간을 굶어 죽게 방치시켜 놓은 인간삶의 권리를 부정하는 이와 같은 만행을 결코 용인하지 않을것으로 믿어마지 않는 바입니다. 세계 정부 위치에 있는 유엔인권 위원회가 만약에 이와 같은 천부인권인 인간삶의 권리를 부정한 인권유린 만행을 용인 한다면 인간사회는 유지 보존되여질 수 없고 국가나 인류사회가 유지 운영되여 질 수 없다는 것은 당연한 이치란 것입니다. 때문에 유엔으로서는 단호한 제재조치를 단행 해야만 된다는 것입니다.

4. 때문에 이와 같은 인간삶을 부정하는 무자비하고 무책임한 정치 행정 상황하에서는 삶을 갈구하는 힘 없는 어민들로서는 불가피 전 인류들에게 구원을 요청하지 않을 수 없기 때문에 대한민국 국민으로서 수모감을 무릅쓰고 세계제국들의 헌법정신이나 국제연합 헌장이나 국제인권 장전이나 인류들이 다같이 추구하는 인도주의 정신에 따라 유엔인권위원회에 청원을 올

— 4 —

리어 전인류들의 규탄과 재재속에서 천부인권의 인간 삶의 권리를 부정하는 국제적으로도 유례없는 최악의 상태에 이른 우리의 정치행정에 경종을 울려주심이 인간다운삶을 보장하는 자유국가 본연의 정치행정을 실현해 나갈수 있게 적극 제재조치 지원 협조해 주심과 아울러 공권력을 구사하여 생존권을 박탈당하고 어언 6 년간 기아선상에서 생사의 지로에서 헤매는 1 만 2 천여 천수만어민들의 생존권을 보장시켜 주실것을 청원 드리나이다.

이상과 같은 청원사항은 다같은 인간조건인 유엔인권위원회 위원님 제위께서는 충분한 이해가 있으실것으로 믿어마지 않는 바입니다. 그리고 인간의 생명을 존중하고 삶을 갈구하는 인류들로서는 다같이 동정하고 협조하고 규탄제재 할것으로 믿어마지 않는바입니다.

1990 년 4 월 30 일

한국서산 A . B 지구어민생존권쟁취위원회

위원장 이 상

— 5 —

0062

관리 번호	91 -514

외 무 부

종 별 :

번 호 : GVW-0945

일 시 : 91 0523 1900

수 신 : 장관(국연)

발 신 : 주 제네바 대사

제 목 : 아국 인권관련 진정서

대: 국연 2031-26002

금 5.23 대호 정부 답변서를 유엔 인권사무국에 제출함. 끝

(대사 박수길-국장)

예고 91.6.30 까지

1991. 6.30 에 ~~~~
~~~ 일반문서로 ~~~

국기국

PAGE 1

관리
번호 91-3996

주 제 네 바 대 표 부

재네(정) 2031-21   1991. 5.31

수 신 : 외무부장관

참 조 : 국제기구조약국장

제 목 : 유엔인권 사무국 접수 아국관련 진정서 (91-2)

1. 당지 유인 인권사무국은 91. 5. 24자 당관앞 공한을 통해 1503 절차에 의거,
   아국인권 상황관련 진정서 2건이 접수되었음을 알려온바, 이를 별첨
   송부합니다.

2. 상기 진정서 제출자는 비밀이며, 이중 1건은 임수경등 "정치범"석방,
   국가보안법철폐를 요청하는 내용이며, 또다른 1건은 홍성담 사건 관련
   입니다.

3. 상기 진정서중 임수경등 "정치범"관련 건은 인권사무국에 제출한
   아국답변서에 의거, 당관에서 조치하고, 홍성담 사건은 본부에서
   답변자료(영문)를 관계부처와 협의작성하여 91.6.25까지 인권사무국에
   제출할수 있도록 조치하여 주시기 바랍니다.

첨부 : 상기 공한 1부. 끝.

일반문서로 재분류(1991. 12. 31.)

예고: 91.12.31 일반

진 관			결재 (공람)		
접수일시	1991. 6. 4.	번호 2297			
처 리 과	0게				

주 제 네 바 대 사

검 토 필(1991. 6.30.)

0064

OFFICE DES NATIONS UNIES À GENÈVE

UNITED NATIONS OFFICE AT GENEVA

CENTRE POUR LES DROITS DE L'HOMME

CENTRE FOR HUMAN RIGHTS

Téléfax: (022) 733 98 79
Télégrammes: UNATIONS, GENÈVE
Télex: 412 962 UNO CH
Téléphone: 734 60 11   731 02 11

RÉF N°: G/SO 215/1 KOREA REP
(à rappeler dans la réponse)

Palais des Nations
CH-1211 GENÈVE 10

The Secretariat of the United Nations (Centre for Human Rights) presents
its compliments to the Office of the Permanent Observer of the Republic of
Korea to the United Nations Office at Geneva and with reference to its note
No. G/SO 215/1 KOREA REP, dated 7 July 1980, has the honour to transmit
herewith copies of two communications dated 12 February and 18 March 1991,
concerning human rights, which refer to the Republic of Korea.

Since the authors of the communications have not stated that they have
already divulged their names or that they have no objection to their names
being divulged, the communications are being forwarded, as required by the
resolution, without disclosing their identity.

A brief indication of the substance of the communications will be included
in a confidential list of communications which is to be submitted to the
Commission on Human Rights and the Sub-Commission on Prevention of
Discrimination and Protection of Minorities under Economic and Social Council
resolutions 728 F (XXVIII) and 1503 (XLVIII).

Any reply which the Permanent Observer may wish to transmit on behalf of
its Government under the above-mentioned resolutions should be forwarded to
the Centre for Human Rights, United Nations Office at Geneva, with an
indication as to whether the reply is to be presented to the Commission and
the Sub-Commission in summary form or in full.

24 May 1991   0065

JAVIER PEREZ de CUELLAR
SECRETARY GENERAL
THE UNITED NATIONS
NY, NY 10017

6/20 215/1 KOR RER

MARCH 18 '91

    / AM WRITING FOR THE IMMEDIATE RELEASE OF
IM SU KYUNG AND FATHER MOON AND ALL THE OTHER
KOREAN POLITICAL PRISONERS (1,300 PLUS). TODAY, THERE ARE
LIMITED CONTACTS ALLOWED BETWEEN NORTH & SOUTH
KOREANS, AND MANY OF THE PRISONERS WERE INCARCERATED
WHEN SEGREGATION WAS STRICTLY ENFORCED.

    / STRONGLY URGE THE REPEAL OF THE NATIONAL
SECURITY LAW WHICH IS THE MEANS OF FALSELY CREATING
POLITICAL PRISONERS FROM THEIR DESIRE FOR THE BASIC
HUMAN NEED OF A UNIFIED FAMILY.

    / URGE THE REMOVAL WITHOUT DELAY OF ALL US
TROOPS AND WEAPONS FROM SOUTH KOREA AND ALLOW
NORTH & SOUTH KOREA TO REUNIFY INTO ONE COUNTRY
AND THUS ALLOW THE DIVIDED FAMILIES TO ONCE AGAIN
BECOME WHOLE. / URGE THAT THIS BE DONE
WITHOUT THE SLIGHTEST UNITED STATES INTERFERENCE;
ALLOW THE KOREAN PEOPLE (BOTH NORTH & SOUTH) THE
SELF DETERMINATION THAT PEOPLE THE WORLD
OVER DESERVE AND DESIRE SO STRONGLY.

                  SINCERELY

                              (Signed)
                           [signature deleted]

P.S. IM SU KYUNG & FATHER MOON WERE SENTENCED TO
8 & 10 YEARS (LATER REDUCED TO 5 YEARS) JUST FOR
CROSSING THE DEMILITARIZED ZONE (AFTER ALMOST
40 YEARS AFTER THE KOREAN WAR).

                                       0066

·OFFICE DES NATIONS UNIE≡ GENÈVE

CENTRE POUR LES DROITS DE L'HOMME

Téléfax: (022) 733 98 79
Télégrammes: UNATIONS, GENÈVE
Télex: 412 962 UNO CH
Téléphone: 734 60 11   731 02 11

RÉF. N°:
(à rappeler dans la réponse)

UNIT ≡NATIONS OFFICE AT GENEVA

CENTRE FOR HUMAN RIGHTS

Palais des Nations
CH-1211 GENÈVE 10

COMMUNICATION

From: [Name deleted]   Address:

To: The United Nations

Mission concerned: Republic of Korea   Language: German

Date: 12 February 1991

Unofficial Summary Translation

The author alleges that Hong Song-Dam was arrested on 31 July 1989 in the Republic of Korea for having painted on a wall and sent pictures of it to the Peoples Democratic Republic of Korea. He was later sent to 7 years' imprisonment on grounds of infringement of the national security law. United Nations intercession is sought on his behalf and on behalf of others alleged political detainees.

0067

Kommission für Menschenrechte
der Vereinten Nationen
Palais des Nations

CH - 1211 Geneve

Betr.: Menschenrechtsverletzung in der Republik Korea

Sehr geehrte Damen und Herren,

durch eine Menschenrechtsorganisation habe ich von folgendem
Fall einer Menschenrechtsverletzung erfahren und möchte ihn
Ihnen vortragen:

Am 1. Juni 1990 wurde der 35jährige Hong Song-Dam, Vorsitzender
der Gruppe Kwangju der "Korean Nationalistic Artists
Federation" vom Berufungsgericht in Seoul zu sieben Jahren Haft
verurteilt. Ihm wurde ein Verstoß gegen das nationale
Sicherheitsgesetz (National Security Law, NSL) vorgeworfen. Er
soll eine Mauer bemalt haben und Fotos davon nach Nord-Korea
geschickt haben. Außerdem soll er als Spion eines in
Deutschland lebenden koreanischen Pfarrers tätig gewesen sein.
Nach seiner Verhaftung am 31. Juli 1989 wurde er im Gefängnis
gefoltert.

Ich bitte Sie, sich des Falles von Hong Song-Dam anzunehmen und
bei der koreanischen Regierung gegen seine Folterung und
Verurteilung zu protestieren und seine Freilassung zu fordern.
Sollten Ihre Interventionen zu einem Ergebnis führen,
informieren Sie mich bitte darüber.

Ich bedanke mich für Ihre Bemühungen und verbleibe

mit freundlichen Grüßen,

(Signed)
[Signature deleted]

0068

기 안 용 지

분류기호 문서번호	국연 2031 **22307**	(전화:)	시 행 상 특별취급	
보존기간	영구·준영구· 10. 5. 3. 1	장	관	

수 신 처 보존기간		

시행일자	1991. 6. 17.

보 조 기 관	국 장	전결	협 조 기 관	문서통제 경유 1991. 6. 17
	과 장			발 송 인
기안책임자		송영완		발송 1991. 6. 17 외무부

경 유 수 신 참 조	주제네바대사	발신명의

제 목	아국관련 진정서(91-2)

대 : 제네(정) 2031-21(91.5.31.)

대호, 법무부에서 작성한 홍성담 관련 설명자료를 별첨

송부하오니 영문으로 작성하여 인권사무국에 제출후 결과

보고바랍니다.

첨부 : 상기 설명자료 1부. 끝.

0069

공   란

공   란

공   란

공　　　　　란

공　　　란

공　　　란

관리 번호	91 -693

외 무 부

종 별 :

번 호 : GVW-1259   일 시 : 91 0705 1900

수 신 : 장관(국연)

발 신 : 주 제네바 대사

제 목 : 아국관련 진정서(91-2)

　　대: 국연 2031-22307

　　대호, 답변서를 금 7.5 인권 사무국에 재출함. 끝

　　(대사 박수길-국장)

　　예고 91.12.31. 까지

일반문서로재분류(1991.12.31.)

검 토 필(1991. 6. 30.)

국기국　　차관　　1차보

관리 번호	91 -4565

외 무 부

종 별 :

번 호 : GVW-1485   일 시 : 91 0807 1100

수 신 : 장 관(국연)

발 신 : 주 제네바 대사

제 목 : 유엔 인권 진정서

대: WGV-0094, 국연 2031-26002, 22307

금 8.6 MOLLER 유엔 인권 사무국 진정서 담당관에게 확인한바에 의하면 8.2종료된 진정서 실무소위 심의결과 대호 아국 관계 진정서 3 건은 기각되었다고함. 끝

(대사 박수길-국장)

예고 91.12.31. 일반

일반문서로재분류 (1991.12.31.)

국기국

PAGE 1

정 리 보 존 문 서 목 록					
기록물종류	일반공문서철	등록번호	2019030060	등록일자	2019-03-25
분류번호	734.22	국가코드		보존기간	영구
명 칭	유엔인권소위원회, 제43차. Geneva, 1991.8.5-30				
생 산 과	국제연합과	생산년도	1991~1991	담당그룹	
내용목차	* 수석대표 : 박수길 주제네바대사 * 유엔인권소위원회 : 유엔인권위원회 소수민 차별방지 및 보호에 관한 소위원회				

0001

주 제 네 바 대 표 부

제네 (정) 2031-473   1991. 5. 3

수신 : 외무부장관

참조 : 국제기구조약국장

제목 : 제 43차 유엔 인권 소위 잠정 의제

     91. 8. 5 - 8. 30간 당지에서 개최되는 제 43차 유엔 인권 소위

잠정 의제를 별첨 송부합니다.

첨 부 : 동 잠정의제 (E/CN.4/Sub.2/1991/1) 1부. 끝.

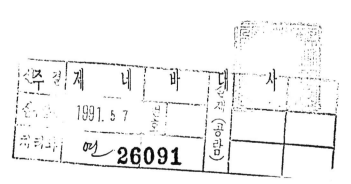

0002

UNITED
NATIONS

Economic and Social Council

Distr.
GENERAL

E/CN.4/Sub.2/1991/1
19 April 1991

Original: ENGLISH

COMMISSION ON HUMAN RIGHTS
Sub-Commission on Prevention
   of Discrimination and
   Protection of Minorities
Forty-third session

PROVISIONAL AGENDA

<u>Note by the Secretary-General</u>

<u>Duration and venue of the session</u>

1.   The forty-third session of the Sub-Commission on Prevention of
Discrimination and Protection of Minorities will be held at the United Nations
Office at Geneva from 5 to 30 August 1991. The first meeting will be convened
at 10.30 a.m. on Monday, 5 August 1991.

<u>Provisional agenda</u>

2.   The provisional agenda, prepared in accordance with rule 5 of the rules
of procedure of the functional commissions of the Economic and Social Council,
is reproduced below.

<u>Pre-sessional working groups</u>

3.   In accordance with previous decisions, the forty-third session of the
Sub-Commission will be preceded by three working groups as follows:

   (a) <u>Working Group on Communications</u>, established pursuant to paragraph 1
of Economic and Social Council resolution 1503 (XLVIII) of 27 May 1970. This
Working Group of five members of the Sub-Commission will meet for two weeks
prior to the forty-third session, that is from 22 July to 2 August 1991;

   (b) <u>Working Group on Contemporary Forms of Slavery</u>, established pursuant
to Economic and Social Council decisions 16 (LVI) and 17 (LVI)

0003

GE.91-11884/6040a

of 17 May 1974. This Working Group of five members of the Sub-Commission will meet for one week prior to the forty-third session, that is from 29 July to 2 August 1991;

(c) <u>Working Group on Indigenous Populations</u>, established pursuant to Economic and Social Council resolution 1982/34. At its forty-second session, the Sub-Commission, by its resolution 1990/26 of 31 August 1990 endorsed by Commission on Human Rights resolution 1991/59 of 6 March 1991, recommended to the Economic and Social Council that the Working Group on Indigenous Populations should be authorized to meet for 10 working days prior to the forty-third session, for the purpose of intensifying its efforts to complete a draft declaration on indigenous rights in consultation with interested Governments and organizations of indigenous peoples, that is from 22 July to 2 August 1991.

<u>In-session working groups</u>

4.   Since its thirty-fourth session in 1981, the Sub-Commission has established a sessional working group to assist it in relation to its annual review of developments concerning the human rights of persons subjected to any form of detention or imprisonment. The Sub-Commission may wish to consider establishing such a working group at its forty-third session.

5.   At its forty-first session, the Sub-Commission by its decision 1989/104 decided that, at the beginning of its forty-second session, it would establish a sessional working group of five of its members, appointed by the various regional groups and open to the participation of other members of the Sub-Commission, to prepare an overview and an analysis of the suggestions and proposals which have been made in order to enable the Sub-Commission to better discharge its responsibilities in dealing with violations of human rights as discussed under item 6 of its agenda, taking also into account the functions and duties of the Commission on Human Rights in the matter. At its forty-sixth session the Commission on Human Rights, by its resolution 1990/64 of 7 March 1990, invited the Sub-Commission to request this Working Group to include in its deliberations an examination of ways and means to avoid any proliferation of studies as well as of draft resolutions or decisions on issues already being dealt with by the Commission. By its decision 1990/125 of 31 August 1990, the Sub-Commission decided that the Working Group should continue its work at the forty-third session.

6.   By its decision 1990/123 of 31 August 1990, the Sub-Commission decided to establish, at its forty-third session, a sessional open-ended working group with the view to continuing to work on the preparation of a revised version of the draft declaration on freedom and non-discrimination in respect of the right of everyone to leave any country, including his own, and to return to his country (E/CN.4/Sub.2/1988/35 and Add.11, annex I). The Sub-Commission also decided to ask Mr. W. Sadi to prepare, without financial implications, the revised version of the above-mentioned draft declaration, on the basis of the discussions in the open-ended working group at its forty-second session and the comments and proposals contained in document E/CN.4/Sub.2/1990/47, to be submitted in 1991 for analysis and discussion by the working group with a view, if possible, to its submission to the Sub-Commission at its forty-third session. The Sub-Commission further decided, if appropriate, to invite the Special Rapporteur, Mr. Mubanga-Chipoya to be present in Geneva during the meetings of the working group.

0004

7.   Any decisions or resolutions affecting the provisional agenda of the forty-third session of the Sub-Commission which may be taken by the Economic and Social Council at its first regular session of 1991 will be brought to the attention of the Sub-Commission in an addendum to the present document.

8.   The annotations to the items listed in the provisional agenda will be issued as an addendum to the present document.

0005

<u>Provisional agenda</u>

1. Election of officers.

2. Adoption of the agenda.

3. Review of the work of the Sub-Commission.

4. Review of further developments in fields with which the Sub-Commission has been concerned.

5. Elimination of racial discrimination:

    (a) Measures to combat racism and racial discrimination and the role of the Sub-Commission;

    (b) Adverse consequences for the enjoyment of human rights of political military, economic and other forms of assistance given to the racist and colonialist régime of South Africa.

6. Question of the violation of human rights and fundamental freedoms, including policies of racial discrimination and segregation and of apartheid, in all countries, with particular reference to colonial and other dependent countries and territories: report of the Sub-Commission under Commission on Human Rights resolution 8 (XXIII).

7. The new international economic order and the promotion of human rights.

    (a) The role and equal participation of women in development.

8. The realization of economic, social and cultural rights.

9. Communications concerning human rights: report of the Working Group established under Sub-Commission resolution 2 (XXIV) in accordance with Economic and Social Council resolution 1503 (XLVIII).

10. The administration of justice and the human rights of detainees:

    (a) Question of human rights of persons subjected to any form of detention and imprisonment;

    (b) Question of human rights and states of emergency;

    (c) Individualization of prosecution and penalties, and repercussions of violations of human rights on families;

    (d) The right to a fair trial.

11. Independence and impartiality of the judiciary, jurors and assessors and the independence of lawyers.

12. Human Rights and disability.

13. Elimination of all forms of intolerance and of discrimination based on religion or belief.

0006

14. International peace and security as an essential condition for the enjoyment of human rights, above all the right to life.

15. Discrimination against indigenous peoples.

16. Contemporary forms of slavery.

17. Promotion, protection and restoration of human rights at national, regional and international levels:

    (a) Prevention of discrimination and protection of children: human rights and youth;

    (b) Prevention of discrimination and protection of women.

18. Protection of minorities.

19. The right of everyone to leave any country, including his own, and to return to his country.

20. Consideration of the future work of the Sub-Commission and of the draft provisional agenda for the forty-fourth session of the Sub-Commission.

21. Adoption of the report of the forty-third session.

0007

기 안 용 지

분류기호 문서번호	국연 2031-	(전화 :　　　)	시 행 상 특별취급	
보존기간	영구·준영구. 10. 5. 3. 1.	장　　　관		
수 신 처 보존기간				
시행일자	1991. 5. 10.			

보 조 기 관	국 장	전 결	협 조 기 관			문 서 통 제 (1991. 5. 11)
	과 장	*uy*				
						발 송 인 (1991. 5. 11)
기안책임자		송 영 완				

경 유 수 신 참 조	법무부장관 법무실장	발 신 명 의	

제 목	제43차 유연인권소위 잠정의제

　　　　91.8.5-8.30간 제네바에서 개최되는 제 43차 유연인권

소위원회 잠정의제를 별첨 송부하니 검토하시기 바라며, 귀부직원의

출장이 필요하다고 인정될 경우 동 회의 아국대표단 명단 통보에

참고코자 하니 출장직원의 직.성명을 91.6.30.한 당부로 통보하여

주시기 바랍니다.

　　　　첨 부 : 표제 잠정의제 사본 1부.　　　　끝.

0008

주 제 네 바 대 표 부

제네(정) 2031-544   1991. 6. 14

수신 : 외무부장관

참조 : 국제기구조약국장

제목 : 제 43차 유엔 인권소위 잠정의제 주석 자료

91.8.5 - 8.30 간 당지에서 개최되는 제 43차 유엔인권소위
잠정의제 주석 자료를 별첨 송부합니다.

첨부 : 동 자료 (E/CN.4/Sub.2/1991/1/Add.1) 1부. 끝.

주 제 네 바 대 사

0009

UNITED NATIONS

Economic and Social Council

Distr.
GENERAL

E/CN.4/Sub.2/1991/1/Add.1
17 May 1991

Original: ENGLISH

COMMISSION ON HUMAN RIGHTS
Sub-Commission on Prevention
   of Discrimination and
   Protection of Minorities
Forty-third session

ANNOTATIONS TO THE PROVISIONAL AGENDA

Prepared by the Secretary-General

CONTENTS*

* This table of contents is based upon the provisional agenda of the forty-third session of the Sub-Commission with the addition of the indicative sub-headings found in the text of the annotations for ease of reference.

GE.91-12092/3194B

0010

CONTENTS (continued)

0011

CONTENTS (continued)

0012

CONTENTS (continued)

0013

Item 1. Election of officers

1.   Rule 15 of the rules of procedure of the functional commissions of the Economic and Social Council provides that "at the commencement of its first meeting of a regular session", the Sub-Commission "shall elect, from among the representatives of its members, a Chairman, one or more Vice-Chairmen and such other officers as may be required".

Item 2. Adoption of the agenda

2.   Rule 7 of the rules of procedure provides that the agenda shall be adopted at the beginning of each session, after the election of officers, on the basis of the provisional agenda. The provisional agenda for the present session of the Sub-Commission is contained in document E/CN.4/Sub.2/1991/1.

3.   At its thirty-eighth session, the Sub-Commission, by its decision 1985/109, decided to observe at the commencement of its future annual sessions, beginning with the thirty-ninth session, a minute of silence in honour of the victims of apartheid in South Africa.

4.   Since 1985, the Sub-Commission has taken a number of decisions regarding the consideration, on a biennial basis, of certain agenda items (see resolutions 1985/34 and 1989/1 and decision 1988/104).

5.   As a result of those decisions, the Sub-Commission considers at odd-numbered sessions, such as the present, the following items:

    (a) Elimination of all forms of intolerance and of discrimination based on religion or belief;

    (b) International peace and security as an essential condition for the enjoyment of human rights, above all the right to life;

    (c) Review of the work of the Sub-Commission;

and at even-numbered sessions, the following items:

    (d) Human rights and disability;

    (e) Human rights and scientific and technological developments;

    (f) Encouragement of universal acceptance of human rights instruments.

6.   By its decision 1990/113, adopted at its forty-second session, the Sub-Commission decided to suspend the debate on the agenda item "Human rights and disability" and to include it in the provisional agenda for its forty-third session as a matter of the highest priority.

7.   At its forty-first session, by its resolution 1989/1, the Sub-Commission, recalling its resolution 1985/34 and Commission on Human Rights resolution 1985/28, decided that the item entitled "The new international economic order and the promotion of human rights" would be considered on an annual basis.

0014

8.   At its forty-first session, by its resolution 1989/41, the Sub-Commission decided to consider matters related to slavery and slavery-like practices in subsequent sessions under the agenda item entitled "Contemporary forms of slavery".

9.   The Sub-Commission may wish to recall the following decisions that it took at its forty-second session:

     (a) By its resolution 1990/106, the Sub-Commission decided to postpone consideration of draft resolution E/CN.4/Sub.2/1990/L.7 and the relevant amendments thereto until its forty-third session. For the text of the draft resolution and the amendments thereto see paragraphs 69 and 70 of the report of the Sub-Commission on its forty-second session (E/CN.4/1991/2);

     (b) By its decision 1990/115, the Sub-Commission decided to suspend further consideration of draft resolution E/CN.4/Sub.2/1990/L.40 until its forty-third session. For the text of the draft resolution see paragraph 77 of the report of the Sub-Commission on its forty-second session (E/CN.4/1991/2);

     (c) By decision 1990/116, the Sub-Commission decided to suspend further consideration of draft resolution E/CN.4/Sub.2/1990/L.45 until its forty-third session. For the text of the draft resolution see paragraph 101 of the report of the Sub-Commission on its forty-second session (E/CN.4/1991/2);

     (d) By its decision 1990/121, the Sub-Commission decided to discuss the situation in Lebanon at its forty-third session (see annotations to item 6).

Organization of work

10. With regard to the question of the organization of work of the present session, the Sub-Commission may recall that paragraph 2 of rule 24 of the rules of procedure of the Economic and Social Council provides that, except for the regional commissions, the commissions and committees of the Council shall not create either standing or ad hoc intersessional subsidiary bodies without prior approval of the Council.

11. As authorized by the Council, three working groups are scheduled to meet prior to the forty-third session of the Sub-Commission: the Working Group on Communications (see annotations to item 9), the Working Group on Indigenous Populations (see annotations to item 15) and the Working Group on Contemporary Forms of Slavery (see annotations to item 16). In this regard, the Sub-Commission may recall that, by its resolution 1990/26, the Sub-Commission recommended to the Commission on Human Rights that it recommend to the Economic and Social Council that the Working Group on Indigenous Populations be authorized to meet for 10 working days prior to the forty-third session of the Sub-Commission. In its resolution 1991/59, the Commission recommended that the Economic and Social Council authorize the Working Group to meet for 10 working days prior to the forty-third session of the Sub-Commission.

12. At its thirty-fourth and subsequent sessions, the Sub-Commission had established a sessional working group to assist it in relation to its annual review of developments concerning the human rights of persons subjected to any form of detention or imprisonment. The Sub-Commission may wish to consider establishing such a working group at the present session (see annotations to item 10 (a)).

0015

13. By its decision 1990/125, the Sub-Commission decided that the sessional working group of five of its members, appointed by Sub-Commission decision 1989/104, should continue its work at the forty-third session (see annotations to items 3 and 6).

14. By its decision 1990/123, the Sub-Commission also decided to establish, at its forty-third session, a sessional open-ended working group with the view to continuing to work on the preparation of the revised version of the draft declaration on freedom and non-discrimination in respect of the right of everyone to leave any country, including his own, and to return to his country (see annotations to item 19).

15. When considering its organization of work, the Sub-Commission may wish to take into account Commission resolution 1991/56, by which the Commission, _inter alia_,

(a) Requested the Sub-Commission to give priority to those topics on which standards are being prepared;

(b) Recommended that the Sub-Commission should propose a new study only when a previously authorized one was fully completed;

(c) Recommended that the Sub-Commission should restrict the number of studies undertaken at any one time in order to give the opportunity to all members to participate in an in-depth discussion among experts;

(d) Urged the Sub-Commission to concentrate its attention on those specific human rights issues to which it can make a distinctive contribution as an expert body;

(e) Invited the Sub-Commission to continue to give due regard to new developments in the field of human rights;

(f) Encouraged the Sub-Commission to continue and finalize its discussions on the best way to improve the efficiency of the debate, while attaching high priority to the efforts to rationalize and streamline its work.

16. The Commission, by the same resolution, invited its Chairman to inform the Sub-Commission on the debate of the Commission on the work of the Sub-Commission.

17. The Commission further requested the Sub-Commission, at its forty-third session, to consider its practice of forwarding draft resolutions and decisions to the Commission for attention, action or consideration.

18. The Sub-Commission will recall its decision 1990/122, by which it decided that draft resolutions and decisions should not be introduced by one of the sponsors, and urged members not to make general comments on the draft, but offer only concrete proposals on the texts.

19. With regard to documentation, the attention of the Sub-Commission is drawn to Economic and Social Council resolution 1986/33, adopted upon recommendation by the Commission in its resolution 1986/31, by which the Council requested the Sub-Commission henceforth to submit to the Commission, after a thorough examination, the studies and reports prepared by the

0016

special rapporteurs of the Sub-Commission with a brief written introductory
statement by the special rapporteur, and to discontinue the practice of
requesting special rapporteurs to introduce their reports personally to the
Commission. The Council further requested the Sub-Commission to adhere
strictly to the guidelines governing the limitation of documents and to ensure
that special rapporteurs responsible for preparing reports and studies were
brief and concise and that their reports and studies, as far as possible, did
not exceed 32 pages. The Council also decided that henceforth studies prepared
by special rapporteurs of the Sub-Commission should be printed only following
an express decision to that effect taken by the Commission and subsequently by
the Council, which should have an opportunity to study the relevant financial
implications. In this connection, reference should be made to Economic and
Social Council resolution 1982/50 and the annex thereto, Commission
resolution 17 (XXXVII) of 10 March 1981, 1983/22, 1983/28, 1988/43, 1989/32
and 1991/56, as well as the instructions issued by the Secretary-General
with respect to documentation for meetings (ST/SGB/184/Add.1 and
ST/AI/189/Add.20/Rev.1).

Item 3. <u>Review of the work of the Sub-Commission</u>

20. This item was first on the Sub-Commission's agenda at its thirty-fifth
session, in accordance with its decision 2 (XXXIV) of 3 September 1981.
Subsequently, the Economic and Social Council, by resolution 1983/32 and
1986/35; the Commission, by resolutions 1983/21, 1983/22, 1984/60, 1985/28,
1986/37, 1986/38, 1987/35, 1988/43, 1989/36 and 1990/64 and decision 1986/102;
and the Sub-Commission, by resolutions 1983/21, 1984/37 and 1985/24, provided
a number of general and specific directives and suggestions concerning the
Sub-Commission's role, title and methods of work, as well as the election of
its members. Commission resolution 1990/64 requested the Chairman of the
Sub-Commission to report to the Commission on the implementation of the
guidelines provided by the Commission in that resolution. The Chairman of the
Sub-Commission submitted his report to the Commission's forty-seventh session
(E/CN.4/1991/48).

21. The Commission on Human Rights, at its forty-seventh session, adopted
resolution 1991/56 entitled "Work of the Sub-Commission on Prevention of
Discrimination and Protection of Minorities". In that resolution, the
Commission, <u>inter alia</u>, reaffirmed that the Sub-Commission can best assist the
Commission by providing it with recommendations based on the different views
and perspectives of independent experts, which should be appropriately
reflected in the report of the Sub-Commission as well as in the expert studies
carried out under its auspices; called upon the Sub-Commission, in the
fulfilment of its functions and duties, to be guided by the relevant
resolutions of the Commission and the Economic and Social Council; requested
the Sub-Commission to give priority to those topics on which standards are
being prepared, in accordance with decisions taken by the Commission and
within the time frames set by the Commission; urged all the special
rapporteurs of the Sub-Commission to submit their reports by the deadline
given by the Secretariat so that these reports can be available in all
languages well before the meeting; recommended that the Sub-Commission should,
as a general rule, propose a new study only when a study previously authorized
is fully completed; and reminded the Sub-Commission that new studies or other
reports involving financial implications can only be undertaken after
authorization by its superior bodies.

22. In that same resolution, the Commission recommended that the Sub-Commission should restrict the number of studies undertaken at any one time to give the opportunity to all members to participate in an in-depth discussion among experts and should consider elaborating procedures with a view to ensuring the earliest possible completion of studies.

23. The Commission further requested the Sub-Commission to restrict its requests to the Secretary-General to ask Governments, intergovernmental organizations, specialized agencies and other such bodies for their views and comments to requests relating to those studies which have received prior explicit approval from the Commission; invited the Sub-Commission to give due consideration to draft resolutions proposed for adoption, bearing in mind that such draft resolutions should be proposed only on subjects that have been thoroughly discussed in the Sub-Commission or in its working groups; and requested the Sub-Commission to consider its practice of forwarding draft resolutions or decisions to the Commission. The Commission recognized that working groups constituted an invaluable element in the expert work of the Sub-Commission, noted the steps taken so far by the Sub-Commission to rationalize and streamline its work and encouraged the Sub-Commission to continue this process, and called upon States to nominate as members and alternates persons meeting the criteria of independent experts who should discharge in that capacity their functions as members of the Sub-Commission. The Commission invited the Chairman of the Commission to inform the Sub-Commission on the debate under its item concerning the work of the Sub-Commission. Finally, the Commission requested the Chairman of the Sub-Commission to report to it on the implementation of the guidelines which it provided in that resolution. With respect to the subject of rationalizing its work, the Sub-Commission may wish to take note of Commission decision 1991/109, containing guidelines for a revised provisional agenda for its forty-ninth session.

24. With respect to standard-setting activities, the Sub-Commission will recall Commission resolution 1987/24, by which the Commission invited the Sub-Commission, when engaged in developing international instruments in the field of human rights, to bear in mind the guidelines established in General Assembly resolution 41/120 of 4 December 1986. In that resolution, the Assembly urged Member States and United Nations bodies engaged in developing new international human rights standards to give due consideration in that work to the established international legal framework, and invited Member States and United Nations bodies to bear in mind the following guidelines in developing international instruments in the field of human rights. Such instruments should, _inter alia_:

     (a) Be consistent with the existing body of international human rights law;

     (b) Be of fundamental character and derive from the inherent dignity and worth of the human person;

     (c) Be sufficiently precise to give rise to identifiable and practicable rights and obligations;

     (d) Provide, where appropriate, realistic and effective implementation machinery, including reporting systems;

     (e) Attract broad international support.

0018

Various possibilities of implementing paragraphs 2 and 6 of
resolution 8 (XXIII) of the Commission

25. At its fortieth session, the Sub-Commission decided to continue
the discussion at its forty-first session of this subject, without prejudice
to the confidential procedure provided for in resolution 1503 (XLVIII) of
the Economic and Social Council or to other procedures instituted since the
adoption of that resolution by the Council (decision 1988/104).

26. At its forty-first session, by its decision 1989/104, the Sub-Commission
decided that, at the beginning of its forty-second session, it would establish
a sessional working group of five of its members, appointed by the various
regional groups and open to the participation of other members of the
Sub-Commission, to prepare an overview and an analysis of the suggestions and
proposals which have been made in order to enable the Sub-Commission to better
discharge its responsibilities in dealing with violations of human rights as
discussed under item 6 of its agenda, taking also into account the functions
and duties of the Commission on Human Rights in the matter. At its
forty-second session, by its decision 1990/125, the Sub-Commission decided
that the working group should continue its work at the forty-third session.

27. At its forty-seventh session, the Commission on Human Rights, by its
resolution 1991/56, invited the working group of the Sub-Commission to
intensify its discussions on reform issues and to examine ways and means to
avoid any proliferation of studies as well as draft resolutions and decisions
on issues already being dealt with by the Commission.

28. At the present session, the Sub-Commission will have before it the report
of the Working Group (see also item 6) (E/CN.4/Sub.2/1991/16).

Item 4. Review of further developments in fields with which the
         Sub-Commission has been concerned

29. This item has been regularly considered by the Sub-Commission since 1962,
in conformity with resolution 5 (XIV). The Sub-Commission, at its forty-third
session, will have before it a note of the Secretary-General containing a
review of further developments in fields with which the Sub-Commission has
been concerned (E/CN.4/Sub.2/1991/2).

30. Under this item, the Sub-Commission has discussed recent activities of
the International Labour Organisation and the United Nations Educational,
Scientific and Cultural Organization relating to matters dealt with by the
Sub-Commission. The reports of ILO and UNESCO on their activities relating
to these matters will be available in documents E/CN.4/Sub.2/1991/3 and
E/CN.4/Sub.2/1991/4 respectively.

Compensation for victims of gross violations of human rights

31. The Sub-Commission, at its forty-first session, by its
resolution 1989/13, entrusted Mr. Theo van Boven with the task of
undertaking a study concerning the right to restitution, compensation and
rehabilitation for victims of gross violations of human rights and fundamental
freedoms, taking into account relevant existing international human rights

norms on compensation and relevant decisions and views of international human rights organs, with a view to exploring the possibility of developing some basic principles and guidelines in this respect.

32. The Sub-Commission, at its forty-second session, by its resolution 1990/6, requested Mr. van Boven to prepare for the Sub-Commission, at its forty-third session, a progress report on the subject.

33. At the present session, the Sub-Commission will have before it the progress report of the Special Rapporteur (E/CN.4/Sub.2/1991/7).

<u>Human rights and the environment</u>

34. At its forty-second session, having considered the concise note of Ms. Fatma Zohra Ksentini on the subject (E/CN.4/Sub.2/1990/12), the Sub-Commission adopted resolution 1990/7, by which it entrusted Ms. Ksentini with the task of preparing a study on human rights and the environment and requested her to submit a preliminary report to the Sub-Commission at its forty-third session. It recommended to the Commission that it should endorse Ms. Ksentini's appointment as Special Rapporteur.

35. At its forty-seventh session, the Commission on Human Rights, by its resolution 1991/44, endorsed the appointment by the Sub-Commission of Ms. Ksentini as Special Rapporteur and recommended to the Preparatory Committee for the United Nations Conference on Environment and Development that Ms. Ksentini be invited to participate as an observer at the sessions of the Preparatory Committee and the Conference. The Special Rapporteur was requested to complete the study and to submit a report to the Sub-Commission at its forty-third session with a view to making a timely contribution to the Preparatory Committee. The Commission further recommended that the Economic and Social Council should endorse the appointment of Ms. Ksentini as Special Rapporteur.

36. At its present session, the Sub-Commission will have before it the preliminary report of the Special Rapporteur (E/CN.4/Sub.2/1991/8).

<u>Right to freedom of opinion and expression</u>

37. At its fortieth session, the Sub-Commission, by its decision 1989/110, requested Mr. Danilo Türk to prepare a working paper containing a proposal for carrying out a study called for by the Commission on Human Rights in its resolution 1988/37 concerning the right to freedom of expression and opinion, with the aim of clarifying conceptual and methodological questions and to serve as a basis on which future decisions could be taken by the Sub-Commission on this matter.

38. At its forty-first session, the Sub-Commission, by its resolution 1989/14, decided to entrust Mr. Louis Joinet and Mr. Türk with the preparation of a study on the right to freedom of opinion and expression, the current problems of its realization and on measures necessary for its strengthening and promotion.

0020

39. At its forty-second session, having considered the preliminary report submitted by the Special Rapporteurs (E/CN.4/Sub.2/1990/11), the Sub-Commission, by its decision 1990/117, decided to give priority consideration to the updated report on the subject at its forty-third session.

40. The Commission, at its forty-seventh session, adopted resolution 1991/32, by which it welcomed the intention of the Special Rapporteurs to study in greater details measures necessary for the strengthening and promotion of this right and decided to review this question on the basis, _inter alia_, of the updated report of the Special Rapporteurs.

41. At the present session, the Sub-Commission will have before it the updated report of the Special Rapporteur (E/CN.4/Sub.2/1991/9).

Traditional practices affecting the health of women and children

42. The Sub-Commission, at its thirty-sixth session, in its resolution 1983/1, made recommendations concerning a study relating to traditional practices affecting the health of women and children. The Commission, for its part, in resolution 1984/48, recommended to the Economic and Social Council that a working group of experts should undertake such a study. The Council endorsed that recommendation (resolution 1984/34) and the report was presented to the Commission at its forty-second session, in 1986 (E/CN.4/1986/42). The Commission, by its resolution 1986/28, took note of the report of the working group and requested the Secretary-General to transmit the report to Governments, competent organizations and specialized agencies, drawing their attention to the recommendations contained therein. At its forty-fourth session, the Commission, by its resolution 1988/57, requested the Sub-Commission to consider measures to be taken at the national and international levels to eliminate such practices, and to submit a report to the Commission at its forty-sixth session.

43. The Sub-Commission, at its fortieth session, by its resolution 1988/34, requested Ms. Halima Embarek Warzazi to study, on the basis of information to be gathered from Governments, specialized agencies and other intergovernmental and non-governmental organizations concerned, recent developments with regard to traditional practices affecting the health of women and children, and to bring the results of her study to the attention of the Sub-Commission at its forty-first session. The Commission, at its forty-fifth session, by its decision 1989/107, approved the Sub-Commission's request.

44. At its forty-first session, by its resolution 1989/16, the Sub-Commission took note of Ms. Warzazi's preliminary report (E/CN.4/Sub.2/1989/42 and Add.1) and made the following recommendations to the Commission on Human Rights:

    (a) The mandate of the Special Rapporteur should be extended for two years so as to enable her to present a more complete report;

    (b) Field missions should be undertaken by Ms. Warzazi, if possible to two countries where harmful traditional practices are prevalent;

    (c) International regional seminars should be held on the subject of harmful traditional practices in Africa and Asia;

0021

(d) All efforts should be made by the Centre for Human Rights to provide necessary support, including a full-time professional assistant, to liaise with Governments, United Nations agencies and Economic and Social Commissions, non-governmental organizations and other concerned institutions, with special emphasis on data-gathering from the many organizations currently working to eliminate harmful traditional practices, but which are not mentioned in the current report;

(e) The subject of traditional practices should be on the agenda of the Sub-Commission for sustained follow-up.

45. The recommendations were endorsed by the Commission (decision 1990/109) and the Economic and Social Council (decision 1990/247).

46. The Sub-Commission at the present session will have before it the report of the Special Rapporteur (E/CN.4/Sub.2/1991/6).

Discrimination against HIV-infected people or people with AIDS

47. The Sub-Commission, by its decision 1988/111, decided that the information provided to the Sub-Commission at its fortieth session by the World Health Organization, the International Commission of Jurists and certain members on the problem of discrimination against persons with the HIV virus or suffering from AIDS, together with the consideration set forth in General Assembly resolution 42/8 of 26 October 1987 and World Health Assembly resolution WHA 41.24 of 13 May 1988, justified consideration of the question whether the Sub-Commission should study that problem. Consequently, the Sub-Commission asked Mr. Luis Varela Quirós to prepare, for submission to the Sub-Commission at its forty-first session, a concise note setting forth methods by which such a study could be made.

48. The Commission, by its resolution 1989/11, invited the Sub-Commission to examine, using the opportunity provided by the study on discrimination against persons with the HIV virus or suffering from AIDS envisaged in its decision 1988/111, the possibility of extending the scope of such a study to other kinds of discrimination against sick or disabled persons, in consultation with WHO and giving Governments that wished to express their views the opportunity to do so.

49. At its forty-first session, the Sub-Commission entrusted Mr. Varela Quirós with a study of problems and causes of discrimination against HIV-infected people or people with AIDS. The Sub-Commission recommended that the Special Rapporteur take into account Commission resolution 1989/11 and the issues and guidelines of the 1989 International Consultation on HIV/AIDS and Human Rights convened in Geneva.

50. At its forty-second session, the Sub-Commission, by its decision 1990/118, decided to continue consideration of the progress report of the Special Rapporteur at its forty-third session.

51. At the present session, the Sub-Commission will have before it the progress report of the Special Rapporteur (E/CN.4/Sub.2/1991/10).

0022

Human rights in times of armed conflict

52. At its forty-first session, the Sub-Commission adopted resolution 1989/24, by which it recommended to the Commission that the Secretary-General should be called upon to request information from Governments on the scope of education provided to members of the police and the armed forces and to submit a report to the Sub-Commission. The Sub-Commission should study the matter further at its forty-second session.

53. At its forty-sixth session, by its resolution 1990/66, the Commission endorsed the recommendation of the Sub-Commission.

54. At its forty-second session, the Sub-Commission took no action on this question.

55. At its present session the Sub-Commission will have before it the report of the Secretary-General (E/CN.4/Sub.2/1991/5).

Status of special rapporteurs and representatives, members of the Sub-Commission and members of working groups established by the Commission

56. The Sub-Commission will recall Commission resolution 1991/33, which requested the Secretary-General to take the necessary measures to ensure that all special rapporteurs and representatives, independent experts, members of the Sub-Commission and members of working groups established by the Commission are considered as "experts on mission" within the context of article VI, section 22, of the Convention on the Privileges and Immunities of the United Nations, and in this regard urged States to comply with their obligations under the Convention. The Commission further requested the Secretary-General to take the necessary measures to ensure the prescribed protection for officials of the United Nations Secretariat accompanying special rapporteurs and representatives, independent experts, members of the Sub-Commission and members of working groups established by the Commission, on field missions, and to report to the Commission at its forty-eighth session on the measures taken in this regard.

Provisional suspension of rule 59 of the rules of procedure of the functional commissions of the Economic and Social Council

57. At its forty-second session, the Sub-Commission decided to suspend temporarily rule 59 of the rules of procedure for the purpose of protecting the independence of experts during the time necessary to vote on the draft resolutions under agenda item 6 (decision 1990/105) and agenda item 9 (decision 1990/111) of the forty-second session of the Sub-Commission.

58. At the same session, the Sub-Commission adopted resolution 1990/4, by which it recommended to the Commission the adoption of a draft resolution recommending that the Economic and Social Council should add the following footnote to rule 59 of the rules of procedure of its functional commissions:

"It is understood that the Sub-Commission on Prevention of Discrimination and Protection of Minorities will vote on resolutions pertaining to allegations of violations of human rights in countries by secret ballot."

0023

59. At its forty-seventh session, the Commission, by its resolution 1991/81, proposed that the Economic and Social Council interpret the rules of procedure of the functional commissions as they pertain to the Sub-Commission and recommended to the Council that it interpret rule 59 of the rules of procedure as follows: it is understood that the Sub-Commission on Prevention of Discrimination and Protection of Minorities may vote on resolutions pertaining to allegations of violations of human rights in countries by secret ballot, when it so decides by a majority of its present and voting members.

Movement and dumping of toxic and dangerous products and wastes

60. The Sub-Commission will recall Commission resolution 1991/47, by which the Commission invited the United Nations Environment Programme and the Organization of African Unity to intensify their collaboration on the problem of transboundary movements of hazardous wastes and their disposal, and decided to consider this question further.

Item 5. Elimination of racial discrimination

Sub-item (a) Measures to combat racism and racial discrimination and the role of the Sub-Commission

61. The Sub-Commission decided to include this item in its agenda at its thirty-first session, in 1978, and the item has since remained on its agenda.

Implementation of the Programme for the Decade for Action to Combat Racism and Racial Discrimination

62. In resolution 3057 (XXVIII) of 2 November 1973, the General Assembly designated the 10-year period beginning on 10 December 1973 as the Decade for Action to Combat Racism and Racial Discrimination; the Programme was annexed to that resolution. Since that time, the question of the implementation of the Programme has been discussed at each session of the General Assembly, the Economic and Social Council, the Commission on Human Rights and the Sub-Commission.

63. The Second World Conference to Combat Racism and Racial Discrimination, which took place from 1 to 12 August 1983 in Geneva, adopted a Declaration and a Programme of Action for a Second Decade. Upon the recommendation of the Conference, the General Assembly, by its resolution 38/14 of 22 November 1983, proclaimed the period beginning on 10 December 1983 as the Second Decade to Combat Racism and Racial Discrimination and approved the Programme of Action annexed to that resolution.

64. The General Assembly, at its forty-second session, adopted resolution 42/47 of 30 November 1987 by which it approved a plan of activities for the period 1990-1993, the second half of the Second Decade.

65. At its forty-fifth session, the General Assembly adopted resolution 45/105 of 14 December 1990, by which it took note of the report submitted by the Secretary-General containing information on the activities of Governments, specialized agencies, regional intergovernmental organizations and non-governmental organizations, as well as United Nations organs, to give effect to the Programme of Action for the Second Decade to Combat Racism and Racial Discrimination (A/45/443). The Assembly also noted and commended the

efforts made to coordinate all the programmes currently under implementation by the United Nations system that relate to the objectives of the Decade and encouraged the Coordinator for the Second Decade to Combat Racism and Racial Discrimination to continue his efforts.

66. In the same resolution, the Assembly took note of the study of the results achieved and the obstacles encountered during the first Decade for Action to Combat Racism and Racial Discrimination and the first half of the Second Decade and requested the Secretary-General to publish the study and distribute it on as wide a scale as possible. The Assembly further requested the Secretary-General to continue the study on the effects of racial discrimination on the children of minorities, in particular those of migrant workers, in the field of education, training and employment, and to submit recommendations for the implementation of measures to combat the effects of that discrimination.

67. At its forty-second session, the Sub-Commission, by its resolution 1990/1, requested the Secretary-General to consider ways and means necessary to respond to urgent situations and new trends involving racism and racial discrimination and to prepare an outline, for consideration by the Sub-Commission at its forty-third session, of possible activities for increasing the effectiveness of United Nations actions to combat racism and racial discrimination. The Sub-Commission also requested the Secretary-General to organize, at the forty-third session, a joint meeting for one day with the Committee on the Elimination of Racial Discrimination.

68. By its resolution 1990/2, the Sub-Commission expressed its appreciation to the Special Rapporteur for his study (E/CN.4/Sub.2/1989/8 and Add.1), decided to transmit the recommendations contained in the study to the Secretary-General so that they might be taken into account in further actions to combat racism and racial discrimination. The Sub-Commission requested the Secretary-General to prepare, on the basis of replies obtained from Governments, specialized agencies and other intergovernmental organizations, as well as from non-governmental organizations, an overview of current trends of racism, discrimination, intolerance and xenophobia affecting the above-mentioned groups, as well as of measures taken by Governments against those phenomena and the effects of such measures and to submit the overview for consideration by the Sub-Commission at its forty-third session, under item 5 (a) of its agenda. The Sub-Commission also decided to give thorough consideration at its forty-third session to the recommendation of the Special Rapporteur to update the study on racial discrimination prepared in 1976 by Mr. Hernán Santa Cruz.

69. The Commission, at its forty-seventh session, by its resolution 1991/11, urged all States and international organizations to cooperate with the Secretary-General in the implementation of those activities for the period 1985-1989 (see A/39/167-E/1983/33 and Add.1 and 2) not yet undertaken and of the plan of activities for the period 1990-1991 listed in the annex to General Assembly resolution 42/47 of 30 November 1987. The Commission decided that the thematic topic for 1992 would be "Treatment of political prisoners and detainees in South Africa, particularly women and children" and for 1993 "Global survey on the extent of dissemination of the International Convention on the Elimination of All Forms of Racial Discrimination"; it took note with

0025

satisfaction of the report of the Seminar on political, historical, economic, social and cultural factors contributing to racism, racial discrimination and apartheid, held at Geneva from 10 to 14 December 1990 (E/CN.4/1991/63 and Add.1) and recommended to the General Assembly that it take appropriate steps, in due course, to launch a Third Decade to Combat Racism and Racial Discrimination, to begin in 1993.

70. At its present session, the Sub-Commission will have before it the outline prepared by the Secretary-General (E/CN.4/Sub.2/1991/11 and the report of the Secretary-General (E/CN.4/Sub.2/1991/12 and Add.1).

Sub-item (b) Adverse consequences for the enjoyment of human rights of political, military, economic and other forms of assistance given to the racist and colonialist régime of South Africa

71. This question has been considered by the Sub-Commission since its twenty-sixth session when, in resolution 3 (XXVI) of 19 September 1973, it affirmed the importance of evaluating the consequences for the enjoyment of human rights of assistance to the colonial and racist régimes of southern Africa. At its fifty-sixth session, in 1974, the Economic and Social Council approved the decision of the Commission on Human Rights to authorize the Sub-Commission to appoint a special rapporteur on this issue (resolution 1864 (LVI)). Since then, the Sub-Commission, the Commission on Human Rights and the General Assembly have regularly examined this question at various sessions and have adopted a number of resolutions pertaining thereto. Particular reference may be made to: (a) resolution 1 (XXX) of 26 August 1977, by which the Sub-Commission, in implementation of Commission on Human Rights resolution 7 (XXXIII) of 4 March 1977, invited Mr. Ahmed Khalifa, the Special Rapporteur on the question, to prepare the necessary material for a provisional general list identifying those whose activities constituted assistance to the colonial and racist régimes in southern Africa; (b) Sub-Commission resolutions 2 (XXXIII) of 2 September 1980 and 6 (XXXIV) of 9 September 1981 and resolutions 1982/16, 1983/6, 1984/4, 1985/3, 1987/7, 1988/3 and 1989/18, in which Mr. Khalifa was invited to continue, subject to annual review, to update the list and submit it through the Sub-Commission to the Commission.

72. At its forty-second session, the Sub-Commission considered the updated report submitted by the Special Rapporteur (E/CN.4/Sub.2/1990/13 and Add.1) and adopted resolution 1990/3 which recommended the Commission should adopt a resolution calling for the Economic and Social Council to welcome the Commission's invitation to the Special Rapporteur to continue to update his list.

73. At its forty-fifth session, the General Assembly also considered the updated report of the Special Rapporteur and adopted resolution 45/84 of 14 December 1990. By this resolution, the Assembly expressed its appreciation to the Special Rapporteur for his updated report and welcomed with satisfaction the intention of the Commission and the Sub-Commission to invite the Special Rapporteur to continue to update his list of banks, transnational corporations and other organizations assisting South Africa. The Assembly invited the Sub-Commission at its forty-third session to consider the Special Rapporteur's updated report.

0026

74. The Commission on Human Rights, at its forty-seventh session, adopted resolution 1991/9 recommending that the Economic and Social Council should welcome the invitation to the Special Rapporteur and should request the Secretary-General to contact the Government of South Africa with a view to enabling the Special Rapporteur to visit that country within the perspective of the next update of his report. The attention of the Sub-Commission is also drawn to Commission resolution 1991/17 on adverse consequences for the enjoyment of human rights of political, military, economic and other forms of assistance given to South Africa. At the present session, the Sub-Commission will have before it the updated report of the Special Rapporteur (E/CN.4/Sub.2/1991/13 and Add.1).

Item 6. <u>Question of the violation of human rights and fundamental freedoms, including policies of racial discrimination and segregation and of apartheid, in all countries, with particular reference to colonial and other dependent countries and territories: report of the Sub-Commission established under Commission on Human Rights resolution 8 (XXIII)</u>

75. By resolution 8 (XXIII) of 16 March 1967, the Commission on Human Rights decided to give annual consideration to the item entitled "Question of violations of human rights and fundamental freedoms, including policies of racial discrimination and segregation and of apartheid, in all countries, with particular reference to colonial and other dependent countries and territories". In paragraph 2 of that resolution, the Commission requested the Sub-Commission to prepare a report containing information on violations of human rights and fundamental freedoms from all available sources for the use of the Commission. The Secretary-General was requested, in paragraph 3, to provide assistance and facilities to the Sub-Commission in accomplishing its task. In paragraph 6, the Commission invited the Sub-Commission to bring to the attention of the Commission any situation which it had reasonable cause to believe revealed a consistent pattern of violations of human rights and fundamental freedoms in any country, including policies of racial discrimination, segregation and apartheid, with particular reference to colonial and other dependent territories.

76. The Economic and Social Council, in resolution 1235 (XLII) of 6 June 1967, welcomed the decision of the Commission to give annual consideration to the item and concurred with the requests for assistance addressed to the Sub-Commission and the Secretary-General in Commission resolution 8 (XXIII). The Council authorized the Commission and the Sub-Commission to examine information relevant to gross violations of human rights and fundamental freedoms contained in the communications listed by the Secretary-General pursuant to Economic and Social Council resolution 728 F (XXVIII) of 30 July 1959, and further authorized the Commission to make a thorough study of situations which revealed a consistent pattern of violations of human rights.

<u>Situation in South Africa</u>

77. By its resolution 1990/10, the Sub-Commission, at its forty-second session, welcomed the introduction of the policy measures by the Government of South Africa which has resulted, <u>inter alia</u>, in the unbanning of the African

National Congress, the Pan Africanist Congress of Azania and other political
parties; the release of Mr. Nelson Mandela and some political prisoners;
and the partial lifting of the state of emergency. It called upon opponents
of apartheid in South Africa to form a broad united front and demonstrate
unity of purpose and concerted action for the elimination of apartheid and the
establishment of a non-racial democratic South Africa and strongly urged the
international community to maintain sanctions and other forms of international
pressure against the Pretoria régime in order to compel it to eradicate
apartheid. The Sub-Commission also urged those Governments that had recently
established or were contemplating the establishment of diplomatic relations to
reconsider their decision.

78. By its resolution 1991/21, the Commission, at its forty-seventh session,
commended the positive change which took place in South Africa in 1990 and
took note of the recent major political pronouncements by the Government
of South Africa. It urged the South African Government to repeal all
discriminatory and repressive legislation under apartheid without delay
or exception and to proceed to negotiate in good faith for a democratic
non-racial government. The Commission further called upon the Government
of South Africa to negotiate an agreement with all parties on transitional
arrangements and modalities on the process of drawing up a new constitution.
It decided to extend for a further two years the mandate of the Ad Hoc Working
Group of Experts on South Africa and renewed its request to the Government of
South Africa to allow the Group to visit the country.

79. The attention of the Sub-Commission is drawn to General Assembly
resolution 45/176 of 19 December 1990 entitled "Policies of apartheid of
the Government of South Africa".

Situation in the Palestinian and other Arab territories occupied by Israel

80. By resolution 1990/12, the Sub-Commission, at its forty-second session,
requested the Secretary-General to provide it, at its forty-third session,
with an updated list of reports, studies, statistics and other documents
relating to the question of Palestine and other occupied Arab territories,
with the texts of the relevant United Nations decisions and resolutions, as
well as with the report of the Special Committee to Investigate Israeli
Practices Affecting the Human Rights of the Population of the Occupied
Territories, and with all other information relevant to the implementation
of the resolution.

81. The Commission on Human Rights, at its forty-seventh session, adopted
resolutions 1991/1 A and B entitled "Question of the violation of human rights
in the occupied Arab territories, including Palestine"; 1991/2 entitled "Human
rights in the occupied Syrian Arab territory" and 1991/3 entitled "Israeli
settlements in the occupied Arab territories". The Commission also adopted
resolution 1991/6 on the situation in occupied Palestine.

Situation of human rights in the Islamic Republic of Iran

82. By resolution 1990/9, the Sub-Commission requested the Secretary-General
to inform the Sub-Commission, at its forty-third session, of relevant reports
by other special rapporteurs or bodies in the field of human rights, as well

0028

as of steps which have been and are being taken by the General Assembly, the
Economic and Social Council and the Commission on Human Rights to prevent
violations of human rights in the Islamic Republic of Iran and decided to
consider the situation of human rights in the Islamic Republic of Iran,
including the situation of minority groups such as the Baha'i, at its
forty-third session.

83. By its resolution 1990/8, the Sub-Commission strongly condemned the
assassination of Professor Kazem Rajavi and expressed the wish that the
Special Rapporteur on the situation of human rights in the Islamic Republic
of Iran would include information available to him in this regard in his next
report.

84. The Commission on Human Rights, at its forty-seventh session, adopted
resolution 1991/82 by which it requested the Special Representative to
maintain his contacts and cooperation with the Government of the Islamic
Republic of Iran and to report on further progress to the Commission at its
forty-eighth session. The Commission would consider his report with a view
to discontinuing his mandate if further progress regarding his recommendations
has been made.

85. The attention of the the Sub-Commission is further drawn to
General Assembly resolution 45/173 of 18 December 1990 on the same subject.

Situation of human rights in Guatemala

86. The Sub-Commission, by its resolution 1990/11, exhorted the Government
of Guatemala to intensify its efforts to ensure that the human rights and
fundamental freedoms of its citizens are respected, to adopt and implement
energetic measures to prevent violations of these rights and freedoms, to
protect and promote the organizations which safeguard human rights, and
to undertake investigations of violations of human rights. It urged the
Government to adopt practical measures to improve the economic, social and
political conditions of the indigenous peoples, taking into account their
petitions and proposals, together with all relevant international standards
in this field; encouraged it to continue to support the process of national
reconciliation and especially the talks between the various sectors of
Guatemalan society and Guatemalan National Revolutionary Unity, organized by
the National Reconciliation Commission with the aim of achieving a peaceful
solution to the long process of confrontation which Guatemala has experienced;
and called upon all parties concerned to continue the talks established
under the Oslo Agreement, and to create the appropriate conditions for the
achievement of national reconciliation and the cessation of armed actions
contrary to that objective.

87. The Commission on Human Rights, at its forty-seventh session, expressed
its gratitude to the Government of Guatemala for its collaboration with the
Centre for Human Rights. It further requested the Secretary-General to
continue to provide the Government of Guatemala with advisory services in the
field of human rights and to extend the mandate of the independent expert so
that he may continue to examine the human rights situation in that country
(resolution 1991/51).

0029

Situation in Iraq and in occupied Kuwait

88. By its resolution 1990/13, the Sub-Commission recommended to the Commission that it consider the appointment of an individual of recognized international standing as special rapporteur with the mandate to examine the human rights situation in Iraq.

89. In this context, the Sub-Commission will recall its decisions 1990/108 and 109 on the situation in the Gulf.

90. The Commission, at its forty-seventh session, decided to appoint a special rapporteur to examine the human rights violations committed in occupied Kuwait by the invading and occupying forces of Iraq (resolution 1991/67).

91. At the same session, the Commission adopted resolution 1991/74 on the situation of human rights in Iraq by which it requested its Chairman to appoint a special rapporteur with the mandate to undertake a thorough study of the violations of human rights by the Government of Iraq (resolution 1991/74).

92. The General Assembly, at its forty-fifth session, adopted resolution 45/170 of 18 December 1990 on the situation of human rights in occupied Kuwait.

Situation of human rights in El Salvador

93. By resolution 1990/14, the Sub-Commission at its forty-second session expressed its deep concern over the persistent increase in the number of human rights violations being committed for political reasons in El Salvador and over the continued failure to observe the humanitarian rules of war; welcomed the fact that the Government of El Salvador and the Frente Farabundo Martí para la Liberación Nacional have concluded agreements and taken verification measures on human rights, since strict compliance with these rights is essential for guaranteeing a just and lasting peace; and urged the immediate adoption of all necessary actions and measures, as were agreed, to avoid any type of act or practice prejudicial to the life, integrity, security and freedom of persons and to eliminate any form of disappearances and abductions, as well as to give priority to investigating any cases of this kind which might occur and identifying and punishing the culprits. The Sub-Commission recommended to the Special Representative of the Commission on Human Rights, in his report to the General Assembly, to place special emphasis on verifying whether the commitments and measures set out in the agreement on human rights signed by the two parties on 26 July 1990 have been implemented.

94. At its forty-seventh session, the Commission, by its resolution 1991/75, commended the Special Rapporteur for his report (E/CN.4/1991/34) and endorsed the recommendations contained therein. It decided to extend the mandate of the Special Representative for a further year.

95. The General Assembly, at its forty-fifth session, having considered the report of the Special Representative, adopted resolution 45/172 of 18 December 1990 on the situation of human rights and fundamental freedoms in El Salvador.

0030

Situation in East Timor

96. In its resolution 1990/15, the Sub-Commission recommended that the Commission on Human Rights should consider, at its forty-seventh session, the human rights situation in East Timor.

97. At its forty-seventh session, the Commission took no action on this subject.

Situation in Lebanon

98. By its decision 1990/121, the Sub-Commission decided to discuss the situation at its forty-third session.

99. At its forty-seventh session, the Commission considered the human rights situation in southern Lebanon and adopted resolution 1991/66, by which it decided to continue its consideration of the situation on human rights in southern Lebanon at its next session.

Establishment of a sessional working group

100. By decision 1989/104, the Sub-Commission decided to establish, at the beginning of its forty-second session, a sessional working group of five of its members, appointed by the various regional groups and open to the participation of other members of the Sub-Commission, to prepare an overview and an analysis of the suggestions and proposals which have been made in order to enable the Sub-Commission to better discharge its responsibilities in dealing with violations of human rights as discussed under item 6 of its agenda, taking also into account the functions and duties of the Commission on Human Rights in the matter.

101. The Sub-Commission further decided to request the same sessional working group, in preparing the overview and analysis, to submit to the Sub-Commission its views and recommendations as to the possible advantages and disadvantages of the various suggestions and proposals referred to above, and to present its findings in the light of the deliberations of the Sub-Commission at its forty-second session under the agenda item relating to the question of the violations of human rights and fundamental freedoms.

102. At its forty-second session, the Sub-Commission established the working group and took note of its report (E/CN.4/Sub.2/1990/14). By its decision 1990/125, the Sub-Commission decided to continue the work of the Group at its forty-third session.

103. The Commission on Human Rights, in its resolution 1991/56, invited the Sub-Commission to instruct its working group to intensify its discussions on reform issues and to include in its deliberations an examination of ways and means to avoid any proliferation of studies as well as of draft resolutions or decisions on issues already being dealt with by the Commission.

Other matters

104. In discussing this item, the Sub-Commission may wish to take into account the following resolutions and decisions adopted by the Commission on Human Rights at its forty-seventh session:

Resolutions

1991/4   Situation in Afghanistan

1991/5   Question of Western Sahara

1991/29   Consequences on the enjoyment of human rights of acts of violence committed by armed groups that spread terror among the population and by drug traffickers

1991/68   Situation of human rights in Cuba

1991/69   Situation of human rights in Romania

1991/76   Situation of human rights in Albania

1991/77   Situation of human rights in Haiti

1991/78   Situation of human rights in Afghanistan

1991/80   Situation in Equatorial Guinea

Decisions

1991/104   Situation in Cambodia

1991/106   Question of human rights in Cyprus.

105. At its present session, the Sub-Commission will have before it the following documents in connection with this item:

(a) Note by the Secretary-General pursuant to Sub-Commission resolution 1990/9 (E/CN.4/Sub.2/1991/14);

(b) Note by the Secretary-General pursuant to Sub-Commission resolution 1990/12 (E/CN.4/Sub.2/1991/15);

(c) Report of the sessional working group (E/CN.4/Sub.2/1991/16).

Item 7. The New International Economic Order and the promotion of human rights

106. The Sub-Commission, at its thirty-first session, by decision 6 of 15 September 1978, added to the agenda for its thirty-second session an item entitled "The New International Economic Order and the promotion of human rights". By its resolution 1985/34, the Sub-Commission decided to consider this item on a biennial basis. By its resolution 1989/1, the Sub-Commission decided to consider this item on an annual basis.

0032

Sub-item (a) The role and equal participation of women in development

107. The Sub-Commission first proposed to include the topic "Prevention of discrimination and protection of women" as a sub-item of its agenda during its thirty-seventh session, in 1984 (E/CN.4/Sub.2/1984/SR.39).

108. At its thirty-ninth session, the Sub-Commission adopted resolution 1987/26 entitled "The role and equal participation of women in development", in which it decided to consider, at its forty-first and future sessions, and in connection with the item on its agenda entitled "The New International Economic Order and the promotion of human rights", a sub-item entitled "The role and equal participation of women in development". The Sub-Commission also requested the Secretary-General to make available to it, at each of its future sessions, the reports of the Committee on the Elimination of Discrimination Against Women and of the Commission on the Status of Women.

109. At the present session, the Sub-Commission will have before it the most recent reports of the Committee on the Elimination of Discrimination Against Women and of the Commission on the Status of Women.

Item 8. The realization of economic, social and cultural rights

110. The Commission, at its forty-third session, by resolution 1987/19, requested the Sub-Commission to examine the conclusions and recommendations of the report of the Commission entitled The Realization of Economic, Social and Cultural Rights: Problems, Policies, Progress (United Nations publication, Sales No. 75.XIV.2) and to submit to the Commission, at its forty-fourth session, a proposed timetable for updating those conclusions and recommendations, taking into account the activities of the specialized agencies, other United Nations bodies and organs, other intergovernmental organizations, Governments and non-governmental organizations, and keeping in mind the importance of maintaining a specific human rights focus in examining the issues raised in that report. The Commission also requested the Sub-Commission to consider, in accordance with its resolution 1983/35, the preparation of a study on the impact on human rights of the policies and practices of the major international financial institutions, most notably the International Monetary Fund and the World Bank.

111. The Sub-Commission, at its thirty-ninth session, in its resolution 1987/29 A, recommended to the Commission on Human Rights and the Economic and Social Council, in response to Commission resolution 1987/19, that the Sub-Commission be authorized to appoint, from its members to be elected in 1988, a special rapporteur to study problems, policies and progressive measures relating to a more effective realization of economic, social and cultural rights; the special rapporteur would be requested to present a substantial progress report to the Sub-Commission at its forty-first session. The Commission, in its resolution 1988/22, invited the Sub-Commission to appoint a special rapporteur for that purpose.

112. At its fortieth session, the Sub-Commission, by its resolution 1988/33, decided to entrust Mr. Danilo Türk with a study of problems, policies and progressive measures relating to the more effective realization of economic, social and cultural rights, and recommended that the Special Rapporteur should

take account of the guidelines and issues contained in resolution 1987/29 A of the Sub-Commission. The resolution of the Sub-Commission was endorsed by Commission resolution 1989/13 and Economic and Social Council decision 1989/138.

113. By its resolution 1990/16, the Sub-Commission, having considered the progress report of the Special Rapporteur (E/CN.4/Sub.2/1990/19), endorsed the preliminary recommendations contained therein, requested the Special Rapporteur to prepare a second progress report and encouraged him to establish direct contact with international financial institutions as well as United Nations agencies utilizing social and economic data and indicators relevant to his study. The Sub-Commission invited the Commission on Human Rights, at its forty-seventh session, to consider requesting the Secretary-General to organize a seminar under the United Nations programme of human rights activities in 1992-1993 for discussion of appropriate indicators to measure achievements in the progressive realization of economic, social and cultural rights.

114. By its resolution 1990/17, the Sub-Commission decided to consider the human rights dimensions of population transfer, including the policy and practice of the implantation of settlers and settlements, at its future sessions under the agenda item "The realization of economic, social and cultural rights".

115. By its resolution 1991/13, the Commission, at its forty-seventh session, invited interested Governments to provide the Special Rapporteur with their comments and information at their disposal about their experience concerning the impact of economic adjustment policies arising from foreign debt on the enjoyment of human rights and requested the Special Rapporteur to take these views into account.

116. In its resolution 1991/18, the Commission on Human Rights welcomed the progress report of the Special Rapporteur and invited him, when preparing a progress report, to take into account comments made in the Commission, and requested that in the report priority be given to identifying practical strategies to promote for everyone the economic, social and cultural rights contained in the Covenant, paying particular attention to the most vulnerable and disadvantaged.

Human rights and extreme poverty

117. At its forty-sixth session, the Commission on Human Rights adopted resolution 1990/15, in which it reaffirmed that extreme poverty and exclusion from society constitute a violation of human dignity and that urgent national and international action is therefore required to eliminate them; it requested the Sub-Commission, when giving attention, in accordance with its resolution 1989/20, to problems, policies and progressive measures relating to more effective realization of economic, social and cultural rights, to examine the question of extreme poverty and exclusion from society in greater depth and to carry out a specific study of this question.

118. By its decision 1990/119, the Sub-Commission decided to request Mr. Eduardo Suescún Monroy to prepare the method and plan of work for the study on human rights and extreme poverty.

0034

119. At its forty-seventh session, the Commission, in resolution 1991/14, recommended that the Sub-Commission, when considering, in accordance with its decision 1990/119, the method and plan of work for the study on human rights and extreme poverty, should give attention more particularly to the conditions in which the poorest themselves can convey their experience and so contribute to a better understanding of the harsh reality of their lives and its causes.

Other matters

120. With regard to the issues under this item, the Sub-Commission may wish to note the following resolutions of the Commission adopted at its forty-seventh session:

1991/15 Right to development

1991/19 Respect for the right of everyone to own property alone as well as in association with others.

121. At the present session, the Sub-Commission will have before it the second progress report by the Special Rapporteur (E/CN.4/Sub.2/1991/17) and the report by Mr. Suescún Monroy (E/CN.4/Sub.2/1991/18).

Item 9. Communications concerning human rights: report of the Working Group established under Sub-Commission resolution 2 (XXIV) in accordance with Economic and Social Council resolution 1503 (XLVIII)

122. By resolution 1503 (XLVIII) of 27 May 1970, the Economic and Social Council authorized the Sub-Commission to appoint a working group of not more than five of its members to meet annually and consider all communications received by the Secretary-General under Council resolution 728 F (XXVIII) of 30 July 1959 with a view to bringing to the attention of the Sub-Commission those communications, together with replies of Governments, if any, which appear to reveal a consistent pattern of gross and reliably attested violations of human rights and fundamental freedoms. As an initial step in the implementation of Council resolution 1503 (XLVIII), the Sub-Commission adopted provisional procedures for dealing with the question of admissibility of communications in resolution 1 (XXIV) of 13 August 1971. The Working Group on Communications was established by Sub-Commission resolution 2 (XXIV) of 16 August 1971. The Working Group has met prior to each session of the Sub-Commission and presented to the Sub-Commission a confidential report.

123. Under the terms of Council resolution 1503 (XLVIII), the Sub-Commission is called upon to consider at private meetings the communications brought before it in accordance with the decision of a majority of the members of the Working Group and any replies of Governments relating thereto, and other relevant information, with a view to determining whether to refer to the Commission on Human Rights particular situations which appear to reveal a consistent pattern of gross and reliably attested violations of human rights requiring consideration by the Commission. Pursuant to paragraph 8 of Council resolution 1503 (XLVIII), the Sub-Commission communicates its conclusions on the item confidentially to the Commission.

0035

124. By decision 4 (XXXIV) of 3 March 1978, the Commission decided that the Sub-Commission and its Working Group on Communications should thenceforth have access to the records of the closed meetings of the Commission covering its examination of situations referred to it under Council resolution 1503 (XLVIII), together with all other confidential documents relating thereto that had been before the Commission.

125. By decision 3 (XXXIV) of 3 March 1978 the Commission decided that, when dealing with communications under Council resolution 1503 (XLVIII) and situations which the Commission had decided to keep under review, it would invite the Chairman-Rapporteur of the Working Group on Communications of the Sub-Commission to be present during the deliberations of the Commission on that item and to take the floor if he so wished.

126. A number of procedural steps have been taken at the Commission level with regard to the application of the procedure governed by Council resolution 1503 (XLVIII). Since 1974, the Commission has every year established a working group (Working Group on Situations) to assist it in examining the situations referred to it by the Sub-Commission and to make recommendations thereon to it. By resolution 1990/41, the Economic and Social Council, authorized the establishment of the Commission's Working Group on Situations, on a permanent basis, instead of the earlier ad hoc basis. The Working Group's recommendations are communicated to the Governments directly concerned (see Commission decision 14 (XXXV) of 12 March 1979), which are invited to participate in the meetings of the Commission at which the situations in question are examined (see Commission decisions 5 (XXXIV) of 3 March 1978 and 9 (XXXVI) of 7 March 1980).

127. By decision 1990/112, the Sub-Commission, wishing to modify its decision 1989/102, decided that the Working Group on Communications, acting under operative paragraph 1 of Council resolution 1503 (XLVIII), should in the future consider only those communications that had been transmitted to the Governments concerned under Council resolution 728 F (XXVIII) not later than 12 weeks prior to the meetings of the Working Group. At its forthcoming session, to be held from 22 July to 2 August 1991, the Working Group on Communications will, accordingly, consider communications received and processed by the Secretariat since the last session of the Sub-Commission and forwarded to the Governments concerned not later than 29 April 1991.

128. At its forty-second session, the Sub-Commission decided to suspend rule 59 of the rules of procedure of the functional commissions of the Economic and Social Council, so as to allow for voting by secret ballot on decisions at that session on proposals under Council resolution 1503 (XLVIII) (decision 1990/111).

129. The Sub-Commission's attention is also drawn to paragraph 5 of its last confidential report, which relates to matters kept pending until its forty-third session.

130. At the present session, the Sub-Commission will have before it the following documents:

    (a) The confidential report of the Working Group on Communications of the Sub-Commission on its meetings from 22 July to 2 August 1991;

(b) Relevant documentation referred to in paragraph 5 of the
Sub-Commission's last confidential report;

(c) The confidential summary records of the forty-seventh session of
the Commission on Human Rights, the text of the Commission's confidential
decisions and other documents relating thereto;

(d) Resolutions and decisions adopted by the Council, the Commission and
the Sub-Commission that are of relevance to the work of the Sub-Commission
under Council resolution 1503 (XLVIII);

(e) Confidential lists of communications compiled by the
Secretary-General under Council resolutions 728 F (XXVIII) and 1503 (XLVIII)
since the Sub-Commission's forty-second session, as well as replies received
from Governments during the period July 1990 - June 1991.

131. The above-mentioned confidential documents will be handed to the members
of the Sub-Commission.

Item 10. The administration of justice and the human rights of detainees

Sub-item (a) Question of the human rights of persons subjected to any
form of detention or imprisonment

Annual review

132. By resolution 7 (XXVII) of 20 August 1974, the Sub-Commission decided to
review annually developments concerning the human rights of persons subjected
to any form of detention or imprisonment, taking into account any reliably
attested information from Governments, specialized agencies, regional
intergovernmental organizations and non-governmental organizations in
consultative status, provided that such non-governmental organizations acted
in good faith and that their information was not politically motivated,
contrary to the principles of the Charter of the United Nations.

133. At its thirty-fourth and subsequent sessions, the Sub-Commission
established a sessional working group to consider the question of the
human rights of detained persons.

134. In its resolution 1988/33, paragraph 6, the Commission on Human Rights
reminded the Sub-Commission of the request made in its resolution 1987/33
that, when carrying out its annual review of the human rights of persons
subjected to any form of detention or imprisonment, it should include in its
consideration the work of the Human Rights Committee and the Committee on the
Elimination of Racial Discrimination, the developments elsewhere in the human
rights programme and the activities within the United Nations programme on
crime prevention and control bearing upon the subject, and requested the
Secretary-General to continue to make available to the Sub-Commission succinct
information on these matters.

135. In connection with the matters dealt with under item 10, the attention of
the Sub-Commission is drawn to General Assembly resolutions 45/107 to 45/119
of 14 December 1990 which endorsed the various instruments and resolutions
adopted at the Eighth United Nations Congress on the Prevention of Crime and
the Treatment of Offenders.

0037

136. The Sub-Commission will further recall Commission on Human Rights resolution 1991/38 entitled "Torture and other cruel, inhuman or degrading treatment or punishment: report of the Special Rapporteur" and the report of the Special Rapporteur on Torture (E/CN.4/1990/17).

137. At the present session, under this item, the Sub-Commission will have before it:

(a) A report of the Secretary-General containing information received from Governments pursuant to Sub-Commission resolution 7 (XXVII) (E/CN.4/Sub.2/1991/19 and Add.1);

(b) A report of the Secretary-General containing information from specialized agencies and intergovernmental organizations pursuant to Sub-Commission resolution 7 (XXVII) (E/CN.4/Sub.2/1991/20);

(c) A synopsis of material submitted by non-governmental organizations pursuant to Sub-Commission resolutions 7 (XXVII) and 4 (XXVIII) (E/CN.4/Sub.2/1991/21);

(d) A report by the Secretary-General giving succinct information on the work of the Human Rights Committee and the Committee on the Elimination of Racial Discrimination, the developments elsewhere in the human rights programme and the activities within the United Nations programme on crime prevention and control, in accordance with Commission on Human Rights resolution 1988/33 (E/CN.4/Sub.2/1991/22);

(e) The report of the sessional Working Group on Detention to the Sub-Commission (E/CN.4/Sub.2/1991/27).

Question of model legislation

138. The Sub-Commission may wish to refer to General Assembly resolution 45/166 of 18 December 1990, entitled "Human rights in the administration of justice", which contains a number of specific elements relevant to the matter dealt with under the present agenda item. In that resolution, the General Assembly drew the attention of the Commission on Human Rights and the Sub-Commission to the issues raised in the resolution in order to accord priority to issues related to human rights in the administration of justice.

139. The General Assembly, in the same resolution, requested the Commission on Human Rights to invite the Sub-Commission to study the implementation of United Nations norms and standards in the administration of justice and human rights; to identify problems that may impinge on their effective implementation; and to recommend viable solutions with action-oriented proposals to the Commission. It requested the Secretary-General to prepare, on the basis of comments by Member States and relevant international organizations and bodies, a draft model text for national legislation in the field of human rights in the administration of justice and to coordinate these activities of the Commission and the Sub-Commission with the Committee on Crime Prevention and Control. The Commission was further requested to invite the Sub-Commission to consider this draft model with a view to further elaboration of model texts and to propose such texts to the Commission for adoption.

0038

140. The Commission, at its forty-seventh session, by resolution 1991/34, requested the Secretary-General to establish a consolidated list of provisions in the various United Nations standards relating to human rights in the administration of justice with a view to drafting model texts for national legislation. It invited the Sub-Commission, on the basis of this consolidated list, to study the implementation of United Nations norms and standards in this field; to identify problems that may impinge on their effective implementation; to recommend viable solutions with action-oriented proposals to the Commission; to take the necessary action with a view to elaborating model texts for national legislation for the effective implementation of standards relating to human rights in the administration of justice; to take the necessary action with a view to elaborating model texts for national legislation for the effective implementation of standards relating to human rights in the administration of justice; and to consider the question of the effectiveness of habeas corpus and similar remedies during states of emergency and to formulate suggestions thereon. The Sub-Commission was requested to report to the Commission at its forty-eighth session on the implementation of the resolution.

141. At the present session, the Sub-Commission will have before it the note by the Secretary-General containing the consolidated list of United Nations standards in the field of human rights in the administration of justice and comments received regarding model legislation (E/CN.4/Sub.2/1991/26).

Protection of staff members of the United Nations system

142. The Commission and the Sub-Commission have concerned themselves in recent years with the detention, disappearance, and death in detention of United Nations staff members from the point of view of respect for their human rights as laid down in international instruments. Both bodies have asked for reports from the Secretary-General on this subject (Sub-Commission resolution 1987/21 and Commission resolutions 1988/41, 1989/28, 1990/31 and 1991/37).

143. The Sub-Commission at its fortieth session had before it the report on this subject requested in its resolution 1987/21 (E/CN.4/Sub.2/1988/17). At that session, it adopted resolution 1988/9, pursuant to which Ms. María Concepción Bautista was entrusted with the task of undertaking an examination of the violations of the human rights of staff members of the United Nations system, their families and experts as well as of the repercussions of those violations on the functioning of United Nations organs and agencies. The Sub-Commission requested that a preliminary report be presented to its forty-first session.

144. At its forty-first session, the Sub-Commission adopted resolution 1989/30 by which it requested the Special Rapporteur to continue to study the subject and to submit an updated version to its forty-second session.

145. At its forty-second session, having considered the updated version of Ms. Bautista's report (E/CN.4/Sub.2/1990/30), the Sub-Commission adopted resolution 1990/20, by which it invited Ms. Bautista to submit a final version of the report as well as practical recommendations for the improvement of the protection of personnel of the United Nations system and their families, including experts and consultants. The Sub-Commission also adopted decision 1990/120 on this subject.

0039

146. By resolution 1991/37, the Commission, for its part, requested the Secretary-General to submit an updated version of the report on the situation of United Nations staff members, experts and their families detained, imprisoned, missing or held in a country against their will. At the present session, the Sub-Commission will have before it the final report by Ms. Bautista (E/CN.4/Sub.2/1991/23).

Application of international standards concerning the human rights of detained juveniles

147. By its resolution 1989/31, the Sub-Commission requested the Secretary-General to update document E/CN.4/Sub.2/1987/30 on the incarceration of children under the age of 18 with adult prisoners and to submit the revision to the forty-second session of the Sub-Commission. In addition, it decided to appoint Ms. María Concepción Bautista to prepare a report, without financial implications, on the application of international standards concerning the human rights of detained juveniles, in particular the separation of juvenile and adult offenders in penal institutions, detention pending trial, least possible use of institutionalization, and the objectives of institutional treatment; further requested the Secretary-General to submit the resolution to Governments, specialized agencies and non-governmental organizations requesting their comments; and decided to continue to study these questions at its forty-second session. At its forty-second session, the Sub-Commission, by its resolution 1990/21, extended the mandate of Ms. Bautista until its forty-third session.

148. At its present session, the Sub-Commission will have before it the report of Ms. Bautista pursuant to resolution 1989/31 (E/CN.4/Sub.2/1991/24).

Report on the practice of administrative detention

149. By its resolution 1990/22, the Sub-Commission again expressed its appreciation to Mr. Louis Joinet for his revised report on the subject (E/CN.4/Sub.2/1990/29 and Add.1), invited the Commission to consider the different proposals contained in the report for the purpose of either acting upon one of them or requesting the Sub-Commission to elaborate further upon the proposal which the Commission deemed the most appropriate, and requested the Secretary-General to inform the Sub-Commission, at its forty-third session, of the action taken by the Commission pursuant to the resolution.

150. At its forty-seventh session, by resolution 1991/42, the Commission decided to create, for a three-year period, a working group composed of five independent experts with the task of investigating cases of detention imposed arbitrarily or in a manner otherwise inconsistent with the international standards set forth in the Universal Declaration of Human Rights or in the relevant international legal instruments accepted by the States concerned. The Working Group would seek and receive information from Governments and intergovernmental and non-governmental organizations, as well as from the individuals concerned, their families or their representatives, and carry out its mandate with discretion, objectivity and independence. It was requested to present a comprehensive report to the Commission at its forty-eighth session. The Commission recommended to the Economic and Social Council that it approve the creation of such a working group.

0040

151. At its present session, the Sub-Commission will have before it a note by the Secretary-General (E/CN.4/Sub.2/1991/25) pursuant to resolution 1990/22.

Draft declaration on the protection of all persons from enforced or involuntary disappearances

152. At its forty-second session, by resolution 1990/33, the Sub-Commission adopted the draft declaration on the subject (E/CN.4/Sub.2/1990/32, annex) and decided to transmit it to the Commission for consideration. At its forty-seventh session, the Commission, by its resolution 1991/41, expressed its appreciation to the Sub-Commission for its work and decided to establish an open-ended intersessional working group to consider the draft declaration with the view to its adoption by the Commission at its forty-eighth session in 1992. The Commission recommended to the Economic and Social Council that it authorize this working group to meet for a period of two weeks prior to the forty-eighth session. If so authorized, the working group is scheduled to meet for two weeks in November 1991.

Privatization of prisons

153. At its forty-first session, by decision 1989/110, the Sub-Commission requested Mr. Miguel Alfonso Martínez to prepare, without financial implications, a working paper containing proposals on the best way for the Sub-Commission to study further the issue of privatization of prisons, and to submit the working paper to the Sub-Commission at its forty-second session.

154. The sessional Working Group on Detention established by the Sub-Commission at its forty-second session decided to postpone consideration of this item until 1991 (see E/CN.4/Sub.2/1990/32, para. 32).

Sub-item (b) Question of human rights and states of emergency

155. By resolution 10 (XXX) of 31 August 1977, the Sub-Commission expressed its concern at the manner in which certain countries applied the provisions relating to situations known as states of siege or emergency. Convinced that a connection existed between such application and the situation regarding human rights in the said countries, the Sub-Commission considered that a comprehensive study of the implications for human rights of recent developments in that sphere would be conducive to the achievement of the aims pursued by the United Nations in the field of human rights. The comprehensive study was presented by Ms. Nicole Questiaux at the thirty-fifth session of the Sub-Commission (E/CN.4/Sub.2/1982/15).

156. In resolution 1983/18, the Commission requested the Sub-Commission to propose, for the Commission's consideration at its fortieth session, measures designed to ensure respect throughout the world for human rights and fundamental freedoms in situations where states of siege or emergency existed.

157. At the Sub-Commission's request (resolutions 1983/30 and 1984/27), the Economic and Social Council, by resolution 1985/37, authorized the Sub-Commission to appoint a special rapporteur to carry out the work referred to in Commission resolution 1983/18 and Sub-Commission resolution 1983/30 for the purpose of (a) drawing up and updating annually a list of countries which proclaim or terminate a state of emergency; and (b) submitting an annual

0041

special report to the Commission containing reliably attested information on compliance with the rules, internal and international, guaranteeing the legality of the introduction of a state of emergency. By its resolution 1985/32, the Sub-Commission requested Mr. Leandro Despouy, the Special Rapporteur for that task, to present his first report to the Sub-Commission at its thirty-ninth session.

158. The Sub-Commission, at its forty-second session, had before it the third annual report and list of States prepared by the Special Rapporteur (E/CN.4/Sub.2/1989/30 and Add.1 and Add.2/Rev.1). By its resolution 1990/19, it invited the Special Rapporteur to continue his work and to submit to the Sub-Commission the next annual report and list updated on the basis of information received. It recommended to the Commission that it recommend to the Economic and Social Council the adoption of a decision endorsing the Sub-Commission's request to the Special Rapporteur.

159. The Commission, by its decision 1991/108, decided to recommend to the Economic and Social Council the endorsement of Mr. Despouy's mandate.

160. At the present session, the Sub-Commission will have before it the next annual report and list proposed by the Special Rapporteur (E/CN.4/Sub.2/1991/28).

Sub-item (c) Individualization of prosecution and penalties, and repercussions of violations of human rights on families

161. In resolution 26 (XXXVI) of 11 March 1980, the Commission on Human Rights called upon Governments to observe the strict application of the principle that no one can be prosecuted or persecuted merely because of his connection, particularly family connection, with a suspect, an accused person or a person who has been convicted. The Sub-Commission was requested to study the question and to submit recommendations to the Commission for its consideration. The question was discussed at the thirty-seventh session of the Sub-Commission (E/CN.4/1985/3, paras. 235-237) but no action was taken.

Sub-item (d) The right to a fair trial

162. The Sub-Commission, at its forty-first session, adopted resolution 1989/27 by which it decided to appoint Mr. Stanislav Chernichenko and Mr. William Treat as rapporteurs to prepare a report on existing international norms and standards pertaining to the right to a fair trial for submission to the Working Group on Detention and to the Sub-Commission.

163. Having considered the report of the two Special Rapporteurs (E/CN.4/Sub.2/1990/34), the Sub-Commission, by resolution 1990/18, recommended to the Commission that it ask the Economic and Social Council to endorse its decision to entrust Messrs. Chernichenko and Treat with the preparation of a study entitled "The right to a fair trial: current recognition and measures necessary for its strengthening". The Special Rapporteurs would be requested to prepare a questionnaire for submission to Governments and organizations concerned and to submit a preliminary report based upon their study to the Sub-Commission and the Commission, at its forty-third and forty-eighth sessions respectively.

0042

164. The Commission, by its resolution 1991/43, endorsed the request of the Sub-Commission.

165. At the present session, the Sub-Commission will have before it the preliminary report of the two Special Rapporteurs (E/CN.4/Sub.2/1991/29).

Item 11. <u>Independence and impartiality of the judiciary, jurors and assessors and the independence of lawyers</u>

166. By its decision 1980/124, the Economic and Social Council authorized the Sub-Commission to entrust Mr. L.M. Singhvi with the preparation of a report on the independence and impartiality of the judiciary, jurors and assessors, and the independence of lawyers.

167. The Special Rapporteur accordingly submitted preliminary and progress reports on the subject in 1980, 1981 and 1982 (E/CN.4/Sub.2/L.731, E/CN.4/Sub.2/481 and Add.1, and E/CN.4/Sub.2/1982/23). He presented his final report on the subject (E/CN.4/Sub.2/1985/18 and Add.1-6) to the Sub-Commission at its thirty-eighth session and drew attention, in particular, to the draft declaration on the independence of justice (E/CN.4/Sub.2/18/Add.5/Rev.1).

168. The Special Rapporteur submitted a report containing comments and suggestions on the draft declaration (E/CN.4/Sub.2/1988/20) and a revised version of the draft declaration (E/CN.4/Sub.2/1988/20/Add.1 and Add.1/Corr.1) to the Sub-Commission at its fortieth session.

169. At its forty-first session, the Sub-Commission adopted resolution 1989/22 on the subject, by which it invited Mr. Louis Joinet to prepare, without financial implications, a working paper on means in the area of monitoring by which the Sub-Commission could assist in ensuring respect for the independence of the judiciary and the protection of practising lawyers, as requested in Commission resolution 1989/32.

170. The Commission on Human Rights endorsed Sub-Commission resolution 1989/22 and requested the Sub-Commission to study the working paper with a view to recommending to the Commission any initiatives which could be taken to effectuate the implementation of the Basic Principles on the Independence of the Judiciary and the protection of practising lawyers (resolution 1990/33).

171. At its forty-second session, the Sub-Commission considered the working paper prepared by Mr. Joinet (E/CN.4/Sub.2/1990/35) and decided, by its resolution 1990/23, to entrust Mr. Joinet with the preparation of a report:

(a) To make a system-wide analysis of the advisory service and technical assistance programmes of the United Nations as regards the independence of the judiciary and the protection of practising lawyers, propose means by which the cooperation between the programmes could be enhanced, and set forth guidelines and criteria to be taken into account in the provision of these services;

(b) To bring to the attention of the Sub-Commission information on legislative or judicial measures or other practices which have served to strengthen or to undermine the independence of the judiciary and the protection of practising lawyers in accordance with United Nations standards.

0043

172. By the same resolution, it decided to consider this report at its forty-third session and recommended to the Economic and Social Council, through the Commission, that it endorse its decision.

173. At its present session, the Sub-Commission will have before it the report of the Special Rapporteur (E/CN.4/Sub.2/1991/30).

Item 12. Human rights and disability

174. By its resolution 1984/20, the Sub-Commission decided to inscribe on the agenda of its thirty-eighth session an item entitled "Human rights and disability".

175. By the same resolution, the Sub-Commission further decided to appoint Mr. Leandro Despouy as Special Rapporteur to undertake the comprehensive study requested by the Economic and Social Council in its resolution 1984/26. The Sub-Commission requested the Special Rapporteur to consider a number of specific aspects of disability in his study and to present it to the Sub-Commission for consideration at its thirty-eighth session and to the Commission on Human Rights at its forty-second session.

176. At its thirty-eighth session, the Sub-Commission considered the preliminary report of the Special Rapporteur (E/CN.4/Sub.2/1985/32) and, by its resolution 1985/34, decided to consider this item on a biennial basis beginning at its fortieth session.

177. At its fortieth session, the Sub-Commission considered the progress report of the Special Rapporteur (E/CN.4/Sub.2/1988/11) and, by its resolution 1988/8, requested the Special Rapporteur to submit a final report to the Sub-Commission at its forty-second session.

178. At its forty-second session, by decision 1990/113, the Sub-Commission decided to suspend the debate on item 12 and include it on the provisional agenda for its forty-third session as a matter of the highest priority.

179. At its present session, the Sub-Commission will have before it the final report of the Special Rapporteur (E/CN.4/Sub.2/1991/31).

Item 13. Elimination of all forms of intolerance and of discrimination based on religion or belief

180. The General Assembly, by its resolution 37/187 of 18 December 1982, requested the Commission on Human Rights to consider measures to implement the Declaration on the Elimination of All Forms of Intolerance and of Discrimination Based on Religion or Belief, proclaimed by its resolution 36/55 of 25 November 1981. The Commission, by its resolution 1983/40, requested the Sub-Commission to undertake a comprehensive and thorough study of the current dimensions of the problems of intolerance and of discrimination on grounds of religion or belief, using as terms of reference the text of the Declaration.

181. By its resolution 1983/31, the Sub-Commission appointed Mrs. Elizabeth Odio Benito to undertake the study requested in Commission resolution 1983/40. The Special Rapporteur submitted her final report (E/CN.4/Sub.2/1987/26) to the Sub-Commission at its thirty-ninth session.

0044

182. Pursuant to Commission resolution 1988/55, the Sub-Commission considered, at its forty-first session, a working paper prepared by Mr. Theo van Boven (E/CN.4/Sub.2/1989/32) containing a compilation of provisions relevant to the elimination of intolerance and discrimination based on religion or belief contained in the Declaration and other international instruments, and examining, mindful of General Assembly resolution 41/120 of 4 December 1986 and taking into account the provisions of existing international instruments in this field, the issues and factors which should be considered before any drafting of a further binding international instrument on freedom of religion and belief took place.

183. At that session, the Sub-Commission adopted resolution 1989/23, by which it brought to the attention of the Commission certain issues and considerations (operative paragraph 3) and reaffirmed the willingness and interest of the Sub-Commission to make a further contribution to the activities which may be considered by the Commission in this field.

184. The Commission, at its forty-sixth session adopted resolution 1990/27 which, _inter alia_, welcomed with appreciation the working paper prepared by Mr. van Boven.

185. With respect to the present item, the attention of the Sub-Commission is also drawn to General Assembly resolution 45/136 of 14 December 1990 and Commission resolution 1991/48.

Item 14. <u>International peace and security as an essential condition for the enjoyment of human rights, above all the right to life</u>

186. By its decision 4 (XXXIV) of 10 September 1981, the Sub-Commission decided to include in the provisional agenda of its thirty-fifth session a new item entitled "The effects of gross violations of human rights on international peace and security". At its thirty-seventh session, in 1984, the Sub-Commission decided in its resolution 1984/30, to consider the item as a sub-item, entitled "Gross violations of human rights and international peace".

187. By its resolution 1985/34, the Sub-Commission decided that this item would be considered on a biennial basis starting from its thirty-ninth session.

188. At its thirty-eighth session, the Sub-Commission, by its resolution 1985/1, decided that this item of its agenda should be expressed as follows: "International peace and security as an essential condition for the enjoyment of human rights, above all the right to life".

189. At its forty-first session, the Sub-Commission, by resolution 1989/47, invited Mr. Murlidhar Bhandare to prepare a working paper on the interrelationship between international peace and the effective materialization of all human rights, particularly of the rights to life and to development.

190. At its present session, the Sub-Commission will have before it the working paper of Mr. Bhandare (E/CN.4/Sub.2/1991/32).

Item 15.   <u>Discrimination against indigenous peoples</u>

<u>Working Group on Indigenous Populations</u>

191. The creation of the Working Group on Indigenous Populations was
authorized by the Economic and Social Council in its resolution 1982/34 which
authorized the Sub-Commission to establish annually a working group to:

(a)   Review developments pertaining to the promotion and protection
of human rights and fundamental freedoms of indigenous peoples, including
information requested by the Secretary-General to analyse such materials, and
to submit its conclusions to the Sub-Commission, bearing in mind the report
of the Special Rapporteur of the Sub-Commission, Mr. José R. Martínez Cobo
(E/CN.4/Sub.2/1986/7 and Add.1-4, the two final chapters being issued as a
United Nations publication - Sales No. E.86.XIV.3);

(b)   Give special attention to the evolution of standards concerning the
rights of indigenous peoples, taking account of both the similarities and the
differences in the situations and aspirations of indigenous peoples throughout
the world.

192. The Working Group on Indigenous Populations held eight sessions prior
to 1991.   It submitted detailed reports (E/CN.4/Sub.2/1982/33,
E/CN.4/Sub.2/1983/22, E/CN.4/Sub.2/1984/20, E/CN.4/Sub.2/1985/22 and Add.1,
E/CN.4/Sub.2/1987/22 and Add.2, E/CN.4/Sub.2/1988/24 and Add.1,
E/CN.4/Sub.2/1989/36 and E/CN.4/Sub.2/1990/42) to the Sub-Commission.
These reports were also made available to the Commission.

193. At the present session, the Sub-Commission will have before it the report
of the Working Group on its ninth session (E/CN.4/Sub.2/1991/40).

<u>Draft declaration on indigenous rights</u>

194. By resolution 1985/22, the Sub-Commission endorsed the plan of action
adopted by the Working Group for its future work, contained in annex I of its
report on its fourth session (E/CN.4/Sub.2/1985/22), as well as its decision
to emphasize in its forthcoming sessions the part of its mandate relating to
standard-setting activities, with the aim of producing, in due course, a
draft declaration on indigenous rights which might be proclaimed by the
General Assembly.

195. At its forty-second session, by resolution 1990/26, the Sub-Commission
expressed its appreciation to the Working Group, and especially to its
Chairman/Rapporteur, Ms. Erica-Irene A. Daes, for the progress made at
its ninth session in carrying out its standard-setting mandate.   The
Sub-Commission requested the Secretary-General to transmit the report of
the Working Group to Governments, indigenous peoples, intergovernmental and
non-governmental organizations for specific comments and suggestions aimed at
the clarification, simplification and generalization of the texts contained in
the annexes to its report; to ensure that all meetings of the Working Group
at its ninth and future sessions are provided with interpretation and
documentation in both Spanish and English; to prepare a brief note on the

0046

financial implications of convening one or more of the future sessions of the Working Group in Latin America or Asia, for consideration by the Working Group at its ninth session; and to organize a regional training course in Latin America on the United Nations, human rights and indigenous peoples, as a matter of the highest priority and in accordance with Sub-Commission resolution 1989/35, and for this purpose to utilize to the greatest possible extent the expertise of the members of the Working Group and of indigenous peoples' organizations.

196. The Sub-Commission recommended that the Chairman-Rapporteur of the Working Group be entrusted with the task of preparing an extensive analytical commentary on the articles of the draft declaration, based on her first revised text, the reports of the informal drafting groups, the debate at the eighth session of the Working Group, the written observations received, existing international human rights instruments and other available comments.

197. The Sub-Commission, by the same resolution, recommended to the Commission that the Economic and Social Council authorize the Working Group to meet for 10 days prior to the forty-third session of the Sub-Commission.

198. By its resolution 1991/59, the Commission expressed its appreciation to the working group for its valuable work and endorsed the recommendations in operative paragraphs 8 and 9 of Sub-Commission resolution 1990/26. It recommended that by the Economic and Social Council authorize the Working Group to meet for 10 working days prior to the forty-third session of the Sub-Commission.

199. At the present session, the Sub-Commission will have before it the analytical commentary on the articles of the draft declaration prepared by the Chairman/Rapporteur of the Working Group (E/CN.4/Sub.2/1991/36) and a note by the Secretary-General on the financial implications of convening sessions of the Working Group outside of Geneva (E/CN.4/Sub.2/1991/35).

Ownership and control of cultural property of indigenous peoples

200. At its forty-second session, the Sub-Commission, by its resolution 1990/25, entrusted Ms. Erica-Irene A. Daes with the preparation of a working paper on the question of the ownership and control of the cultural property of indigenous peoples for submission to the Working Group on Indigenous Populations at its ninth session, and requested all organs and organizations of the United Nations system with relevant expertise to provide Ms. Daes with the information and assistance she may require for the completion of this task.

201. At its present session, the Sub-Commission will have before it the working paper prepared by Ms. Daes (E/CN.4/Sub.2/1991/34).

Economic and social relations between indigenous peoples and States

202. At its forty-second session, the Sub-Commission, by its resolution 1990/27, recommended that the United Nations Conference on Environment and Development provide indigenous people's organizations with effective means of participating directly in its work, and that any new

0047

conventions which may be adopted regarding biodiversity, or conserving
renewable resources, provide explicitly for the role of indigenous peoples as
resource users and managers, and for the protection of indigenous peoples'
right to control of their own traditional knowledge of ecosystems;
and invited the Special Rapporteur on human rights and the environment to take
into account the special relationship between fragile habitats and indigenous
peoples, especially with respect to sustainability, and also invited the
Special Rapporteur on compensation for human rights violations to address
indigenous concerns in his forthcoming reports to the Sub-Commission. The
Sub-Commission requested the Secretary-General to convene, as soon as
possible, the meeting of experts on indigenous self-government and the
technical conference on achieving environmentally sound and sustainable
self-development for indigenous peoples, and to include indigenous experts
among the invitees in accordance with existing practice; to bring the
resolution to the attention of the Secretary-General of the United Nations
Conference on Environment and Development and the Chairman of the Preparatory
Committee for the Conference, drawing their attention in particular to the
recommendations contained in paragraph 1, and invite them to indicate what
steps they may be able to take in accordance with those recommendations; to
arrange for the Centre for Human Rights to enter into discussions with United
Nations operational programmes in development and environment regarding
possible mechanisms and guidelines for promoting the rights of indigenous
peoples through their direct participation in the planning and implementation
of projects; to invite the World Intellectual Property Organization to
prepare, in consultation with other appropriate specialized agencies and
indigenous peoples' organizations, recommendations concerning the protection
of the intellectual property of indigenous peoples, for discussion at the
Working Group's ninth session; and to submit a report to its forty-third
session on the measures taken to implement the present resolution, and on the
results achieved.

203. At its present session, the Sub-Commission will have before it the report
of the Secretary-General (E/CN.4/Sub.2/1991/37).

Study on the significance of treaties, agreements and other constructive
arrangements

204. By resolution 1987/17, the Sub-Commission recommended the appointment
of Mr. Miguel Alfonso Martínez as Special Rapporteur with the mandate of
preparing a study on the treaties concluded between indigenous peoples and
States in all parts of the world with regard to the contemporary significance
of such treaties for all parties concerned. By the same resolution, the
Sub-Commission requested Mr. Alfonso Martínez to prepare a document analysing
the general outline of such a study and the juridical, bibliographical and
other information sources on which such a study should be based, and to submit
the document to the Sub-Commission for consideration at its fortieth session.

205. In accordance with a recommendation made by the Commission in
resolution 1988/56, the Economic and Social Council, in decision 1988/134,
authorized the appointment of Mr. Alfonso Martínez as Special Rapporteur of
the Sub-Commission with the mandate of preparing an outline on the possible
purposes, scope and sources of a study to be conducted on the potential
utility of treaties, agreements and other constructive arrangements between

0048

indigenous populations and Governments for the purpose of ensuring the promotion and protection of the human rights and fundamental freedoms of indigenous populations. Furthermore, the Special Rapporteur was requested to give particular attention to certain guidelines promulgated in the Council resolution and to submit the outline to the Sub-Commission for consideration by the Working Group on Indigenous Populations at its sixth session.

206. By resolution 1988/20, the Sub-Commission endorsed the outline of the study prepared by the Special Rapporteur. The Economic and Social Council, on the basis of recommendations by the Sub-Commission (resolution 1988/20) and the Commission (resolution 1989/4), adopted its resolution 1989/77, in which it confirmed the appointment of Mr. Miguel Alfonso Martínez as Special Rapporteur of the Sub-Commission authorized to carry out the study, and requested the Special Rapporteur to submit a progress report to the Sub-Commission at its forty-first session.

207. At its forty-second session, in resolution 1990/28, the Sub-Commission requested the Special Rapporteur to submit a preliminary report on his study to the Working Group and the Sub-Commission.

208. At its present session, the Sub-Commission will have before it the preliminary report of the Special Rapporteur (E/CN.4/Sub.2/1991/33).

International Year for the World's Indigenous Peoples

209. The Sub-Commission, in resolution 1987/15, recommended that the General Assembly should proclaim the year 1992 the "International Year of the World's Indigenous Populations". The Commission and the Economic and Social Council, by resolutions 1988/58 and 1988/37 respectively, recommended that the General Assembly should, when appropriate, proclaim such an international year.

210. By its resolution 1988/19, the Sub-Commission recommended that an international year for indigenous rights should be proclaimed to coincide with the end of the Second Decade for Action to Combat Racism and Racial Discrimination in 1993, and requested the Secretary-General to bring that resolution to the attention of the General Assembly in connection with its consideration of resolution 1988/37 of the Economic and Social Council. The resolution was brought to the attention of the Genera Assembly at its forty-third session. No action on the matter was taken by the Assembly at that session.

211. By resolution 1989/36, the Sub-Commission entrusted Mr. Asbjørn Eide and Ms. Christy Mbonu with the task of preparing a working paper on possible United Nations activities for an international year for indigenous rights, with an explicit focus on the development process and on promoting international cooperation with indigenous peoples' organizations.

212. In its decision 1990/113, the Commission decided to recommend that the Economic and Social Council recommend to the General Assembly that it proclaim an International Year for the World's Indigenous Peoples, in 1993 or another appropriate year, in accordance with established procedures governing the proclamation of international years.

213. At its forty-second session in resolution 1990/29, the Sub-Commission requested Mr. Eide and Ms. Mbonu to submit a second working paper providing more specific suggestions for activities that might be carried out at the national and international levels during the international year.

214. At the forty-fifth session, by resolution 45/164, the General Assembly proclaimed 1993 as International Year for the World's Indigenous People. It requested the Commission to consider possible United Nations activities in connection with the Year and requested the Secretary-General to submit to its forty-sixth session a draft programme of activities.

215. The Commission, at the forty-seventh session adopted resolution 1991/57 by which it recommended that the specialized agencies, regional commissions and other organizations of the United Nations system, in their consideration of the contributions that they can make to the success of the International Year for the World's Indigenous People, be guided by how: (a) their operational activities can most effectively contribute to the solution of problems faced by indigenous people; and (b) indigenous people can play an important role in the planning, implementation and evaluation of projects which may affect them. It requested the Secretary-General, in preparing the draft programme of activities for the International Year, requested by the General Assembly in its resolution 45/164, to take into account the ongoing work of the Sub-Commission as well as the Working Group on Indigenous Populations and to consider specific recommendations for the coordination and implementation of the draft programme of activities.

216. The Sub-Commission, at its present session, will have before it the working paper prepared by Mr. Eide and Ms. Mbonu (E/CN.4/Sub.2/1991/39).

United Nations Voluntary Fund for Indigenous Populations

217. As recommended by Sub-Commission resolution 1984/35 C, Commission resolution 1985/29 and Economic and Social Council resolution 1985/38, the General Assembly, by resolution 40/131 of 13 December 1985, established the United Nations Voluntary Fund for Indigenous Populations. The purpose of the Fund is to assist representatives of indigenous communities and organizations to participate in the deliberations of the Working Group on Indigenous Populations by providing it with financial assistance, funded by means of voluntary contributions from Governments, non-governmental organizations and other private or public entities. The Voluntary Fund is administered by the Secretary-General with the advice of a five-member Board of Trustees. The Board of Trustees held its fourth session in April 1991.

218. The General Assembly, by its decision 45/433, called for contributions to the Voluntary Fund and for the wide dissemination of information about the activities of the Fund.

Relocation of Navajo and Hopi families

219. At its forty-second session, by resolution 1990/34, the Sub-Commission requested its Chairman to convey copies of the resolution to the interested parties along with the assurances of the continuing interest of the Sub-Commission in an early and equitable resolution of the situation.

0050

Item 16. <u>Contemporary forms of slavery</u>

<u>Activities of the Working Group on Contemporary Forms of Slavery</u>

220. By its resolution 13 (XXIII) of 21 March 1967, the Commission on Human Rights requested the Sub-Commission to undertake regular consideration of the question of slavery in all its forms, including the slavery-like practices of apartheid and colonialism.

221. Basing itself on a recommendation submitted by the Sub-Commission (resolution 7 (XXVI)) and approved by the Commission (decision 5 (XXX) of 6 March 1974), the Economic and Social Council, by its decisions 16 (LVI) and 17 (LVI) of 17 May 1974, authorized the Sub-Commission to establish a working group composed of five of its members to meet prior to each session of the Sub-Commission to review developments in the field of slavery and the slave trade in all their practices and manifestations, including the slavery-like practices of apartheid and colonialism, the traffic in persons and the exploitation of the prostitution of others as defined in the Slavery Convention of 1926, the Supplementary Convention on the Abolition of Slavery, the Slave Trade and Institutions and Practices Similar to Slavery of 1956, and the Convention for the Suppression of the Traffic in Persons and of the Exploitation of the Prostitution of Others of 1949. The Sub-Commission established the Working Group on Slavery by its resolution 11 (XXVII) of 21 August 1974. By its resolution 1988/42, the Commission on Human Rights endorsed the recommendation of the Sub-Commission that the name of the Working Group on Slavery should be changed to "Working Group on Contemporary Forms of Slavery".

222. At its fortieth session the Sub-Commission adopted resolution 1988/31, by which it approved the programme of work of the Working Group for the period 1989-1991. This programme of work included three main themes to be discussed in successive years: prevention of the sale of children, of prostitution of children and of the use of children in pornography (1989); eradication of the exploitation of child labour and of debt bondage (1990); and prevention of traffic in persons and of the exploitation of the prostitution of others (1991). In addition, at each session, the Working Group will review information received on the status and the implementation of conventions on slavery and slavery-like practices, review developments in other fields of contemporary forms of slavery and consider the recommendations adopted at previous sessions.

223. The Sub-Commission, in its resolution 1989/41, requested, <u>inter alia</u>, the Secretary-General to submit to the Sub-Commission, at its forty-second session, a report on the adoption of children for commercial purposes and on the recruitment of children into governmental and non-governmental armed forces and their participation in hostilities, taking into account the comments of Governments and further information received by him.

224. In the same resolution, the Sub-Commission decided to consider these matters in subsequent sessions under the agenda item "Contemporary forms of slavery".

225. The Working Group on Contemporary Forms of Slavery will hold its sixteenth session from 29 July to 2 August 1991, at Geneva.

226. In its resolution 1991/58, the Commission on Human Rights encouraged the Sub-Commission, including its Working Group, once again to elaborate recommendations on the ways and means of establishing an effective mechanism for the implementation of the Slavery Convention. It recommended to the General Assembly that it establish a voluntary fund on contemporary forms of slavery and requested Governments to pursue a policy of information, prevention and rehabilitation of women victims of the exploitation of prostitution, and to take appropriate economic and social measures deemed necessary to that effect. It further recommended that the Working Group should consider these concerns at its sixteenth session.

Exploitation of child labour and debt bondage

227. At its forty-second session, in resolution 1990/30, the Sub-Commission requested the Commission to authorize it to consider the possibility of updating Mr. Abdelwakhab Bouhdiba's study on child labour, and in resolution 1990/31 endorsed a programme of action for the elimination of the exploitation of child labour.

228. By its resolution 1991/55, the Commission endorsed the views expressed by the Sub-Commission on the need to adopt a concerted programme of action decided to transmit the draft submitted by the Sub-Commission in resolution 1990/31 to Governments and international organizations for their comments. It requested the Secretary-General to submit a report of the replies received to the Commission at its forty-eighth session, at which time the Commission would examine the draft programme along with the report of the Secretary-General.

Sale of children, child prostitution and child pornography

229. Based on the recommendation of the Sub-Commission contained in its resolution 1989/42, the Commission on Human Rights, by its resolution 1990/68, decided to appoint for a period of one year a special rapporteur to consider matters relating to the sale of children, child prostitution and child pornography, including the problem of the adoption of children for commercial purposes. The Special Rapporteur, in fulfilling his mandate, was invited to take account of the need to be in a position to use any credible and reliable information made available to him, to request the Governments concerned to state their views and comment on any information he intended to include in his report and to carry out his task with discretion and independence. The Special Rapporteur was further requested to submit a comprehensive report to the Commission at its forty-seventh session on his activities relating to these matters, including the frequency and extent of such practices, along with his conclusions and recommendations.

230. The Sub-Commission, in its resolution 1990/30, welcomed the appointment of the Special Rapporteur, Mr. Vitit Muntarbhorn, for a term of two years and invited him to examine ways and means of cooperating with the Working Group on Contemporary Forms of Slavery. The Commission, by its resolution 1991/58, endorsed the invitation of the Sub-Commission.

0052

231. By its resolution 1991/54, the Commission requested the Special
Rapporteur to consider the possibility of attending the meetings of the
Working Group and requested the Under-Secretary-General for Human Rights to
provide the Sub-Commission with the necessary cooperation for the fulfilment
of this mandate. The Commission further decided to refer to the
Sub-Commission the draft programme of action for prevention of sale of
children, child prostitution and child pornography so that it might make the
necessary amendments thereto in the light of opinions received from
Governments and organizations contained in the report of the Secretary-General
(E/CN.4/1991/50 and Add.1). The Commission requested the Sub-Commission fully
to reflect the 10-point programme of the World Declaration on the Survival,
Protection and Development of Children (see E/CN.4/1991/59, annex, para. 20)
adopted by the World Summit for Children on 30 September 1990, and to give the
highest priority to the reformulation of the draft programme so that it might
be adopted by the Commission at its forty-eighth session.

Child soldiers

232. In its resolution 1990/30, the Sub-Commission welcomed the decision of
the Working Group on Contemporary Forms of Slavery to place this subject on
the agenda for its sixteenth session.

233. At the present session, the Sub-Commission will have before it the report
of the Working Group on Contemporary Forms of Slavery on its sixteenth session
(E/CN.4/Sub.2/1991/41).

Item 17. Promotion, protection and restoration of human rights at national,
          regional and international levels

    Sub-item (a) Prevention of discrimination and protection of children:
                  human rights and youth

234. At the 30th meeting of its thirty-seventh session, on 31 August 1984,
the Sub-Commission decided to include in its provisional agenda for the
thirty-eighth session a sub-item entitled "Prevention of discrimination and
protection of children".

235. At its thirty-eighth session, the Sub-Commission, by its
resolution 1985/12, referring, inter alia, to Commission resolution 1985/13,
requested Mr. Dimitru Mazilu to prepare a report on human rights and youth
analysing the efforts and measures for securing the implementation and
enjoyment by youth of human rights, particularly the right to life, education
and work, in order to facilitate the Sub-Commission's discussion of the
topic. The Commission, by its resolution 1987/44, took note of the
above-mentioned resolution of the Sub-Commission.

236. The Sub-Commission considered the question of the availability of the
study of the Special Rapporteur at some length at its fortieth and forty-first
sessions, adopting resolutions 1988/37 and 1989/45. It will be recalled that
the personal situation of the Special Rapporteur, Mr. Mazilu, was the subject
of consideration by the Commission on Human Rights and the Economic and Social
Council. At the request of the latter, the International Court of Justice
gave an advisory opinion on 15 December 1989 on the applicability of the

Convention on the Privileges and Immunities of the United Nations in the case of rapporteurs and special rapporteurs of the Sub-Commission (see E/1990/15/Add.1).

237. At its forty-second session, having considered the updated report of the Special Rapporteur, the Sub-Commission decided, by resolution 1990/32, to request Mr. Mazilu to update and complete his report and to present it at its forty-third session.

238. The Commission on Human Rights, by its resolution 1991/64, reaffirmed the role of youth in promoting the full and effective enjoyment of the entire range of human rights and fundamental freedoms for all, as well as the fact that youth attached crucial importance to the promotion of international peace and cooperation and the enjoyment of human rights and fundamental freedoms. It called upon all States, all governmental and non-governmental organizations, the United Nations organs concerned and the specialized agencies to devote constant attention to the exercise by young people of all human rights, including the right to education and vocational training and the right to work, with a view to ensuring full employment and the solution of the problem of unemployment among young people. In addition, the Commission called upon all States to take appropriate legislative, administrative and other action for the exercise by youth of all human rights and fundamental freedoms, including the right to education and the right to work, with a view to creating conditions for the active participation of young people in the formation and implementation of programmes for the overall development of their countries.

239. By its resolution 1991/65, the Commission requested the Secretary-General to report on the question of conscientious objection to military services.

240. At the present session, the Sub-Commission will have before it the report of the Special Rapporteur (E/CN.4/Sub.2/1991/42).

Sub-item (b) Prevention of discrimination and protection of women

241. At its thirty-seventh session, the Sub-Commission decided to include in its provisional agenda a sub-item on the prevention of discrimination and protection of women.

242. The Sub-Commission at its thirty-ninth session adopted resolution 1987/26, entitled "The role and equal participation of women in development", in which it expressed its belief that it should devote greater attention to prevention of discrimination against women, particularly in relation to development, and in coordination with other relevant bodies of the United Nations, and decided to consider, at its forty-first and future sessions, and in connection with the item of its agenda entitled "The New International Economic Order and the promotion of human rights", a sub-item entitled "The role and equal participation of women in development" (see annotations to item 7 (a)).

243. In that resolution, the Sub-Commission also requested the Secretary-General to make available to it, at each of its future sessions, the reports of the Committee on the Elimination of Discrimination against Women and of the Commission on the Status of Women.

0054

Item 18. <u>Protection of minorities</u>

244. The Sub-Commission, at its fortieth session, by resolution 1988/36, invited Ms. Claire Palley to prepare a working paper on possible ways and means to facilitate the peaceful and constructive resolution of situations involving racial, national, religious and linguistic minorities.

245. At its forty-first session, the Sub-Commission, by resolution 1989/44, decided to entrust Mr. Asbjørn Eide with the preparation of a further report on national experience in the protection of minorities, and decided to consider these issues at its forty-second and future sessions under a separate agenda item. By decision 1990/105, the Commission on Human Rights endorsed the decision of the Sub-Commission to entrust Mr. Eide with the task of preparing a study.

246. In its resolution 1990/5, the Sub-Commission, having considered the report prepared by Mr. Eide (E/CN.4/Sub.2/1990/46), requested him to submit a preliminary report to the Sub-Commission at its forty-third session. It recommended to the Commission on Human Rights that it endorse the working methods proposed by the Special Rapporteur and approve the undertaking of his study. In its resolution 1991/62, the Commission endorsed the recommendation of the Sub-Commission.

247. The Sub-Commission will note that the Commission, at each session since the thirty-fourth, has established an open-ended working group to consider the drafting of a declaration on the rights of persons belonging to national, ethnic, religious and linguistic minorities. At its forty-seventh session, the working group began the second reading of the draft declaration (see E/CN.4/1991/53). By resolution 1991/61, the Commission requested the Economic and Social Council to authorize an open-ended working group to meet intersessionally for a period of two weeks at the beginning of December 1991 to complete its second reading.

248. At the present session, the Sub-Commission will have before it the preliminary report of Mr. Eide (E/CN.4/Sub.2/1991/43).

Item 19. <u>The right of everyone to leave any country, including his own, and to return to his country</u>

249. The Sub-Commission, by its resolution 1988/39, decided to consider this matter under a separate item on its agenda at its forty-first session.

250. At its forty-first session, by resolution 1989/25, the Sub-Commission decided to establish a sessional working group with a view to preparing a revised version of the draft declaration on the subject.

251. At its forty-second session, by decision 1990/123, the Sub-Commission decided to establish, at its forty-third session, a working group to continue work on the draft declaration. It requested Mr. W. Sadi to prepare the revised version of the draft declaration, on the basis of the discussions in the open-ended working group at its forty-second session and the comments and proposals contained in document E/CN.4/Sub.2/1990/47, to be submitted in 1991 for analysis and discussion by the working group with a view, if possible, to its submission to the Sub-Commission at its forty-third session. It

further decided, if appropriate, to invite the Special Rapporteur,
Mr. Mubanga-Chipoya, to be present in Geneva during the meetings of the
working group.

252. At its present session, the Sub-Commission will have before it the
revised version of the draft declaration (E/CN.4/Sub.2/1991/44) and the
report of the sessional working groups (E/CN.4/Sub.2/1991/45).

Item 20. <u>Consideration of the future work of the Sub-Commission and of
the draft provisional agenda for the forty-fourth session of
the Sub-Commission</u>

253. The Economic and Social Council, by its resolution 1984 (LVII)
of 1 August 1974, requested the Secretary-General to submit at each session of
a functional commission or subsidiary body of the Council a draft provisional
agenda for its following session, together with an indication, in respect of
each agenda item, of the documents to be submitted under that item and the
legislative authority for their preparation, with a view to enabling the
functional commission or subsidiary body concerned to consider the documents
from the point of view of their contribution to the work of the respective
bodies.

254. Pursuant to that request, the Secretary-General will submit to the
Sub-Commission, towards the end of the forty-third session, a note containing
a draft provisional agenda for the forty-fourth session, together with
information concerning the documentation relating thereto
(E/CN.4/Sub.2/1991/L.1).

Item 21. <u>Adoption of the report on the forty-third session</u>

255. Under rule 37 of the rules of procedure, the Sub-Commission is to report
to the Commission on Human Rights on the work of its session. In this
connection, the Sub-Commission may wish to take account of the revised
guidelines for the format and contents of the report of functional commissions
and standing committees of the Economic and Social Council (E/1979/94) approved
by the Council in its resolution 1979/69. This resolution and the revised
guidelines are available for consultation in the Secretariat.

0056

ANNEX

Members and Alternates of the Sub-Commission on Prevention of Discrimination and Protection of Minorities

Mr. Miguel Alfonso Martínez   (Cuba)
  *Mr. Julio H. Pérez

Mr. Awn Shawkat Al-Khasawneh   (Jordan)
  *Mr. Waleed M. Sadi

Ms. Judith Sefi Attah   (Nigeria)
  *Mrs. Christy Ezim Mbonu

Ms. Mary Concepción Bautista   (Philippines)
  *Ms. Haydee B. Yorac

Mr. Theodoor Cornelis van Boven   (Netherlands)
  *Mr. Cornelis Flinterman

Mr. Stanislav Valentinovich Chernichenko   (Union of Soviet Socialist Republics)
  *Mr. Teimuraz O. Ramishvili

Ms. Erica-Irene A. Daes   (Greece)
  *Mr. Alexis Heraclides

Mr. Leandro Despouy   (Argentina)
  *Mr. Juan Carlos Hitters

Mr. Ion Diaconu   (Romania)
  *Mr. Ioan Maxim

Mr. Asbjørn Eide   (Norway)
  Mr. Jan Helgessen

Mr. El Hadji Guissé   (Senegal)
  *Mr. Ndary Toure

Mr. Ribot Hatano   (Japan)
  *Mr. Yozo Yokota

Mr. Claude Heller   (Mexico)
  *Mr. Hector Fix Zamudio

Mr. Aidid Abdillahi Ilkahanaf   (Somalia)
  *Mr. Mohamed Isa Turunji

Mr. Louis Joinet   (France)
  *Mr. Alain Pellet

---

  *   Alternate.

Mr. Ahmed Khalifa   (Egypt)

Ms. Fatma Zohra Ksentini   (Algeria)
  *Ms. Farida Aiouaze

Ms. Claire Palley   (United Kingdom of Great Britain
  *Mr. John Merills   and Northern Ireland)

Mr. Rafael Rivas Posada   (Colombia)
  *Mr. Eduardo Suescún Monroy

Mr. Gilberto Vergre Saboia   (Brazil)
  *Ms. Marília S. Zelner Gonçalves

Mr. Rajindar Sachar   (India)

Mr. Jin Tian   (China)
  *Mr. Daode Zhan

Mr. William W. Treat   (United States of America)
  *Mr. John Carey

Mr. Danilo Türk   (Yugoslavia)
  *Ms. Lidija R. Basta

Ms. Halima Embarek Warzazi   (Morocco)
  *Mr. Mohamed Laghmari

Mr. Fisseha Yimer   (Ethiopia)

—————

0058

	분류번호	보존기간

발 신 전 보

번 호 : WGV-0948   910725 1400 FO   종별 : _____

수 신 : 주　제네바　대사. 총총총총총

발 신 : 장 관　　(국연)

제 목 : 제43차 유엔인권소위

대 : 주제네(정) 2031-544, 423

　　1.　대호, 표제회의 참가 아국대표단 구성에 관한 귀견 보고바라며 (본부 및 법무부 직원 출장계획 없음) 표제회의에서의 국제민간인권단체 등에 의한 남북한의 인권상황 거론에 관한 대책을 수립, 8.2(금)한 보고 바람.

　　2.　또한, 제46차 총회(91.9.17-12.20.예정) 제3위에서의 인권문제 토의 대책수립에 참고코자 하니 북한인권문제 제기방안등에 관한 귀견을 8.15(목)한 파편 보고바람.　끝.

(국제기구조약국장　문동석)

일반문서로재분류(1991.12.31.)

	보안통제	(서명)

앙고재	91년 7월 25일 UN과	기안자성명 홍병식		과장 (서명)	심의관 (서명)	국장		차관	장관 (서명)	외신과통제

0059

외 무 부

종 별 :

번 호 : GVW-1430

일 시 : 91 0726 2000

수 신 : 장관(국연)

발 신 : 주 제네바 대사

제 목 : 제 43차 유엔 인권 소위

대: WGV-0948

대호, 표제회의 아국 대표단은 본직, 이성주 참사관 및 김종훈 서기관으로
구성하는 것이좋을 것으로 사료됨. 끝

(대사 박수길-국장)

예고 91.12.31. 까지

일반문서로 재분류 (199 / . /ㅗ. 31..

국기국

91.07.27   05:34
외신 2과 통제관 FM

0060

발 신 전 보

번   호 : WGV-0968   910727 1258 DN   종별 : _____

수   신 : 주   제네바   대사. ♣♣♣♣

발   신 : 장 관   (국연)

제   목 : 제43차 유엔 인권소위

대 : GVW-1430

대호, 귀견대로 아국대표단 명단 통보바람. 끝.

(장관대리   유종하)

앙고재	91년 7월 27일	기안자 성명		과 장	심의관	국 장	1차보	차 관	장 관

외신과통제

0061

공　　　　란

공 란

외 무 부

종 별 :

번 호 : GVW-1469   일 시 : 91 0805 1800

수 신 : 장관(국연,법무부)

발 신 : 주 제네바 대사

제 목 : 제 43차 유엔 인권 소위(1)

1. 표제 회의가 금 8.5 오전 제 42 차 회의 의장인 TURK 위원(유고)의 사회로 개최되어 MARTENSEN 유엔 인권 담당 사무총장의 환영사, 의장단 선출 및 의제채택이 있었음.

2. 금차 회의 의장에는 지역 윤번 원칙에 따라 LOUIS JOINET 위원(불란서)이 선출되고, 3 명의 부의장에는 HELLER 위원(멕시코), BAUTISTA 의원(필린핀)및 TURK 위원(유고)이, 라포터에는 BUISSE 위원(세네갈)이 각각 선출됨.

3. JOINET 의장은 의장 취임인사를 겸하여 최근 인권 위원회 및 인권 소위에서 논의되어온 소위의 토의 방식 개선 문제에 언급, 현재 21 개 항에 달하는 방만한 의제를 4-5 개 MAJOR HEADING 으로 재편, 발언 시간 제한, 의제 소개의 간략화, 회의의 정시 시작(결정 사항이 없을 경우 정족수에 관계없이 정시 시작)등 인권 소위 WORKING METHODS 의 개선 문제를 금일 오후 회의에서 논의할 것을 제의하였으나 동 사안의 중요성에 비추어 간단히 처리될 사항이 아니라는 MARTINEZ(쿠바), KAHLIFA(이집트)위원등의 반응에 따라 사무국이 작성한 잠정 의제(E/CN.4/SUB.2/1991/1)을 원안대로 일단 채택하고, 상기 문제는 금일 오후 소집되는 의장단회의 및 비공개 전체회의(PLENARY IN PRIVATE)에서 논의하기로하고 산회함.

4. 금일 회의에는 북한에서는 당지 대표부 참사관 박덕훈이 참석함. 끝
(대사 박수길-국장)

국기국   차관   1차보   2차보   법무부

長 官 報 告 事 項

1991.8.6.
亞 洲 局
東北亞 1課 (63)

題 目 ： 유엔人權小委에서의 在日韓國人 人權問題

91.8.3字 日本 마이니찌新聞은 在日韓國人의 人權問題가 第43次 유엔人權小委員會(8.5-31, 제네바)에서 提起될 것이라고 報道하였는 바, 關聯事項 아래 報告드립니다.

---

1. 마이니찌新聞 報道內容

O 第43次 유엔人權小委에서 在日韓國人·朝鮮人의 人權侵害問題가 提起될 것으로 確實視되고 있음.

　- 指紋捺印義務, 選擧權問題 등을 圍繞한, 人權小委의 對應與否 注目

O 人權小委에 提起되게 된 背景은 "在日韓國人·朝鮮人 人權獲得鬪爭全國聯合會" 代表인 최창화 牧師가 90.6月 및 91.2月等 2回에 걸쳐 유엔人權小委에 報告書를 提出한데서 起因

　- 同報告書는 指紋捺印義務, 强制退去 및 選擧權等 政治參加의 權利不在 등을 强調

　* 최창화 牧師는 日本북큐슈居住 民權運動家로서 指紋捺印制度 撤廢, 出入國의 自由保障等 在日韓國人의 法的地位向上을 위해 活動中 (指紋捺印을 拒否한 딸 "최선애"에 대한 日政府의 再入國 不許事件으로 有名)

0065

2. 유엔人權小委 提起 事例

　　○ 在日韓國人 人權問題는 過去 第36次(83.8) 및 第37次(84.8) 유엔人權小委
　　　에서 國際民間人權團體(NGO)에 의해 提起된 바 있음.

　　　　- "Int'l Human Rights Law Group"은 第36次 人權小委時, 在日韓國人에
　　　　　대한 指紋捺印制度, 强制退去 및 再入國 節次等 差別待遇를 非難

　　　　- "Human Rights Group"은 第37次 人權小委時, 指紋捺印制度 및 民族敎育
　　　　　不許를 非難

　　○ 이에 대해 日政府는 在日韓國人이 65年 法的地位協定으로 인해 餘他外國人에
　　　　비해 有利한 待遇를 받고 있으며, 指紋捺印制度는 在日韓國人뿐아니라
　　　　모든 日本居住 外國人에게 適用되고 있다고 反論

3. 措置事項

　　○ 駐후꾸오카 總領事館을 통해 최창화 牧師의 推進現況을 確認
　　　　* 本件의 유엔人權小委 提起自體는 在日韓國人 人權問題에 대한 國際社會
　　　　　의 關心을 喚起시키는 效果는 있을 것으로 보이나, 91.1.10 韓.日 外務
　　　　　長官間 覺書署名을 契機로 指紋捺印撤廢, 强制退去條項의 事實上 死文化,
　　　　　最大 5年間의 再入國 許容等 在日韓國人의 法的地位와 處遇가 伸張되고
　　　　　있음에 비추어, 本件이 人權小委에 정식으로 提起되지는 않을 것으로
　　　　　觀測

　　○ 必要時, 駐제네바代表部를 통해 유엔人權小委에서의 處理動向을 把握. 끝.

0066

외 무 부

종 별 :

번 호 : GVW-1486 　　　　　　　　　일 시 : 91 0807 1700

수 신 : 장관(아일,국연) 사본:주일대사,주후꾸오카총영사(본부중계필)

발 신 : 주 제네바 대사

제 목 : 재일 한국인 인권문제

대: WGV-1005

1. 대호, 유엔 인권소위 참석차 당지 체류중인 최창화 목사에게 확인 사항을 아래 보고함.

　가. 최목사는 90.6 월 및 91.2 월에 걸쳐 재일 한국인 인권 침해에 관한 재일 한국인 인권 획득 부쟁연합회 명의의 진정서를 유엔 사무총장(유엔 인권 사무국)에게 제출한바 있음. 동 진정서는 유엔의 진정서 비밀심의 절차인 <u>1503 절차</u>에 의거한 것임.

　나. 동 진정서는 7.22-8.2 간 당지에서 열린 유엔 인권소위산하 진정서 실무소위에서 심의된 것으로 알려진바, 동 결과는 상금 확인되지 않고 있으나, 최목사는 실무소위에서 채택되었을 가능성이 많은 것으로 예측하고 있음.

　(상기 실무 소위에서 채택된 진정서들은 인권 소위에서 비고애로 토의되며, 토의 결과 채택된 진정서들은 명년도 유엔 인권 위원회에 회부됨. 상기 절차까지의 모든 토의는 비공개이며, 동 결과는 공표되지 않음)

　다. 현재 최목사는 인권소위에 옵서버로 등록되어 있는 민간인권 단체 <u>MINORITY RIGHTS GROUP</u> 의 대표단의 일원으로 회의 참석중인바, 최목사에 의하면 동단체에서 재일 한국인 문제를 공개회의시 거론할 가능성이 있으며, 세계 교회 협의회 (WWC) 산하 COMMISSION OF THE CHURCHES OF INTERNATIONAL AFFAIRS 에서 일본내 외국인 노동자 인권문제를 제기할 예정이라함. 한편 최목사는 8.9 일 당지 출발 예정임.

　라. 참고로 79.10 월 및 80 년 3 월 최목사가 유엔에 제출한바 있는 진정서는 81.3 월 인권위까지 회부되어 비공개로 토의된바 있으나 동 회의에서 기각되었다고 함.

　2. 진정서 제출에 관한 1503 절차는 비밀절차로서, 진정서 제출과 인권소위공개회의어시 비특정인권문제가 제기되는 것은 별개의 문제임. 참고로 최근

아주국　　차관　　1차보　　2차보　　국기국　　정와대　　안기부　　중계

PAGE 1 　　　　　　　　　　　　　　　　　　　　91.08.08　　08:43
　　　　　　　　　　　　　　　　　　　　　　외신 2과 통제관 CA

0067

수년간 인권위 또는 인권 소위에서 재일 한국인 문제가 제기된 사례는 없었음.

　　3. 대호 진정서 심의 결과 및 회의에서의 재일 한국인 문제 거론 동향은 파악되는대로 추보하겠음.

　　4. 대호 진정서 사본은 정파편 송부함. 끝

(대사 박수길-국장)

예고 91.12.31. 까지

외 무 부

종 별 :

번 호 : GVW-1497   일 시 : 91 0808 1800

수 신 : 장 관(국연,법무부)

발 신 : 주 제네바 대사

제 목 : 제 43차 유엔인권소위(2)

1. 표제 회의는 8.6 의제 2항 (의사일정)을 토의 확정하고 이어서 의제 3항 (소위활동 재검토)을 논의한후 8.7-9 양일간 의제 5항 (인종차별철폐)을 논의하였음.

2. 상기 의사일정에 의하면 의제 6항 (각국인권상황) 및 의제 10항 (재소자인권)은 각각 8.12-15간, 8.20-21 및 28 토의예정이며, 회의 막바지 토의시간 부족현황을 예방키 위해 발언시간을 각각 아래와 같이 제한키로 함.

위원: 10-15분

옵저버: 10분

정부옵저버의 답변권 행사: 1차 5분, 2차 3분

3. 8.6 오후의 의제 3항 (소위활동 재검토) 논의는 8.8-9 예정된 WG 논의를 앞둔 관계로 본격적인 토의보다는 대부분의 위원들이 최근 소위활동에 대한 인권 위원회의 비판과 관련 소위 활동에 전혀 문제점이 없는 것은 아니나 나름대로 유용성이 있다는 일반론을 표명하였음. 특히 KSENTINI (ALGERIA) 위원은 이제까지 소위 활동 결과에 대한 INVENTORY작성, 소위에 대한 시간 및 예산지원 확대, 중장기 계획의 수립, 후속 조치 강화 방안 마련, 개선방향을 제시하였고 CHERNICHENKO (소련)위원은 유엔경사리를 경제이사회와 사회 이사회를 분리, 사회 이사회가 인권문제에 보다 많은관심을 기울이게 하면서 인권소위가 경사리를 직접 보조 (인권위는 폐지)하는 방안도 고려가능하다는 의견과 소위의 탈정치화 노력 및 긴급사태 대응 체제 구비 필요성을 강조하였음.

4. 한편 상기 의제 3항 토의시 PALLEY (영국)위원이 새로운 상황에 대한 소위의 대처 능력제고 필요성을 언급하면서 인도적 간섭권 (RIGHTOF HUMANITARIAN INTERVENTION) 에 관한 연구착수의 시급성을 지적함으로써 동 문제에 관해 상당한 논란이있었는 바, TURK (유고), DAES (그리스), EIDE (놀웨이), DESPOUY (알젠틴)

국기국   법무부

PAGE 1   91.08.09   09:01 WG

외신 1과 통제관

0069

ILKAHANAF (소말리아) 위원등이 이에 동조한 반면, WARZAZI (모로코), KSENTINI, MARTINEZ (쿠바) 위원은 동논의 착수에 반대한바, 특히 WARZAZI 위원은 이는 유엔 6위 및 3위에서도 논의된바 없으며 각국의 특수사정을 고려치 않고 일률적 기준에 따라 적용할 경우 이외에는 인정될 수 없으며 최근 IRAQ 케이스가 유일한 예외이나 이경우에도 KURDS 와 SHITE 간 균형을 상실함으로써 정치적으로 MOTIVATED 되었음을 보여주고 있다고 지적하는등 강한 반론을 제기함.

한편 SADI (요르단) 위원은 무력 간섭과 비무력간섭, SACHAR (인도) 위원은 국가에 의한 간섭과 국제기구에 의한 간섭을 구별할 필요가 있다는 의견을 개진함.

5. 8.8-8 의 의제 5항 토의에서는 남아공의 인종차별 정책과 최근 대두되고 있는 외국인 노동자박해, 피난민, 망명자등에 대한 차별, 무관심등 새로운 형태의 인종차별 문제가 집중거론됨.

6. 남아공 문제 특별 보고자인 KHALIFA (이집트)위원은 자신의 보고서를 설명하면서 최근 남아공에서 많은 변화가 일어나고 있는 것은 사실이나 잉카타에 대한 경찰의 비밀 자금지원등에서 보는 바와같이 사실상의 철폐 (DEFACTO ELIMINATION) 에는 이르지 못하고 있고 언제라도 사태가 발전할 가능성이 있으므로 (REVERSIBLE)국제적 압력을 지속적으로 가할 필요가 있으며, 따라서 최근 EC, 미국, 스위스등의 대 남아공 경제체제 해체 및 완화 조치는 시기상조라고 비판하였음.

7. 대부분의 위원들이 KHALIFA 의원의 보고서를 평가하면서 남아공 인종차별이 완전 철폐되었다는 확실한 증거가 있을때까지 국제적 노력을 중단하지 말아야 할것이라는 입장을 표명하였으나, TREAT (미국) 위원, PALLEY (영국)위원, POSADA (콜롬비아)위원등 일부 위원은 최근 남아공 정부가 취한 일련의 조치는 반전될 가능성이 있는 단계는 넘어섰다고 하면서, 남아공에 대한 국제적 압력은 계속되어야 하지만 남아공의 경제를 파멸시키는 것은 어느 누구에게도 도움이 되지않으므로 반대한다는 입장을 밝혔음. PAN-AFRICAN CONGRESS OF AZANIA 대표는 남아공에서는 아직도 흑인에 대한 생명권의 거부, VIRUS살포, STERILIZATION 등을 통한 흑인 인구 축소정책등이 추진되고 있다고 하면서 최근의 변화는 표면적, 가식적 변화에 불과하다고 주장하고, 핵무기 개발관련 남아공과 이락간의 균형을 잃은 선진국의 대응태도등을 비판하였음.

8. 외국인 노동자에 대한 박해등 새로운 형태의 인종차별 문제는 WARZAZI (모로코), KSENTINI (알제리아)등 중동지역 출신 위원 및 BAUTISTA (필리핀) 위원등에

PAGE 2

0070

의해 집중 거론되었는바, 이들 위원들은 불란서등 서구 선진국 정부의 소극적, 미온적
정책을 강력하게 비판하면서 소위가 이문제에 대한 관심을 더욱 증대시켜야 할것임을
강조함. 동 문제관련 WCC 는 일본내 외국인 노동자 차별대우 문제의 심각성을
제기하였음.끝.

　　(대사 박수길-국장)

PAGE 3

외 무 부

종 별 :

번 호 : GVW-1505 일 시 : 91 0809

수 신 : 장 관(국연,법무부)

발 신 : 주 제네바 대사

제 목 : : 제 43차 유엔인권 소위(3)

연: WGV-14861. 표제회의는 8.9 나이제리아, 쿠바 (대남아 공제제조치의 완화는 인종차별문제에 관한 미국정부의 시각을 반영, 외국인 노동자 문제는 과거 선진국이 제 3세계에 자행한 정복과착취의 결과)등의 발언 및 연호 8항 WCC발언에 대한 일본의 간단한 답변을 끝으로 의제 5항 (인종차별 철폐) 토의를 마치고, 의제 13항 (종교 및 신념을 근거로 한 차별) 토의에 착수함.

2. 상기 의제는 격년제 토의 의제로 41차 소위에 WORKING PAPER 를 제출한 VAN BOVEN (화란)위원은 종교 및 신념에 따른 차별은 인권의 가장 기본적 요소가 되는 다원성 자체를 위협할 뿐만 아니라 NATIONALISM 과 결합할 경우 상승효과를 발휘, 국제평화까지 위협하는 요인이되므로 이에대한 PREVENTIVE ACTION 및 ANTICIPATORY DIPLOMACY 가 필요하다고 강조하고, 동 철폐를 위한 구속력있는 국제협정 마련 문제와 관련해서는 기본적으로 인간양식 (HEART RATHER THAN HEAD) 의 문제이기 때문에 세계인권선언, CCPR 등 기존협정의 테두리내에서 고려되어야 할 것이라는 의견을 개진함.

3. 그밖에 WARZAZI (모로코) 위원은 종교적 광신문제에 관한 검토의 시급성, EIDE(놀웨이) 위원은 인종차별주의 와의 밀접한 연관성, ATTAH (나이제리아)위원은 정치적 MOTIVE 에 의한 종교의 악용 경향의 경계필요성을 각각 언급하고, INT'L ASSOCIATION FOR THEDEFENSE OF RELIGIOUS FREEDOM 등 일부 NOG 가 수단, 사우디등의 개종 자유거부, 카나다 원주민 문화 말살정책등을 거론함.

4. 인권소위는 8.12(월) 회의를 재개, 상기 의제 13항 관련 NGO 발언 청취를 계속한후 의제 6항 (각국 인권상황) 토의에 들어갈 예정임.끝

(대사 박수길-국장)

국기국   1차보   법무부

주 제 네 바 대 표 부

제내(정) 20322-36   1991. 8. 9

수신 : 장관

참조 : 국제기구조약국장

제목 : 제 43차 유엔인권소위 참가대책

91.8. 9

　　　　당관에서 작성한 제 43차 유엔인권소위 참가 대책자료을 별첨 송부 하오니
업무에 참고 하시기 바랍니다.

첨부 : 동 대책 자료 1부. 끝.

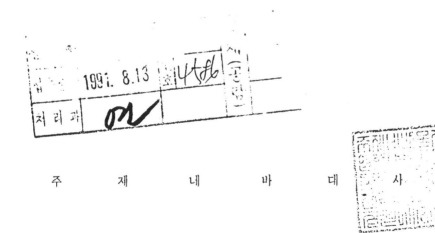

주   제   네   바   대   사

제 4 3 차 유엔인권위 참가대책

(91. 8.5-8.30)

1991. 8

주 제 네 바 대 표 부

- 차   례 -

0075

제 43차 유엔인권 소위 참가대책

----

1. 회의기간 : 91. 8. 5-8.30(4주간)

2. 회의장소 : 유엔회의장 17호실

   - 개회식 : 91. 8.5(월) 10:30

3. 회의참가 규모

   가. 인권소위 위원 : 26명

   나. 옵서버 : 유엔회원국, 비회원국 및 국제민간 단체(NGO)등

      θ 90년도 제 42차 회의시 97개국 정부옵서버, 8개 정부간 기구,
        2개 민족해방 운동기구 및 97개 NGO대표 참가

4. 회의의제

   가. 총 21개 의제 : 별첨 참조

   나. 아국 인권상황 거론 가능 의제

      θ 의제 6항 : 세계인권 상황
      θ 의제 10항 : 법사행정 및 재소자 인권

   다. 북한 문제 거론 가능의제

      θ 의제 6항 : 세계인권 상황
      θ 의제10항 : 법사행정 및 재소자 인권

1

0076

5.   90년도 제 42차 인권소위시 주요토의 내용

   가.   아국 관련 상황

      0 1503절차에 의거한 임수경 사건 관련 진정서는 진정서 실무소위에서
         기각됨
      0 인권소위 위원이나 정부 옵서버의 아국인권 상황 거론은 없었음.
      0 아국 인권 상황을 집중 거론한 NGO는 없었으나 하기 2개 NGO가 간략히
         언급함.
         - Habitat Int'l Coaltion : 주민강제 이주와 관련한 서울시 재개발
                                    문제
         - 세계 노조연맹 : 전노협 결성관련자 구속 문제

   나.   북한 관련 사항

      0 북한 인권 문제에 대한 언급은 없었음.

   다.   일반 토의 사항

      0 이라크 관련 결의안이 19:4:1로 채택 되엇으며, 남아공, 이란, 과테말라,
         팔레스타인 지역, 엘살바돌, 동티몰에 관한 결의안이 채택됨.
      0 그밖에 중국, 미얀마, 스리랑카, 페루, 쿨롬비아, 이디오피아, 라이베리아등의
         인권상황 및 카나다내 인디언이 인권보호 문제에 대해 많은 NGO가 발언함.
      0 의제 6항 결의안 심의시 <u>비밀 투표</u>가 가능하도록 하기 위해 의사 규칙에 주석을
         삽입하도록 경사리에 권고하는 결의안이 채택되엇으며, 인권소위 활동 개선
         방안에 관한 실무위 토의는 큰 진전이 없었음.   그밖에 소수민족 및
         토착민 인권문제가 부각됨.

6.   금차회의시 토의 전망

   가.   아국관련 사항

      0 1503절차에 따른 아국관련 진정서 3건은 진정서 실무 소위애서 기각됨.

                                2   0077

- 임수경 사건
- . 서울 및 목포 교도소내 재소자 인권 문제
- 홍성담 사건

0 일부 NGO에 의한 아국인권 상황 거론 가능성 상존
  - 거론가능 NGO :
    . Int'l League for the Rights and Liberations of Peoples
    . Int'l Union of Students
    . World Federation of Trade Unions
    . World Federation of Democratic Youth
    . Commission of the Churches of International Affairs(WCC 산하)
    . International Commission of Jurists
    . Pax Romana
  - 거론 가능 사건
    . 임수경 사건등 불법 방북사건
    . 학생시위(강경대 사건등)
    . 사회과학 연구소 사건
    . 전노협 및 전교조 관련 사항

나. 북한 관련 사항

0 91. 4월 평양 IPU 총회시 일부 서방 대표들의 북한 인권 문제 제기 사례 및
  많은 NGO가 전체주의 채재의 인권 문제에 관심을 보이고 있음에 비추어
  일부 NGO에 의한 북한 인권문제 거론 가능성이 있음.

다. 일반 토의 사항

0 팔래스타인 지역, 이락, 이란, 쿠바등 중남미 일부 국가, 중국, 미안마 및
  유고등의 인권문제, 소수민족 및 토착민 인권 문제가 거론될 것으로
  예상됨.

0 작년에 이어 인권소위 활동 개선 방안이 실무위에서 토의되며, 특히 의제
  6항 관련 토의 진행방법의 개선을 위한 노력이 있을 것으로 예상됨.

3   0078

공   란

Provisional agenda

1. Election of officers.

2. Adoption of the agenda.

3. Review of the work of the Sub-Commission.

4. Review of further developments in fields with which the Sub-Commission
    has been concerned.

5. Elimination of racial discrimination:

    (a) Measures to combat racism and racial discrimination and the role of
         the Sub-Commission;

    (b) Adverse consequences for the enjoyment of human rights of political
         military, economic and other forms of assistance given to the racist
         and colonialist régime of South Africa.

6. Question of the violation of human rights and fundamental freedoms,
    including policies of racial discrimination and segregation and of
    apartheid, in all countries, with particular reference to colonial and
    other dependent countries and territories: report of the Sub-Commission
    under Commission on Human Rights resolution 8 (XXIII).

7. The new international economic order and the promotion of human rights.

    (a) The role and equal participation of women in development.

8. The realization of economic, social and cultural rights.

9. Communications concerning human rights: report of the Working Group
    established under Sub-Commission resolution 2 (XXIV) in accordance with
    Economic and Social Council resolution 1503 (XLVIII).

10. The administration of justice and the human rights of detainees:

    (a) Question of human rights of persons subjected to any form of
         detention and imprisonment;

    (b) Question of human rights and states of emergency;

    (c) Individualization of prosecution and penalties, and repercussions of
         violations of human rights on families;

    (d) The right to a fair trial.

11. Independence and impartiality of the judiciary, jurors and assessors and
    the independence of lawyers.

12. Human Rights and disability.

13. Elimination of all forms of intolerance and of discrimination based on
    religion or belief.

0080

14. International peace and security as an essential condition for the enjoyment of human rights, above all the right to life.

15. Discrimination against indigenous peoples.

16. Contemporary forms of slavery.

17. Promotion, protection and restoration of human rights at national, regional and international levels:

    (a) Prevention of discrimination and protection of children: human rights and youth;

    (b) Prevention of discrimination and protection of women.

18. Protection of minorities.

19. The right of everyone to leave any country, including his own, and to return to his country.

20. Consideration of the future work of the Sub-Commission and of the draft provisional agenda for the forty-fourth session of the Sub-Commission.

21. Adoption of the report of the forty-third session.

ANNEX

<u>Members and Alternates of the Sub-Commission on Prevention</u>
<u>of Discrimination and Protection of Minorities</u>

Mr. Miguel Alfonso Martínez   (Cuba)
    *Mr. Julio H. Pérez

Mr. Awn Shawkat Al-Khasawneh   (Jordan)
    *Mr. Waleed M. Sadi

Ms. Judith Sefi Attah   (Nigeria)
    *Mrs. Christy Ezim Mbonu

Ms. Mary Concepción Bautista   (Philippines)
    *Ms. Haydee B. Yorac

Mr. Theodoor Cornelis van Boven   (Netherlands)
    *Mr. Cornelis Flinterman

Mr. Stanislav Valentinovich Chernichenko (Union of Soviet Socialist Repub
    *Mr. Teimuraz O. Ramishvili

Ms. Erica-Irene A. Daes   (Greece)
    *Mr. Alexis Heraclides

Mr. Leandro Despouy   (Argentina)
    *Mr. Juan Carlos Hitters

Mr. Ion Diaconu   (Romania)
    *Mr. Ioan Maxim

Mr. Asbjørn Eide   (Norway)
    Mr. Jan Helgessen

Mr. El Hadji Guissé   (Senegal)
    *Mr. Ndary Toure

Mr. Ribot Hatano   (Japan)
    *Mr. Yozo Yokota

Mr. Claude Heller   (Mexico)
    *Mr. Hector Fix Zamudio

Mr. Aidid Abdillahi Ilkahanaf   (Somalia)
    *Mr. Mohamed Isa Turunji

Mr. Louis Joinet   (France)
    *Mr. Alain Pellet

---

    * Alternate.

7

0082

Mr. Ahmed Khalifa   (Egypt)

Ms. Fatma Zohra Ksentini   (Algeria)
   *Ms. Farida Aiouaze

Ms. Claire Palley   (United Kingdom of Great Britain
   *Mr. John Merills   and Northern Ireland)

Mr. Rafael Rivas Posada   (Colombia)
   *Mr. Eduardo Suescúm Monroy

Mr. Gilberto Vergre Saboia   (Brazil)
   *Ms. Marília S. Zelner Gonçalves

Mr. Rajindar Sachar   (India)

Mr. Jin Tian   (China)
   *Mr. Daode Zhan

Mr. William W. Treat   (United States of America)
   *Mr. John Carey

Mr. Danilo Türk   (Yugoslavia)
   *Ms. Lidija R. Basta

Ms. Halima Embarek Warzazi   (Morocco)
   *Mr. Mohamed Laghmari

Mr. Fisseha Yimer   (Ethiopia)

8

0083

외　무　부

종　별 :

번　호 : GVW-1520
일　시 : 91 0814 1100

수　신 : 장관(국연, 법무부)

발　신 : 주 제네바 대사

제　목 : 제 43차 유엔 인권 소위(4)

1. 표제회의는 8.12 오전 의제 13항(종교, 신념에입각한 차별 철폐) 토의를 종료하고 이어서 8.13 현재까지 의제 6항(각국인권 상황)을토의중임.

2. 8.12 의제 13항 토의시 주요 발언 내용은 아래와같음.

- PAX CHRISTI INT'L : 최근 많은 개선이 이루어지고 있음에도 불구 중국의 티벳불교로 탐안, 동유럽의 반유태주의 대두, 일부 회교국의 종교적불관용 정책 지속 현상에 우려 표명.

- INT'LFELLOWSHIP FOR RECONCILIATION : 상이한 종교간 대화의 필요성 을 강조하고, 티벳트, 치타공지역의 불교도 박해를 언급하면서 유엔 감시(MONITORING)제도의 적합성에 의문제기

- WORLD UNION IN PROGRESSIVE JUDAISM : 시리아 정부의 유태인 박해 및 유태여인 출국 불허를 강력 규탄

- 기타 INT'L WOMEN'S LEAGUE FOR PEACE AND FREEDOM 이뉴질랜드내 마우이 원주민 박해문제를, 미국 및캐나다 대표가 연호 8.9 남아공 관련 쿠바 발언 및캐나다 인디안 관련 IWGIA 의 발언에 답변권행사

3. 8.12 오전 부터 현재까지 진행중인 의제 6항토의에는 WARZAZI 위원등 5명의 소위위원,PLO, PAC 의 2개 민족해방기구 및 약 20개 NGO대표가 발언한바, 주요 내용은아래와 같음.(동의제 토의는 8.16 까지 계속될 예정임)

- WARZAZI(모로코)위원: 제 3세계 인권문제만 집중 거론되는 현상은 공정치 못하다고(UNFAIR)하면서, 외국인 노동자, 최근의 알바니아 난민과같은 ASYLUM SEEKERS 에 대한 비인도적 처우,냉담한 반응등 선진국의 인권 경시 현상에대한 관심 촉구-

- KHALIFA(이집트)위원: 냉전이 사려겼음에도 불구하고 세계 도처에서의 수백만난민,무 력충돌에 따른 민간인 희생자, 대규모 기아현상 발생등 인권 상황은

국기국　　차관　　1차보　　구주국　　외정실　　청와대　　안기부　　법무부

91.08.14　20:39 BU

외신 1과 통제관

0084

오히려악화되고있다고 지적하고 탈냉전으로 말미암아 인권문제가 강대국의 자선(CHARITY) 의 대상이 될위험성이 있음을 경고하였으며, IRAQ 에대해서는 즉각적인 무력대응을 하면서도 남아공및 팔레스타인 문제는 방관하는 선진국의DOUBLE STANDARD 를 비난하면서 HUMANITARIANINTERVENTION 은 주권존중 원칙에 반하므로 인정할수 없다는 입장 표명

　- ILKHANAF (소말리아)위원: 소말리아 전정권의 가혹행위를 예로 들면서 HUMANITARIAN INTERVENTION에 관련 상기 KHALIFA 의원 발언에 반론제기

　- AMNESTY INT'L : 인권소위 역할의 중요성을 강조한후 이락(쿠르드, 시아무슬림 박해등, UN감시 실시 촉구), 쿠웨이트(팔레스타인인,이락점령시 부역자 강제추방,박해),미안마(수천명의 양심수 감금 등), 이란(금년중500 명이상 처형등), 중국 (89년 민주화 시위 참가자박해, 수천명의 정치범 감금, 처형, 티벳트의탄압등), 모리타니아(불법감금, 고문, 처형),페루(신정부 수립후에도 인권 유린 현상 계속),시리아의 8개국 인권 상황만을 거론

　- PAX CHRISTI INT'L :

티벳, 동티몰, 사이프러스, 남부 레바논, 이란,버마, 스리랑카등의 인권 위반 사례를 비난하고외국인 노동자, ASYLUM SEEKERS 및 걸프전희생자에 대한 관심 촉구

　- INT'L LEAGUE FOR HUMAN RIGHTS, AMERICAN JURISTASSOCIATION, WORLD UNIVERSIRY SERVICE, INDIAN JURISTCOMMISSION 은 콜롬비아, 칠레, 과테말라 등중남미 제국에서의 납치, 처형, 실종등 인권유린 사태와 관련자에 대한 정부의 미온적 대처(IMPUNITY) 를 규탄

　- 기타 INT'L FIGHTERS AGAINST SLAVERY 및 INT'L UNIONFOR FRIENDSHIP AMONG PEOPLES 가 동티몰에 대한 인니정부의 점령 및인권 탄압을, HUMAN RIGHTSADVOCATES 가소련내 민족갈등에 따른 인권유린문제(특히 아제르바이잔으로 부터의 아르메인아인강제 추방)를, ARAB HUMAN RIGHTS ORGANIZATIONS 가팔레스타인 문제, 이락의 쿠웨이트 침공및동국내 인권 상황, 쿠웨이트 정부의 인권유린등을, INT'L ASSOCIATION FORDEFENSE OF RELIGIOUSFREEDOM 이 이란, 사우디의 RELIGIOUS TOTALITARIANISM을, INT'L SOCIETY FOR EDUCATIONAL DEVELOPMENT 가터어키 정부의 KURDS 인 공격을, BAHAI INT'LCOMMUNITY 가 이란정부의 BAHAI COMMUNITY 박해를,FOUR DIRECTIONS COUNCIL 이 필리핀 정부의 반군 진압가정에서의 원주민 인권 유린을 각각 규탄.끝

(대사 박스길 ─ 국장)

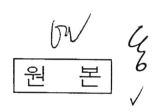

외 무 부

종 별 :

번 호 : GVW-1533　　　　　　　　　　　일 시 : 91 0816 1100

수 신 : 장관(국연, 법무부)

발 신 : 주제네바대사

제 목 : 제 43차 유엔인권 소위(5)

　　　연: GVW-1520

　　1. 표제회의는 의제 6항(각국 인권 상황)토의를 연호에 이어 8월 14-15일 간에도계속, 8.15.동 의제 토의를 종료하였음.

　　2. 토의에 참가한 대부분의 NGO 들이 특히중남미, 중동지역을 중심으로 특정 인권 위반사례를 지적, 동 위반국을 규탄하는데 중점을둔 반면 소위위원들은 신국제질서형성이 인권문제에 미치는 영향, 향후 관심 증대가필요한 인권문제 및 동취급 방향등 일반적문제에 관한 의견을 주로 피력하였음.

　　3. 소위 위원들의 주요 발언 내용은 아래와같음.

　　- VAN BOVEN(화란): 최근 세계 도처에서 민주화신장을 환영하면서도 민주주의는인권 보장의필요 조건은 되나 충분 조건이 되지 못하므로 가식적민주주의(DEMOCRACY IN FACADE) 에 대한 경계를촉구하고, HUMANITARIAN INTERVENTION 문제에 대해서는남용 우려가 없지는 않으나 대규모 인권위반 사태에 대해서는 국제사회의 행동이필요하다는 의견을 피력. 또한 인권 소위에서 일부국의 인권상황만 선별적으로 거론되고있는 문제점과 관련 전혀 거론치 않는 것보다 일부국이라도 계속 관심을 경주하는 것이 낫다고 전제한후, 특히 제 3세계 약소국 인권 문제만집중 표적이 되고 있다는 비판에 대해서는영국, 불란서(외국인 노동자, 피난민,중국(민주탄압, 불법체포 처형,티벳인 권상황), 소련(발틱 3국, 우크라이나,아제르바이잔등 인종 분규에 따른 인권침해) 미국(경제 사회적 불평) 등 안보리 5개상임이사국의 인권문제를 일일이 열거하면서이들 문제에 대한 관심 경주도 필요하다는 의견피력

　　- KSENTINI(알제리아): BIPOLARISM 의 와해가인권규범의 획일적, 선별적 적용등제3세계에 대해 오히려 불리한 상황을 불러일으킬위험성이 있으며, 제 3세계 문제의핵심은빈곤 및 기아로 부터의 해방에 있는 만큼, 이를위해서는 경제적 권리,

---

국기국　　　차관　　　1차보　　　　　　　　분석관　　　청와대　　　안기부　　　법무부

개발권, 환경권등에대한 보다 많은 관심 경주가 필요하다고 언급하고가장 심각한 인권 문제로서는 자결권과 무차별원칙이라는 핵심적(CARDINAL) 인권 요소가거부되고 있는 APRTHEID와 PALESTINE 문제를지적

- SABOIA(브라질): 냉전종식, 민주주의 확대, 중동평화 회담 개최 전망, 캄보디아, 중남미, 남아공등의 변화를 긍정적으로 평가하나 독재추방이 자동적 인권상황 개선 을 가져오는 것은아니므로 새로운 GRIEVANCE 발생 예방을 위한지원, 극단적 민족주의의 대두, 민족분열(FLAGMENTATION) 현상등의 문제에 대한 국제적공동 노력이 필요함 을 언급

- MARTINGZ(쿠바) : 신국제질서와 관련 과연새로운 질서가 형성되고 있는지, 신질서가구질서와 크게 다른점이 있는지 의문표시(동위원은 동 의문의 근거로서 팔레스타인 문제,사이프러스 분쟁, 미국내 인종차별 문제, 북아일랜드 문제, 선진국의 외국 인 노동자문제, 남미의 원주민 문제, 엘살바돌, 과테말라, 한국내 상황등이 크게 달라질 것이없다고 하였음)

- CHERNICHENKO(소련): 정부의 직접개입에 의한 인권 위반과 정부가 통제할 수 없는 인권위반을 구분할 필요성이 있으며 최근소련내 인종분규는 과거 정권의 유산으로 서 정부가 통제할 수 없는 상황인 점을 고려, 당사자간 대화가 가능토록 국제적인지원이 필요함을 언급- TURK(유고슬라비아): 일방적 비난보다는 중재, 대화촉진등을포함한 SOLUTION-ORIENTED 된생산적 토의의 필요성을 강조하고 유고슬라비아KOSOVO지역 내 알비니아 게 주민과 세르비아정부간 대화가 이루어질 수 있도록 소위가 노력해줄 것을 촉구

- DESPOUY(알젠틴): 태국, 홍콩, 쿠웨이트 및서구 제국에서 망명자, 피난민의 강제 수용 추방,걸프전에 있어서의 아동 피해를 언급하면서 남미문제와 아동 문제에 대한 소위의 관심 증대를촉구

4. NGO 대표들의 주요 발언 내용은 아래와 같음

- WORLD ORGANIZATION AGAINST TORTURE: 소련내인종분규, 유고, 알바니아 문제,부탄 정부의왕정유지를 위한 인권탄압, 바레인, 수단,엘살바돌, 멕시코, 브라질 인권상황 언급

- INT'L ORG FOR ELIMINATION OF ALL FORMS OF RACISM:유고의 KOSOVO 지역 문제,터키 정부의 쿠르드족탄압 문제 거론

- UNION OF ARAB LAWYERS: 이락내 민간인 참상을설명하면서 대이락 경제 조치

해제를 촉구

- INT'L MOVEMENT FOR RECONCILIATION : 홍콩내 중국민주화 인사 탄압을 규탄하면서 홍콩의중국반환후 인권이 계속 보장될 수 있도록국제법 및 국내법적 조치 촉구

- HABITAT IN'TL COALITION: 주택 문제도 인권의주요한 요소려 취급하여야 할 것이라고 하고, 많은국가에서 도시 환경, 재개발, 국제행사개최등을 이유로 대규모 주민 강제추방 현상이벌어지고 있는데 대한 예방 조처의 필요성을강조하면서 아국의 올림픽 개최를 포함한18개국의 예를 열거(동 발언문 파편 송부 예정)

- 그밖에 INT'L INDIAN TREATY COUNCIL 이 과테말라문제, INT'L WOMEN'S LEAGUE FOR PEACE AND FREEDOM 이동 TIMOR 문제를, INT'L FALCON MOVEMENT 가 IRAN인권문제를, IN'L MOVEMENT FOR FRATERNAL UNION 이수단, 나이제리아, 모잠비크 문제를 각각 거론

5. 상기 및 연호 NGO 발언에 대해서 이락, 이란,시리아, 미얀마, 터어키, 모로코, 필리핀, 스리랑카,인도네시아, 중국, 콜롬비아, 페루, 부탄등이 발언또는 답변권 행사등을 통하여 자국의 입장을표명하였으며 동 TIMOR 문제와 관련한포루투갈과 인도네시아간, 사이프러스 문제에 관한터어키와 사이프러스간 상호 비난 발언등이있었음.끝

(대사 박수길-국장)

PAGE 3

0088

외 무 부

종 별 :

번 호 : GVW-1551   일 시 : 91 0820 1600

수 신 : 장 관(국연, 법무부)

발 신 : 주 제네바 대사

제 목 : 제 47차 유엔인권소위(6)

1. 표제회의는 8.16(금) 부터 의제 18항 (소수집단보호) 및 12항 (지체부자유자 인권)을 토의중임.

2. 8.16.오후에 있은 의제 12항 토의에서는 지체부자유 발생원인, 동 부자유에 대한 편견, 차별 유형, 동 차별 철폐를 위한 국내적, 국제적조치 및 건의 (각국국내법의 국제수준화, 유엔산하 감시기구의 설치등)를 주요 내용으로 하는 특별보고자 DESPOUY (알젠틴)위원의 보고서 (E/CN/4/SUB 2/1991/31) 설명에 이어, INT'L FELLOWSHIPFOR RECONCILIATION 등 7개 NGO 대표가 발언한바, 대부분 불구자인 이들은 수화 (SIGNAL LANGUAGE)통역을 통해 동등한 교육 기회보장, 고용자의 편견 제게를 위한 노력 필요성, 자신들의 권리신장 운동에 대하 유엔의 적극적인 지원등을 강조 또는 건의함. (동 의제에 대한소위 위원간 토론은 의제 18항 토의 종료후 재개예정)

3. 8.16. 오전 및 8.19 에 있은 의제 18항 토의에서는 특별보고자 EIDE (놀웨이) 위원의잠정 보고서 (E/CN 4/SUB 2/1991/43) 을 토대로 소수집단 정의의 필요성, 소수 집단과 토착민의구분 필요성, 종교적 소수집단의 포함 여부, 특별혜택 제공필요성, 인접국에 의한 개입문제등에 관해 의원들의 개진과 MINORITY RIGHT GROUP등 3개 NGO 의 발언이 있었는바 주요 내용은 아래와 같음.

- EIDE (특별보고자): 동 문제 해결의 최선책은 대화를 통한 평화적 해결임을 강조 하고, 동 문제 검토에 필요한 기본 지침 (GUIDELINE) 으로 무차별 원칙, 국가의 안정 유지,국가안보에 대한 위협, 수동적 보호 (무차별)과적극적 보호 (특혜, 특수지위 보장)등 6개항을 제시함. 또한 각국별로 소수집단에 대한 해석이 다양하므로 현단게에서는 명확한 정의를 내리지않고 검토를 진행함이 바람직하며, 종교적 소수집단도 검토대상 에 포함시켰음을 설명함.

국기국   1차보   법무부

PAGE 1   91.08.21   09:37 WG

외신 1과 통제관

0089

- DAES (그리스): 종교적 소수집단 포함을 지지하고,' 충분한 숫자를 이루는 비지배적 (NON-DONIMANT)집단으로서 소속국에 충성을 서약하는 집단' 으로 정의를 내리는 방안을 검토해 줄것을 제의함.

- BAN BOVEN (화란): 종교적 소수집단 포함을 지지하고, 소수집단과 토착민의 구별 및 소수집단 거주지역 천연자원 개발권의 귀속 (정부 또는 동집단) 문제에 대한 검토가 필요하다는 의결을 표명함.

- KHALIFA (이집트) : 소수민족들이 자결권을 지나치게 추구할 경우 민족국가의 분열에 의한 파멸 (SELF-MUTILATION) 현상을 초래할 위험성이 높다고 경고하면서 엄격한 축소정의 및 종교적 소수집단을 검토 대상에서 제외할 것을 주장함.

- ILKAHANAF (소말리아): 대화를 통해 해결 되지않은 경우의 대안 검토 필요성을 지적하고, 종교적 소수집단을 검토 대상에 포함시킬 것을 지지함.

- SACHAR (인도), KSENTINI (알제리아), MARTINEZ (쿠바) 위원은 인접국의 개입권 인정은 지극히 위험한 발상이므로 받아들일 수 없다는 입장을 표명함.

- 한편 NGO 로서는 MINORITY RIGHTS GROUP 이 동문제 검토과정에서 정부뿐만 아니라 소수집단의 의견을 직접 청취할 필요성과 유엔의 ADVISORY SERVICE 등 현존 제도의 활용 적극화 필요성을, INT'L FED FOR PROTECTION OF THE RIGHTS OF MINORITIES가 이락에서의 쿠르드족 및 SHIITE 무슬림 박해, 쿠웨이트 정부의 이락 부역자 박해 문제 및 그리스계 소수민족에 대한 알바니아 정부의 차별정책을, INT'L FED OF HUMAN RIGHTS 가 동 유럽 특히 루마니아 정부의 집시에 대한 차별 및 박해 문제를 각각 제기함

4. 한편 8.19 상기 의제 18항 토의시에는 동일새벽 발생한 소련정부 전복 사태와 관련, EIDE (놀웨이) 위원이 동 사태는 인권문제에 중대한 영향을 미치는 사건이므로 이에대한 긴급토의 및 고르바쵸프 정권의 원상 회복 긴급사태철회, 군대의 철수등을 촉구하는 결의안을 채택할 것을 제의하고, DESPOUY (알젠틴), DAES (그리스) 위원이 이에 동조하였으나 MARTINEZ (쿠바) 위원이 제 42차 소위시 카나다 모호크인디안 문제 처리 전례에 따라 성급한 행동 (PRECIPITATED ACTION)은 자제해야 한다는 이유를들어 이에 반대 입장을 표명하고, CHERNICHENKO (소련), WARZAZI (모로코), KSENTINI (알제리아),GUISSE (세네갈), ATTAH (나이제리아), JINTIAN (중국) 위원등도 정확한 사태 파악이 되지않은 현단계에서는 시기 상조라는 의견을 표명함으로서, 의장은 TREAT (미국) 위원의절충안을 받아들여 의장단 회의를 조속히 소집, 동 문제 토의

PAGE 2

여부 및 토의방법등을 협의한후 동협의 결과를 전체회의에 다시 회부키로 결정
(동의장단 협의는 명 8.20.오전 개최 예정) 하고 의제 18항 토의를 계속 하였음.끝
　　　(대사 박수길-국장)

외 무 부

종 별 :

번 호 : GVW-1563   일 시 : 91 0822 1100

수 신 : 장 관(국연, 법무부)

발 신 : 주 제네바 대사

제 목 : 제 43차 유엔인권소위(7)

1. 표제 회의는 8.20 야간회의를 속개, 의제 3,5,13 항 관련 3 개 결의안을 부표없이 채택하고 의제 17 항(청소년 및 여성의 인권), 의제 18 항(소수집단 보호) 및 12 항(장애자 인권) 토의를 종료하였으며, 의제 10 항(법사행정 및 비상사태하의 인권등) 토의를 시작한바, 8.20-21 간 주요 토의 내용 아래 보고함.

가. 소련사태 토의

0 8.20 오전 회의시 의장은 소련 사태 토의여부에 관한 의장단 회의 결정에따라 동 문제를 의제 10 항 B(비상사태하의 인권)에서 토의할 것을 제안한바, 채택됨.

0 이에따라 8.21. 오전회의시 EIDE(놀웨이), DAES(그리스), VAN BOVEN(화란), TREAT(미국), SACHAR(인도)등 많은 위원들은 금번 사태가 소련 국내법 뿐만 아니라 국제법상으로도 불법이며, 심각한 인권위반 사태의 발생이 우려되므로 인권소위가 시급히 동 문제를 다뤄야 할 것이라고 강조하고 아래와 같은 조치를 제의함

- DESPOUY 비상사태 특별보고관이 소련 당국에 긴급 전문을 발송, 동 사태에 대한 상세 내용을 회신토록 요청

- 인권위 의장 또는 유엔사무총장을 통해 소련국가 위원회에 금번 사태에 대한 우려와 인권보장을 촉구하는 긴급 APPEAL 을 전달

- 헌정 질서가 회복될때 까지 동 문제를 토의

0   CHERMICHENKO(소련),   MARTINEZ(쿠바),   KSENTINI(알제리), TIANZIN(중국), 위원등은 사태의 유동성, 정확한 정보의 부족, 동 문제가 국내문제이며 인권소위 관할이 아닌 이유등을 내세워 소위의 즉각적인 행동에 반대함.

0 오전 회의 종료직전 DESPOUY 특별보관은, 통상적인 절차에 따라 금번 사태의 상세한 내용을 문의하는 동인의 공한을 8.20 소련당국에 발송하였다고 밝혔음. 또한 MARTENSEN 사무차장은 9.19 자 유엔사무총장 논평을 낭독함.

국기국	차관	1차보	미주국	구주국	분석관	청와대	안기부	법무부

O 의장은 동 문제를 오후 회의시 재론키로 한바, 이날 오후 소련사태의 급진전에 따라 더이상의 토의는 없었음

나. 의제 18(소수집단 보호)

O 미국대표는 금세기초에 이어 현재도 발칸문제가 국제정세 있어 최대의 현안이라고 말하고 인권소위가 소수민족 문제 해결에 선구역할을 함을써 본연의 임무에 충실해야 할때라고 강조함.

동 대표는 특히 코소바, 불가리아내 터키계, 이라크내 쿠르드 및 시아파, 집시의 인권 상황을 제기함.

O 헝가리 대표는 자국정부의 소수민족 정책을 설명하고 해외거주 헝가리인 문제해결을 위해 우쿠라이나 정부와의 합동위원회 구성등 양자적 노력도 경주하고 있다고 언급함.

O 터키대표는 그리스 정부가 터키계 소수민에 대해 교육, 토지정책등에 있어 차별을 계속하고 있다고 강력히 비난한바 그리스 대표는 답변권을 통해 이를 반박함.

O NGO 인 ROMANI INT'L UNION 는 중동 부유럽 특히 루마니아에서의 집시 차별을 비난하고 소수집단 문제해결에는 교육의 역할이 중요하며, 교육의 자유, 학교 선택의 자유등이 보장되어야 한다고 강조함.

INT'L INDIAN TREATY COUNCIL 은 미국의 하와이 점령 및 합병을 비난함.

다. 의제 17(청소년 및 여성의 인권)

O EIDE 위원은 청소년 인권에관한 MAZILU 특별보고관 보고서를 평가하고 청소년의 실업문제 및 강제징집 문제가 검토되어야 한다고 언급함.

O 브라질 대표는 자국내 아동 및 청소년에 대한 살해행위의 빈번한 발생에 우려를 표명하고 동 정부가 담당기구 신설등 강력한 대응조치를 추진중이라고 밝히고 관련 국제기구의 지원을 요청함.

O NGO 대표 주요 발언내용은 아래와 같음

- FRIENDS WORLD COM. FOR CONSULTATION: 무력 분쟁시 청소년 관여, 양심에따른 군복무 거부에 대한 처벌 및 강제징집 조치를 비난

- WONEN'S INT'L LEAGUE FOR PEACE 및 INT'L FALCON MOVEMENT: 이란 여성에대한 복장, 조혼 및 사법제도상의 인권위반

INT'L ABOLITIONIST FED: 브라질내 빈번한 아동 살해행위, 페루내 미성년자금광노역, 미국에서의 미성년에 대한 사형 제도 부활, 이락, 루마니아 내

PAGE 2

청소년 인권 문제
 - DISABLED PEOPLES IN'L: 장애자 아동, 여성에 대한 교육 및 사회적 서비스 박탈
(라항 부터 GVW-1574 로 계속됨)

0094

외 무 부

종 별 :

번 호 : GVW-1574 　　　　　　　　　　　일 시 : 91 0822 1100

수 신 : 장 관(국연, 법무부)

발 신 : 주 제네바 대사

제 목 : 제 43차 유엔인권소위(7)

　　라. 의제 12(장애자 인권)

　　O 위원들은 DESPOUY 위원의 장애자 인권보고서를 평가하고 특히 A 규약 산하의 경제사회 문화 위원회에서 장애자 인권문제를 감시토록 권고하는 제의를 지지함.

　　장애자 인권에 관한 별도 협약 제정문제에 대해 DESPOUY 위원은 유엔 총회시 스웨덴등 일부 국가가 이를 지지한바 있으나 현 상황에서는 기존 협약내 관련조항이 이행이 바람직하다고 언급함.

　　O EIDE 위원은 장애장에 대한 편견 및 차별 타파를 위해 장애자 이익단체가정책결정 과정에 참여해야 한다고 말하였으며 DAES 위원은 토착민 장애자 문제를, KSENTINI 위원은 여성장애자 문제에 대한 심층 연구 필요성을 강조함.

　　O INT'L EDUCATIONAL DEVELOPMENT COR 는 국제옴브즈만 제도 도입을 지지하고, 중국정부의 장애자 강제불임 시술 및 교육제한을 비난함.

　　마. 의제 10(법사행정등)

　　O 8.21. 오후 BAUTISTA 위원의 청소년 재소자 인권에 관한 국제적 기준 적용 문제보고서(1991/24), TREAT 및 CHERNICHENKO 위원의 공정한 재판의 권리 제 2차 보고서(1991/29), DESPOUY 위원의 비상사태하의 인권보고서(1991/28), MARTINEZ 위원의 교도소의 사설화 문제 보고서에 대한 설명에 이어 NGO 대표의 발언이 있었음.

　　O 주요 NGO 발언 내용은 아래와 같음.

　　- AL: IMPUNITY 에 대한 철저 연구가 필요함. 특히 필리핀 및 콜롬비아에서의 보안군의 인권침해, 스리랑카에서의 실종자 가족에 대한 위협문제가 심각함.

　　- ICJ: IMPUNITY 연구 필요

　　- INT'L FED.OF HUMAN RIGHTS: IMPUNITY 및 법관, 증인에 대한 위협 문제, 과테말라, 코소바 상황심각

국기국	차관	1차보	미주국	구주국	분석관	정와대	안기부	법무부

PAGE 1

- COMMISSION OF CHURCHES FOR INT'L AFFAIRS: 아르메니아에서의 민간인 살해행위 반발
- INT'L HUMAN RIGHTS LAW GROUP: 인권소위가 기존 인권 협약으로 IMPUNITY에 대처할 수 있는지 여부등을 연구, 조사할 것을 촉구
- HUMAN RIGHTS ADOVOCATE : 난민 및 ASYLUM SEEKER 의 인권보장 문제
- CENTRE EUROPE: 서사하라에서의 민간인 불법 구금
- INT'L EDUCATIONAL DEVELOPMENT: 일본 경찰서 구치제도(변호인 접견권 제한 및 고문행위등) 문제점

2. 한편 8.20-21 회의에서는 NGO 인 INT'L LEAGUE FOR THE RIGHTS AND LIBERATION OF PEOPLES 대표로 등록된 당지 거주 최기환 및 이좌웅(재일교포로 추정)이 계속 참석중인바, 동 단체는 의제 10 항 관련 8.22. 오전 발언 예정임. 끝

(대사 박수길-국장)

PAGE 2

외　무　부

종　별 :

번　호 : GVW-1584　　　　　　　　　　일　시 : 91 0823 1100

수　신 : 장관(국연,법무부,기정동문)

발　신 : 주 제네바 대사

제　목 : 제 43차 유엔인권소위(8)

연: GVW-1563

1. 연호 보고대로 INT'L LEAGUE FOR THE RIGHTS AND THE LIBERATION FOR PEOPLES 대표 VERONA GRAF 는 금 8.22. 오전 의제 10 항 토의시 아래 요지로 아국인권 상황을 왜곡, 발언을 행함(당지 반한교포 최기환 및 재일조총련 추정 이좌웅은 GRAF 옆 좌석에 착석)

- 현재 한국에는 3,750 명의 정치범과 정치적 행위로 구속된 4,100 명이 수감중임.(KNCC 가 작성한 1,500 명의 명단, 인적사항 리스트를 ANNEX 로 제출)

- 정치범 전원 석방 약속은 지켜지지 않고 있으며 한국정부는 오히려 인권위반의 세계기록을 다시 수립함.

- 상기 인권위반은 사실상의 긴급사태(NON-DECLARED STATE OF EMERGENCY)로밖에 볼수 없는 공안정국 하에서 80,000 명의 전경대, 보안법, 집시법, 노동법 및 안기부, 보안사등 각종 법적, 제도적 장치를 통해 자행됨

- 강경대, 김기정이 경찰에 의해서, 박창수가 안기부에 의해 살해되고 범민련, 전민련, 전대협, 전노련, 진교조가 탄압을 받고 있음.

사법권의 독립은 가식에 불가하며 영장제도의 정상운영 및 공정한 재판은 기대 곤란함.

- 상기 법적, 제도적 장치는 존재치도 않는 북한으로 부터의 위협(NON EXISTENT THREAT)을 위해 필요하다고 주장되나, 사실상 집권세력의 정치적 반대세력탄압 도구에 불과함.

- 한국에서의 법은 자유 및 권리신장을 위해서가 아니라 이의 말살을 위해 존재하며, 인권관련 국제규범 및 민주헌법의 시해을 저해함.

(안기부는 판단 및 국회의원도 영장없이 체포가능하며, 청와대 마져 도청중임)

국기국	차관	1차보	미주국	구주국	분석관	청와대	안기부	법무부

PAGE 1

- 안기부, 보안사, 경찰대공과는 문자그대로 고문의 본부임.(유원호 및 박정수를 예시)

- 이상의 사실 및 80 년 광주사태 경험에 비추어 한국정권은 반민주, 반국민적이며 새로운 국제질서에 역행함.

- 한국정부에 보안법등 반민주 입법철폐, 안기부등 비헌법기관 해체, 정치범 석방, 민주체제 탄압중지, 임수경, 문익환, 문규현등 석방을 탄원함.

2. 상기에 대해 이성주 참사관은 동일 오후 아래요지의 답변권을 행사함.

- 전국제사회가 최근, 특히 1988 년 민선대통령 선출이후의 한국의 민주발전을 찬양하고 있는 시점에서 ILRLP 가 허무맹랑한 중상발언을 한것은 극히 유감이며 놀라운 일임.

- 악의에 찬 발언성격에 비추어 진진한 답변의 가치도 없으나 올바른 이해와 정확한 기록을 위해 답변권을 행사함.

- 발언자는 민선대통령 선출이후 한국의 민주화 발전 사실에 전혀 무지하며, 동 무지는 동인의 발언내용의 황당성에 의해서 여실히 입증됨.

- 한국정부 및 한국의 민주화 발전 이미지를 손상코자 하는 단체(ON ENTITY)의 견해를 그대로 대변(PARROTING)하고 있다는 의구심을 금할 수 없으며 허위와 왜곡은 동인의 소속단체의 편향된 성격을 입증함.

- 동인이 제시한 정치범 숫자는 극단좌익 집단의 주장에도 없는 과장된 숫자로 조작에 불과하고 한국이 인권위반이 세계기록을 세우고 있다는 것은 완전한NON SENSE 에 불과

- 동인이 제출한 리스트에는 7 명의 경찰관을 살해한 동의대 사건 범인들도포함되어 있는 점등 동인은 폭력과 정치적 범죄를 제대로 구분치 못하고 있고 이역시 동인의 무지를 확연히 입증하며, 영장없는 체포 운운은 황당무계의 극치임.

- 동인의 발언 내용은 왜곡과 거짓의 AMALGAM 으로 한국 민주화에 대한 적대감의 표현일 뿐임.

- 동인이 한국의 인권상황을 진저으로 우려한다면 한국의 민주제도를 파괴코자 하는 무명 단체가 제공하는 정보에 입각치 말고 최소한 한번만이라도 한국을 직접 방문, 정확한 실상을 파악하기를 진정으로 기대함.

3. 상기 아측의 답변권은 전체적으로 강한 인상을 주는 것은 사실이나, ILRLP 의 발언이 아국의 전반적인 국내상황 관련, 국내 반정부 집단의 입장을 그대로 대변하는

PAGE 2

0098

악의에 찬 내용이었기 때문에, 한번쯤은 강력한 대응이 필요하다는 판단에 따른 것이나, NGO 등의 아국비난 발언에 일일이 대응 하는 것은 회의분위기 및 성숙한 민주국가의 의미지는 물론 해당 NOG 발언 내용에 대한 관심을 오히려 시킬 가능성을 없지 않은 점을 고려, 잔여 소위기간 또는 향후 인권위, 인권소위에서는 금번 ILRLP 와 같이 극단적 발언이 아닌한 가급적 묵살하는 것이 바람직할 것으로 보임.

4. 상기 ILRLP 가 아국대봉령에 대한 일체의 존칭을 생략한 것과 관련 WARZAZI(모로코) 위원은 NGO 가 특정국가의 국가원수를 지칭할 경우 최소한의 예외는 지켜야 할 것이라는 경고 발언을 하였음.

5. 한편 ILRLP 발언직후 INT'L ORG. FOR THE ELIMINATION OF ALL FORMS OF RACIAL DISCRIMINATION 중공의 사법제도 운영을 비판하는 내용의 발언을 하면서서두에 북한 및 중국과 같이 전국민이 감옥속에 살고 있는 것과 같은 나라가 있다고 언급하였음.

6. 상기 ILRLP 의 발언문 및 아측의 답변권은 정파편 송부하며, 기타 토의내용은 별전 보고 예정임.끝

(대사 박수길-국장)

주 제 네 바 대 표 부

재내(정) 2031-319   1991. 8.23

수신 : 장관

참조 : 국제기구조약국장

제목 : 제 43차 유엔인권소위 자료   91 8. 23

      연 : GVW-1584

      표제 회의 의제 10항 토의관련 8.22 회의시 NGO인 ILRLP의 아국관련
발언문 및 이에 대한 아국대표 반박 발언문을 별첨 송부합니다.

      첨부 : 동 발언문 각 1부. 끝.

            주 제 네 바 대 사

48015

0100

LIGUE INTERNATION▆▆▆ UR LES DROITS ET LA LIBERATION DES PEUPLES
Organisation non gouverne▆▆▆▆▆▆oée ou statut consultatif auprès de l'ONU et de l'UNESCO

INTERNATIONAL LEAGUE FOR THE RIGHTS AND THE LIBERATION OF PEOPLES   Cat. II
Non-governmental organization in consultative status with UNO and UNESCO

LIGA INTERNACIONAL POR LOS DERECHOS Y LA LIBERACION DE LOS PUEBLOS
Organización no gubernamental reconocida como entidad consultiva antes el ONU y el UNESCO

Oral statement
Sub-Commission on Prevention of Discrimination
and Protection of Minorities
43rd session - August 1991 - Geneva
item 10, 10 b): The administration of justice
and the human rights of detainees; Question of
the human rights of persons subjected to any
form of detention or imprisonment

Verena GRAF

ARBITRARY IMPRISONMENT IN SOUTH KOREA

Even though the situation in South Korea seems sometimes to be improving, the *International League for the Rights and Liberation of Peoples* deems it once more necessary to raise the question of the human rights of persons subjected to any form of detention or imprisonment in that country.

First of all, a few figures. According to our calculations there are at present more than 3750 political prisoners and 4100 persons detained for political offenses. Annexed to the present report, we submit a list of more than 1500 political prisoners with occupations, charges, dates of arrest and sentences. It is more than evident that the "democratic promise" of the General President Roh Tai-Ou that not one political prisoner would be left has not been kept, and that on the contrary, the South Korean government has again reached a world record in human right violations.

It must be noted that those violations have taken place under a non-declared state of emergency which is in force since the beginning of 1989; in Korean, it is called "Kong-An-Jong-Guk", which literally means "state of public security". It is a cross between the police state that existed under Sung-Man Rhee and the dictatorial regime of Pak Chung-Hui. The combat police forces, Chun-Gyong-Dai, under which more than 80000 soldiers fulfil permanently the function of a martial force under a state of emergency. All liberties and rights are faced constantly with a frightening array of legal instruments - the National Security Law, Law on Assembly and Demonstration, Labor Relations Law, Media Standard Law, Public Security Inspection Law, etc. - and with the ruthless repression of law-enforcement agencies, especially the Agency for National Security Planning (ex KCIA), the Information Command for Military Security, the Anti-Communist Section of the Korean National Police, etc.

It is under this situation of terror that two students, Mr. Kang Jyong-Dai and Miss Kim Kui-Jong, were killed on the campus by the Combat Police Force, while Mr. Pak Chang-Sou, chairman of the trade union of Hanjin Industries, was murdered by agents of the KCIA in a hospital where he was under treatment for wounds caused by torture. It is under

0101

this situation of repression that the movements of Bum-Min-Ryon (Pan-Korean Alliance for Reunification), Chun-Min-Ryon, Pan-Korean Democratic Union, and Chun-Dai-Hyup (Federation of All Korean Students) are severely persecuted and that the activities of Chun-Ro-Yon (Federation of Democratic Trade Unions), and Chun-Kyo-Jo (Federation of Democratic Teachers), are restrained and now virtually prohibited. The situation of terror and repression is such that it is considered foolish to hope for an effective application of "habeas corpus" and of the right to a fair trial in South Korea. The independence of justice has become a mere travesty because of arbitrary interferences of the above-mentioned law instruments and law-enforcement agencies. All these facts show the real and permanent existence of a state of emergency in South Korea, even though it was not declared, for deceptive purposes.

While the South Korean government defends the above-mentionned law instruments as a necessary safeguard against a non existent "threat" from North Korea, they have been widely used as the ruling power's paramount tool and as institutionalized mechanism for supressing legitimate political dissent and basic freedoms and rights which are protected even by the South Korean Constitution. It is really frightening that there should exist laws in South Korea, not in order to concretize and apply those freedoms and rights, but, on the contrary, to negate them. It is one of the problems which impedes an effective implementation of democratic constitutionalism in South Korea and the implementation of the international and United Nations norms and standard relating to human rights. To give just an example, the Law on the Agency for National Security Planning allows this agency to arrest without a warrant even members of parliament and judges. It is interesting to note that the KCIA is tapping even the telephone of the Blue House, the presidential mansion of General President Roh Tai-Ou. One must also mention the Public Security Inspection Law, which is a surrogate of the former Public Security Law and permits the administrative detention of everybody, including those who have served their term and are considered as a threat to public security, without the benefit of judiciary procedures.

Another obstacle to the effective implementation of human rights consists of the Korean law-enforcement agencies, especially the Agency for National Security Planning, the Information Command for Military Security and the Anti-Communist Section of the Korean National Police. They are literally the headquarters of torture for political prisoners and persons arrested for political reasons; for all Koreans, "Namsan-Mountain" and "Bingo-Hotel" are not only the geographical denominations of these two agencies, but are synonyms of torture to the death, because they know of more than 12 such cases. On the details of ill-treatment and torture, we invite you, in order to save time, to consult the reports presented by the *International League for the Rights and Liberation of Peoples* in the last several

0102

years, even though the situation has notably worsened since then.

We would like in particular to dwell on two cases; the first is that of Mr. You Won-Ho, a companion of Reverend Mun Ik-Whan, who was deprived of sleep for 28 days and suffered various forms of torture. He has recently written a letter to his family, saying : "...Here is my dying wish to you; never go to Namsan-Mountain (namely the Agency for National Security Planning). If you should be obliged in the future to go there, it is better to kill yourselves." It indicates clearly how unbearable are the tortures suffered by political prisoners or detainees in South Korea. The second concerns Mr. Pak Chang-Sou, one of the most devoted leaders of the South Korean labour movement. He was arrested by KCIA on April 14th of this year and detained in a hospital in Anyang because of heavy head injuries caused by torture. On May 5th he was found dead in the yard of the hospital. The Prosecutor-General's Office announced that he had killed himself by throwing himself from the rooftop of the hospital which is 25 meters high. But his dead body had no other wound than the above-mentioned head injury. How could a dead body thrown from a height of 25 meters on a concrete ground not suffer multiple fractures? The victim was probably poisoned, another invention of KCIA for getting rid of political prisoners.

Just a word about the 143 political prisoners sentenced to 20 to 40 years' detention; 23 of them are more than 70 years old and 2 more than 80 years old. We know that even during the medieval dark ages persons so advanced in years were not kept in prison.

After all, what wrong have committed these political prisoners and detainees for political reasons? They have formed study groups, democratic trade unions or other organisations, they have published books, they have failed to report to the authorities crimes committed by members of their family, they have criticised the military presence and nuclear weapons of the USA in South Korea, they have urged the withdrawal of US forces, they have tried to meet North Korean students or to have cultural and scientific contacts there, they have demanded peaceful reunification of Korea, abolition or at least drastic reform of the National Security Law, judicial fairness, they have criticised human right violations, they have proclaimed non-governmental movements for reunification, civil dialogues with North Korea or impartial understanding of North Korea, they have insisted for a simultaneous nuclear inspection in the South and the North, etc. In short, they have exercised democratic civil rights.

Judging from the above-mentioned, and leaving aside the unforgettable massacre of Kwang-Jou in 1980, the South Korean regime is anti-democratic and anti-national and going against the irreversible tendency of our time towards a peaceful and democratic international order free from all kinds of subordination and interference. Here we find also

0103

the basic cause of human rights violations in South Korea, namely the negation of the Korean people's right to free and independent choice and action. The legal and political absurdities based on the archaic cold war logics and logics of dependence must be stopped.

We fervently hope, however, that all is not yet lost. Next month, South Korea will be a member of the United Nations and it is a very good opportunity to demand from its government that it comply with the various United Nations standards, especially those relating to human rights, and with the fundamental principles of the United Nations, namely international peace based on international democracy.

Accordingly, we appeal to the South Korean government :

- To abolish all undemocratic, antinational and repressive laws, beginning with the National Security Law.

- To suppress all the unconstitutional oppressive law-enforcement agencies, beginning with the Agency for National Security Planning;

- To set free all political prisoners and persons arrested for political reasons, beginning with those sentenced to long terms of imprisonment;

- To cease immediately all repressive measures against the organizations Chun-Mib-Ryon, Chun-Dai-Hyup, Chun-Ro-Ryon, Chun-Kyo-Jo and other democratic organizations, beginning with the liberation of Mr. Pak No-Hai and other workers;

- To abolish immediately all measures against activists of non-governmental movements for reconciliation and reunification, beginning with the immediate liberation of Miss Rim Sou-Gyong, Reverend Mun-Ik-Wan, Mr. You Won-Ho and the catholic pastor Mun Gyou-Hyon. (We wish to add that the *International League for the Rights and Liberation of Peoples* has submitted to the Human Rights Center's Secretariat in March 1990 a petition signed by no less than 726 organizations and 46.385 individuals for the release of the above-mentioned persons).

22 August 1991

Mr. Chairman,

It is extremely deplorable that an NGO representative made
highly slanderous remarks about the alleged human right
violations in my country. It is also quite surprising that she
has the audacity to make such a statement full of falsehood and
distortions, at a time when the international community widely
applauds the remarkable progress my country has made in the
development of democratic institutions, including human rights
particularly since we popularly elected our President with strong
democratic platform in 1988.

I consider that the blatantly malicious nature of the
statements made by the representative of the International League
for the Rights and the Liberation of Peoples this morning renders
it unworthy of serious or substantial response. Nevertheless,
because it is replete with unfounded accusations, falsehoods and
gross distortions of fact, I feel it is necessary to make a brief
comment to set the record straight.

The speaker is ignorant of the significant democratization
which the Republic of Korea has undertaken particularly since the
adoption of its new Constitution in 1988 under the popularly
elected President with democratic platform, and her ignorance is
reflected in the absurdity of her statements. I am convinced
that she has never been to the Republic of Korea. If she had,
she would have realized herself the ludicrousness of her charges.

I suspect the speaker was not parroting the hostile views
of an entity determined to denigrate the good image of the
Government of the Republic of Korea and its programme of

1

0105

democratization which includes concrete progress in the promotion of fundamental human rights. The falsehoods and distortions in her statement are ample proof to convince all of us of the biased nature and true identity of the organization she allegedly represents.

The speaker claims to have based her proposals on "facts and figures". But such figures on political prisoners and detainees are rarely found even in documents of the farthest-left radicals. It is therefore most probable that her "calculations" are actually pure fabrication.

Certainly no one in this room would consider the human rights record of the Republic of Korea any kind of a "world record", in a positive or negative sense. The speaker's contention to that effect is pure nonsense. The Republic of Korea fully realizes that guaranteeing fundamental human rights to all citizens is a basic obligation of all democratic societies. We admit that there are areas which require improvement in our country. Our recent adhesion to the International Covenant on Economic, Social and Cultural Rights and the International Covenant on Civil and Political Rights and its Optional Protocol represents only one example of the concrete steps in this direction, as does prosecution and punishment of police officers who overreacted during student riots.

The speaker has muddled the crucial distinction, made in all democratic societies, between violence and political crimes. Would she consider radical and violent demonstrators who have been prosecuted for violent crimes, including throwing firebombs, attacking police stations and other public buildings, and setting fire to public property, which have resulted in deaths and serious injuries, as political prisoners? Surely no democratic country would, and if such a country exists at all, it would exist, I presume, only in the imaginary world of the NGO representative herself. Ironically enough, in her list of the so-called political prisoners, she had the audacity to include

2

those who set fire to a school library resulting in the death of 7 policemen and many injured in May 1989. The speaker's confusion of violence and the concept of political prisoners is yet another example of her ignorance.

The speaker's preposterous contention that anyone could be arrested or detained without a warrant reaches a new height of absurdity. Even the most radical students would not make such a statement, knowing that outright lies, when they are perpetrated, only serve to discredit a cause.

In summary, the speaker's assertions are void of the essential elements of truth necessary for them to be seriously considered. They form a messy amalgam of gross distortions of fact and outright lies and reflect only the speaker's ignorance and the hostility towards democratization held by the organization she represents.

My advice to her would be to beware of being used as an instrument of an organization dedicated to denigrating the good image of Korea, and with the aim of destabilizing my country. Even if she is not being used as an instrument, her statement full of falsehoods will serve only to destroy whatever credibility the organization she represents has.

If she is truly interested in the human rights situation in the Republic of Korea, I would like to suggest that she visits my country at least once and sees for herself the true situation there, instead of relying on distorted information and concotion emanating from obscure entities which attempt to destroy our democratic system, or exercising her gift of imagination.

Thank you.

3

0107

주 제 네 바 대 표 부

제네(정) 2031-749   1991. 8. 27

수신 : 외무부장관

참조 : 국제기구조약국장

제목 : 제 43차 유엔인권 소위   91. 8. 30

        연 : GVW-1548

        연호 8.22 인권소위 회의시 NGO인 ILRLP의 아국 비방 발언시 함께 제출한
한국기독교 교회협의회 인권위원회 작성 구속자 현황을 별첨 송부합니다.

        첨부 : 상기 구속자 현황 1부.   끝.

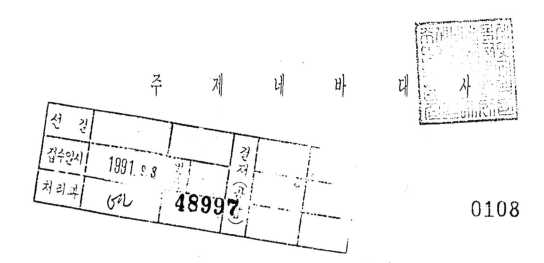

주 제 네 바 대 사

선결			결재	
접수일시	1991. 9 8			
처리과	6L	48997		

0108

공 란

공 란

공   란

공   란

공   란

공　　　란

공　　　란

공   란

공　　　　란

공   란

공　　　란

공 란

공 란

공 란

공   란

공   란

공　　　　란

공   란

공   란

공   란

공 란

공 란

공   란

공   란

공 란

공 란

공   란

공   란

공 란

공　　　란

공 란

공　　　란

외 무 부

종 별 :

번 호 : GVW-1604
일 시 : 91 0827 1030

수 신 : 장관(국연, 법무부)

발 신 : 주 제네바 대사

제 목 : 제 43차 인권 소위

8.22 표제회의에서의 ILRLP 발언문과 아국의 반박 발언문을 별첨 송부함. 끝

첨부: GVW(F)-310

(대사 박수길-국장)

국기국   2차보   법무부

PAGE 1

LIGUE INTERNATIONALE P——ES DROITS ET LA LIBERATION DES PEUPLES
Organisation non gouvernementale dotée du statut consultatif auprès de l'ONU et de l'UNESCO

INTERNATIONAL LEAGUE FOR THE RIGHTS AND THE LIBERATION OF PEOPLES
Non-governmental organization in consultative status with UNO and UNESCO

LIGA INTERNACIONAL POR LOS DERECHOS Y LA LIBERACION DE LOS PUEBLOS
Organización no gubernamental reconocida como entidad consultiva antes el ONU y el UNESCO

Cat. II

Gưw(카)-3/0 / 082718~
6уw-1 사 겁 5

Oral statement
Sub-Commission on Prevention of Discrimination
and Protection of Minorities
43rd session - August 1991 - Geneva
item 10, 10 b): The administration of justice
and the human rights of detainees; Question of
the human rights of persons subjected to any
form of detention or imprisonment

Verena GRAF

ARBITRARY IMPRISONMENT IN SOUTH KOREA

Even though the situation in South Korea seems sometimes to
be improving, the *International League for the Rights and
Liberation of Peoples* deems it once more necessary to raise
the question of the human rights of persons subjected to any
form of detention or imprisonment in that country.

First of all, a few figures. According to our calculations
there are at present more than 3750 political prisoners and
4100 persons detained for political offenses. Annexed to the
present report, we submit a list of more than 1500 political
prisoners with occupations, charges, dates of arrest and
sentences. It is more than evident that the "democratic
promise" of the General President Roh Tai-Ou that not one
political prisoner would be left has not been kept, and that
on the contrary, the South Korean government has again
reached a world record in human right violations.

It must be noted that those violations have taken place
under a non-declared state of emergency which is in force
since the beginning of 1989; in Korean, it is called "Kong-
An-Jong-Guk", which literally means "state of public
security". It is a cross between the police state that
existed under Sung-Man Rhee and the dictatorial regime of
Pak Chung-Hui. The combat police forces, Chun-Gyong-Dai,
under which more than 80000 soldiers fulfil permanently the
function of a martial force under a state of emergency. All
liberties and rights are faced constantly with a frightening
array of legal instruments - the National Security Law, Law
on Assembly and Demonstration, Labor Relations Law, Media
Standard Law, Public Security Inspection Law, etc. - and
with the ruthless repression of law-enforcement agencies,
especially the Agency for National Security Planning (ex
KCIA), the Information Command for Military Security, the
Anti-Communist Section of the Korean National Police, etc.

It is under this situation of terror that two students, Mr.
Kang Jyong-Dai and Miss Kim Kui-Jong, were killed on the
campus by the Combat Police Force, while Mr. Pak Chang-Sou,
chairman of the trade union of Hanjin Industries, was
murdered by agents of the KCIA in a hospital where he was
under treatment for wounds caused by torture. It is under

7-1

0142

2

this situation of repression that the movements of Bum-Min-Ryon (Pan-Korean Alliance for Reunification), Chun-Min-Ryon, Pan-Korean Democratic Union, and Chun-Dai-Hyup (Federation of All Korean Students) are severely persecuted and that the activities of Chun-Ro-Yon (Federation of Democratic Trade Unions), and Chun-Kyo-Jo (Federation of Democratic Teachers), are restrained and now virtually prohibited. The situation of terror and repression is such that it is considered foolish to hope for an effective application of "habeas corpus" and of the right to a fair trial in South Korea. The independence of justice has become a mere travesty because of arbitrary interferences of the above-mentioned law instruments and law-enforcement agencies. All these facts show the real and permanent existence of a state of emergency in South Korea, even though it was not declared, for deceptive purposes.

While the South Korean government defends the above-mentionned law instruments as a necessary safeguard against a non existent "threat" from North Korea, they have been widely used as the ruling power's paramount tool and as institutionalized mechanism for supressing legitimate political dissent and basic freedoms and rights which are protected even by the South Korean Constitution. It is really frightening that there should exist laws in South Korea, not in order to concretize and apply those freedoms and rights, but, on the contrary, to negate them. It is one of the problems which impedes an effective implementation of democratic constitutionalism in South Korea and the implementation of the international and United Nations norms and standard relating to human rights. To give just an example, the Law on the Agency for National Security Planning allows this agency to arrest without a warrant even members of parliament and judges. It is interesting to note that the KCIA is tapping even the telephone of the Blue House, the presidential mansion of General President Roh Tai-Ou. One must also mention the Public Security Inspection Law, which is a surrogate of the former Public Security Law and permits the administrative detention of everybody, including those who have served their term and are considered as a threat to public security, without the benefit of judiciary procedures.

Another obstacle to the effective implementation of human rights consists of the Korean law-enforcement agencies, especially the Agency for National Security Planning, the Information Command for Military Security and the Anti-Communist Section of the Korean National Police. They are literally the headquarters of torture for political prisoners and persons arrested for political reasons; for all Koreans, "Namsan-Mountain" and "Bingo-Hotel" are not only the geographical denominations of these two agencies, but are synonyms of torture to the death, because they know of more than 10 such cases. On the details of ill-treatment and torture, we invite you, in order to save time, to consult the reports presented by the *International League for the Rights and Liberation of Peoples* in the last several

-2

years, even though the situation has notably worsened since then.

We would like in particular to dwell on two cases; the first is that of Mr. You Won-Ho, a companion of Reverend Mun Ik-Whan, who was deprived of sleep for 28 days and suffered various forms of torture. He has recently written a letter to his family, saying : "...Here is my dying wish to you; never go to Namsan-Mountain (namely the Agency for National Security Planning). If you should be obliged in the future to go there, it is better to kill yourselves." It indicates clearly how unbearable are the tortures suffered by political prisoners or detainees in South Korea. The second concerns Mr. Pak Chang-Sou, one of the most devoted leaders of the South Korean labour movement. He was arrested by KCIA on April 14th of this year and detained in a hospital in Anyang because of heavy head injuries caused by torture. On May 5th he was found dead in the yard of the hospital. The Prosecutor-General's Office announced that he had killed himself by throwing himself from the rooftop of the hospital which is 25 meters high. But his dead body had no other wound than the above-mentioned head injury. How could a dead body thrown from a height of 25 meters on a concrete ground not suffer multiple fractures? The victim was probably poisoned, another invention of KCIA for getting rid of political prisoners.

Just a word about the 143 political prisoners sentenced to 20 to 40 years' detention; 23 of them are more than 70 years old and 2 more than 80 years old. We know that even during the medieval dark ages persons so advanced in years were not kept in prison.

After all, what wrong have committed these political prisoners and detainees for political reasons? They have formed study groups, democratic trade unions or other organisations, they have published books, they have failed to report to the authorities crimes committed by members of their family, they have criticised the military presence and nuclear weapons of the USA in South Korea, they have urged the withdrawal of US forces, they have tried to meet North Korean students or to have cultural and scientific contacts there, they have demanded peaceful reunification of Korea, abolition or at least drastic reform of the National Security Law, judicial fairness, they have criticised human right violations, they have proclaimed non-governmental movements for reunification, civil dialogues with North Korea or impartial understanding of North Korea, they have insisted for a simultaneous nuclear inspection in the South and the North, etc. In short, they have exercised democratic civil rights.

Judging from the above-mentioned, and leaving aside the unforgettable massacre of Kwang-Jou in 1980, the South Korean regime is anti-democratic and anti-national and going against the irreversible tendency of our time towards a peaceful and democratic international order free from all kinds of subordination and interference. Here we find also

0144

7-3

4

the basic cause of human rights violations in South Korea,
namely the negation of the Korean people's right to free and
independent choice and action. The legal and political
absurdities based on the archaic cold war logics and logics
of dependence must be stopped.

We fervently hope, however, that all is not yet lost. Next
month, South Korea will be a member of the United Nations
and it is a very good opportunity to demand from its
government that it comply with the various United Nations
standards, especially those relating to human rights, and
with the fundamental principles of the United Nations,
namely international peace based on international democracy.

Accordingly, we appeal to the South Korean government :

- To abolish all undemocratic, antinational and
  repressive laws, beginning with the National Security
  Law.

- To suppress all the unconstitutional oppressive law-
  enforcement agencies, beginning with the Agency for
  National Security Planning;

- To set free all political prisoners and persons
  arrested for political reasons, beginning with those
  sentenced to long terms of imprisonment;

- To cease immediately all repressive measures
  against the organizations Chun-Mib-Ryon, Chun-Dai-
  Hyup, Chun-Ro-Ryon, Chun-Kyo-Jo and other democratic
  organizations, beginning with the liberation of Mr.
  Pak No-Hai and other workers;

- To abolish immediately all measures against activists
  of non-governmental movements for reconciliation and
  reunification, beginning with the immediate
  liberation of Miss Rim Sou-Gyong, Reverend Mun-Ik-
  Wan, Mr. You Won-Ho and the catholic pastor Mun Gyou-
  Hyon. (We wish to add that the *International League
  for the Rights and Liberation of Peoples* has
  submitted to the Human Rights Center's Secretariat in
  March 1990 a petition signed by no less than 726
  organizations and 46.385 individuals for the release
  of the above-mentioned persons).

7-4

0145

Right of Reply
by the Delegation of the
Republic of Korea,

22 August 1991

Mr. Chairman,

It is extremely deplorable that an NGO representative made highly slanderous remarks about the alleged human right violations in my country. It is also quite surprising that she has the audacity to make such a statement full of falsehood and distortions, at a time when the international community widely applauds the remarkable progress my country has made in the development of democratic institutions, including human rights particularly since we popularly elected our President with strong democratic platform in 1988.

I consider that the blatantly malicious nature of the statements made by the representative of the International League for the Rights and the Liberation of Peoples this morning renders it unworthy of serious or substantial response. Nevertheless, because it is replete with unfounded accusations, falsehoods and gross distortions of fact, I feel it is necessary to make a brief comment to set the record straight.

The speaker is ignorant of the significant democratization which the Republic of Korea has undertaken particularly since the adoption of its new Constitution in 1988 under the popularly elected President with democratic platform, and her ignorance is reflected in the absurdity of her statements. I am convinced that she has never been to the Republic of Korea. If she had, she would have realized herself the ludicrousness of her charges.

I suspect the speaker was not parroting the hostile views of an entity determined to denigrate the good image of the Government of the Republic of Korea and its programme of

1

7-5

0146

democratization which includes concrete progress in the promotion
of fundamental human rights. The falsehoods and distortions in
her statement are ample proof to convince all of us of the biased
nature and true identity of the organization she allegedly
represents.

The speaker claims to have based her proposals on "facts and
figures". But such figures on political prisoners and detainees
are rarely found even in documents of the farthest-left radicals.
It is therefore most probable that her "calculations" are
actually pure fabrication.

Certainly no one in this room would consider the human
rights record of the Republic of Korea any kind of a "world
record", in a positive or negative sense. The speaker's
contention to that effect is pure nonsense. The Republic of
Korea fully realizes that guaranteeing fundamental human rights
to all citizens is a basic obligation of all democratic
societies. We admit that there are areas which require
improvement in our country. Our recent adhesion to the
International Covenant on Economic, Social and Cultural Rights
and the International Covenant on Civil and Political Rights and
its Optional Protocol represents only one example of the concrete
steps in this direction, as does prosecution and punishment of
police officers who overreacted during student riots.

The speaker has muddled the crucial distinction, made in all
democratic societies, between violence and political crimes.
Would she consider radical and violent demonstrators who have
been prosecuted for violent crimes, including throwing firebombs,
attacking police stations and other public buildings, and setting
fire to public property, which have resulted in deaths and
serious injuries, as political prisoners? Surely no democratic
country would, and if such a country exists at all, it would
exist, I presume, only in the imaginary world of the NGO
representative herself. Ironically enough, in her list of the
so-called political prisoners, she had the audacity to include

2

7-6

0147

those who set fire to a school library resulting in the death of 7 policemen and many injured in May 1989.   The speaker's confusion of violence and the concept of political prisoners is yet another example of her ignorance.

The speaker's preposterous contention that anyone could be arrested or detained without a warrant reaches a new height of absurdity. Even the most radical students would not make such a statement, knowing that outright lies, when they are perpetrated, only serve to discredit a cause.

In summary, the speaker's assertions are void of the essential elements of truth necessary for them to be seriously considered. They form a messy amalgam of gross distortions of fact and outright lies and reflect only the speaker's ignorance and the hostility towards democratization held by the organization she represents.

My advice to her would be to beware of being used as an instrument of an organization dedicated to denigrating the good image of Korea, and with the aim of destabilizing my country. Even if she is not being used as an instrument, her statement full of falsehoods will serve only to destroy whatever credibility the organization she represents has.

If she is truly interested in the human rights situation in the Republic of Korea, I would like to suggest that she visits my country at least once and sees for herself the true situation there, instead of relying on distorted information and concotion emanating from obscure entities which attempt to destroy our democratic system, or exercising her gift of imagination.

Thank you.

3

7-2

0148

외 무 부

종 별 :

번 호 : GVW-1606   일 시 : 91 0829 1100

수 신 : 장 관(국연, 법무부)

발 신 : 주 제네바 대사

제 목 : 제 43차 유엔인권소위(9)

연: GVW-1563

표제 회의는 8.22.부터 금 8.26 오전까지의 제10항(법사행정) 및 의제 11항(사법부의 독립)문제를 토의 하였으며, 8.23. 야간회의 및 8.26 오전회의에서는 의제 6항(각국 인권상황) 관련 9개 결의안을 채택한바, 동 주요 내용을 아래 보고함.

1. 의제 10항(법사 행정)

0 연호 NGO 에 이어 PAX CHRISTI INT'L 등 18개NGO 로 부터 아래 요지의 발언이있었으며, 이에 대해 아국, 필리핀,모로코,유고,인니,일본,이집트,칠레, 미얀마, 터어키, 모리타니아의 답변권 행사가 있었음.

- PAX CHRISTI INT'L: 중국정부의 티벳 주민에대한 불법구금, 고문, 즉결처형등사법절차 거부,KUWAIT 의 계엄하 사법권 유린 및 미국의 걸프전 참전 거부자에 대한 처벌을 비난

- INT'L ASSOC OF EDUCATORS: 티벳에서의 사법권문제 규탄

- WORLD ORG AGAINST TORTURE: 터어키, 나이제리아,이집트등의 열악한 형무소 실태지적,

- INT'L ASSOCFOR DEMOCRATIC LAWYERS: 일본의 제 3야당 간부에 대한 경찰의 도청과 동 도청에 대한 일본정부의 불기소 처분등 미온적 처벌 규탄

- INT'L LEAGUE FOR RIGHTS AND LIBERATION OF PEOPLES:아국인권 상황 왜곡 비난(기보고)

- LIBERATION: 동티몰 주민에 대한 인니정부의 학대행위

- MOVEMENT AGAINST RACISM: 터어키의 쿠르드인,세르비아의 KOSOVO 박해등 거론

- LATIN AMERICAN FED OF RELATIVES OFDISAPPEARED-DETAINEES: 칠레, 멕시코, 페루등 남미제국의 불법 체포, 구금, 처형, 실종사건 및 터어키내 쿠르드인, 동티몰

국기국   1차보   외정실   분석관   청와대   안기부   법무부

91.08.28   05:35 FN

외신 1과 통제관

0149

문제 거론

2. 의제 11항(사법부의 독립)

0 특별보고자 JOINET 위원으로 부터 사법부 독립침해에 대한 유엔의 감시기능 강화를 위해 유엔의 자문 및 기술제공 프로그램의 개선을 권고하는 내용의 보고서 설명에 이어, EIDE(놀웨이) 위원등 5명의 위원 및 INT'LCOMMISSION OF JURISTS 등 10개 NGO 가 발언한바,주요 내용은 아래와 같음

- EIDE 위원: 의제 10항, 11항은 법치주의(RULE OF LAW) 의 근간이 되는 사항으로 이에대한 UN 의 감시강화가 중요함.

특히 군사재판에 관한 관심 증대가 필요함.

- VAN BOVEN(화란) 위원: 유엔의 자문 및기술제공도 중요하나, 철저한 보호노력이 앞서야할것임.

- GUISSE(세네갈) 위원: 법관의 부정(CORRUPTION) 에 의한 독립성 침해에도 관심을 경주해야 함.

- INT'L COMMISSION OF JURISTS: 사법부의 독립이 침해되고 있는 국가로 콜롬비아, 수단,팔레스타인지역, 유고, 루완다, 페루, 파라과이등 약20개국 및 동 침해 사례를 지적

- INT'L UNION OF LAWYER: 코소보지역 상황의 심각한 특히 강조

- LAWYERS COMMITTEE FOR H.R.: 수단, 케냐, 미얀마, 페루, 이스라엘, 스리랑카,터어키등의 침해 사례를 지적하고, 유엔의 자문 및 기술제공의 실효성에 의문을 제기함

- INT'L LEAGUE FOR RIGHTS AND LIBERATION OF PEOPLES:알바니아계 판사 해직등코소보 문제 지적

- INT'L EDUCATION DEVELOPEMNT: 중국 민주화 시위관련자에 대한 공정한 재판의거부 및 파키스탄에서의 정치적 이유로 인한 판사 해직 사례비난

0 상기에 대해 케냐,터어키,뷔니지아, 인니가 답변권을 행사함

3. 의제 6항 관련 결의안 채택

0 남아공,과테말라, 이스라엘 점령지역, 강제퇴거,쿠웨이트, 캄보디아,이란,티벳,이락, 엘살바돌 인권상황에 관한 결의안이 채택되었음

0 동 티몰 인권상황에 관해서는 폴투갈 의회사절단의 금년말 현지 방문 예정 및현재진행중인 유엔측 중재 노력등을 감안,금년도에는 결의안을 채택치 않기로

PAGE 2

합의함.

0 반면 티벳 인권 상황에 관한 결의안은 금년 최초로 채택된바, 중국대표는 동 결의안 채택이 문제 해결에 하등의 도움이 되지 않는다고 하면서, 동 결의채택에 강력한 유감의 뜻을 표명함.

0 한편 EIDE 위원등에 의해 BALTIC 3 국의 인권상황에 대한 결의안도 제출된바 있으나, 소련 쿠테타이후의 사태진전으로 인하여 철회되었음.

0 상기 결의안들은 MARTINEZ(쿠바) 위원의 주장에 따라 강제퇴거(L.15) 관련 결의안 외에는 모두 비밀 투표에 회부된바 동 투표결과는 아래와 같음.

(찬, 반, 기권, 불참의 순)
- 남아공(L.5): 20-0-1-2
- 과테말라(L.13): 19-1-1-2
- 이스라엘 점령지역(L.14): 16-2-4-1
- 쿠웨이트(L.16): 16-4-2-1
- 캄보디아(L.17): 14-4-4-1
- 이란(L.18): 19-2-1-1
- 티벳(L.19): 9-7-4-2-1(무효)
- 이락(L.20): 16-2-4-2
- 엘살바돌(L.22): 18-1-3-1.끝
(대사 박수길-국장)

원 본

외 무 부

종 별 :

번 호 : GVW-1630

일 시 : 91 0830 1900

수 신 : 장관(이규형 유엔 과장)

발 신 : 주 제네바 대사(이성주 참사관)

제 목 : 업연

1. 제 43차 인권 회의는 금 8.30 예정대로 종료되었으나, 금주내내 심야회의가 계속된 관계로 9호 이후 전문 보고를 못하였음.

2. 9호 보고 이후의 토의 내용은 9.2(월) 전문으로 일괄 보고할 예정이니 양승 바람.

3. 건승기원함. 끝

국기국

PAGE 1

91.08.31   08:10 DQ

외신 1과 통제관

0152

외 무 부

종 별 :

번 호 : GVW-1664   일   시 : 91 0903 0940

수 신 : 장 관(국연,법무부)

발 신 : 주 제네바 대사

제 목 : 제 43차 유엔 인권 소위(10)

표제회의는 전 의제 항목에 관한 토의를 마치고8.30 예정대로 폐막한바, 8.27-30간 주요 토의 내용및 금차 회의 주요 결의 및 결정 사항을 아래와같이 보고함.

1. 의제 15항(토착민에 대한 차별)- 토착민 관련 WG 의장인 DAES(그리스)위원은 동 WG 보고서 설명을 통해 '토착민의 권리에 관한 선언' 성안 작업 계속 필요성,토착민 그룹, 정부 및 인권 소위간 3자간 대화의 계속 및 헌법질서 테두리내에서의 권리 추구등을 강조함.

- HATANO(일본) 위원이 구속력이 없는 선언 작성에 지나친 노력을 경주하는 것은 바람직하자못하다고 하고, 아이누족에 대한 일본정부의 정책경험을 예로 들면서토착민에 대하 정의 설정이필요하다는 의견을 개지난데 대해, EIDE(놀웨이) 위원등은 토착민의 개념도 시대와 장소에 따라 수시 변해가고 있으므로 정확한 개념정의는사실상 불가능하다는 입장을 피력함.

- 그밖에 KSENTINI(알제리), WARZAZI(모로코),POSADA(알젠틴) 위원등이 정부와 토착민 사이에 상호 인정 및 타협등 대화를 통한 문제해결 자세의 중요성을 강조하고, 특히 POSADA위원은 자결권의 지나친 추구는 위험하다는의견을 피력함.

- NGO 중에는 FOUR DIRECTIONS COUNCIL 이 세계토착민의 해 (1993) 선포와 관련 UN 의적극적인 조정 및 예산 지원을 요청하고,토착민의 문화 유산 보존에 관한 UNESCO등 유엔 기구 활동 개선에 대해 소위가 적극지원해 줄것을 요청하였고 기타 다수의NGO 가 아마존의 금광 개발에 따른 YANOMANI 원주민피해, 인도네시아, 말련등의 산림 개발에 따른 토착민 피해, 호주 원주민에 대한 호주 정부의 차별정책등의 문제를 지적함.

2. 의제 7항(신국제 경제 질서) 및 8항(경제적,사회적, 문화적 권리의 실현)

- TURK(유고) 위원의 경제적, 사회적, 문화적권리 실현에 관한 제 2차 보고서(

종가름   1자브   의정실   분석관   청와대   안기부   법무부

E/CN 4/SUB.2/1991/17) 및 MBONU(나이제리아) 위원의 주민강제 이주에 관한 보고서(E/CN4/SUB2/1991/47)설명이 있었음.

- TURK 위원은 상기 보고서 설명을 통해 90년UNDP 발간 HUMAN DEVELOPMENT REPORT 상의 HUMANDEVELOPMENT INDEX(HDI) 가 많은 문제점을 안고있다고 언급하고, 경제적, 사회적, 문화적 권리실현도의 객관적 측정을 위한 지수(INDICATOR)개발을 위해 92년중 전문가 회의의 개최등관련 노력을 계속 경주할 예정임을 밝히고,국제 금융기관자금 지원하에 실시되는 각국의개발정책이 상기 권리의 실현에 미치는 다대한 영향력을 감안할때 IBRD, IMF 등은 개발 노력지원에 있어 단순한 경제 개발 측면 뿐만아니라 교육, 인적 자원 개발등 각종 사회적영역에 대해 보다 많은 관심을 경주해야할것 이라느 의견을 피력함

- MBONU 위원의 자신의 보고서 설명시, 지역개발, 천재지변 대처등 주민 강제 이주가 불가피한 경우가 많으나, 동 과정에서 인권침해 가능성이 높으므로, 주민 강제 이주와 관련한 경제, 사회,정치적 충격에 관한 철저한 연구와 예방책이 필요함을 강조함.

- ZHAN(중국의 교체위원), SACHAR(인도),GUISSE(세네갈), WARZAZI(모로코), KSEUINI(알제리) 위원등은 상기 UNDP 의 HDI 의부당성을 강력히 비판하였고 이들중 일부 위원은동 INDICATOR 개발 노력 자체에 대한 의문도 표시함. MARTINEZ(쿠바) 위원 은 인권 소위에서도경제적, 사회적 ,문화적 권리는 정치적, 시민적권리에 비학 등한 시 되고 있다고 하면서, 양권리간의 균형된 취급 필요성을 강조함.

O 그밖에 FLINTERMAN(화란의 교체 위원)이주택문제 해결의 시급성, DESPOUY (알젠틴)위원이 개도국에서 고위 정부 관리의부정 및 이에 따른 자금의 해외 유출 문제의심각성을 지적함.

- NGO 로 부터는 아래 내용의 발언이 있었음.

. HABITAT COALITION INTERNATIONAL: 전세계 10억 무주택자를 위한 주거 문제(ADEQUATE HOUSING)해결

. INT'L EDUCATIONAL DEVELOPMENT: 일본에서의 KAROSI(과로사)문제 및 이에 대한 일본정부의 미온적 대처

- PAXCHRISTI INT'L : 터어키, 이락, 탄자니아, 인니,중국, 미국등에서의 주민 강제이주 사례 지적 및차기 인권소위부터 동문제를 별도 의제로 설정,취급할 것을 요청

PAGE 2

0154

- EFORD 등 9개 NGO 는 연명으로 대 이락 경제제재조치로 인한 이락 민간인의 참상을 지적하고, 동 제재 조치의 해제를 촉구하는 호소문을 낭독함.

3. 의제 16항(현대적 노예형태)
- KSENTINI(알제리)위원의 보고서를 기초로, 아동및 여성매매, 장기(HUMAN ORGANS) 거래, 소년병(CHILD SOLDIERS), 아동 노동 및 BONDAGE LABOUR등에 대한 논의가진행된바, ILO, WHO, UNICEF,인터폴 등 관련 기구와의 긴밀한 협조하에 상기유형의인권 침해 사례 예방 및 철폐를 위한국제적 노력의 활성화 필요성이 강조됨.

4. 의제 4항(인권소위 관심 분야 현황 평가)
- 인권 침해 피해자에 대한 보상, 인권과환경, 의견 및 표현의 자유, 여성 및 아동 건강에유해한 전통 관습, AIDS 환자에 대한 차별문제등에 관한 토의가 진행됨.
- 의견 및 표현의 자유 관련, 보고자 TURK 위원은 동 자유는 기본적(FUNDAMENTAL)권리의 하나이기 때문에 여타 권리와 상충시 우선해야 한다는 것을 기본 원칙으로는 하되, 무제한의 행사를 방임할 수만도 없으므로 일정한기준(정당성, 비례성, 입법기관에 의한입법조치, 민주주의와의 양립성등)에 의해합리적 제한을 가하는 것을인정해 야 한다는의견을 피력하고, 따라서 동 제한을 여하히 엄격히축소(RESTRICTIONS ON RESTRICTIONS) 하느냐 하는점을 집중 검토해야 한다고 언급함.
- 상기에 대해 미국 대표(BLACKWELL 본부대사)는 동 자유는 여하한 경우에도 제한해서는 안된다는 반대 입장을 피력하였으나, EIDE 위원은 양심의 자유등 행동을수반하지 않는 자유는 절대적 자유로서 무제한 인정이 가능하나, 행동이 수반됨으로써 타인의 자유와 권리와 충돌할 가능성이 있는 자유에는 일정 제한이 필요하다고하면서 TURK 위운의 입장을 전폭 지지함.
- 기타 PALLEY(영국) 위원은 인권과환경관련 걸프전에서 쌍방에 의해 화학무기가사용되었다는 증거가 있다고 하면서 동 무기 사용의 전면적 금지 필요성을 강조함.
- NGO 중에서는 FREE PRESS FEDERATION 이 언론자유에 대한 여하한 제한도 받아들일수 없다는 입장을I 표명한 이외에는 대부분의 NGO 가 환경문제에 관한 소위 활동에 지지 의사를 표명하는 발언을 함.

5. 의제 14항(인권의 기본 조건으로서 국제평화와 안전)
- 차기 회의로 토의를 연기키로 결정

PAGE 3

0155

6. 의제 3항(인권 소위활동 재검토)

 - 소위 활동 재검토 WG 의장인 VAN BOVEN 위원은 도 WG 보고서를 설명하면서 소위 활동의 합리화(RATIONALIZATION) 시킬 필요성은 명백하다고 전제한후, 금차회의 기간중에도 시간부족으로 실질적 논의를 진행할 수 없었던점(8.8-9 양일간 활동)을 고려, 92년에는 INTERSESSIONAL WG 회의를 개최할 것을 주장하면서, 이를 위해결정문안 (L 74) 를 제출하였음을 밝힘.

 - 상기 보고에 이어 미국대표(ABRAM 인권대사)는 인권위원회의 거듭된 요구에도 불구하고 인권소위는 금년에는 오히려 작년보다 원래의 MANDATE를 일탈(STRAYED)하고 있다고 비난하면서 인권소위가 인권위원회등 여타 유엔 기관의 역할과 중복되어서는 곤란하므로 각종 인권협약 및 기준 시행상의 문제점 검토등 전문가적 입장에서 인권 소위 본연의 지성적(INTELLECTUAL) 활동에 치중하고 각국의 인권상황등 정치적 논의는 인권위원회에 맡겨야 할 것이며, 따라서 소위 위원들도 소속국 정부내에서 여타 공적 직위를 보유해서는 안 될 것이라는 점등을 언급함.

 - 이에 대해 SACHOU, MARTINEZ, ALKASAWNEH 위원등이동 대사의 발언에 강력히 항의하였고 EIDE위원은 인권소위의 설립 및 변모 과정을 설명하면서 미대사의 의견을그대로 받아들이기는 어렵다는 입장을 표명함. 특히 동 위원 및 VANBOVEN 위원은 최근 수년간 소위활동에 대한 NGO 및 각국정부의 관심 및 참여도 에 비추어볼때 소위가 안고 있는 여러가지 문제점에도 불구하고 소위가 인권문제에 대해 많은 기여를하고 있는 점은 틀림없는 사실이라고언급함으로써 미대사의 발언은 지나치다는 뜻을표시함.

7. 결의안 및 결정문안의 심의 및 채택

(가) 의제 4항 관련

 - 여성 및 아동 건강에 유해한 전통 관습(L.5), 인권과 환경(L.28), 인권침해피해자보상(L.33), 팔레스타인등 이스라엘 점령자(L.43), 의견 및 표현의 자유(L.77) 에 관한 결의안을 투표없이 채택

 - 최소한의 인도적 기준에 관한 선언(L.37),이락 민간인 관련 호소 (L 52), AIDS 환자차별(L.64), 인권 침해범에 대한 차별면제(L.71) 에 관한 결정을 투표없이 채택

 - 화학무기 철폐(L.2) 에 관한 결의안(PALLEY 의원 제출)은 이에 대한 CHERNICHENKO 위원의 토의 연기제안이 11-4-5-1 로 통과함으로써 차기 회의로 연기된바, PALLEY 위원은 내년도에는 모든 대량 학살 무기를포함하는 결의안을 제출할

PAGE 4

0156

예정이라고언급함.

(나) 의제 7항 관련

- 국가 고위 관리에 인한 부정(L.23) 에 관한 결의안을 부표없이 채택

(다) 의제 8항 관련

- 주택(HOUSING) 에 관한 권리 실현 촉진(L.26), 경제적, 사회적, 문화적 권리의 실현(L.34), 주민 강제 이주의 인권 관련 측면(L.38), 소말리아 상황(L.50) 에 관한결의안을 부표없이 채택

- 인권과 극빈 (L.53) 에 관한 결의안은철회

(라) 의제 11항 관련

- 법관등의 독립 및 공정성(L.31) 에 관한 결의안을 부표없이 채택

(마) 의제 15항 관련

- 토착민에 대한 선언 초안(L.44), 토착민과 국가간 경제, 사회적 관계(L.46), 토착민문화재의 소유 및 관리(L.47), 세계 토착민의해 (L.48) 에 간한 결의안을부표없이 채택

- 토착민과 국가간 재협정에 관한 연구(L.45),세계 토착민의 해 (L.48) 에 관한 결정을 토의없이 채택

(바) 의제 16항 관련

- 현대적 노예 형태에 관한 WG 보고(L.40),인신매매 방지 해동 계획 (L.42) 에관한결의안을 부표없이 채택

- 아동 매매 방지 행동 계획(L.41) 에 관한결정을 부표없이 채택

- 여성 차별 철폐 협약에 대한 유보의 효력(L.49)에 관한 결의안을 내년 회의로연기키로함으로써 철회

(사) 의제 14항 관련

- 출국 및 입국의 자유(L.65) 에 관한 결정을 부표없이 채택

(아) 의제 3항 관련

- 인권소위 작업 재검토 WG (L.74) 에 관한결정(INTERSESSIONAL 회의 개최)을 부표없이채택

8. 금차 회의 보고서 채택

- 회의 폐막일까지 보고서 준비 작업이 완료되지 않음으로서 동 보고서 준비가완료되는 데로 RAPPORTEUR (GUISSE 위원)가 검토한후 위원들에게 봉보하기로

PAGE 5

0157

합의함. 끝

(대사 박수길-국장)

관리 번호	9/ -/

외 무 부

종 별 :

번 호 : GVW-1691   일 시 : 91 0906 1930

수 신 : 장관(국연,법무부)

발 신 : 주 제네바 대사

제 목 : 제 43차 유엔 인권 소위(11)

　　90.8.5-30 간 개최된 표제회의에 관한 종합 관찰 평가 및 건의를 아래와 같이 보고함.

　　1. 회의 참가

　　가. 인권소위 위원 36 명(정위원 26 명 프러스 교체위원 10 명), 90 개국 정부 옵서버, 3 개 민족해방기구, 12 개 유엔 및 정부간 기구, 111 개 민간 인권단체(NGO)가 참석함. 특히 NGO 의 참가가 계속 확대되는 추세를 보임.

　　나. 북한측에서는 이철대사, 박덕훈 참사관 및 김철수, 정용웅 서기관이 참가 등록을 했으나 주로 박덕훈이 참석함.

　　2. 아국 및 북한 인권 관련 사항

　　가. 1503 절차에 의거 금차 회의에 제출된 임수경, 홍성담, 서울 및 목포 교도소 난동사건 관련 진정서 3 건은 진정서 실무소위 심의결과 기각된 것으로 파악됨.

　　나. 민간인권 단체인 INT'L LEAGUE FOR RIGHTS AND LIBERATION OF PEOPLES 가 기 보고한대로 아국의 국내 인권 상황을 왜곡 비난 하였는바, 동 발언 수일전부터 당지 반한 교포 최기환 및 재일 조총련 소속으로 추정되는 김좌웅이 회의장에 참석, ILRIP 와 해동을 같이 한 점에 비추어 재일 조총련의 강한 사주가 있었던 것으로 추정됨.

　　다. 기타 HABITAT INT'L COALITION 이 18 개국의 주민 강제 이주 사례 거론시 아국 OLYMIC 개최 관련 재개발 사업을 함께 거론하였고, MARTINEZ 위원이 신국제 질서를 비난하면서 미국과 우호관계에 있는 국가의 인권 상황에 문제가 있음을 언급시 영국등 8-9 개국과 함께 아국의 이름도 거명한바 있으나, 상기 발언들은 아국을 직접적 또는 집중적인 비난대상으로 한 것은 아니였음.

　　라. 북한에 대해서는 INT'L ORG FOR THE ELIMINATION OF ALL FORMS OF RACIAL DISCRIMINATION 이 지구상에 전주민이 감옥생활을 하고 있는 것과 같은 국가가 있다고

국기국	장관	차관	1차보	2차보	분석관	정와대	안기부	법무부

PAGE 1

하면서 그 예로 중국과 북한을 거명한 바 있음.

3. 일반 토의 사항 평가

0 금차 회의 기간중에는 8.19 의 소련 쿠데타 발생관련, 동 구데타 결과 예상되는 인권 문제에 대한 영향의 토의 여부를 놓고 서방 출실위원 및 제 3 세계 출신 위원들간 첨예한 의견 대립이 있었으나 8.21 이후 사태가 안정됨으로써 더이상의 토의 없이 진정되었음.

0 국별 인권 상황으로는 TIBET 인권, 동티몰 인권, 남아공의 인종차별, 팔레스타인등 이스라엘 점령지, 엘살바돌, 과테말라 등 남미 제국에 있어서의 인권유린과 동 관련자 처벌 면제(IMPUNITY)문제, 미얀마 인권 YUGO(코소보 지역)인권, KURDS 족에 대한 이락, 터어키 양국의 박해 문제, 기타 토착민(호주, 미국, 중남미, 동남아)에 대한 박해문제등이 집중 거론된바, 예년과 다른 특이 사항으로서는 동 TIMOR 문제에 대해서는 금년말 예정인 폴부갈 의회 사절단의 현지 방문 문제가 합의되는등 최근의 사태 호전을 고려 결의안을 제출지 않기로 합의된 반면, TIBET 인권 상황과 관련해서는 중국 정부 옵서버 및 중국 출신 TIAN JIN 위원의 강력한 반대에도 불구 결의안이 채택되었음.(티벳 망명정부가 주관하는 시위가 회의기간중 회의장 주변에서 계속됨)

0 회의 주제별로는 최근의 남아공 정부의 정책 변화등의 영향으로 APARTHEID 에 대한 실질적 인 관심은 비교적 저조해진 반면, 선진국에서의 이주 노동자 처우 문제와 피난민 및 망명자(ASYLUM SEEKERS)외면 문제등 새로운 형태의 인종 차별 문제 소수집단 보호문제, 토착민 보호문제, 주민의 강제이주 문제, 중대한 인권 위반 사태 발생시 주변국의 인도적 간첩 문제등에 대한 관심이 부각되는 현상을 보였음.

0 인권소위 활동 개선 방안에 관해서는 금차 회의 기간중에도 실무위가 2 차례 회의 밖에 개최할수 없게 된 결과, 보고서 및 연구서 작성에 관한 문제만을검토한 이외에는 큰 진전이 없었는바, 이를 고려 <u>92 년중 INTERSSESSIONAL WG 을 개최키로 합의함.</u>

4. 기타

0 금차 회의기간중 90.6 및 91.2. 2 회에 걸쳐 재일 한국인 인권문제 관련 UN 에 진정서를 제출한 재일 한국인 인권획득 투쟁위원회 최창화 목사가 MONORITY RIGHTS GROUP 의 일원으로 회의에 참석하며, NGO 및 소위 위원과의 비공식 접촉등을 통해 동 문제에 관한 관심을 촉구하는 노력을 경주하였으나, 금차 회의기간중 특별한 성과는

PAGE 2

0160

없었던 것으로 관측됨.

5. 건의

0 금차 회의 ILRLP 의 아국인권 상황 왜곡 비난발언에 대해서는 일단 강하게 대응하였으나 NGO 의 아국 비난 발언에 일일이 대응하는 것은 성숙한 민주 국가로서의 이미지 및 회의 분위기에도 맞지 않고 해당 NGO 발언 내용에 대한 관심을 오히려 증대시킬 가능성도 없지 않은 점을 고려, 앞으로 특별한 경우가 아니면 묵살하는데신 적절한 회의의제 토의에 일반 발언 형식으로 토의에 참여하면서 아국의 관련 인권 신장 노력을 설명하는 방식으로 회의 참가 전략을 수정하는문제를 검토할 필요가 있음.

0 또한 금차 회의에는 일본의 각종 민간 인권 단체 소속원이 다수 참석하여회의에서의 공개 발언 및 각종 비공식 설명회 개최등을 통해 자국내 외국인 노동자 처우, 노동인권, 도청문제등 각종 일본국내 인권 문제를 제기하는 현상이 두드러진바, 아국도 국력의 신장과 함께 국내 인권 단체가 인권 회의에 직접 참가할 가능성에 대한 장기적 대비책도 강구해야 할 것임. 끝

(차석대사 김삼훈-국장)

예고 92.12.31. 일반

검토필 (1992. 6 .30.)

長官報告事項

報告畢

1991. 9. 9.
國際機構局
國際聯合2課(1)

題 目 : 第43次 유엔 人權小委員會 會議結果

    91.8.5-30間 제네바에서 開催된 第43次 유엔 人權小委員會 會議
結果 및 南北韓 人權問題 擧論內容을 아래 報告드립니다.

1. 會議參加

  가. 韓國代表團(옵서버)

    ○ 首席代表 : 박수길 駐제네바 大使

    ○ 代 表 : 駐제네바 代表部 職員 2名

    * 北韓側 이철 大使外 駐제네바代表部 職員 2名 參席

  나. 各國 代表團

    ○ 人權小委 委員 36名(정위원 26명 및 교체위원 10명)

    ○ 90개국 政府옵서버, 3개 民族解放機構, 12개 유엔 및 政府間 機構,
      11개 民間 人權團體(NGO)

앙고재	년9월9일	담당	과장	국장
		이	소	12

0162

2. 南北韓 人權問題 擧論

　가. 韓 國

　　o 實務小委, 임수경 關係等 陳情書 3건 棄却

　　o ILRLP, 韓國의 人權狀況 歪曲非難 (조총련 사주 추정)

　나. 北 韓

　　o 人種差別 撤廢를 위한 國際機構, 中國, 北韓 거명, 全住民의
　　　감옥생활 指摘

3. 主要 討議事項

　가. 國別 人權狀況

　　o Tibet 및 東Timor 人權, 남아공 人種差別, 이스라엘 占領地,
　　　엘살바돌 및 과테말라 人權蹂躪, 미얀마 및 유고 人權,
　　　쿠르드族 및 其他 土着民 迫害問題 討議

　　o 東Timor 問題 決議案 생략, Tibet 問題는 決議案 採擇

　나. 아파타이트 問題 關心低調 대신 先進國에서의 移住勞動者 處遇,
　　　亡命者 외면, 小數集團保護, 土着民 保護問題等 關心 浮刻

　다. 92년중 Intersessional Working Group 開催 合意

4. 其他事項

　　o 在日韓國人 人權獲得 鬪爭委員會 최창화 牧師, Monority Rights
　　　Group의 一員으로 會議參席, 積極 活動했으나, 成果 別無

5. 建 議

　　o NGO의 我國非難 發言에 個別對應 止揚, 적절한 議題討議時 一般發言
　　　形式으로 韓國 人權伸張努力을 說明하는 方式으로의 戰略 修正

　　o 國內人權團體의 人權會議 直接 參加 可能性 對備

6. 言論對策 : 해당 없음. 끝.

기 안 용 지

분류기호 문서번호	연이 2031 - **3614**전화:)		시 행 상 특별취급	
보존기간	영구·준영구· 10. 5. 3. 1	장		관
수 신 처 보존기간				
시행일자	1991.10.5.			

보조기관	국 장	전결	협조기관		문서통제
	심의관				
	과 장				
기안책임자		김종훈			발 송 인

경 유	
수 신	주제네바 대사
참 조	

발신명의

제 목   유엔인권위 강제실종실무위 회의

1. 유엔사무총장은 별첩 91.9.23자 본직 앞 공한을

통해 유엔인권위 산하 강제실종실무위 회의가 91.10.28-11.8간

귀지에서 개최됨을 알려왔습니다.

2. 상기회의에서는 인권소위가 작성한 강제실종으로

부터의 보호에 관한 선언 초안이 검토될 예정인 바, ~~귀관~~

~~판제관의 동의의예 적의 참가~~, 회의결과 및 관련자료를

보고~~하도록 조치하여~~ 주시기 바랍니다.

첨부 : 유엔사무총장 공한사본 1부. 끝.

0164

OFFICE DES NATIONS UNIES A GENÈVE

CENTRE POUR LES DROITS DE L'HOMME

Téléfax: (022) 733 98 79
Télégrammes: UNATIONS, GENÈVE
Télex: 412 962 UNO CH
Téléphone: 734 60 11   731 02 11

RÉF. N°: G/SO 219/1
(à rappeler dans la réponse)

UNITED NATIONS OFFICE AT GENEVA

CENTRE FOR HUMAN RIGHTS

Palais des Nations
CH-1211 GENÈVE 10

The Secretary-General of the United Nations presents his compliments to the Minister for Foreign Affairs of the Republic of Korea and has the honour to draw the attention of His Excellency's Government to Commission on Human Rights resolution 1991/41 of 5 March 1991 entitled "Question of enforced or involuntary disappearances". A copy of the resolution is attached.

In paragraph 19 of the resolution, the Commission decided to establish an open-ended inter-sessional working group of the Commission to consider the draft declaration on protection of all persons from enforced or involuntary disappearances submitted by the Sub-Commission, with a view to its adoption by the Commission at its forty-eighth session. Further, it invited, inter alia, all Governments to participate in the activities of the working group. It also requested the working group to meet for a period of two weeks before the forty-eighth session of the Commission.

The Economic and Social Council in its resolution 1991/27 of 31 May 1991 authorized an open-ended working group on the question to meet for a period of two weeks prior to the forty-eighth session of the Commission. A copy of the resolution is attached.

After consultations with interested delegations and participants, the Secretary-General wishes to inform His Excellency's Government that the Working Group on the Question of a Draft Declaration on the Protection of All Persons from Enforced or Involuntary Disappearances will hold its first session at the Palais des Nations, Geneva, from 28 October to 8 November 1991.

23 September 1991

0165

COMMISSION ON HUMAN RIGHTS

Resolution

1991/41. Question of enforced or involuntary disappearances

The Commission on Human Rights,

Bearing in mind General Assembly resolution 33/173 of 20 December 1978, in which the Assembly requested the Commission on Human Rights to consider the question of disappeared persons with a view to making appropriate recommendations, and all other United Nations resolutions concerning missing or disappeared persons,

Convinced of the need to continue the implementation of the provisions of General Assembly resolution 33/173 and of the other United Nations resolutions on the question of enforced or involuntary disappearances,

Recalling its resolution 20 (XXXVI) of 29 February 1980, by which it decided to establish a working group consisting of five of its members, to serve as experts in their individual capacity, to examine questions relevant to enforced or involuntary disappearances, and its resolutions 1987/27 of 10 March 1987, 1988/34 of 8 March 1988, 1989/27 of 6 March 1989 and 1990/30 of 2 March 1990,

Recalling also its decision 1986/106 of 13 March 1986, by which it invited the Sub-Commission on Prevention of Discrimination and Protection of Minorities to reconsider the question of a declaration against unacknowledged detention of persons,

Recalling further its resolution 1990/76 on co-operation with representatives of United Nations human rights bodies,

Recalling General Assembly resolution 45/165 of 18 December 1990,

Profoundly concerned at the fact that the practice of enforced or involuntary disappearances is continuing in various regions of the world,

Concerned also at the reports concerning harassment of witnesses of disappearances or relatives of disappeared persons,

Having considered the report of the Working Group (E/CN.4/1991/20),

1.   Expresses its appreciation to the Working Group on Enforced or Involuntary Disappearances for the way in which it has done its work, and thanks the Group for submitting to the Commission at its forty-seventh session a report in accordance with its resolution 1990/30;

2.   Takes note of the report of the Working Group, and thanks it for continuing to improve its methods of work and for recalling the humanitarian spirit underlying its mandate;

3.   Requests the Working Group to report on its work to the Commission at its forty-eighth session and reminds the Group of the obligation to discharge its mandate in a discreet and conscientious manner;

RES/HR/91/7
GE.91-15711

0166

4. Further requests the Working Group, in its efforts to help eliminate the practice of enforced or involuntary disappearances, to present to the Commission all appropriate information it deems necessary and all concrete suggestions and recommendations regarding the fulfilment of its task;

5. Reminds the Working Group of the need to observe, in its humanitarian task, United Nations standards and practices regarding the receipt of communications, their consideration, their evaluation, their transmittal to Governments and the consideration of government replies;

6. Notes with concern that some Governments have never provided substantive replies concerning disappearances alleged to have occurred in their country;

7. Deplores the fact that, as the Working Group points out in its report, some Governments have not acted on the recommendations contained in the Group's reports concerning them or replied to the Group's requests for information on those matters;

8. Urges the Governments concerned, particularly those which have not yet responded to communications transmitted to them by the Working Group, to co-operate with and assist the Group so that it may carry out its mandate effectively, and in particular to answer expeditiously requests for information addressed to them by the Group;

9. Also urges the Governments concerned to intensify their co-operation with the Working Group in regard to any measure taken in pursuance of recommendations addressed to them by the Group;

10. Once again urges the Governments concerned to take steps to protect the families of disappeared persons against any intimidation or ill-treatment to which they might be subjected;

11. Encourages the Governments concerned to give serious consideration to inviting the Working Group to visit their country, so as to enable the Group to fulfil its mandate even more effectively;

12. Urges Governments to take steps to ensure that, when a state of emergency is introduced, the protection of human rights is guaranteed, particularly as regards the prevention of enforced or involuntary disappearances;

13. Reminds Governments of the need to ensure that their competent authorities conduct prompt and impartial inquiries when there is reason to believe that an enforced or involuntary disappearance has occurred in a territory under their jurisdiction;

0167

14. **Expresses its profound thanks** to the Governments which have co-operated with the Working Group and responded to its requests for information;

15. **Also expresses its profound thanks** to the Governments which have invited the Working Group to visit their country, asks them to give all necessary attention to its recommendations and invites them to inform the Group of any action they take on the recommendations;

16. **Requests** the Secretary-General to ensure that the Working Group receives all necessary assistance, in particular the staff and resources it requires to perform its functions, especially in carrying out missions or holding sessions in countries which would be prepared to receive it;

17. **Expresses its satisfaction** to the Sub-Commission's Working Group on Detention, which has completed preparation of the draft Declaration on enforced or involuntary disappearance;

18. **Expresses its thanks** to the Sub-Commission, which has finalized the draft and is transmitting it to the Commission;

19. **Decides** to establish an open-ended inter-sessional working group of the Commission on Human Rights to consider the draft Declaration submitted by the Sub-Commission, with a view to its adoption by the Commission at its forty-eighth session;

20. **Invites** all Governments, the intergovernmental agencies and the non-governmental organizations to participate in the activities of the working group;

21. **Requests** the Working Group to meet for a period of two weeks before the forty-eighth session of the Commission on Human Rights;

22. **Requests** the Secretary-General to invite comments, for consideration by the Working Group, from Governments, intergovernmental agencies and non-governmental organizations on the draft Declaration and to circulate these comments to Governments in advance of the meeting of the Working Group;

23. **Requests** the Secretary-General to extend all facilities to the Working Group for its meeting prior to the Commission's forty-eighth session;

24. **Recommends** the following draft resolution to the Economic and Social Council for adoption:

0168

"The Economic and Social Council,

Recalling Commission on Human Rights resolution 1991/41 of 5 March 1991,

1. Authorizes an open-ended working group of the Commission on Human Rights to meet for a period of two weeks prior to the forty-eighth session of the Commission to consider the draft Declaration on the protection of all persons from enforced or involuntary disappearance, submitted by the Sub-Commission on Prevention of Discrimination and Protection of Minorities (see E/CN.4/Sub.2/1990/32, annex), with a view to its adoption by the Commission at its forty-eighth session;

2. Requests the Secretary-General to extend all facilities to the Working Group for its meeting prior to the Commission at its forty-eighth session."

———

0169

ECONOMIC AND SOCIAL COUNCIL

Resolution 1991/27

The Economic and Social Council,

Recalling Commission on Human Rights resolution 1991/41 of 5 March 1991,

1. Authorizes an open-ended working group of the Commission on Human Rights to meet for a period of two weeks prior to the forty-eighth session of the Commission to consider the draft declaration on the protection of all persons from enforced or involuntary disappearances prepared by the Sub-Commission on Prevention of Discrimination and Protection of Minorities, with a view to its adoption by the Commission at its forty-eighth session.

2. Requests the Secretary-General to extend all facilities to the working group for its meeting prior to the forty-eighth session of the Commission.

RES/HR/91/15
GE.91-17471

0170

OFFICE DES NATIONS UNIES A GENÈVE

CENTRE POUR LES DROITS DE L'HOMME

Téléfax: (022) 733 98 79
Télégrammes: UNATIONS, GENÈVE
Télex: 412 962 UNO CH
Téléphone: 734 60 11   731 02 11

RÉF. N°: **G/SO 214 (3-3-16)**
(à rappeler dans la réponse)

UNITED NATIONS OFFICE AT GENEVA

CENTRE FOR HUMAN RIGHTS

Palais des Nations
CH-1211 GENÈVE 10

22 November 1991

Excellency,

We should like to draw your attention to resolution 1991/28 entitled "Right to a fair trial", adopted by the Economic and Social Council on 31 May 1991. A copy of the resolution is attached.

After having taken into account the brief report on the right to a fair trial prepared by the two Special Rapporteurs, the Economic and Social Council requested the Secretary-General to transmit the questionnaire together with the brief report prepared by Mr. Chernichenko and Mr. Treat to Governments, the specialized agencies and non-governmental organizations for their response and comments, and to transmit the responses to the Special Rapporteurs for consideration in connection with their study.

On 19 April 1991, a preliminary questionnaire prepared by the Special Rapporteurs was forwarded to you by the Secretary-General. We realize that it was difficult for your Government to respond because the questionnaire is quite comprehensive and there was very little time before the Sub-Commission. Hence, we fully understand the reasons why your Government may not have been able to reply.

At the forty-third session of the Sub-Commission on Prevention of Discrimination and Protection of Minorities, in August 1991, the two Special Rapporteurs presented their second report together with a slightly revised and improved questionnaire. Sub-Commission members urged the rapporteurs to obtain Government replies to the questionnaire. In its resolution 1991/14, the Sub-Commission again recommended that the Secretary-General should send the questionnaire to Governments which had not yet been able to respond, along with the second report.

The questionnaire is contained in annex II to the second report on the right to a fair trial (E/CN.4/Sub.2/1991/29). A copy of this report is enclosed. We would greatly appreciate your response to the questionnaire.

You will note that the questionnaire recognizes that such inquiries are time-consuming for respondent Governments. Accordingly, the questionnaire contains two parts. In the first part Governments are simply asked to send copies of the relevant codes, rules, regulations, and decisions setting forth procedures in civil courts, criminal courts, emergency/special courts, military courts, and certain administrative processes. Governments are not asked to provide substantive responses to part I.

./...

H.E. the Minister for Foreign Affairs
77 Sejong-Ro
Chongro-ku
Seoul
Republic of Korea

0171

OFFICE DES NATIONS UNIES A GENÈVE

CENTRE POUR LES DROITS DE L'HOMME

UNITED NATIONS OFFICE AT GENEVA

CENTRE FOR HUMAN RIGHTS

Téléfax: (022) 733 98 79
Télégrammes: UNATIONS, GENÈVE
Télex: 412 962 UNO CH
Téléphone: 734 60 11   731 02 11

RÉF. N°:
(à rappeler dans la réponse)

Palais des Nations
CH - 1211 GENÈVE 10

- 2 -

If Governments are able to provide more substantive responses, they are requested to consider the questions raised in part II. Here again, it is recognized that answering the questions may be time-consuming. Accordingly, Governments may wish to answer only those questions beginning with arabic numbers. If Governments are able to provide more complete responses, they may answer the questions beginning with small letters and which ask for more detailed information.

We would appreciate it if any responses to the questionnaire you may wish to communicate could be forwarded to the Centre for Human Rights, United Nations Office at Geneva, CH-1211 Geneva 10, if possible by 31 January 1992.

Accept, Excellency, the assurances of our highest consideration.

pp. Stanislav Chernichenko
and William Treat

0172

OFFICE DES NATIONS UNIES A GENÈVE

CENTRE POUR LES DROITS DE L'HOMME

Téléfax: (022) 733 98 79
Télégrammes: UNATIONS, GENÈVE
Télex: 412 962 UNO CH
Téléphone: 734 60 11   731 02 11
RÉF. N°:   G/SO 211 (4)
(à rappeler dans la réponse)

UNITED NATIONS OFFICE AT GENEVA

CENTRE FOR HUMAN RIGHTS

Palais des Nations
CH - 1211 GENÈVE 10

The Secretary-General of the United Nations presents his compliments to the Minister for Foreign Affairs of the Republic of Korea and has the honour to refer to resolution 1991/22 of 5 March 1991 entitled "Co-ordinating role of the Centre for Human Rights", whereby the Commission on Human Rights:

"Invites again the Secretary-General to request Governments, United Nations specialized agencies and intergovernmental and non-governmental Organizations to express their views on the strengthening of the activities of the Centre for Human Rights, with special emphasis on new directions and forms, including increasing the representation of under-represented group of States, notably the developing countries, in senior and policy-formulating posts in the Centre, while safeguarding the principle of equitable geographical distribution, in accordance with the relevant resolutions of the General Assembly, particularly resolution 45/125 on the improvement of the status of women in the Secretariat, and to submit a report setting out those views and opinions to the Commission at its forty-eighth session.

The Secretary-General would appreciate if any information relating to the request of the Commission was communicated, preferably by 31 January 1992.

29 November 1991

0173

OFFICE DES NATIONS UNIES A GENÈVE

CENTRE POUR LES DROITS DE L'HOMME

UNITED NATIONS OFFICE AT GENEVA

CENTRE FOR HUMAN RIGHTS

Téléfax: (022) 733 98 79
Télégrammes: UNATIONS, GENÈVE
Télex: 412 962 UNO CH
Téléphone: 734 60 11   731 02 11

RÉF. N°: G/SO 234 (19-2)
(à rappeler dans la réponse)

Palais des Nations
CH-1211 GENÈVE 10

The Secretary-General of the United Nations presents his compliments to the Minister for Foreign Affairs of the Republic of Korea and has the honour to refer to Sub-Commission on Prevention of Discrimination and Protection of Minorities resolution 1991/22 of 28 August 1991, entitled "Possible ways and means of facilitating the peaceful and constructive solution of problems involving minorities".

The attention of His Excellency's Government is drawn to paragraph 4 of the resolution, which calls on the Secretary-General to transmit a reminder with the questionnaire annexed to the Special Rapporteur's progress report (E/CN.4/Sub.2/1990/46) if they have not yet done so, and paragraph 7 of the resolution, which requests the Special Rapporteur, in updating his report to take into consideration the replies submitted by Governments. A copy of the questionnaire is enclosed.

The Secretary-General would appreciate it if any information which His Excellency's Government wished to submit pursuant to the above-mentioned request could be sent to the Centre for Human Rights, United Nations Office at Geneva, CH-1211 Geneva 10, no later, if possible, than 28 February 1992.

29 November 1991

0174

주 제 네 바 대 표 부

제네(정) 2031- 1021   1991. 11. 26

수신 : 장관

참조 : 국제기구국장

제목 : 유엔인권소위 요청자료 목록

　　　유엔인권사무국은 인권소위가 결의등을 통하여 각국에 요청한바 있는

자료 목록표를 보내온바, 이를 별첨 송부합니다.

첨부 : 상기 목록표 1부.　　끝.

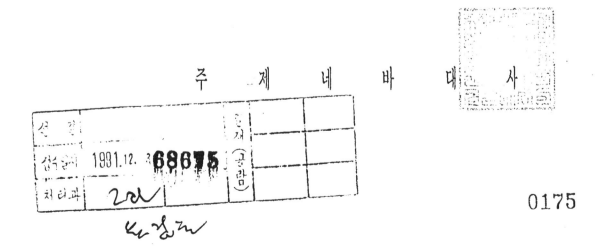

0175

OFFICE DES NATIONS UNIES À GENÈVE

CENTRE POUR LES DROITS DE L'HOMME

UNITED NATIONS OFFICE AT GENEVA

CENTRE FOR HUMAN RIGHTS

Téléfax: (022) 733 98 79
Télégrammes: UNATIONS, GENÈVE
Télex: 28 96 96
Téléphone: 734 60 11   731 02 11

RÉF. N°: G/SO 232/24-43rd
(à rappeler dans la reponse)

Palais des Nations
CH-1211 GENÈVE 10

15 November 1991

Dear Mr. Ambassador,

    I am writing to draw your attention to the attached table of resolutions adopted by the Sub-Commission on Prevention of Discrimination and Protection of Minorities at its forty-third session which invite Governments to provide information in regard to the drafting of certain studies and reports.

    An explanatory note gives further details of the purpose of the table. As stated in this note, the table has been prepared in an effort to simplify the task of delegations in determining what contributions of information are expected of them and by which dates.

    It would be much appreciated if any information which your Government wishes to submit pursuant to the requests could be sent to the Centre for Human Rights, Palais des Nations, 1211 Geneva 10, Switzerland, bearing in mind the dates indicated for the individual requests.

    In anticipation of your response, I remain, dear Mr. Ambassador,

Yours sincerely,

John Pace
Chief
Legislation and Prevention
of Discrimination Branch

His Excellency
Mr. Soo Gil Park
Ambassador
Permanent Representative of the Republic of Korea to
the United Nations Office at Geneva
20 route de Pré-Bois
Case postale 566
1215 Genève 15

0176

EXPLANATORY NOTE

At its forty-seventh session, the Commission on Human Rights adopted resolution 1990/70 by which it requested the Secretary-General to prepare a list containing operative paragraphs of all resolutions which require the preparation of reports and studies.

In response to this request, the Secretariat is proposing a new approach in the communication of requests for information from United Nations human rights bodies. The list attached to the present note refers to the resolutions and decisions adopted by the Sub-Commission at its forty-third session.

This new approach is intended to reduce the present excessive number of notes verbales and letters and to assist delegations in determining their schedules for furnishing replies and/or information in response to the requests from United Nations human rights bodies.

The list covers resolutions and decisions containing requests of a general nature, such as those addressed to "all Governments". It does not extend to requests addressed to individual persons or bodies.

The list is intended to serve only as a guide and will be used as a reminder when necessary. It indicates the number of the resolution or decision, its title and the paragraph(s) where the request is contained. It also specifies the type of information that is requested, and the ultimate use of this information. Finally, the list gives the deadline for the receipt of the information. The dates are calculated on the estimated time required for preparation of the final document by the Secretariat for submission to the meetings of the body concerned.

15.11.91/E

0177

INFORMATION REQUESTED FROM GOVERNMENTS BY THE SUB-COMMISSION ON PREVENTION OF DISCRIMINATION AND PROTECTION OF MINORITIES

RESOLUTION OR DECISION	TITLE	OP. PARA.	ISSUES ON WHICH INFORMATION IS REQUESTED	PURPOSE FOR WHICH THE INFORMATION IS REQUESTED	INFORMATION REQUIRED BY
7 (XXVII)	The question of the human rights of persons subjected to any form of detention or imprisonment	1	The human rights of persons subjected to any form of detention or imprisonment.	Report containing analysis of information received to be submitted to the Sub-Commission at its 44th session	30-Mar-92
4 (XXVIII)	Ibid	5	Ibid	Ibid	Ibid
1991/02	Measures to combat racism and racial discrimination and the role of the Sub-Commission	11	Trends of racism, discrimination, intolerance and xenophobia affecting indigenous peoples, migrant workers and other vulnerable groups in society. Measures taken by Governments against these phenomena, as well as the effects of such measures.	An overview by the Secretary-General of the issues for consideration by the Sub-Commission at its 44th session.	27-Mar-92
—— /02	Measures to combat racism and racial discrimination and the role of the Sub-Commission	12	Serious incidents attributable to racism, racial discrimination and xenophobia that take place in any part of the world, including the measures taken by the Governments concerned in response to these incidents.	A report by the Secretary-General for consideration by the Sub-Commission at its 44th session.	27-Mar-92

0178

Page 1

			10-Apr-92
1991/105	Study of the issue of the privatization of prisons	(a)	The privatization of prisons.	A working paper, containing a systematic compilation of views and analytical comments thereon to be submitted by the Secretary-General to the 44th session of the Sub-Commission.
1991/16	The application of international standards concerning the human rights of detained juveniles	2	Successful efforts to implement, and practices that are not compatible with international standards on the human rights of detained juveniles.	Updated report by the Special Rapporteur to be submitted to the 44th session of the Sub-Commission.	31-Jan-92
1991/17	Violations of the human rights of staff members and other persons acting under the authority of the United Nations	6	Cases of arrest, detention or abduction of officials of the United Nations or the specialized agencies since 1980, provided by member States.	Final version of the report by the Special Rapporteur to be submitted to the 44th session of the Sub-Commission.	28-Feb-92
1991/18	Question of human rights and states of emergency	3	The question of human rights and states of emergency.	Updating the Special Rapporteur's present report and the submission of the next annual report and updated list to the 44th session of the Sub-Commission.	28-Feb-92
22	Possible ways and means of facilitating the peaceful and constructive solution of problems involving minorities	4	The questionnaire annexed to the Special Rapporteur's progress report (E/CN.4/Sub.2/1990/46).	Submission by the Special Rapporteur of an updated report to the Sub-Commission at its 44th session and his final report to the Sub-Commission at its 45th session.	28-Feb-92

1991/24	Human rights and the environment	5	Information relevant to the preparation of the Special Rapporteur's report.	A progress report on human rights and the environment for the 44th session of the Sub-Commission; and the final study.	21-Feb-92
1991/25	The right to restitution, compensation and rehabilitation for victims of gross violations of human rights and fundamental freedoms	3	Relevant decisions and views of international human rights organs, as well as national law and practice.	A second progress report to the 44th session and a final report to the 45th session.	28-Feb-92
1991/30	Draft universal Declaration of indigenous rights	7 (a)	Comments and suggestions on the text of the draft Declaration as it has so far been elaborated by the Working Group.	The completion of the first reading of the text and the begining of the second reading at the tenth session of the Working Group.	16-Mar-92
1991/110	Study on treaties, agreements and other constructive arrangements between States and indigenous populations		The questionnaire submitted by the Special Rapporteur in 1990, (E/CN.4/Sub.2/1990/42, annex VI).	A progress report on the Study to be submitted to the Working Group on Indigenous Populations at its 10th session and to the Sub-Commission at its 44th session.	16-Mar-92
1991/132	Ownership and control of the cultural property of indigenous peoples	3	The laws and traditions of indigenous peoples with respect to the definition, ownership and control of cultural property.	A study of the measures which should be taken by the international community to strengthen respect for the cultural property of indigenous peoples, for submission to the Sub-Commission at its 45th session.	27-Mar-92

0180

1991/34	Report of the Working Group on Contemporary Forms of Slavery	13	The recruitment of children into government and non-governmental armed forces.	Update the Secretary-General's report on the recruitment of children into government and non-governmental armed forces (E/CN.4/Sub.2/1990/43 and Add. 1 & 2), for submission to the Sub-Commission at its 44th session.	16-Mar-92
1—/34	Report of the Working Group on Contemporary Forms of Slavery	15	Views and suggestions on the possibility of preparing guiding principles for combating the various contemporary forms of slavery, as well as spheres in which such guiding principles could be applied.	Consideration of this matter by the Working Group at its future sessions.	16-Mar-92
1991/35	Independence and impartiality of the judiciary, jurors and assesors and the independence of lawyers	8	Practices and measures which have served to strengthen or to weaken the independence of the judiciary and the legal profession.	A report on practices which have served to strengthen or to weaken the independence of the judiciary and the legal profession in accordance with United Nations standards, for submission to the 44th session of the Sub-Commission.	31-Jan-92

0181

Page 4

정 리 보 존 문 서 목 록

기록물종류	일반공문서철	등록번호	2020080026	등록일자	2020-08-20
분류번호	734.21	국가코드		보존기간	영구
명 칭	유엔 인권위원회, 제48차. Geneva, 1992.1.27-3.6. 전2권				
생 산 과	국제연합2과	생산년도	1992~1992	담당그룹	
권 차 명	V.1 1월-2.24				
내용목차	* 수석대표 : 박수길 주제네바 대사				

0001

。   귀

주 제 네 바 대 표 부

제네(정) 2031-30   1992. 1. 6.

수신 : 장관

참조 : 국제기구국장

제목 : 48차 유엔인권위 회의

　　　　92.1.27-3.6간 당지에서 개최될 예정인 표제 회의 관련 문서를 별첨

송부합니다.

　　　　첨부 : 의제 설명자료등 회의문서 7점.　　끝.

주　　제　　네　　바　　대　　　　사

선　결			결 재 (공람)		
접수일시 1992.1.14	편 호				
처리과 2차 02481					

0002

Economic and Social Council

Distr.
GENERAL

E/CN.4/1992/1/Add.1
7 November 1991

Original: ENGLISH

COMMISSION ON HUMAN RIGHTS
Forty-eighth session
27 January-6 March 1992

ANNOTATIONS TO THE PROVISIONAL AGENDA

Prepared by the Secretary-General

CONTENTS*

---

 * This table of contents is based upon the provisional agenda of the forty-eighth session of the Commission with the addition of the indicative subheadings found in the text of the annotations for ease of reference.

GE.91-14061/3928B

0003

CONTENTS (continued)

0004

CONTENTS (continued)

0005

CONTENTS (<u>continued</u>)

0006

CONTENTS (continued)

0007

CONTENTS (<u>continued</u>)

0008

Item 1. Election of officers

1. Rule 15 of the rules of procedure of the functional commissions of the Economic and Social Council provides that "at the commencement of its first meeting of a regular session the Commission shall elect, from among the representatives of its members, a Chairman, one or more Vice-Chairmen and such other officers as may be required".

Item 2. Adoption of the agenda

2. Rule 7 of the rules of procedure provides that "the Commission shall at the beginning of each session, after the election of its officers, ... adopt the agenda for that session on the basis of the provisional agenda".

3. The Commission will have before it the provisional agenda (E/CN.4/1992/1) prepared by the Secretary-General in accordance with rule 5 of the rules of procedure, as well as the present annotations relating to the items included in the provisional agenda.

Item 3. Organization of the work of the session

4. The attention of the Commission is drawn to the relevant resolutions concerning control and limitation of documentation (inter alia, General Assembly resolution 33/56 and Economic and Social Council resolutions 1981/83 and 1982/50). Furthermore, the Commission will recall that at its last eight sessions it set time-limits for statements. At its forty-seventh session, for example, members of the Commission were limited to one statement of 15 minutes or two statements of 10 minutes per item, observers and non-governmental organizations were limited to one statement of 10 minutes per item, while observer States mentioned in a report and liberation movements could make one statement of 15 minutes or two statements of 10 minutes per item. It was also agreed that, with regard to rights of reply, the practice followed by the General Assembly, namely limitation to two replies, the first of 10 minutes and the second of 5 minutes, would again be observed. In view of the existing financial constraints and the overall reductions imposed, the session must be most carefully planned from the outset, bearing in mind the absolute need for maximum effectiveness in the use of the resources available.

5. The attention of the Commission is also drawn to Economic and Social Council decision 1991/263 of 31 May 1991, by which the Council, taking note of Commission on Human Rights decision 1991/110 of 8 March 1991, decided to authorize, if possible within existing financial resources, 40 fully serviced additional meetings, with summary records, for the forty-eighth session of the Commission. The Council took note of the Commission's decision to request the Chairman, at its forty-eighth session, to make every effort to organize the work of the session within the time normally allotted, the additional meetings to be held only if they prove absolutely necessary.

6. The attention of the Commission is also drawn to item 12 (c) of the provisional agenda (E/CN.4/1992/1), under which the Commission should provide for a special closed meeting in connection with a decision relating to a particular situation.

7.   The attention of the Commission is also be drawn to Economic and Social
Council resolution 1990/48 of 25 May 1990 in which the Council authorized the
Commission to meet exceptionally between its regular sessions, provided that a
majority of States members of the Commission so agreed. In addition, the
Council recommended that the mandates of the thematic rapporteurs and working
groups established or to be established by the Commission should, unless
otherwise decided, be of three years' duration. Further, the Council decided
that, in the week following the forty-eighth session of the Commission, the
Bureau should meet to make suggestions about the organization of the work of
the Commission, including the effective use of conference time and facilities.

Working groups

8.   The session will be preceded by meetings of the four presessional working
groups referred to in E/CN.4/1992/1, paragraph 3 (a) to (d).

Composition of the Commission

9.   The composition of the Commission for 1992 is the following. The term of
membership of each State expires on 31 December of the year indicated in
brackets.

    Angola (1995), Argentina (1993), Australia (1993), Austria (1993),
    Bangladesh (1995), Barbados (1995), Brazil (1992), Bulgaria (1995),
    Burundi (1993), Canada (1995), Chile (1995), China (1993),
    Colombia (1995), Costa Rica (1995), Cuba (1995), Cyprus (1995),
    Czechoslovakia (1993), France (1992), Gabon (1995), Gambia (1993),
    Germany (1993), Ghana (1992), Hungary (1992), India (1995),
    Indonesia (1993), Iran (Islamic Republic of) (1995), Iraq (1992),
    Italy (1992), Japan (1993), Kenya (1995), Lesotho (1995), Libyan Arab
    Jamahiriya (1995), Madagascar (1992), Mauritania (1993), Mexico (1992),
    Netherlands (1995), Nigeria (1995), Pakistan (1992), Peru (1993),
    Philippines (1992), Portugal (1993), Senegal (1992), Somalia (1992),
    Sri Lanka (1995), Syrian Arab Republic (1995), Tunisia (1995), Union of
    Soviet Socialist Republics (1995), United Kingdom of Great Britain and
    Northern Ireland (1995), United States of America (1992), Uruguay (1995),
    Venezuela (1993), Yugoslavia (1992) and Zambia (1993).

Assistance to Guatemala in the field of human rights

10. The Commission may wish to recall its resolution 1991/51, adopted at its
forty-seventh session, in which it requested the Secretary-General to extend
the mandate of the independent Expert, Mr. C. Tomuschat, so that he might
continue to examine the human rights situation in Guatemala and provide
assistance to the Government in the field of human rights, reporting to the
Commission on the subject at its forty-eighth session, and decided to consider
the question under an item of its agenda to be determined in the light of the
above-mentioned report and of the situation of human rights in Guatemala. The
Economic and Social Council, in its decision 1991/246 of 31 May 1991, approved
the Commission's request.

11. The report of the independent Expert will be before the Commission, at
its present session (E/CN.4/1992/5).

0010

Item 4. Question of the violation of human rights in the occupied Arab
         territories, including Palestine

12. The Commission has been seized of the human rights situation in the
territories occupied by Israel as a result of the hostilities of June 1967
every year since its twenty-fourth session (1968).

13. At its forty-seventh session, the Commission adopted resolution 1991/1 A
and B and 1991/2 in which it decided to place this item on the agenda of the
forty-eighth session as a matter of high priority.

14. The Commission also adopted resolution 1991/3 relevant to this item.

15. At its forty-third session, the Sub-Commission on Prevention of
Discrimination and Protection of Minorities adopted resolution 1991/6 on the
situation in the Palestinian and other Arab territories occupied by Israel.

16. Attention is also drawn to Economic and Social Council resolution 1991/19
on the situation of and assistance to Palestinian women.

17. In accordance with paragraphs 5 and 6 of resolution 1991/1 A, paragraph 5
of resolution 1991/1 B and paragraph 6 of resolution 1991/2, the Commission
will have before it the report of the Secretary-General on the implementation
of the said resolutions (E/CN.4/1992/6) and a note by the Secretary-General
listing United Nations reports issued between sessions of the Commission that
deal with the condition in which the population of the Palestinian and other
occupied Arab territories is living (E/CN.4/1992/7). The Commission will also
have before it draft resolution X, contained in chapter I, section A of the
report of the Sub-Commission (E/CN.4/1992/2-E/CN.4/Sub.2/1991/65).

Item 5. Violations of human rights in southern Africa: report of the Ad Hoc
         Working Group of Experts

18. The Ad Hoc Working Group of Experts on southern Africa was established by
the Commission on Human Rights in accordance with resolution 2 (XXIII) of
6 March 1967. Since then, the Commission has renewed the mandate of the
Ad Hoc Working Group regularly, and most recently at its forty-seventh session
by resolution 1991/21. The renewal of the mandate was endorsed by the
Economic and Social Council in decision 1991/237. The Ad Hoc Working Group is
composed of Mr. Leliel Mikuin Balanda (Zaire), Mr. Armando Entralgo (Cuba),
Mr. Felix Ermacora (Austria), Mr. Mulka G. Reddy (India), Mr. Elly E.E. Mtango
(United Republic of Tanzania) and Mr. Zoran Pajic (Yugoslavia).

19. At its forty-seventh session, by resolution 1991/21, the Commission
requested the Group to continue to examine the situation regarding the
violations of human rights in South Africa including, in particular, reports
of torture, ill-treatment and deaths of detainees, as well as infringements
of trade union rights in South Africa, and submit its interim report to
the Commission at its forty-eighth session and its final report at its
forty-ninth session. It also requested the Group to submit a brief
preliminary report to the General Assembly at its forty-sixth and
forty-seventh sessions.

0011

20. By resolution 1991/8, the Commission requested the Group to pay special attention to the question of detention, torture and other inhuman treatment of children in South Africa. On the same matter, the General Assembly, at its forty-fifth session, adopted resolution 45/144, entitled "Torture and inhuman treatment of children in detention in South Africa".

21. In pursuance of these resolutions, the Commission will have before it the Ad Hoc Working Group's interim report (E/CN.4/1992/8).

Item 6. The adverse consequences for the enjoyment of human rights of political, military, economic and other forms of assistance given to the racist regime in southern Africa

22. This item has been considered by the Commission since its thirtieth session (1974). The item has also been regularly considered by the General Assembly and the Sub-Commission on Prevention of Discrimination and Protection of Minorities.

23. At its forty-seventh session, the Commission adopted resolutions 1991/9 and 1991/17, in which it expressed its appreciation to Mr. Ahmed Khalifa, Special Rapporteur of the Sub-Commission on Prevention of Discrimination and Protection of Minorities, for his updated report containing the list of banks, transnational corporations and other organizations assisting the racist regime of South Africa.

24. Upon the recommendation of the Commission on Human Rights in its resolution 1991/9, the Economic and Social Council, by its resolution 1991/26 of 31 May 1991, invited the Special Rapporteur to continue to update his list and invited the Sub-Commission at its forty-third session and the Commission at its forty-eighth session to consider the revised report.

25. At its forty-third session, the Sub-Commission had before it the updated report of the Special Rapporteur and adopted resolution 1991/1, by which it recommended, through the Commission, that the Economic and Social Council should invite the Special Rapporteur to continue to update his list.

26. It further recommended that the Secretary-General be requested to contact the Government of South Africa with a view to enabling the Special Rapporteur to visit South Africa on a special mission for the puposes of the next updating of the report.

27. At the present session, the Commission will have before it the updated report by the Special Rapporteur (E/CN.4/Sub.2/1991/13 and Add.1).

28. The Commission will also have before it draft resolution I contained in chapter I, section A, of the report of the Sub-Commission (E/CN.4/1992/2-E/CN.4/Sub.2/1991/65).

0012

Item 7. Question of the realization in all countries of the economic, social
         and cultural rights contained in the Universal Declaration of
         Human Rights and in the International Covenant on Economic, Social
         and Cultural Rights, and study of special problems which the
         developing countries face in their efforts to achieve these human
         rights, including: problems related to the right to enjoy an
         adequate standard of living; foreign debt, economic adjustment
         policies and their effects on the full enjoyment of human rights and,
         in particular, on the implementation of the Declaration on the Right
         to Development

29. The Commission, by its resolution 2 (XXXI) of 10 February 1975, decided
to keep this item on the agenda as a standing item with high priority.
In 1989, it modified the original sub-item (a) entitled "Problems related to
the right to enjoy an adequate standard of living; the right to development"
and decided to consider the right to development under a separate agenda item
at its forty-sixth session; it also decided to add to the original
sub-item (a) a specific point entitled "Foreign debt, economic adjustment
policies and their effects on the full enjoyment of human rights and, in
particular, on the implementation of the Declaration on the Right to
Development".

30. The Commission, at its forty-seventh session, adopted resolution 1991/13,
in which it invited Governments which so desired to provide the Special
Rapporteur of the Sub-Commission with their comments and the information at
their disposal about their experience concerning the impact of economic
adjustment policies arising from foreign debt on the enjoyment of human rights
and invited the Sub-Commission to submit the third report of the Special
Rapporteur to the Commission at its forty-eighth session. Also, at its
forty-seventh session, the Commission adopted resolution 1991/18 in which it
welcomed the contribution of the Committee on Economic, Social and Cultural
Rights, which continued to give impetus to the implementation of the economic,
social and cultural rights contained in the Covenant. Further, it requested
the Secretary-General to organize, under the United Nations programme of human
rights activities in 1992-1993, an expert seminar for discussion of
appropriate indicators to measure achievements in the progressive realization
of economic, social and cultural rights.

31. Reference may also be made to Commission resolution 1991/19 entitled
"Respect for the right of everyone to own property alone as well as in
association with others", in which the Commission requested its Chairman to
entrust an independent expert with the task of preparing a study, within the
existing financial resources, on the means whereby and the degree to which
respect for the right to own property alone as well as in association with
others contributed to the development of individual liberty and initiative,
which served to foster, strengthen and enhance the exercise of other human
rights and fundamental freedoms, and requested that a preliminary report be
submitted to the Commission at its forty-eighth session and the final report
at its forty-ninth session. The Economic and Social Council endorsed
the Commission's request. On 29 August 1991, the Chairman appointed
Mr. Luis Valencia Rodriguez (Ecuador) as Special Rapporteur of the Commission.

32. At its forty-third session, the Sub-Commission had before it the second progress report of the Special Rapporteur on realization of economic, social and cultural rights, Mr. Danilo Türk, (E/CN.4/Sub.2/1991/17) and adopted resolution 1991/27. In that resolution, the Sub-Commission endorsed the preliminary recommendations contained in paragraphs 229 to 236 of the Special Rapporteur's report and requested him to submit his final report to the Sub-Commission at its forty-fourth session.

33. The Sub-Commission also adopted resolution 1991/28 entitled "Human rights dimensions of population transfer, including the implantation of settlers and settlements".

34. In regard to this item, the Commission will have before it the second progress report of the Special Rapporteur (E/CN.4/Sub.2/1991/17) and the preliminary report of the independent Expert (E/CN.4/1992/9).

Item 8. <u>Question of the realization of the right to development</u>

35. The Commission in its resolution 1989/45 decided to include this item on the agenda of its forty-sixth session.

36. The Declaration on the Right to Development was proclaimed by the General Assembly at its forty-first session in resolution 41/128 of 4 December 1986. The Working Group of Governmental Experts on the Right to Development, established by the Commission on Human Rights in 1981, had held nine sessions in the period preceding the adoption of the Declaration, to the content of which it contributed. Subsequent to the proclamation of the Declaration, the Working Group has held three sessions, in January 1987, 1988 and 1989, prior to the sessions of the Commission on Human Rights.

37. In accordance with Commission resolution 1989/45, endorsed by the Economic and Social Council in decision 1989/141, the Secretary-General organized a global consultation on the right to development which took place from 8 to 12 January 1990, at Geneva.

38. At its forty-seventh session, the Commission adopted resolution 1991/15, in which it requested the Secretary-General to submit to the Commission on Human Rights at its forty-eighth session concrete proposals on the effective implementation and promotion of the Declaration on the Right to Development, taking into account the views expressed on the issue at the forty-seventh session of the Commission as well as any further comments and suggestions that might be submitted on the basis of paragraph 3 of Commission resolution 1990/18.

39. At its present session, the Commission will have before it in connection with this item the report of the Secretary-General in accordance with resolution 1991/15 (E/CN.4/1992/10 and Add.1).

Item 9. <u>The right of peoples to self-determination and its application to peoples under colonial or alien domination or foreign occupation</u>

40. This item has been on the Commission's agenda since 1975. At its forty-seventh session, the Commission adopted the following resolutions under

0014

this item: 1991/4, entitled "Situation in Afghanistan"; 1991/5, entitled "Question of Western Sahara"; 1991/6, entitled "Situation in occupied Palestine"; 1991/7, entitled "Use of mercenaries as a means of impeding the exercise of the right of peoples to self-determination"; and decision 1991/104, entitled "Situation in Cambodia". In resolutions 1991/4, 1991/5, 1991/6, 1991/7 and decision 1991/104, the Commission decided to keep these situations under review at its forty-eighth session.

41. The Commission will have before it a report of the Secretary-General prepared in accordance with Commission resolution 1991/6 (E/CN.4/1992/11).

Special Rapporteur on the question of mercenaries

42. At its forty-third session, the Commission, by resolution 1987/16, decided to appoint for one year a Special Rapporteur to examine the question of the use of mercenaries as a means of violating human rights and of impeding the exercise of the right of peoples to self-determination. On 1 September 1987, the Chairman of the Commission appointed Mr. Enrique Bernales Ballesteros (Peru) as Special Rapporteur of the Commission on the question of mercenaries.

43. At its forty-sixth session, the Commission adopted resolution 1990/7, in which it extended the mandate of the Special Rapporteur for two years. At its forty-seventh session, the Commission adopted resolution 1991/7, entitled "Use of mercenaries as a means of impeding the exercise of the right of peoples to self-determination", in which it requested the Special Rapporteur to submit his report to the Commission at its forty-eighth session, and a preliminary report to the General Assembly at its forty-sixth session. The Economic and Social Council approved this request by its decision 1991/233.

44. The report of the Special Rapporteur to the Commission is contained in document E/CN.4/1992/12.

Item 10. Question of the human rights of all persons subjected to any form of detention or imprisonment, in particular:

    (a) Torture and other cruel, inhuman or degrading treatment or punishment;

    (b) Status of the Convention against Torture and Other Cruel, Inhuman or Degrading Treatment or Punishment;

    (c) Question of enforced or involuntary disappearances;

    (d) Question of a draft optional protocol to the Convention against Torture and Other Cruel, Inhuman or Degrading Treatment or Punishment.

Question of human rights and states of emergency

45. The attention of the Commission is drawn to the work of the Sub-Commission on this question. A fourth annual report and a list of States which, since 1 January 1985, have proclaimed, extended or terminated a state of emergency, was submitted by the Special Rapporteur on human rights and states of emergency, Mr. Leandro Despouy, to the Sub-Commission at its

0015

forty-third session (E/CN.4/Sub.2/1991/28). In its resolution 1991/18, the
Sub-Commission invited the Special Rapporteur to update his report so that the
Commission, at its forty-eighth session, would have before it the most recent
and accurate information available, and recommended, through the Commission on
Human Rights, to the Economic and Social Council that it endorse the request
of the Sub-Commission to the Special Rapporteur to continue to update the list
of states of emergency and to include in his annual report to the
Sub-Commission and the Commission the completed draft standard provisions on
emergency situations.

46. The Commission will have before it the revised and updated report
(E/CN.4/Sub.2/1991/28/Rev.1), and draft decision 1, contained in chapter I,
section B of the report of the Sub-Commission (E/CN.4/1992/2-
E/CN.4/Sub.2/1991/65).

Staff members of the United Nations and specialized agencies in detention

47. Both the Commission and the Sub-Commission have dealt with the detention,
disappearance and death in detention of United Nations staff members. In its
resolution 1991/37, the Commission requested the Secretary-General to continue
his efforts to ensure that the human rights, privileges and immunities of
United Nations staff members, experts and their families were fully
respected. It also requested him to submit to the Commission, at its
forty-eighth session, an updated version of the report on the situation of
United Nations staff members, experts and their families detained, imprisoned,
missing or held in a country against their will, including those cases which
had been successfully settled since the presentation of the last report.

48. The Sub-Commission, at its fortieth session, had before it, pursuant to
its resolution 1987/21, a report of the Secretary-General on this subject. It
adopted resolution 1988/9, in which it decided to entrust one of its members,
Mrs. Maria Concepción Bautista, with the task of undertaking an examination of
violations of human rights of staff members of the United Nations system.

49. At its forty-third session, the Sub-Commission adopted
resolution 1991/17, in which it invited Ms. Bautista to continue her study in
order to submit to the Sub-Commission, at its forty-fourth session, a final
report which would include practical recommendations for measures to improve
on a long-term basis the protection of personnel of the United Nations system
and their families, as well as of experts and consultants.

Right to freedom of opinion and expression

50. At its forty-sixth session, the Commission adopted resolution 1990/32, in
which it endorsed the appointment by the Sub-Commission of Mr. Louis Joinet
and Mr. Danilo Türk to prepare a study on the right to freedom of opinion and
expression and decided to review the question at its forty-seventh session on
the basis, inter alia, of a preliminary report of the Special Rapporteurs.
The Economic and Social Council endorsed the recommendation of the Commission
in its resolution 1990/35.

51. At its forty-seventh session, the Commission adopted resolution 1991/32,
in which it welcomed the intention of the Special Rapporteurs to study in

0016

greater detail measures necessary for the strengthening and promotion of the
right to freedom of expression, _inter alia_, the concept of a democratic
society, the relationship between the right to freedom of opinion and
expression and the right to freedom of association and peaceful assembly and
the right to take part in Government. It also decided to review the question
at its forty-eighth session on the basis, _inter alia_, of the updated
preliminary report submitted by the Special Rapporteurs to the Sub-Commission
at its forty-third session.

52. The Sub-Commission, at its forty-third session, had before it the updated
preliminary report of the Special Rapporteurs (E/CN.4/Sub.2/1991/9). In its
resolution 1991/39, the Sub-Commission decided to invite the Special
Rapporteurs to continue the work with which they had been entrusted and to
submit to the Sub-Commission, at its forty-fourth session, a report which
includes conclusions and recommendations, taking into account all the comments
made during the discussion on the updated preliminary report.

53. At the present session, the Commission will have before it the updated
preliminary report of Mr. Joinet and Mr. Türk (E/CN.4/Sub.2/1991/9) and draft
decision 15, contained in chapter I, section B of the report of the
Sub-Commission (E/CN.4/1992/2-E/CN.4/Sub.2/1991/65).

**The independence and impartiality of the judiciary, jurors and assessors and
the independence of lawyers**

54. At its forty-fifth session the Commission adopted resolution 1989/32, in
which it expressed its appreciation and thanks to the Special Rapporteur of
the Sub-Commission, Mr. L.M. Singhvi, for his study on this subject
(E/CN.4/Sub.2/1985/18 and Add.1-6) and for his draft declaration
(E/CN.4/Sub.2/1988/20/Add.1 and Add.1/Corr.1), and invited Governments to take
into account the principles set forth in the draft declaration in implementing
the Basic Principles on the Independence of the Judiciary. The Commission
also recommended that Governments should provide for the protection of
practising lawyers against undue restrictions and pressures in the exercise of
their functions, and welcomed the decision of the Sub-Commision to consider
the agenda item entitled "Draft declaration on the independence and
impartiality of the judiciary, jurors and assessors and the independence of
lawyers" at its forty-first session. The Commission further requested the
Sub-Commission, under the said agenda item, to consider effective means of
monitoring the implementation of the Basic Principles on the Independence of
the Judiciary and the protection of practising lawyers.

55. At its forty-seventh session, the Commission adopted resolution 1991/39
in which it endorsed the decision of the Sub-Commission to entrust
Mr. Louis Joinet with the preparation of a report on strengthening the
independence of the judiciary and the protection of practising lawyers.

56. At its forty-third session, the Sub-Commission had before it the report
prepared by Mr. Joinet (E/CN.4/Sub.2/1991/30 and Add.1-4) and adopted
resolution 1991/35, in which it endorsed the recommendations contained in
paragraphs 303 to 305 of that report. The Sub-Commission also decided to
entrust Mr. Joinet with the preparation of a report to bring to the attention

0017

of the Sub-Commission information on practices and measures which had served
to strengthen or to weaken the independence of the judiciary and the legal
profession.

57. At its present session, the Commission will have before it draft
resolution VII contained in chapter I, section A, of the report of the
Sub-Commission (E/CN.4/1992/2-E/CN.4/Sub.2/1991/65).

Draft declaration on enforced or involuntary disappearances

58. The question of a draft declaration against unacknowledged detention
of persons was examined at the thirty-ninth and fortieth sessions of
the Sub-Commission by its sessional Working Group on Detention (see
E/CN.4/Sub.2/1987/15 and E/CN.4/Sub.2/1988/28) pursuant to Commission
decision 1986/106 and Commission resolutions 1987/33 and 1988/33,
paragraph 5. In paragraph 7 of the latter resolution, the Commission called
upon its special rapporteurs and working groups to give particular attention
to questions relating to the effective protection of human rights in the
administration of justice, in particular with regard to unacknowledged
detention of persons.

59. The Working Group on Detention, at its 1988 and 1989 sessions, gave
consideration to a draft declaration on the protection of all persons from
enforced or involuntary disappearances (see E/CN.4/Sub.2/1988/28, annex I and
E/CN.4/Sub.2/1989/29/Rev.1, annex I). At its 1990 session, the Working Group
adopted the draft declaration (E/CN.4/Sub.2/1990/32, annex) and submitted it
to the Sub-Commission, which, in its resolution 1990/33, adopted the draft
declaration and transmitted it to the Commission with the recommendation that
it be endorsed and submitted to the Economic and Social Council and the
General Assembly for final adoption.

60. At its forty-seventh session, the Commission adopted resolution 1991/41,
in which it decided to establish an open-ended inter-sessional working group
to consider the draft declaration submitted by the Sub-Commission, with a view
to its adoption by the Commission at its forty-eighth session. The Economic
and Social Council endorsed the decision of the Commission in its
resolution 1991/27.

61. At the present session the Commission will have before it the report of
the Working Group on the Draft Declaration on Enforced or Involuntary
Disappearances (E/CN.4/1992/19).

Hostage-taking

62. At its forty-seventh session, the Commission adopted resolution 1991/40,
in which it decided to remain seized of the question at its forty-eighth
session.

Human rights in the administration of justice

63. At its forty-fourth session, the General Assembly adopted
resolution 44/162, in which it requested the Commission to invite the

0018

Sub-Commission to study the practical implementation of United Nations
norms and standards in the administration of justice and human rights.

64.   At its forty-seventh session, the Commission adopted resolution 1991/34,
in which it requested the Secretary-General to establish a consolidated list
of provisions in the various United Nations standards relating to human rights
in the administration of justice with a view to drafting model texts for
national legislation. The Commission also invited the Sub-Commission, on the
basis of the consolidated list, to study the implementation of United Nations
norms and standards in that field; to identify problems that might impinge on
the effective implementation of those norms and standards; to recommend viable
solutions with action-oriented proposals to the Commission; to take the
necessary action with a view to elaborating model texts for national
legislation for the effective implementation of standards relating to human
rights in the administration of justice; and to consider the question of the
effectiveness of habeas corpus and similar remedies during states of emergency
and to formulate suggestions thereon. It further requested the Sub-Commission
to report to the Commission at its forty-eighth session on the implementation
of the above-mentioned resolution.

Right to a fair trial

65.   At its forty-seventh session, the Commission adopted resolution 1991/43,
in which it endorsed the decision of the Sub-Commission to entrust
Mr. Stanislas Chernichenko and Mr. William Treat with the preparation of a
study entitled "The right to a fair trial: current recognition and measures
necessary for its strengthening". It also requested the Special Rapporteurs
to draft a questionnaire on the right to a fair trial and requested the
Secretary-General to transmit the questionnaire with the brief report to
Governments, the specialized agencies and non-governmental organizations and
to transmit the responses to the Special Rapporteurs for consideration in
connection with their study. The Economic and Social Council, in its
resolution 1991/28, requested the Special Rapporteurs to submit a preliminary
report to the Sub-Commission at its forty-third session and to the Commission
at its forty-eighth session.

66.   At its forty-third session, the Sub-Commission adopted resolution 1991/14,
in which it requested the Special Rapporteurs to continue the preparation of
their study.

67.   At the present session the Commission will have before it the report of
Mr. Chernichenko and Mr. Treat (E/CN.4/Sub.2/1991/29) and draft resolution II
contained in chapter I, section A of the report of the Sub-Commission
(E/CN.4/1992/2-E/CN.4/Sub.2/1991/65).

Question of arbitrary detention

68.   At its forty-seventh session, the Commission adopted resolution 1991/42,
in which it decided to create, for a three-year period, a working group
composed of five independent experts, with the task of investigating cases of
detention imposed arbitrarily or otherwise inconsistently with relevant
international standards and that the working group, in carrying out its
mandate, should seek and receive information from Governments,

0019

intergovernmental and non-governmental organizations, and should receive
information from the individuals concerned, their families or their
representatives. It also requested the working group to present a
comprehensive report to the Commission at its forty-eighth session. The
Economic and Social Council, in its decision 1991/243, approved the
Commission's decision. On 3 July 1991, the Chairman of the Commission
appointed the following persons as members of the Working Group:
Mr. Roberto Garreton (Chile), Mr. Louis Joinet (France), Mr. Laïty Kama
(Senegal), Mr. Kapil Sibal (India) and Mr. Peter Uhl (Czechoslovakia). At its
first session, the Working Group elected Mr. L. Joinet as its
Chairman/Rapporteur and Mr. R. Garreton as its vice-chairman. The report of
the Working Group is contained in document E/CN.4/1991/20.

Other matters

69. In connection with agenda item 10, the Commission may wish to note the
following resolutions adopted by the Sub-Commission at its forty-third
session: resolution 1991/16, entitled "The application of international
standards concerning the human rights of detained juveniles", and
resolution 1991/25, entitled "The right to restitution, compensation and
rehabilitation for victims of gross violations of human rights and fundamental
freedoms".

Sub-item (a)   Torture and other cruel, inhuman or degrading treatment or
               punishment

70. This item has been considered annually since 1984 by the Commission and
has also been regularly considered by the General Assembly and the
Sub-Commission on Prevention of Discrimination and Protection of Minorities.
Action taken by the General Assembly so far has included adoption of a
declaration and a convention against torture, adoption of the Code of Conduct
for Law Enforcement Officials, the Principles of Medical Ethics Relevant to
the Role of Health Personnel, particularly Physicians, in the Protection of
Prisoners and Detainees against Torture and Other Cruel, Inhuman or Degrading
Treatment or Punishment, the Body of Principles for the Protection of all
Persons under any Form of Detention or Imprisonment, and the Second Optional
Protocol to the International Covenant on Civil and Political Rights aiming at
the abolition of the death penalty.

Special Rapporteur on torture

71. At its forty-first session, the Commission, in its resolution 1985/33,
decided to appoint for one year a special rapporteur to examine questions
relevant to torture. The Chairmen of the Commission subsequently appointed
Mr. Peter Kooijmans (Netherlands) as Special Rapporteur of the Commission on
the question of torture. His mandate was subsequently renewed in Commission
resolutions 1986/50, 1987/29, 1988/32 and most recently in resolution 1990/34
for two years.

72. The Commission, at its forty-seventh session, adopted resolution 1991/38,
in which it decided that the Special Rapporteur, in carrying out his mandate
should continue to seek and receive credible information from Governments, the
specialized agencies, and intergovernmental and non-governmental organizations.

0020

73. At its present session the Commission will have before it the main report of the Special Rapporteur (E/CN.4/1992/17) and a report on his visit to Indonesia following an invitation from the Government of that country (E/CN.4/1992/17/Add.1).

United Nations Voluntary Fund for Victims of Torture

74. The United Nations Voluntary Fund for Victims of Torture was established in December 1981 by the General Assembly (resolution 36/151) for the purpose of receiving voluntary contributions for distribution, through established channels of assistance, as humanitarian, legal and financial aid to individuals who had been tortured and to their relatives. In its resolution 1991/36, the Commission expressed its gratitude and appreciation to those Governments, organizations and individuals that had already contributed to the Fund and appealed to those in a position to do so to respond favourably to requests for contributions, if possible on a regular basis. The Commission also requested the Secretary-General to keep it informed of the operations of the Fund on an annual basis.

75. The Commission will have before it the report of the Secretary-General on the United Nations Voluntary Fund for Victims of Torture presented to the General Assembly at its forty-sixth session (A/46/   ) and a further report (E/CN.4/1992/16) covering any developments that may have occurred following the submission of the report to the Assembly.

Sub-item (b)   Status of the Convention against Torture and Other Cruel, Inhuman or Degrading Treatment or Punishment

76. In its resolution 1991/35, the Commission requested the Secretary-General to continue submitting to the General Assembly and to the Commission annual reports on the status of the Convention against Torture and Other Cruel, Inhuman or Degrading Treatment or Punishment, which was opened for signature on 4 February 1985 and entered into force on 26 June 1987. The Commission will have before it the report of the Secretary-General on the status of the Convention (E/CN.4/1992/15).

Sub-item (c)   Question of enforced or involuntary disappearances

77. In pursuance of General Assembly resolution 33/173, the Commission, by resolution 20 (XXXVI) of 29 February 1980, decided to establish for a period of one year a working group consisting of five of its members, to serve as experts in their individual capacities, to examine questions relevant to enforced or involuntary disappearances of persons. At its thirty-seventh to forty-first sessions, the Commission extended the term of the Working Group's mandate by one year.

78. At its forty-sixth session, in resolution 1990/30, the Commission decided to extend the Working Group's mandate for two years. At the forty-seventh session, in resolution 1991/41, the Working Group was requested to report on its work to the Commission at its forty-eighth session. The Working Group is made up of Mr. Toine van Dongen (Netherlands), Mr. Jonas K.D. Foli (Ghana), Mr. Aga Hilaly (Pakistan), Mr. Diego García-Sayán (Peru) and Mr. Ivan Tosevski (Yugoslavia).

0021

79. The Commission will have before it the report of the Working Group on Enforced or Involuntary Disappearances (E/CN.4/1992/18 and Add.1).

Sub-item (d)   Question of a draft optional protocol to the Convention against Torture and Other Cruel, Inhuman or Degrading Treatment or Punishment

80. The draft optional protocol to the Convention against Torture and Other Cruel, Inhuman or Degrading Treatment or Punishment was submitted by Costa Rica on 6 March 1980 and is designed to establish a system of visits by a committee of experts to places of detention within the jurisdiction of the States parties to the protocol. At its forty-fifth session, in decision 1989/104, the Commission, deferred until its forty-seventh session consideration of the draft optional protocol, which it believed could represent a major step forward towards the effective prevention of torture. At its forty-seventh session, in decision 1991/107, the Commission, having taken note of the draft optional protocol as updated and submitted by Costa Rica on 22 January 1991, decided, in order to give States an opportunity to study it, to consider the draft optional protocol at its forty-eighth session.

Item 11.   Further promotion and encouragement of human rights and fundamental freedoms, including the question of the programme and methods of work of the Commission:

(a)   Alternative approaches and ways and means within the United Nations system for improving the effective enjoyment of human rights and fundamental freedoms

(b)   National institutions for the promotion and protection of human rights

(c)   Coordinating role of the Centre for Human Rights within the United Nations bodies and machinery dealing with the promotion and protection of human rights

81. The item on the further promotion and encouragement of human rights and fundamental freedoms has been on the agenda of the Commission since 1963 (Commission resolution 8 (XIX)). The title of the item was modified by the addition of the subject of alternative approaches in pursuance of General Assembly resolution 32/130 of 16 December 1977. Regional arrangements and national institutions are also considered by the Commission under this item.

Sub-item (a)   Alternative approaches and ways and means within the United Nations system for improving the effective enjoyment of human rights and fundamental freedoms

82. At its forty-seventh session, the Commission adopted resolution 1991/23, entitled "Developments relating to the activities of the Centre for Human Rights" in which it requested the Secretary-General to submit, through the Economic and Social Council, a report on developments relating to the Centre for Human Rights, to the forty-sixth session of the General Assembly and decided to reconsider the question at its forty-eighth session.

83. The attention of the Commission is also drawn to its resolution 1991/24, entitled "Development of public information activities in the field of human rights, including the World Public Information Campaign for Human Rights", in which it requested the Secretary-General to submit to the Commission, at its forty-eighth session, a report on public information activities with special emphasis on the activities of the World Campaign, including details of the costs incurred in 1991 and the budget envisaged for future activities, as well as a further assessment of the impact of the World Campaign activities undertaken by the United Nations in the field of human rights and decided to continue its consideration of the question at its forty-eighth session.

84. The attention of the Commission is also drawn to its resolution 1991/25, entitled "Internally displaced persons", in which it requested the Secretary-General to submit to the Commission at its forty-eighth session an analytical report on internally displaced persons, taking into account the protection of human rights of internally displaced persons, based on information submitted by Governments, the specialized agencies, relevant United Nations organs, regional and intergovernmental organizations, the International Committee of the Red Cross and non-governmental organizations, and decided to consider this matter at its forty-eighth session.

85. The attention of the Sub-Commission should also be drawn to its resolution 1991/26, entitled "International cooperation in solving international problems of a social, cultural or humanitarian character, and in promoting and encouraging universal respect for, and observance of, human rights and fundamental freedoms", in which it invited all States and international organizations to submit to the Secretary-General their comments and views on ways and means of strengthening international cooperation in solving international problems of a social, cultural or humanitarian character, and in promoting and encouraging universal respect for and observance of human rights and fundamental freedoms, for consideration by the Commission at its forty-eighth session.

86. At its forty-seventh session, the Commission also adopted resolution 1991/28, entitled "Regional arrangements for the promotion and protection of human rights in the Asian-Pacific region", in which the Commission requested the Secretary-General to consult the States in the Asian-Pacific region on the widest possible basis in the implementation of that resolution and to submit a further report to the Commission at its forty-eighth session.

87. The attention of the Commission is drawn to its resolution 1991/29, entitled "Consequences on the enjoyment of human rights of acts of violence committed by armed groups that spread terror among the population and by drug traffickers", in which it requested all special rapporteurs and working groups to continue paying particular attention to the adverse effect on the enjoyment of human rights of acts of violence committed by armed groups and by drug traffickers, in their forthcoming reports to the Commission on the situation of human rights in those countries where such acts occur. In accordance with the request made in the resolution the Secretary-General continued to collect information on this question and has made it available to the special rapporteurs and working groups.

88. The attention of the Commission is also drawn to resolution 1991/31, entitled "Human rights and thematic procedures" in which the Commission encouraged thematic Special Rapporteurs and the Working Group on Enforced or Involuntary Disappearances to follow closely the progress made by Governments in their investigations carried out within their respective mandates. The Secretary-General brought resolution 1991/31 to the attention of the Special Rapporteurs/Representatives and Working Groups concerned. Attention is also drawn to resolution 1991/79, entitled "Strengthening of United Nations action in the field of human rights through the promotion of international cooperation and the importance of non-selectivity, impartiality and objectivity".

89. At its present session, the Commission will have before it the reports of the Secretary-General pursuant to resolutions 1991/22 (E/CN.4/1992/21), 1991/24 (E/CN.4/1992/22), 1991/25 (E/CN.4/1992/23) and 1991/28 (E/CN.4/1992/24).

Sub-item (b)   National institutions for the promotion and protection of human rights

90. At its forty-fourth session, the General Assembly adopted resolution 44/64, in which it requested the Secretary-General to prepare, with the assistance of experts, if necessary, and including materials submitted by Governments, a report containing conceptual models of national institutions for the promotion and protection of human rights, to be submitted to the Commission on Human Rights at its forty-seventh session. It invited the Secretary-General to include in his updated report all the information provided by Governments and any additional information that Governments might wish to provide, with particular emphasis on the functioning of various models of national institutions in implementing international standards on human rights, as well as a list of existing national institutions with contact points and a bibliography of relevant materials.

91. At its forty-seventh session, the Commission adopted resolution 1991/27, in which it requested the Centre for Human Rights to continue its efforts in order to enhance cooperation between the United Nations and regional and national institutions. It welcomed the decision of the Secretary-General to convene a workshop in 1991 and requested the Secretary-General to publicize the proceedings of that meeting and to make use of the results in the finalization of the manual on national institutions under preparation by the Centre for Human Rights.

Sub-item (c)   Co-ordinating role of the Centre for Human Rights within the United Nations bodies and machinery dealing with the promotion and protection of human rights

92. At its forty-seventh session, the Commission adopted resolution 1991/22, in which it decided to discuss the question of the coordinating role of the Centre for Human Rights within the United Nations bodies and machinery dealing with the promotion and protection of human rights at its forty-eighth session.

0024

Item 12.   <u>Question of the violation of human rights and fundamental freedoms in
            any part of the world, with particular reference to colonial and
            other dependent countries and territories, including:</u>

   (a) <u>Question of human rights in Cyprus</u>;

   (b) <u>Situation of human rights in occupied Kuwait</u>;

   (c) <u>Study of situations which appear to reveal a consistent
        pattern of gross violations of human rights as provided for in
        Commission resolution 8 (XXIII) and Economic and Social Council
        resolutions 1235 (XLII) and 1503 (XLVIII): report of the Working
        Group on Situations.</u>

93. By resolution 1164 (XLI) of 5 August 1966, the Economic and Social
Council welcomed the decision of the Commission in its resolution 2 B (XXII)
of 25 March 1966 to consider, at its twenty-third session, the question of its
tasks and functions and its role in relation to violations of human rights.
In resolution 2144 A (XXI) of 26 October 1966, the General Assembly invited
the Council and the Commission to give urgent consideration to ways and means
of improving the capacity of the United Nations to put a stop to violations of
human rights wherever they might occur. Pursuant to these resolutions, the
Commission adopted resolution 8 (XXIII) of 16 March 1967, in which it decided
to give annual consideration to an item on the question of violations of
human rights and fundamental freedoms. The title of the item was later
modified by the Commission. Subsequently, the Economic and Social Council
adopted resolutions 1235 (XLII) and 1503 (XLVIII) on the question of
violations of human rights and fundamental freedoms.

94. In resolution 32/130, the General Assembly decided that, in approaching
human rights questions within the United Nations system, the international
community should accord, or continue to accord, priority to the search for
solutions to the mass and flagrant violations of human rights of peoples
and persons affected by various situations referred to in the resolution.
The Assembly reiterated those views in subsequent resolutions, including
resolution 37/199. In resolution 34/175, entitled "Effective action against
mass and flagrant violations of human rights", the Assembly urged the
appropriate United Nations bodies, within their mandates, particularly the
Commission, to take timely and effective action in existing and future cases
of mass and flagrant violations of human rights. By resolution 37/200, the
General Assembly urged all States to cooperate with the Commission in its
study of violations of human rights and fundamental freedoms in any part of
the world and requested the Commission to continue its efforts to improve the
capacity of the United Nations system to take urgent action in cases of
serious violations of human rights.

Sub-item (a)   <u>Question of human rights in Cyprus</u>

95. This question was first considered by the Commission at its thirty-second
session, when it adopted resolution 4 (XXXIII) of 27 February 1976. The
Commission has had this question on its agenda since then; at its
forty-seventh session, by decision 1991/106, the Commission decided to
postpone debate on the sub-item to its forty-eighth session and to give it due

0025

priority. It requested the Secretary-General to provide a report to the Commission regarding the implementation of its previous resolutions on the subject. At its present session the Commission will have before it the report of the Secretary-General (E/CN.4/1992/25).

Sub-item (b) Situation of human rights in occupied Kuwait

96. At its forty-seventh session, the Commission adopted resolution 1991/67, in which it decided to appoint an individual of recognized international standing as special rapporteur with a mandate to examine human rights violations committed in occupied Kuwait by the invading and occupying forces of Iraq and to report to the General Assembly as soon as possible and to the Commission at its forty-eighth session. The Economic and Social Council, in its decision 1991/251, approved the Commission's decision. On 3 May 1991, the Chairman of the Commission appointed Mr. Walter Kalin (Switzerland) as Special Rapporteur on the situation of human rights in occupied Kuwait. At the present session the Commission will have before it the report of the Special Rapporteur (E/CN.4/1991/26).

Sub-item (c) Study of situations which appear to reveal a consistent
pattern of gross violations of human rights as provided for
in Commission resolution 8 (XXIII) and Economic and Social
Council resolutions 1235 (XLII) and 1503 (XLVIII): report of
the Working Group on Situations

97. By resolution 1503 (XLVIII) of 27 May 1970, the Economic and Social Council established a procedure for dealing with communications concerning alleged violations of human rights. Particular situations referred to the Commission by the Sub-Commission on Prevention of Discrimination and Protection of Minorities under Council resolution 1503 (XLVIII) were placed before the Commission for the first time at its thirtieth session in 1974. Since then, particular situations relating to 47 countries have been placed before the Commission under the procedure.

98. Since its thirtieth session in 1974 (see Commission decision 3 (XXX) of 6 March 1974), the Commission annually set up a working group of five of its members, due account being taken of considerations of geographical distribution, to meet for one week prior to the Commission's following session to examine the particular situations referred to the Commission by the Sub-Commission under Council resolution 1503 (XLVIII) and those situations of which the Commission was seized under that procedure, and to make recommendations to the Commission on the course of action to take in respect of each particular situation. By resolution 1990/41 of 25 May 1990, the Economic and Social Council, acting on the recommendation contained in Commission resolution 1990/55 of 7 March 1990, authorized the establishment of the working group, to be referred to as the Working Group on Situations, on a permanent basis, instead of the earlier ad hoc basis.

99. At its thirtieth session, the Commission decided that the Governments concerned should henceforth be invited to submit written observations relating to the particular situations referred to the Commission (decision 3 (XXX), para. 4).

0026

100. In 1978, the Commission decided to issue invitations, during the first week of each session, to the States directly concerned, asking them to send representatives to address the Commission and to answer any questions put by members of the Commission (decision 5 (XXXIV)).

101. In 1979, the Commission decided to authorize its Working Group on Situations in future to communicate the text of the relevant recommendations as soon as possible to the Governments directly concerned, in order to facilitate their participation in the examination of the situations concerning their countries, as provided for in Commission decision 5 (XXXIV) (decision 14 (XXXV)).

102. In 1980, the Commission decided that the States invited to attend the closed meeting of the Commission under Council resolution 1503 (XLVIII) should have the right to attend and to participate in the entire discussion of the situation concerning them, and to be present during the adoption of the final decision taken in regard to that situation (decision 9 (XXXVI) of 7 March 1980).

103. All actions taken under the procedure governed by Council resolution 1503 (XLVIII) remain confidential until such time as the Commission may decide to make recommendations to the Council. The documentation pertaining to the procedure is also confidential.

104. At its forty-eighth session, the Commission will have before it the report of the Working Group on Situations, as well as other confidential documents pertaining to the sub-item, including the confidential report of the forty-third session of the Sub-Commission (E/CN.4/1992/R.1 and addenda), a report relating to the implementation of a confidential decision adopted at the Commission's last session and such observations as may be received from the Governments concerned (to be issued in the E/CN.4/1992/R series). In addition, the Commission will have before it the relevant earlier material relating to the situations of which the Commission is seized. The above-mentioned confidential documents will be handed to the members of the Commission at the session.

105. Chapter X of the report of the Sub-Commission on the work of its forty-third session (E/CN.4/1992/2-E/CN.4/Sub.2/1991/65) is also relevant to this sub-item. In that connection, attention may be drawn to Sub-Commission decision 1991/104 of 27 August 1991, by which it concurred with the view of its Working Group on Communications that the procedure governed by Council resolution 1503 (XLVIII) could not be applied as a reparation or relief mechanism in respect of claims of compensation for human suffering or other losses which occurred during the Second World War.

Situation of human rights in various countries

106. At its forty-seventh session, the Commission considered, and took action on, the situation of human rights in the following countries:

(a) Situation of human rights in southern Lebanon. In its resolution 1991/66, the Commission decided to continue its consideration of the subject at its forty-eighth session. The Commission will have before it the report of the Secretary-General (E/CN.4/1991/36);

0027

(b) <u>Situation of human rights in Cuba</u>. In its resolution 1991/68, the Commission requested the Secretary-General, after consultations with the Chairman and the Bureau of the Commission, to appoint a special representative, in accordance with Commission decision 1989/113, to maintain direct contact with the Government and citizens of Cuba on the issues and questions contained in, and associated with, the report of the mission which took place in Cuba and requested the special representative to report the results to the Commission at its forty-eighth session. The Economic and Social Council, in its decision 1991/252, approved the Commission's requests. On 2 July 1991, the Secretary-General appointed Mr. Rafael Rivas Posada (Colombia) as Special Representative of the Commission. The Commission will have before it the report of the Special Representative (E/CN.4/1991/27);

(c) <u>Situation of human rights in Romania</u>. In its resolution 1991/69, the Commission decided to extend the mandate of the Special Rapporteur, Mr. J. Voyame (Switzerland), for a further year and requested him to report to the Commission, at its forty-eighth session. The Economic and Social Council, in its decision 1991/253 approved this decision. The Commission will have before it the report of the Special Rapporteur (E/CN.4/1991/28);

(d) <u>Situation of human rights in Iraq</u>. In its resolution 1991/74, the Commission requested its Chairman, after consultations with the Bureau, to appoint an individual of recognized international standing in the field of human rights as special rapporteur of the Commission whose mandate would be to make a thorough study of the violations of human rights by the Government of Iraq and to submit an interim report thereon to the General Assembly at its forty-sixth session and a report to the Commission at its forty-eighth session. The Economic and Social Council, in its decision 1991/256 approved the Commission's requests. On 25 June 1991, the Chairman of the Commission appointed Mr. Max van der Stoel (Netherlands) as Special Rapporteur on the situation of human rights in Iraq. The Commission will have before it the report of the Special Rapporteur (E/CN.4/1991/31);

(e) <u>Situation of human rights in El Salvador</u>. In its resolution 1991/75, the Commission decided to extend the mandate of the Special Representative, Mr. José Antonio Pastor Ridruejo (Spain), for a further year and to consider at its forty-eighth session the situation of human rights in El Salvador and the mandate of the Special Representative, taking into account developments of the human rights situation in that country. The Economic and Social Council, in its decision 1991/257 endorsed these decisions. The Commission will have before it the report of the Special Representative (E/CN.4/1991/32);

(f) <u>Situation of human rights in Albania</u>. In its resolution 1991/76, the Commission requested the Secretary-General to bring the resolution to the attention of the Government of Albania and to invite it to provide information regarding its implementation; the Commission also decided to continue its consideration of the situation of human rights in Albania at its forty-eighth session. The Commission will have before it the report of the Secretary-General (E/CN.4/1991/35);

(g) <u>Situation of human rights in Afghanistan</u>. In its resolution 1991/78, the Commission decided to extend the mandate of the Special Rapporteur, Mr. Felix Ermacora (Austria), for one year and requested him to report to

0028

the General Assembly at its forty-sixth session and to the Commission at its forty-eighth session. The Economic and Social Council, in its decision 1991/259, approved the Commission's decision. The Commission will have before it the report of the Special Rapporteur (E/CN.4/1991/33);

(h) Situation of human rights in the Islamic Republic of Iran. In its resolution 1991/82, the Commission requested the Special Representative, Mr. Reynaldo Galindo Pohl (El Salvador), to maintain his contacts and cooperation with the Government of the Islamic Republic of Iran and to submit a report to be considered by the Commission at its forty-eighth session. The Economic and Social Council, in its decision 1991/261, approved the Commission's requests. The Commission will have before it the report of the Special Representative (E/CN.4/1991/34 and Add.1);

Cooperation with representatives of United Nations human rights bodies

107. In its resolution 1991/70, the Commission invited the Secretary-General to submit a report on alleged reprisals against witnesses or victims of human rights violations and decided to consider the question again at its forty-eighth session. The Commission will have before it the report of the Secretary-General (E/CN.4/1991/29);

Summary or arbitrary executions

108. At its forty-seventh session, the Commission adopted resolution 1991/71, in which it requested the Special Rapporteur, Mr. S. Amos Wako (Kenya), to continue to examine situations of summary and arbitrary executions and to report to the Commission at its forty-eighth session. At its present session the Commission will have before it the report of the Special Rapporteur (E/CN.4/1991/30 and Add.1).

Responsibility for violations of human rights and fundamental freedoms

109. In its resolution 1991/72, the Commission invited the competent United Nations bodies to consider the question of State responsibility for violations of international obligations in the field of human rights and fundamental freedoms and decided to consider the question again at its forty-eighth session.

Human rights and mass exoduses

110. At its forty-seventh session, the Commission adopted resolution 1991/73 in which the Commission, urged again the Secretary-General to allocate the necessary resources to consolidate and strengthen the system for undertaking early warning activities in the humanitarian area. At its meeting in April 1991, the Administrative Committee on Coordination (ACC) decided to establish an ad hoc working group on early warning, which was mandated to develop an effective early warning system relating to possible flows of refugees and displaced persons. This working group is composed of representatives of relevant specialized agencies and United Nations offices, including the Centre for Human Rights. It will report to the ACC at its second regular session in 1992.

0029

Action of the Sub-Commission at its forty-third session

111. At its forty-third session, the Sub-Commission adopted resolution 1991/9, entitled "Situation of human rights in the Islamic Republic of Iran", in which it called upon the Commission, at its forty-eighth session, to extend the mandate of the Special Representative and the monitoring of the situation of human rights in the Islamic Republic of Iran.

112. At the same session, the Sub-Commission adopted resolution 1991/10, entitled "Situation in Tibet", in which it requested the Secretary-General to transmit to the Commission information on the situation in Tibet provided by the Government of China and by other reliable sources. At the present session the Commission will have before it a note by the Secretary-General transmitting the requested information.

113. Attention is also drawn to Sub-Commission decision 1991/108, entitled "Appeal concerning the civilian population in Iraq".

114. In the framework of the present item, the attention of the Commission is also drawn to the following resolutions adopted by the Sub-Commission, at its forty-third session: 1991/4 "Situation in South Africa", 1991/5 "Situation of human rights in Guatemala", 1991/6 "Situation in the Palestinian and other Arab territories occupied by Israel", 1991/7 "Situation of human rights in Kuwait", 1991/8 "Situation in Cambodia", 1991/11 "Situation of human rights in El Salvador" and 1991/13 "Situation of human rights in Iraq".

Documentation

115. Pursuant to its own resolutions, adopted at the forty-seventh session, as well as, in some instances, resolutions of the General Assembly, the Economic and Social Council and the Sub-Commission on Prevention of Discrimination and Protection of Minorities, the Commission will have before it the following documentation:

(a) Report of the Secretary-General on the human rights situation in Cyprus (decision 1991/106), (E/CN.4/1992/25);

(b) Report of the Special Rapporteur on the situation of human rights in Kuwait under Iraqi occupation (resolution 1991/67, para.9), (E/CN.4/1992/26);

(c) Report of the Special Representative on the situation of human rights in Cuba (resolution 1991/68, para. 6), (E/CN.4/1992/27);

(d) Report of the Special Rapporteur on the human rights situation in Romania (resolution 1991/69, para. 6), (E/CN.4/1992/28);

(e) Report of the Secretary-General on reprisals against witnesses or victims of human rights violations (resolution 1991/70, para. 5), (E/CN.4/1991/29);

(f) Report of the Special Rapporteur on summary or arbitrary executions (resolution 1991/71, para. 4), (E/CN.4/1992/30 and Add.1);

0030

(g) Report of the Special Rapporteur on the situation of human rights in Iraq (resolution 1991/74, para. 5), (E/CN.4/1992/31);

(h) Report of the Special Representative on the situation of human rights in El Salvador (resolution 1991/75, para. 13), (E/CN.4/1991/32);

(i) Report of the Special Rapporteur on the situation of human rights in Afghanistan (resolution 1991/78, para. 14), (E/CN.4/1992/33);

(j) Report of the Special Representative on the situation of human rights in the Islamic Republic of Iran (resolution 1991/82, para. 8), (E/CN.4/1992/34 and Add.1);

(k) Report of the Secretary-General on the human rights situation in Albania (resolution 1991/76, para. 4 (b)), (E/CN.4/1992/35);

(1) Report of the Secretary-General on the human rights situation in southern Lebanon (resolution 1991/66, para. 5 (b)), (E/CN.4/1992/36);

(m) Note by the Secretary-General on the situation in Tibet (pursuant to Sub-Commission resolution 1991/10, para. 2), (E/CN.4/1992/37).

Item 13. _Measures to improve the situation and ensure the human rights and dignity of all migrant workers_

116. Questions concerning the human rights of migrant workers have been the subject of attention at several sessions of the Commission. In its resolution 34/172 of 17 December 1979, the General Assembly decided to create at its thirty-fifth session a working group open to all member States to elaborate an international convention on the protection of the rights of all migrant workers and their families. Accordingly, at its thirty-fifth session, the General Assembly established an open-ended working group on this subject, whose mandate has since been renewed regularly.

117. The Working Group completed its task in June 1990 and transmitted the draft convention to the General Assembly for action in accordance with General Assembly resolution 44/155. The General Assembly, in resolution 45/158 of 18 December 1990, adopted the International Convention on the Protection of the Rights of All Migrant Workers and Members of Their Families.

118. At its forty-seventh session, in resolution 1991/60, the Commission requested the Secretary-General to report on the status of the Convention to the Commission at its forty-eighth session.

119. At its present session, the Commission will have before it the report of the Secretary-General on the status of the Convention (E/CN.4/1992/38).

Item 14. _Implementation of the Programme of Action for the Second Decade to Combat Racism and Racial Discrimination_

120. In resolution 1991/11, adopted at its forty-seventh session, the Commission requested the Secretary-General to continue to inform the

0031

Commission of the measures taken, pursuant to General Assembly resolution 42/47 of 30 November 1987, 44/52 of 8 December 1989 and 45/105 of 14 December 1990, to ensure that the necessary and additional resources are included in the programme budget for the biennium 1992-1993 to provide for the implementation of the activities of the Second Decade to Combat Racism and Racial Discrimination; to inform the Commission annually of the progress made in carrying out the plan of activities for 1992-1993 so that the Commission can make its contribution thereto; and to organize in 1991 a meeting of representatives of national institutions and organizations promoting tolerance and harmony and combating racism and racial discrimination with a view to exchanging experience on the promotion of such objectives. The Economic and Social Council, in its decision 1991/234, approved the latter request of the Commission.

121. Pursuant to Commission resolution 1991/11, the Secretary-General organized a meeting of representatives of national institutions and organizations, which took place from 7 to 9 October 1991, in Paris.

122. At its first regular session of 1991, the Economic and Social Council adopted resolution 1991/2 on the subject, in which it requested the Secretary-General to continue with the implementation of the activities for the period 1990-1993 and further requested him to continue to accord the highest priority to measures to combat apartheid. The Council also requested the Secretary-General, in his reports, to continue to pay special attention to the situation of migrant workers and their families.

123. At its present session, the Commission will have before it:

(a) The report of the Secretary-General on the implementation of the Programme of Action for the Second Decade to Combat Racism and Racial Discrimination (E/CN.4/1992/39);

(b) The annual report on racial discrimination submitted by the International Labour Organisation (E/CN.4/1992/40);

(c) The annual report on racial discrimination submitted by the United Nations Educational, Scientific and Cultural Organization (E/CN.4/1992/41);

(d) The report of the Meeting of Experts held at Nuuk, Greenland (E/CN.4/1992/42 and Add.1);

(e) The report of the Workshop on National Institutions (E/CN.4/1992/43).

Item 15. Status of the International Covenants on Human Rights

124. In its resolution 1991/16, the Commission requested the Secretary-General to submit to it, at its forty-eighth session, a report on the status of the International Covenant on Economic, Social and Cultural Rights, the International Covenant on Civil and Political Rights and the Optional Protocols to the International Covenant on Civil and Political Rights, including all reservations and declarations, and to include in that report information on the work of the Economic and Social Council and the Committee

0032

on Economic, Social and Cultural Rights. Accordingly, the Commission will have before it information on the status of the International Covenants on Human Rights and the work of the Council and the Committee on Economic, Social and Cultural Rights (A/46/   ), as well as the reservations, declarations, notifications and objections relating to the International Covenant on Economic, Social and Cultural Rights (E/C.12/1988/1) and the International Covenant on Civil and Political Rights and the Optional Protocol thereto (CCPR/C/2/Rev.2).

Item 16. Effective functioning of bodies established pursuant to United Nations human rights instruments

125. This item is included in the provisional agenda of the Commission pursuant to its resolution 1991/20, entitled "Effective functioning of bodies established pursuant to United Nations human rights instruments".

126. In resolution 1991/20, adopted at the forty-seventh session, the Commission requested the Secretary-General to report to the current session of the Commission on the comments of treaty bodies other than the Human Rights Committee on the study of possible long-term approaches to enhancing the effective operation of existing and prospective bodies established under United Nations human rights instruments; requested the Secretary-General to give consideration to the proposal endorsed by the second and third meetings of persons chairing the human rights treaty bodies and by the Committee on Economic, Social and Cultural Rights, to establish a committee resource room for the purpose of gathering and facilitating access to the various sources of information that were indispensable for the effective functioning of various treaty bodies; requested the General Assembly to mandate the Secretary-General to take the appropriate steps in order to finance the meetings of persons chairing the human rights treaty bodies from the available resources of the regular budget of the United Nations, when necessary, with the proviso that reimbursement should eventually be made in every instance from the contributions of States parties to those conventions or from other appropriate sources; requested the Secretary-General to submit to the General Assembly at its forty-sixth session a report examining the financial, legal and other implications of providing full funding for the operation of all human rights treaty bodies; and requested the Secretary-General to prepare an inventory of all international human rights standard-setting activities in order to facilitate better informed decision-making.

127. At its forty-eighth session the Commission will have before it the report of the Secretary-General pursuant to Commission resolution 1991/20 (E/CN.4/1992/44).

Item 17. Report of the Sub-Commission on Prevention of Discrimination and Protection of Minorities on its forty-third session

128. The report of the Sub-Commission is considered annually by the Commission. The report of the Sub-Commission on its forty-third session is contained in document E/CN.4/1992/2-E/CN.4/Sub.2/1991/65.

129. At its forty-third session, the Sub-Commission adopted 39 resolutions and 19 decisions, which are reproduced in the report.

0033

Draft resolutions and decisions for action by the Commission on Human Rights

130. Chapter I, sections A and B, of the report of the Sub-Commission contains 10 draft resolutions and 15 draft decisions proposed to the Commission for action. They are as follows:

Draft resolutions

I. Adverse consequences for the enjoyment of human rights of political, military, economic and other forms of assistance given to the racist regime of South Africa

II. The right to a fair trial

III. Habeas corpus

IV. Human rights and disability

V. Human rights and youth

VI. Protection of minorities

VII. Independence and impartiality of the judiciary, jurors and assessors and the independence of lawyers

VIII. Fraudulent enrichment of top State officials prejudicial to the public interest

IX. Draft programme of action for the prevention of traffic in persons and the exploitation of the prostitution of others

X. Question of the Palestinian and other Arab territories occupied by Israel

Draft decisions

1. Question of human rights and states of emergency

2. Possible ways and means of facilitating the peaceful and constructive solution of problems involving minorities

3. Traditional practices affecting the health of women and children

4. Human rights and the environment

5. The right to restitution, compensation and rehabilitation for victims of gross violations of human rights and fundamental freedoms

6. Realization of economic, social and cultural rights

7. Draft universal declaration of indigenous rights

8. Economic and social relations between indigenous peoples and States

0034

9.   Ownership and control of the cultural property of indigenous peoples

10. Working Group on Contemporary Forms of Slavery

11. Study on problems and causes of discrimination against HIV-infected
     people or people with AIDS

12. Study on treaties, agreements and other constructive arrangements between
     States and indigenous populations

13. International Year for the World's Indigenous Peoples

14. Working Group on the methods of work of the Sub-Commission

15. The right to freedom of opinion and expression

Resolutions and decisions of the Sub-Commission drawn to the attention
of the Commission on Human Rights

131. Chapter I, section C, of the Sub-Commission's report, lists the
resolutions and decisions of the Sub-Commission which are drawn to the
Commission's attention for its consideration or action.

Report of the Chairman of the Sub-Commission

132. In its resolution 1991/56, the Commission called upon the Sub-Commission,
in the fulfilment of its functions and duties, to be guided by the relevant
resolutions of the Commission and the Economic and Social Council. The
Commission reaffirmed that the Sub-Commission could best assist the Commission
by providing it with recommendations based on the different views and
perspectives of independent experts, which should be appropriately reflected
in the Sub-Commission's report as well as in the expert studies carried out
under its auspices. Further, the Commission requested the Chairman of the
Sub-Commission to report to the Commission on the implementation of the
guidelines contained in Commission resolution 1991/56.

133. In the same resolution, the Commission invited its Chairman,
Mr. Bernales Ballesteros, to inform the Sub-Commission on the debate at the
forty-seventh session of the Commission under this item. The Chairman of
the Commission addressed the forty-third session of the Sub-Commission, at
its 14th meeting, on 15 August 1990 (see E/CN.4/Sub.2/1991/SR.14).

134. At the present session, the Commission will have before it under this
item the following documents:

     (a) Report of the Sub-Commission on its forty-third session
(E/CN.4/1992/2-E/CN.4/Sub.2/1991/65);

     (b) Report of the Secretary-General containing an analytical summary of
replies concerning the draft programme of action for prevention of sale
of children, child prostitution and child pornography and the draft programme
of action for the elimination of the exploitation of child labour
(E/CN.4/1992/45);

0035

(c) Report of the Chairman of the Sub-Commission pursuant to Commission resolution 1991/56 (E/CN.4/1992/46);

(d) Note by the Secretary-General transmitting the report of the Working Group on a draft declaration on the right of everyone to leave any country, including his own, and to return to his country (E/CN.4/1992/47).

Item 18. Rights of persons belonging to national, ethnic, religious and linguistic minorities

135. At its thirty-fourth session, the Commission established an informal open-ended working group to consider questions related to the drafting of a declaration on the rights of members of minority groups, on the basis of a text proposed by Yugoslavia (E/CN.4/L.1367) which was intended to serve as a starting-point for an exchange of views. The Commission has continued to examine this question at each of its subsequent sessions, at which a sessional open-ended working group has been established by the Commission to consider the matter.

136. At its forty-seventh session, in resolution 1991/61, the Commission decided to consider this question again at its forty-eighth session. In the same resolution, the Commission recommended to the Economic and Social Council that it authorize an open-ended working group of the Commission to meet for 20 fully-serviced meetings in an inter-sessional session at the beginning of December 1991 to complete its second reading of the draft declaration, with a view to submitting the text to the Commission at its forty-eighth session. The Council, in resolution 1991/30, endorsed this request.

137. The Sub-Commission also examined the question, at its thirty-second, thirty-third, thirty-seventh, thirty-eighth, fortieth and forty-first sessions (Sub-Commission decisions 1 (XXXII), 1 (XXXIII) and 1984/101 and resolutions 1985/6, 1988/36 and 1989/44).

138. At its fortieth session, the Sub-Commission adopted resolution 1988/36, in which it invited Mrs. Claire Palley to prepare a working paper on possible ways and means to facilitate the peaceful and constructive resolution of situations involving racial, national, religious and linguistic minorities. At its forty-first session, the Sub-Commission adopted resolution 1989/44, in which it decided to entrust Mr. Asbjørn Eide with the preparation of a further report on national experience in facilitating the peaceful and constructive solution of problems involving minorities.

139. At its forty-third session, having considered the preliminary report submitted by Mr. Eide (E/CN.4/Sub.2/1991/43), the Sub-Commission adopted resolution 1991/22, in which it requested the Special Rapporteur to submit an updated report to the Sub-Commission at its forty-fourth session and his final report at its forty-fifth session. The Sub-Commission also requested the Secretary-General to prepare, with the cooperation of the Special Rapporteur, the technical meeting of experts on minorities provided for in Commission resolution 1991/62, with a view to it taking place in 1992.

140. At its forty-eighth session, the Commission will have before it the report of the Working Group established under Economic and Social Council resolution 1991/30 (E/CN.4/1992/48), and draft resolution VI contained in chapter I, section A, of the report of the Sub-Commission (E/CN.4/1992/2-E/CN.4/Sub.2/1991/65).

Item 19. Advisory services in the field of human rights

141. At its forty-seventh session, in resolution 1991/49, the Commission requested the Secretary-General to continue to elaborate comprehensive programmes of advisory services and technical cooperation financed under the Voluntary Fund for Technical Cooperation in the Field of Human Rights and to report annually to the Commission on the operation and administration of the Fund.

142. In resolution 1991/50, the Commission requested the Secretary-General to report to the Commission, at its forty-seventh session, on the progress made in the implementation of the programme of advisory services in the field of human rights.

143. In resolution 1991/77, the Commission requested its Chairman to appoint an independent Expert to examine the developments in the human rights situation in Haiti and report to the Commission at its forty-eighth session. The Economic and Social Council, in decision 1991/258 approved the Commission's request. On 3 May 1991, the Chairman appointed Mr. Bruni Celli (Venezuela) as Special Rapporteur of the Commission.

144. In resolution 1991/80, the Commission requested the Secretary-General to extend the mandate of the Expert, Mr. Fernando Volio Jiménez, responsible for cooperating with the Government of Equatorial Guinea in the full implementation of the Plan of Action proposed by the United Nations and accepted by the Government. It requested the Expert to report to the Commission at its forty-eighth session. The Economic and Social Council, in decision 1991/260, approved the Commission's request to the Secretary-General.

145. At its present session, the Commission, under this item, will have before it the following documents:

     (a) The report of the Secretary-General on advisory services and technical cooperation in the field of human rights, including the operation and administration of the Voluntary Fund (E/CN.4/1992/49);

     (b) The report of the independent Expert on the situation of human rights in Haiti (E/CN.4/1992/50);

     (c) The report of the Expert on Equatorial Guinea (E/CN.4/1992/51).

Item 20. Implementation of the Declaration on the Elimination of All Forms of Intolerance and of Discrimination Based on Religion or Belief

146. After the proclamation by the General Assembly in 1981 of the Declaration on the Elimination of All Forms of Intolerance and of Discrimination Based on Religion or Belief (resolution 36/55), the consideration of measures to

0037

implement the Declaration was taken up, at the request of the Assembly, by the Commission and the Sub-Commission on Prevention of Discrimination and Protection of Minorities.

147. At its forty-second session, in its resolution 1986/20, the Commission decided to appoint a special rapporteur to examine incidents and governmental actions which were inconsistent with the provisions of the Declaration on the Elimination of All Forms of Intolerance and of Discrimination Based on Religion or Belief. Mr. Angelo Vidal D'Almeida Ribeiro (Portugal) was appointed Special Rapporteur; his mandate was extended by the Commission at subsequent sessions and most recently, in resolution 1990/27, for two years.

148. At its forty-seventh session, the Commission adopted resolution 1991/48, in which it invited the Special Rapporteur, in carrying out his mandate, to continue to bear in mind the need to be able to respond effectively to credible and reliable information that came before him and to seek the views and comments of the Government concerned on any information which he intended to include in his report.

149. At its present session, the Commission will have before it the report of the Special Rapporteur (E/CN.4/1992/52).

Item 21. Drafting of a declaration on the right and responsibility of individuals, groups and organs of society to promote and protect universally recognized human rights and fundamental freedoms

150. This item was included in the agenda of the forty-eighth session in accordance with Commission resolution 1991/63, adopted at its forty-seventh session. In the same resolution, the Commission decided to continue at its forty-eighth session its work on the elaboration of the draft declaration. The Commission recommended to the Economic and Social Council that it authorize an open-ended working group to meet for a period of two weeks prior to the forty-eighth session of the Commission. The Council, in its resolution 1991/31, gave its authorization.

151. At its forty-eighth session, the Commission will have before it the report of the working group (E/CN.4/1992/53), scheduled to meet from 13 to 24 January 1991.

Item 22. Rights of the Child, including:

(a) Status of the Convention on the Rights of the Child;

(b) Report of the Special Rapporteur on the sale of children;

(c) Programme of action for the elimination of the exploitation of child labour;

(d) Draft programme of action for the prevention of the sale of children, child prostitution and child pornography.

152. This item was included in the agenda of the forty-eighth session in accordance with Commission resolutions 1991/52, 1991/53, 1991/54 and 1991/55.

Sub-item (a) Status of the Convention on the Rights of the Child

153. At its forty-seventh session, the Commission adopted resolution 1991/52, in which it requested the Secretary-General to submit a report on the status of the Convention on the Rights of the Child to the Commission at its forty-eighth session.

154. At the present session, the Commission will have before it the report of the Secretary-General on the status of the Convention on the Rights of the Child (E/CN.4/1992/54).

Sub-item (b) Report of the Special Rapporteur on the sale of children

155. At its forty-sixth session, the Commission adopted resolution 1990/68, in which it decided to appoint a Special Rapporteur to consider matters relating to the sale of children, child prostitution and child pornography, including the problem of the adoption of children for commercial purposes. The Economic and Social Council, in decision 1990/240, requested the Chairman of the Commission to appoint, for a period of two years, a Special Rapporteur on the subject. On 10 September 1990, the Chairman of the Commission appointed Mr. Vitit Muntarbhorn (Thailand) as Special Rapporteur of the Commission on the sale of children.

156. The Commission at its forty-seventh session adopted resolution 1991/53, in which it requested the Special Rapporteur to continue to carry out his work in the light of the mandate as enunciated in Commission resolution 1990/68. It also requested the Special Rapporteur to report on his activities to the Commission at its forty-eighth session.

157. At its present session, the Commission will have before it the report of the Special Rapporteur (E/CN.4/1992/55 and Add.1).

Sub-item (c) Programme of action for the elimination of the exploitation of
              child labour

158. At its forty-seventh session, the Commission adopted resolution 1991/55, in which it endorsed the views expressed by the Sub-Commission on the need to adopt a concerted programme of action to combat the exploitation of child labour. The Commission further decided to transmit to Governments, the specialized agencies and intergovernmental and non-governmental organizations for their comments the programme of action for the elimination of the exploitation of child labour and requested the Secretary-General to submit an analytical summary of the replies received to the Commission at its forty-eighth session.

159. At its present session, the Commission will have before it the report of the Secretary-General containing an analytical summary of replies concerning the draft programme of action (E/CN.4/1992/45).

0039

Sub-item (d) Draft programme of action for the prevention of the sale of
children, child prostitution and child pornography

160. At its forty-seventh session, the Commission adopted resolution 1991/54,
in which it decided to refer to the Sub-Commission the draft programme of
action so that it might make the necessary amendments in the light of
the opinions received from Governments, the specialized agencies and
intergovernmental and non-governmental organizations. The Commission further
requested the Sub-Commission, in its reformulation of the programme of action,
fully to reflect the 10-point programme of the World Declaration on the
Survival, Protection and Development of Children adopted by the World Summit
for Children on 30 September 1990, and requested the Sub-Commission to give
the highest priority to the reformulation of the programme of action so that
it might be adopted by the Commission at its forty-eighth session.

Item 23. Election of members of the Sub-Commission on Prevention of
Discrimination and Protection of Minorities

161. In accordance with Economic and Social Council resolutions 1334 (XLIV)
of 31 May 1968 and 1986/35 of 23 May 1986 and decisions 1978/21 of 5 May 1978
and 1987/102 of 6 February 1987, the Commission on Human Rights, at its
forty-fourth session in 1988, elected 26 members of the Sub-Commission, as
well as their alternates, from nominations of experts made by States Members
of the United Nations on the following basis: (a) seven members from African
States; (b) five members from Asian States; (c) three members from Eastern
European States; (d) five members from Latin American States; (e) six members
from Western European and other States.

162. Pursuant to the procedure established in Council resolution 1986/35,
members of the Sub-Commission were to be elected for a term of four years and
a half of its membership and the corresponding alternates, if any, were to be
elected every two years. The Chairman of the forty-fourth session of the
Commission on Human Rights drew lots to select the members and, as applicable,
their corresponding alternates whose term of office should expire after
two years in accordance with the following pattern: three members from
African States; three members from Asian States; one member from Eastern
European States; three members from Latin American States; and three members
from Western European and other States.

163. As the term of office of half of the membership of the Sub-Commission has
expired, the Commission on Human Rights is called upon to elect Sub-Commission
members and alternates in accordance with the following pattern: three
members from African States; three members from Asian States; one member from
Eastern European States; three members from Latin American States; and three
members from Western European and other States.

164. At its forty-eighth session, the Commission will have before it a note by
the Secretary-General (E/CN.4/1992/56 and Add.   ) containing the names and
biographical data of the candidates nominated for election by member States.

165. In its resolution 1991/56, the Commission on Human Rights called upon
States to nominate as members and alternates persons meeting the criteria of
independent experts who should discharge in that capacity their functions as

0040

members of the Sub-Commission. The Sub-Commission, in its resolution 1987/32, recommended that the Commission on Human Rights try and prevail upon all Governments to nominate more women for election to the Sub-Commission.

166. The attention of the Commission is further drawn to Economic and Social Council resolution 1983/32, by which the Council decided that, notwithstanding rule 13, paragraph 2, of the rules of procedure of the functional commissions of the Council, certain rules should henceforth apply to the Sub-Commission. Under these rules, the nomination of a candidate for membership of the Sub-Commission may be accompanied by a nomination of an expert of the same nationality to be elected simultaneously with the candidate for membership and who may serve temporarily as an alternate if the member is unable to attend, the qualifications for alternates are to be the same as for members and no person may serve as an alternate for a member except the expert so elected.

Item 24. World Conference on Human Rights

167. The item was included in the provisional agenda of the forty-eighth session of the Commission in accordance with Commission resolution 1991/30, in which it also requested the Secretary-General to report on progress in the preparations for the World Conference.

168. At its present session, the Commission will have before it a note by the Secretary-General on progress in the preparations for the World Conference on Human Rights (E/CN.4/1991/57).

Item 25. Draft provisional agenda for the forty-ninth session of the Commission

169. Rule 9 of the rules of procedure provides that, at each session of the Commission, the Secretary-General shall submit a draft provisional agenda for the Commission's subsequent session, indicating in respect of each agenda item the documents to be submitted under that item and the legislative authority for their preparation, in order to enable the Commission to consider the documents from the point of view of their contribution to its work and of their urgency and relevance in the light of the current situation.

170. The Commission will have before it, before the conclusion of the forty-eighth session, a note for its consideration containing a draft provisional agenda for its forty-ninth session, together with information concerning the corresponding documentation (E/CN.4/1992/L.1).

Item 26. Report to the Economic and Social Council on the forty-eighth session of the Commission

171. Rule 37 of the rules of procedure provides that the Commission shall submit to the Council a report, which shall normally not exceed 32 pages, on the work of each session containing a concise summary of recommendations and a statement of issues requiring action by the Council. It shall as far as practicable frame its recommendations and resolutions in the form of drafts for approval by the Council.

0041

발 신 전 보

	분류번호	보존기간

번   호 : WGV-0056   920111 1034 FO 종별 : 암호송신

수   신 : 주   제네바   대사. 총영사

발   신 : 장   관 (연이)

제   목 : 제48차 유엔 인권위 대표단 구성

　　　92.1.27-3.6간 귀지에서 개최되는 표제회의 아국대표단 구성에

관한 귀견 보고바람. 끝.

　　　　　　　　　　　　　　　　　　（국제기구국장　문동석）

									보안통제	
앙고재	92년 1월 10일	유엔 2과	기안자 성명 76정보	과장	심의관	국장		차관	장관	외신과통제

0042

외 무 부

종 별 :

번 호 : GVW-0076   일 시 : 92 0114 1030

수 신 : 장관(연이, 법무부)

발 신 : 주 제네바 대사

제 목 : 48차 인권위 대비

1. 유엔 인권 사무국은 표제회의와 관련하여 1985.1.1 이래 비상 사태(STATE OF EMERGENCY)를 선포, 연장 또는 종료한 국가 리스트를 작성하고 있는바, 동 기록중 아국관련 사항이 아래와 같이 포함되어있음.

- 아래 -

- 내용: 서울에서 학생과 경찰간 충돌로 인해 발생한 가두 소요와 관련 비상조치(EMERGENCY MEASURES)가 취해졌음.

- 소스: 언론보도인바, 보다 정확한 정보가 (한국)정부측으로부터 제시되기를 기대함.

2. 상기 내용은 '비상사태' 대신 '비상조치'라는 애매한 표현을 사용하고 있고, 시기가 불명하며, 소스도 언론보도인바, 그간 85.1.1 이래 여사한 비상사태가 선포된적이 없었던 것으로 알고있던 당관의 인식과 상위하니, 사실여부를 확인, 통보 바람. 사실이 아닐 경우 인권 사무국 관계관을 접촉, 시정조치토록 할것임. 끝

(대사 박수길-국장)

국기국   1차보   법무부

관리 번호 92-37

원 본

외 무 부

종 별 : 지급

번 호 : GVW-0083

일 시 : 92 0114 1830

수 신 : 장관(연이)

발 신 : 주 제네바 대사

제 목 : 인권위 대표단 구성

대: WGV-0056

대호 표제회의 대표단 구성에 대한 당관 의견을 아래 보고함.

1. 수석대표: 박수길대사

2. 대표: 당관 이성주 참사관, 위성락 1 등 서기관

본부직원

관계부처 직원. 끝

(대사 박수길-국장)

예고 92.6.30 까지

2 6 30

국기국

PAGE 1

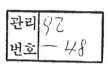

외   무   부

110-760 서울 종로구 세종로 77번지   /   (02) 723-8934   /   (02) 723-3505

문서번호 연이 20314-

시행일자 1992.1.16.

(경유)

수신 법무부장관

참조 법무실장

취급		장 관	
보존			
국 장	전결		
심의관			
과 장			
기안	김종훈		협조

제목 제48차 인권위원회 대책

1. 1992.1.27-3.6간 제네바에서 개최예정인 제48차 유엔 인권위원회(Commission
    on Human Rights) 회의에 당부는 정부옵서버 대표단을 파견할 예정인바,
    동 대표단에 포함될 귀부 인권업무 담당직원을 가급적 조속히 당부로 추천하여
    주시기 바랍니다.

2. 금번 회의에서 아국 인권상황이 거론될 가능성에 대비, 아래사항에 대한 귀부
    의견을 가능한 상세히 작성, 92.1.24까지 회보하여 주시기 바랍니다.

                            - 아   래 -

    가. 아국의 전반적 인권상황 관련 정부입장

    나. 간첩죄 및 국가보안법 위반 장기수 현황 및 고령.장기수형자 석방을
        요청하는 민간인권단체 주장에 대한 정부입장

    다. 남북합의서 서명이후 국가보안법등 관련 국내입법의 개정 또는 운용
        문제에 대한 정부입장

    라. 기타 참고자료. 끝.

0045

주 제 네 바 대 표 부

제네(정) 2031-58   1992. 1. 18

수신 : 장관

참조 : 국제기구국장

제목 : 48차 유엔인권위 회의

            연 : 제네(정) 2031-30

            92.1.27-3.6간 당지에서 개최될 예정인 표제 회의 관련 문서를 별첨

송부합니다.

            첨부 : 1. E/CN.4/1992/10,24,62

                    2. E/CN.4/1992/1/Add.1/Corr.1   끝.

주 제 네 바 대 사

선결			결재(공담)		
접수일시 1992.1.21	번호				
처리과	04038				

0046

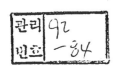

신뢰받는 정부되고 받쳐주는 국민되자

주 코 스 타 리 카 대 사 관

코스타(정) 20400-5   1992. 1. 21
수 신 장 관
참 조 국제기구국장, 미주국장
제 목 주재국정부, 고문등 방지 국제 협약에 관한 의정서안 지지 요청

　　　연 : COW- 0023 (92.1.22)

　　　연호 표제 관련 공한 사본을 별첨 송부합니다.

첨 부 동 공한 사본 1부. 끝.

예고 : 92.12.31까지

주 코 스 타 리 카 대

0047

The Ministry of Foreign Affairs and Religion of the Republic of Costa Rica presents its compliments to the Honourable Embassy of the Republic of Korea on the occasion of bringing to the attention of that distinguished Mission the decision of the Government of Costa Rica to present the "Facultative Protocol Project" to the International Convention against Torture and other Cruel, Inhuman or Degrading Treatment or Punishment, which will be discussed in the Agenda of the 48th Period of Sessions of the Human Rights Commission of the United Nations, to be held from January 28th to March 8, 1992 in Geneva, Switzerland.

As the Government of Costa Rica requests the valuable support of the Honourable Government of the Republic of Korea, it allows itself the opportunity to emphasize the importance of protecting human dignity and the proscription of all forms of torture, so that it has promoted initiatives tending to guarantee the integrity of human beings and their well-being, in a regional and a world-wide scope, as it is presented in the annexed document "A major efficacy in the fight against Torture: The Project of a Facultative Protocol to the Convention."

The Facultative Protocol Project proposed by Costa Rica, is based on the principle of cooperation, and basically proposes the creation of a Sub-Committee for the prevention of torture and of cruel, inhuman or degrading treatments; this Sub-Committee will be in charge of organizing missions in the territories of State Members with the purpose of visiting the imprisonment sites. The execution of the missions will be in charge of a Delegation composed of members of the Sub-Committee and experts. Upon conclusion of the mission, the Sub-Committee will prepare a report based on the conclusions of the delegation, including the necessary recommendations to the State Member concerned. This report, as well as the consultations, will be treated as confidential.

The objective of the Sub-Committee will not be to condemn the States, but under a situation of arrest of an individual, to strengthen the protection measures of the persons deprived of their liberty. Its task is totally preventive.

The Project does not duplicate the duties of the Convention against Torture of the United Nations, nor the European Convention Against Torture, it is a complement of the existing systems. The Project is seeking the establishment of preventive controls which consists in making visits without necessarily existing any suspicion that a determined State is in fact torturing.

0048

Awaiting a favourable response to this proposal, the Ministry of Foreign Affairs and Religion of the Republic of Costa Rica avails this opportunity to reiterate the Honourable Embassy of the Republic of Korea, the assurances of its highest consideration.

San José, January 16, 1992

The Honourable
Embassy of the Republic of Korea
City.-

0049

Solicitud de apoyo del Gobierno de Costa Rica al Gobierno de la República de Corea al Proyecto de Protocolo Facultativo a la Convención Internacional contra la Tortura y otros Tratos o Penas Crueles, Inhumanos o Degradantes en ocasión de ser discutida en la Agenda del 48 Período de Sesiones de la Comisión de Derechos Humanos de Naciones Unidas, a celebrarse del 28 de enero al 8 de marzo del año en curso, en Ginebra, Suiza.

(RESUMEN)

TITULO: "UNA MAYOR EFICACIA EN LA LUCHA CONTRA LA TORTURA: EL PROYECTO DE UN PROTOCOLO FACULTATIVO A LA CONVENCION"

El Proyecto propone la creación de un Subcomité para la prevención de la tortura y de los tratos o penas crueles inhumanos o degradantes encargado de organizar misiones en el territorio de los Estados Partes con el fin de visitar los lugares de detención.

En la Convención contra la Tortura de 1984, artículo 20. Según éste el Comité contra la Tortura está autorizado a llevar a cabo una visita al territorio de un Estado Parte con el consentimiento de este último, en el contexto de una investigación confidencial si existe una información que parezca indicar de forma fundamentada que se practica sistemática la tortura. En este sentido se da un gran paso en la lucha internacional contra la tortura, pero no es propiamente una medida de prevención debido a que es un mecanismo que se activa una vez que se han recibido las noticias de forma fundamentada que la tortura se está aplicando de manera sistemática y la realidad internacional demuestra que cuando sucede una denuncia de este tipo es porque ya han sido muchos los torturados. Es un control "a posteriori" o "post facto".

El Gobierno de Costa Rica, el Comité Suizo contra la Tortura y la Comisión Internacional de Juristas, reunieron en el mes de noviembre de 1990 a un grupo de expertos internacionales y salieron las siguientes ideas para ser incluidas en el Proyecto Facultativo:

-Creación de un subcomité para la prevención de la tortura y de los tratos o penas crueles inhumanos y degradantes. Una vez que diez Estados hayan ratificado el protocolo, el Comité contra la Tortura establecerá un subcomité y elegirá sus miembros. Los miembros del Subcomité ejercerán sus funciones a título personal y serán escogidos entre personas de gran autoridad moral, con reconocida competencia en la administración penitenciaria o policial, o en las especialidades médicas relevantes para el tratamiento de las personas privadas de libertad, o en el campo de la protección internacional de los derechos humanos.

El Subcomité se encargará, por su parte, de organizar misiones en el territorio de los Estados Partes a fin de visitar los lugares de detención. Al ratificar el Protocolo los Estados Partes se comprometerán a permitir tales visitas a cualquier lugar sometido a su jurisdicción donde se encuentre por cualquier causa alguna persona detenida por una autoridad pública, o bajo su instigación o consentimiento expreso o tácito.

El nuevo sistema propuesto por Costa Rica está basado al igual que la Convención Europea en el principio de la cooperación. El objetivo del Subcomité no será condenar a los Estados, sino llegado el momento, tratar de fortalecer la protección de las personas privdas de la libertad.

El Proyecto de Protocolo Facultativo fue presentado por Costa Rica en el 47mo Período de Sesiones de la Comisión de Derechos Humanos (1991) Doc. No. E/C.N. 4/1991/66. Antes de discutirlo en plenario fue presentado a los diferentes grupos regionales que lo acogieron con entusiasmo (grupo europeo occidental y oriental, excepción de la Unión Soviética). Expresaron indiferencia: América Latina, con excepción de Chile, Venezuela, Panamá y Bolivia. Africa y Asia se mostraron poco favorables al mismo, con la excepción de Senegal que lo acogió positivamente.

0050

En sesión plenaria Australia hizo pública su reserva de tipo económico sobre el proyecto. En dicho proyecto de resolución se solicitó que en el 48 período de Sesiones de la Comisión de Derechos Humanos (1992) se reestablezca un grupo de trabajo Ad Hoc para que comience el respetivo análisis del Proyecto de Protocolo Facultativo, contenido en el Doc E/C.N. 4/1991.66.

Conclusión

La única manera de evitar el terrible flagelo que es la tortura es mediante un sistema de visitas a los lugares de detención que es donde es praticada la tortura. De los diferentes sistemas expuestos en este trabajo se ha visto que el más eficaz es sin duda el sitema de visitas que tiene tanto la Cruz Roja Internacional (CICR), como la Convención Europea contra la Tortura, que se basó en parte en las ideas presentadas por Costa Rica en 1990. La modalidad del sistema propuesto por Costa Rica es interesante porque se basa en el principio de cooperación con los Estados y en la confidencialidad. No se trata de un sistema destinado a denunciar a los Gobiernos que practican la tortura, se trata tan sólo de someter a los Estados afetados, recomendaciones específicas sobre cómo evitar tan degradante y nefasta práctica. Sólo si el Estado concernido no sigue las indicaciones del Subcomité, entonces éste sí puede hacer una declaración pública.

El proyecto presentado no duplica las labores de la convención contra la Tortura de Naciones Unidas o la misma Convención Euorpea, se da un complemento entre los sistemas expuestos. El proyecto como tal lo que busca es un control de tipo preventivo debido a que el sistema de visitas se realizará sin que exista ninguna sospecha que un determinado Estado está torturando.

DGPE/SGPM/007/92

El Ministerio de Relaciones
Exteriores y Culto de la República de Costa Rica saluda muy
atentamente a la Honorable Embajada de la República de Corea,
en ocasión de elevar a conocimiento de su distinguida Misión
la decisión del Gobierno de Costa Rica de presentar el
Proyecto de Protocolo Facultativo a la Convención
Internacional contra la Tortura y otros Tratos o Penas
Crueles, Inhumanos o Degradantes, cuya discusión está
incluida en la Agenda del Cuadragésimo Octavo Período de
Sesiones de la Comisión de Derechos Humanos de Naciones
Unidas, a celebrarse del 28 de enero al 8 de marzo del año en
curso, en Ginebra, Suiza.

Al solicitar el valioso apoyo del
Ilustrado Gobierno de la República de Corea, el Gobierno de
Costa Rica se permite destacar la importancia que atribuye a
la protección de la dignidad de la persona y la proscripción
de la tortura, razón por la cual ha promovido iniciativas
tendientes a garantizar la integridad de la persona humana y
su bienestar integral tanto en el ámbito regional como
mundial, como se puede apreciar en el documento anejo "Una
mayor Eficacia en la lucha contra la Tortura: El Proyecto de
un Protocolo Facultativo a la Convención".

El Proyecto de Protocolo Facultativo
propuesto por Costa Rica, basado en el principio de
cooperación, fundamentalmente propone la creación de un
Subcomité para la prevención de la tortura y de los tratos o
penas crueles inhumanos o degradantes, encargado de organizar
misiones en el territorio de los Estados Partes con el fin de
visitar los lugares de detención. La ejecución de las
misiones estará a cargo de una Delegación compuesta de
miembros del Subcomité y expertos. Al término de la misión,
el Subcomité elaborará un informe sobre la base de las
conclusiones de la delegación, informe que transmitirá, con
las recomendaciones que estime necesarias, al Estado Parte de
que se trate. Ese Informe, así como las consultas tendrán
carácter confidencial.

El objetivo del Subcomité no será
condenar a los Estados, sino llegado el momento, tratar de
fortalecer la protección de las personas privadas de
libertad. Su tarea será totalmente preventiva.

0052

-2-

El Proyecto presentado no duplica las labores de la Convención contra la Tortura de Naciones Unidas o la misma Convención Europea, se da un complemento entre los sistemas expuestos. El Proyecto como tal lo que busca es un control de tipo preventivo debido a que el sistema de visitas se realizara sin que exista ninguna sospecha que un determinado Estado está torturando.

En espera de una respuesta favorable a esta gestión, el Ministerio de Relaciones Exteriores y Culto de la República de Costa Rica hace propicia la oportunidad para reiterar a la Honorable Embajada de la República de Corea, las seguridades de su más alta y distinguida consideración.

San José, 16 de enero de 1992

A LA HONORABLE
EMBAJADA DE LA REPUBLICA DE COREA
CIUDAD.-

VM/CBA/gemr

cc: Archivo

Anexo: Lo indicado

0053

법   무   부

인권 20314-/6   503-7045   1992. 1. 22

수신 외무부장관

제목 제48차 유엔 인권위원회

　　1. 연어 20314-90 ('92.1.20)과 관련입니다.

　　2. 당부에서는 제48차 유엔 인권위원회에 참가할 대상자로 당부소속
검사 정기용 (Chung Ki-Yong) 을 추천합니다.　　끝.

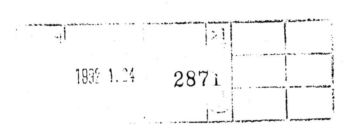

법   무   부   장   관

0054

원 본

외 무 부

종 별 :

번 호 : COW-0023   일 시 : 92 0122 1750

수 신 : 장관(국이,미중)

발 신 : 주 코스타리카 대사

제 목 : 주재국 정부, 고문방지 국제협약에 관한 의정서안 지지요청

1. 주재국 외무성은 공한으로 금년 1.28-3.8 일간 제네바 개최 유엔인권위 제48 차 회기에서 논의될 고문 및 여타 잔인행위 또는 처벌에 대한 국제협약(84.12.10 유엔채택)에 관한 의정서안과 관련하여 아국 정부의 지지를 요청하여 왔음.

2. 주재국은 상기 의정서안을 91 년 인권위 제 47 차 회기에서 "DOC.NO. E/C.N. 4/1991/66"로 제안하였으며, 동 본회의에서 주재국은 베네주엘라 대표를 통해 92 년 제 48 차 회의에서 동 의정서안 분석을 위한 특별 실무진 구성에 관한 결의안(DOC. NO. E/C.N. 4/1991/L.37)을 제안 승인되었음.

3. 동 의정서안 주요요지 아래와 같음

0 고문등 예방을 위한 SUBCOMITTEE (원칙적으로 10-25 명)구성, 동 사절단의고문등 행위 회원국 방문과, 동 관련 회원국에 대한 권고사항 포함 보고서 작성(동 보고서는 원칙적으로 비공개, 관련 회원국이 비협조시 공개)

0 동 SUBCOMITTEE 활동은 기존 유엔 및 유럽의 고문등에 대한 협약에 따른 활동 체제와는 중복되지 않도록하며, 이들 체제를 보완하는 성격을 가짐

0 동 SUBCOMITTEE 사절단 방문은 고문등 행위 혐의가 반드시 없는 경우에도가능하므로 예방적 조치 수립을 목적으로 함.

4. 동 공한 사본 23 일 정파편 송부하겠음.

아국정부 입장 회시바람. 끝.

검토필 (1992. 6. 10.)

(대사 김창근-국장)

예고:92.12.31 까지

국기국 안기부	장관	차관	1차보	2차보	미주국	외정실	분석관	청와대

외 무 부

110-760 서울 종로구 세종로 77번지 / (02) 723-8934 / (02) 723-3505

문서번호 연이 20314-

시행일자 1992.1.24.

(경유)

수신 건 의

참조

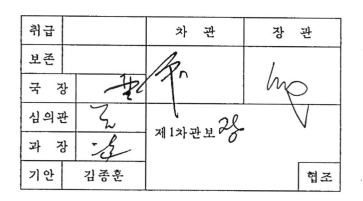

취급		차 관	장 관
보존			
국 장		제1차관보	
심의관			
과 장			
기안	김종훈		협조

제목 제48차 유엔 인권위원회 대표단 파견

　　　　1992.1.27-3.6간 제네바에서 개최예정인 제48차 유엔 인권위원회 회의에
정부대표 및 특별사절의 임명과 권한에 관한 법률 제3758호에 의거, 아래와 같이
정부 옵서버 대표단을 임명, 파견하고자 하오니 재가하여 주시기 바랍니다.

- 아　　　　　　래 -

1. 회 의 명 : 제48차 유엔 인권위원회

　　　　　　　(Commission on Human Rights, Forty-Eighth Session)

2. 회의기간 및 장소 : 1992.1.27-3.6, 제네바

3. 참가목적

　　○ 인권보장문제에 대한 각국의 입장 및 국제적 동향 파악

　　○ 주요의제에 대한 정부입장 표명

　　○ 일부 인권단체의 아국 인권상황 거론시 이에 대한 적극 대처

/ 계속 /

0056

4. 대 표 단

　　ㅇ　수석대표 : 주제네바 대사　　　　　　박수길

　　ㅇ　대　　표 : 주제네바대표부 참사관　　이성주

　　　　　　　　　국제연합2과장　　　　　　정달호(92.2.18-2.29간 참석)

　　　　　　　　　주제네바대표부 1등서기관　위성락

　　　　　　　　　법무부 인권과 검사　　　　정기용(92.2.16-2.27간 참석)

첨부 : 1. 제48차 유엔 인권위원회 대책(안)

　　　　2. 유엔 인권위원회 개요. 끝.

0057

제48차 유엔인권위원회 대책(안)

1. 기본대책

- 세계인권상황에 대한 각국의 입장 및 국제적 동향파악
- 아국인권상황 거론시 적극 대응
- 아국관련 인권문제, 특히 정신대문제 토의내용 파악 및 필요시 발언
- 아국의 인권위원국 입후보 지지기반 확충을 위하여 회의참가 정부 대표와의 긴밀한 접촉

2. 세부대책

가. 아국인권상황 거론시 대응

1) 민간단체 거론시

- 다수국의 인권상황을 거론하는 가운데 아국인권상황이 포함될 경우 답변권 불행사
- 아국인권문제를 집중거론할 경우, 답변권을 행사하여 오류 지적 및 아국정부 인권보장 노력 설명

2) 북한대표 거론시

- 90.2월이래 북한대표가 아국인권문제를 직접 거론한바가 없이 금차 회의에서 직접 발언할 가능성은 희박함.
- 다만 이인모 사건등 북한 관심사항을 거론할 경우에는 동 내용에 대하여 구체적으로 반박하고, 북한인권문제를 적극 제기함.

0058

나. 정신대문제 토의 대응

　　ㅇ 국제 민간단체인 국제법률가위원회(ICJ) 또는 세계교회협의회(WCC)가
　　　 정신대문제를 거론할 가능성에 대비, 아국정부의 세부입장 준비

다. 인권위원국 입후보 지지기반 확충

　　ㅇ 주요의제 토의참여 및 각국대표와의 긴밀한 접촉을 통하여 아국의
　　　 인권위원국 입후보에 대한 지지기반 확충 노력 전개.　　끝.

0059

인권위원회(Commission on Human Rights) 개요

1. 설립근거

○ 1946년 ECOSOC 결의에 의하여 설치

2. 구 성

○ ECOSOC에서 선출하는 임기 3년의 53개 위원국으로 구성

○ 60여개국 정부 및 1백여개 국제민간인권단체(NGO) 대표가 옵서버로
  회의 참가

3. 회의일정

○ 매년 1-3월중 6주간 일정으로 제네바에서 개최

4. 기능 및 권한

○ 아래사항에 관한 제안, 권고 및 보고서를 ECOSOC에 제출
  - 세계인권상황 검토
  - 고문등 재소자 인권문제 검토
  - 각종 인권협약 평가
  - 아동, 소수민족, 이주노동자등 인권취약계층의 인권보호문제
  - 발전의 권리, 법조인 독립보장문제등 특정 인권분야에 대한 성문화
    작업

0060

5. 아국과의 관계

o 아국은 매년 주제네바대사를 수석대표로 외무부, 법무부 담당관으로 구성된 옵서버 대표단을 파견

o 92.4월 ECOSOC 조직회의에서 있을 인권위원국 선거에 입후보함.

6. 유엔 인권위원회 위원국 현황(92.1월 현재)

지 역	국 가 명
아 시 아 (12개국)	방글라데시, 중국, 사이프러스, 인도, 인니, 이란, 이라크, 일본, 파키스탄, 필리핀, 스리랑카, 시리아
서구 및 기 타 (10개국)	호주, 오지리, 카나다, 프랑스, 독일, 이태리, 화란, 폴루갈, 영국, 미국
중 남 미 (11개국)	알젠틴, 바베이도스, 브라질, 칠레, 콜롬비아, 코스타리카, 쿠바, 멕시코, 페루, 우루과이, 베네주엘라
아프리카 (15개국)	앙골라, 부룬디, 가봉, 감비아, 가나, 케냐, 레소토, 리비아, 마다가스칼, 모리타니아, 나이제리아, 세네갈, 소말리아, 튀니지, 잠비아
동 구 (5개국)	불가리아, 체코, 헝가리, 러시아, 유고

0061

분류번호	보존기간

발 신 전 보

번 호 : WCO-0010   920124 1813   DW   종별 : ___

수 신 : 주   코스타리카   대사. ♣♣♣♣

발 신 : 장 관 (연이)

제 목 : 고문방지협약 선택의정서 초안 토의

대 : COW-0023

대호 표제토의 관련, 정부입장은 아래와 같음.

1. 제48차 유엔 인권위에서의 표제 초안 토의와 관련, 아국은 인권위원국이 아니므로 동 초안 채택등의 표결에는 참여할수 없음.

2. 다만 양국간 우호관계에 비추어 가능한 지원을 제공할것임. 끝.

(국제기구국장   김재섭)

보 안 통 제	

앙 고 재	92년 1월 24일	유엔 2 과	기안자 성명 김종술		과 장	집의관	국 장	차 관	장 관	외신과통제

0062

주 튀 니 지 대 사 관

2
김
회신
1992. 1. 24. 해명

튀니지(정)20352 - 27

수 신 : 장 관

참 조 : 국제 기구 국장

제 목 : 제48차 세계 인권위

주 재국 외무성은 별첨 공한을 통해 제48차 인권 위원회에서 선출 하는
인종 차별및 소수 민족 보호 분과 위원에 2명의 주재국 인사를 입후보시킬
계획을 알려오면서 아국의 지지를 요청하여왔으니 검토해주시고 검과를
회시하여 주시기바랍니다.

첨 부 : 상기 공한및 약력서 끝.

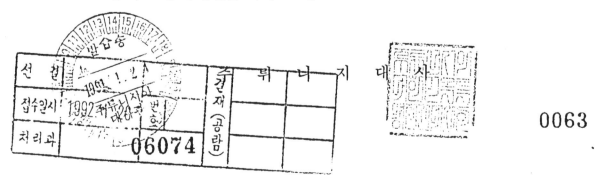

0063

REPUBLIQUE TUNISIENNE

MINISTERE
DES
AFFAIRES ETRANGERES

N° 004328

· 3 1 DEC. 1991

Tunis, le _____

OCI/NU
NBA/ND

/_e Ministère des Affaires Etrangères présente ses compliments à l'Ambassade de la République de Corée et a l'honneur de l'informer de la décision du Gouvernement tunisien de présenter sa candidature à la Sous-Commission de la lutte contre les mesures discriminatoires et de la protection des minorités dont les élections se dérouleront lors de la 48ème session de la Commission des Droits de l'Homme qui se tiendra du 27 janvier au 6 mars 1992 à Genève.

A cet effet l'Ambassade de la République de Corée voudra bien trouver le curriculum vitae de MM :

- Saïd RAMADHANE
- Amor ABDELFATEH

Le Ministère des Affaires Etrangères, dans l'esprit des relations amicales et de coopération qui l'unissent aux autorités coréennes ex
la sous-Commission de la lutte contre les mesures discriminatoires et de la protection des minorités sera favorablement examinée par les autorités compétentes.

Le Ministère des Affaires Etrangères remercie l'Ambassade de la République de Corée de son aimable soutien et lui saurait gré de lui faire connaître la suite que son Gouvernement voudrait bien apporter à ce sujet. Il saisit cette occasion pour lui renouveler les assurances de sa haute considération.

AMBASSADE DE LA REPUBLIQUE DE COREE
TUNIS

0064

Curiculum Vitae

_ Nom   : Ramadhane

_ Prénoms   : Said Naceur

_ Date et lieu de naissance : 08/04/1946 à Tataouine (Tunisie) .

_ Etat civil : Marié et père de trois enfants .

_ Licencié en Droit Public

_ Diplomé d'études approfondies en sciences politiques .

_ Détenteur du certificat d'aptitude à la profession d'avocat .

_ Avocat auprès de la cour de cassation .

_ Conseiller politique du Secrétaire Général du R.C.D du 15/02/90 au 16/03/9

_ Directeur Général des affaires politiques au Ministère de l'Intérieu
  du 17/03/90 au 27/01/91 .

_ Directeur du Journal " El Horria " organe du R.C.D du 28/01/91 à ce jou

_ Vice président de l'association Tunisienne des jeunes avocats
  de 1977 à 1979 .

_ Membre du bureau politique du M.D.S (Parti Toléré puis légalisé)
  de 1981 à 1985 .

_ Directeur de Rédaction du journal" El Mostakbel " organe du M.D.S jusqu e
  1985 .

_ Membre du comité central du R.C.D depuis 1988 .

_ Adhérant et militant de la ligue tunisienne des droits de l'homme depuis
  sa création jusqu'a ce jour .

_ A publié plusieurs articles et éditoriaux aux journaux ." Essabah ".
  (depuis 1972) , " Errai " , " El Mostakbel " , " Essaada " , " El Horria

* M : Ramadhan est Chevalier de l'Ordre de la République .

0065

CURRICULUM VITAE

Nom   :   AMOR

Prénom   :   abdelfattah

Date de naissance   :   4 Mars 1943 à Ksar-Hellal

Situation Familiale   :   Marié - 2 enfants

ADRESSE PERSONNELLE

5, impasse 3 Rue 7122 - Manar II- 1004 Tunis

Tél. :   230 396

ADRESSE PROFESSIONNELLE

Faculté des Sciences Juridiques, Politiques et Sociales de Tunis

14, Rue Hédi KARRAY - 2049 Ariana - Tunisie

Tél.   :   238 220

             :   238 010

             :   230 235

Fax   :   717 255

TITRES ET DIPLOMES

- Professeur de l'enseignement supérieur depuis 1979
- agrégé en Droit Public et Sciences Politiques (1974)
- Docteur en Droit (1973)
- Titulaire d'un D.E.S de Droit Public et d'un D.E.S. de Sciences Politiques (1968)
- Titulaire d'une licence en Droit (1967)
- Titulaire du diplôme du cycle moyen de l'E.N.A (1967)
- Maître de conférences en Droit Public et Sciences Politiques 1974-1979
- Maître Assistant : 1973

0066

- Assistant : 1970-1972
- Professeur invité à Paris I - Paris V - Nantes, Limoges,
  Varsovie, Belgrade, Alger, Annaba, Rabat, Casablanca, Fès,
  ect...

FONCTIONS

- Doyen de la Faculté des Sciences Juridiques Politiques et
  Sociales de Tunis depuis 1987.
- Membre du Conseil Constitutionnel depuis 1987.
- Vice-Doyen de la Faculté de Droit et des Sciences Politiques
  de Tunis 1980-1984.
- Directeur du l'UER de Droit et des Sciences Politiques à la
  Faculté de Droit de Tunis 1978-1979.

AUTRES RESPONSABILITES ET ACTIVITES

- Secrétaire Général Fondateur de l'Académie Internationale de
  Droit Constitutionnel 1984-1988.
- Président de l'Association Tunisienne de Droit
  Constitutionnel depuis 1982.
- Vice Président (depuis 1991) et membre du comité exécutif de
  l'Association Internationale de Droit Constitutionnel (depuis
  1987).
- Expert auprès de la Ligue des Etats Arabes 1979-1983.
- Président du Jury Tunisien d'agrégation en droit public et
  sciences politiques 1986.
- Membres de différents Jurys de recrutement pour le grade
  d'assistant, de maître assistant et de maître de conférences
  en droit public et sciences politiques.
- Directeur de nombreuses thèses et mémoires de recherche.
- Membre du Jury algérien d'agrégation en droit public d'une
  part et science politique d'autre part (1984).

0067

TRAVAUX ET RECHERCHES

- Manuel de Droit Constitutionnel 1987.
- Recueil de constitutions et documents politiques tunisiens (avec K. Saïed) 1987.
- Manuel de droit administratif (ouvrage collectif)1975.
- Le régime politique de la Tunisie 1973.
- Problèmes et perspectives de l'unité maghrébine 1968.
- Une cinquantaine d'articles de recherche en droit constitutionnel, droits de l'homme et relations Internationales (en langue française).
- Une vingtaine d'articles de recherche en langue arabe portant notamment sur des questions de droit constitutionnel et de droits de l'homme.

PRINCIPAUX ENSEIGNEMENTS ASSURES DEPUIS 1970

- Droit Constitutionnel.
- Droits de l'homme et libertés publiques.
- Histoire des idées politiques.
- Droit administratif.
- Droit International et Relations Internationales

0068

법 무 부

2
7h.

427-760 경기도 과천시 중앙동 1번지   /   (02) 503-7045   /   (02) 503-7046

문서번호 인권 0076-2/

시행일자 1992. 1. 25

수신 외무부장관

참조

선결			지시		
접수	일자시간	92.1.27	결재		
	번호	3162	공람		
	처리과				
	담당자				

제목 제 48차 유엔인권위 대비

---

1. GVW-0076('92.1.14)과 관련 입니다.

2. 귀부에서 요청한 비상조치(EMERGENCY MEASURES)에 관한 사실여부
   확인요청에 대하여 당부가 확인한 바, 그러한 사실이 없음을 회신
   합니다. 끝.

법   무   부   장

0069

외 무 부

종 별 :

번 호 : GVW-0186 　　　　　　　일　시 : 92 0127 1600

수 신 : 장관(연이)

발 신 : 주제네바대사

제 목 : 48차 인권위 일정

표제 인권회의 의제별 토이일정을 별첨 송부하니 참고바람.

첨부: GVW(F)-0046

(대사 박수길-국장)

국기국

　　　　　　　　　　　　　　　　　92.01.28　09:43 WG

　　　　　　　　　　　　　　　　　외신 1과 통제관

　　　　　　　　　　　　　　　　　0070

주 제 네 바 대 표 부

번 호 : GVW(F) - 0046   년월일 : 20/27   시간 : 1600
수 신 : 장   관 (으기)
발 신 : 주 제네바대사
제 목 : GVW - 0186

총 2 매(표지포함)

보 안 통 제	∠

외신과 통 재	

0071

46-2-1

		1ST WEEK	2ND WEEK	3RD WEEK	4TH WEEK	5TH WEEK	6TH WEEK
MONDAY		27 JANUARY	3 FEBRUARY	10 FEBRUARY	17 FEBRUARY	24 FEBRUARY	2 MARCH
	a.m.	1 2	5 6 14	10	11	12	23
	p.m.	---	5 6 14	10	11	12	13 21
TUESDAY		28 JANUARY	4 FEBRUARY	11 FEBRUARY	18 FEBRUARY	25 FEBRUARY	3 MARCH
	a.m.	3 4	5 6 14	10	12 C	12	13 21
	p.m.	4	7 8 15 16	10	12 C	12	Voting 12
WEDNESDAY		29 JANUARY	5 FEBRUARY	12 FEBRUARY	19 FEBRUARY	26 FEBRUARY	4 MARCH
	a.m.	4 9	7 8 15 16	10	12	12	Voting 22 19 / 13 21
	p.m.	4 9	7 8 15 16	10	12	22	Voting on remaining items
THURSDAY		30 JANUARY	6 FEBRUARY	13 FEBRUARY	20 FEBRUARY	27 FEBRUARY	5 MARCH
	a.m.	4 9	7 8 15 16	18	12	22 19	---
	p.m.	4 9	17	24	12	19	---
FRIDAY		31 JANUARY	7 FEBRUARY	14 FEBRUARY	21 FEBRUARY	28 FEBRUARY	6 MARCH
	a.m.	5 6 14	17 20	Voting 4 9 / 5 6 14	Voting 7 8 15 16 / 17 20	Voting 10 18 / 24 11	25 26
	p.m.	5 6 14	20	Voting 4 9 / 5 6 14	Voting 7 8 15 16 / 17 20	Voting 10 18 / 24 11	25 26

0072

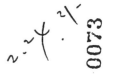

0073

		1ST WEEK	2ND WEEK	3RD WEEK	4TH WEEK	5TH WEEK	6TH WEEK
MONDAY		27 JANUARY	3 FEBRUARY	10 FEBRUARY	17 FEBRUARY	24 FEBRUARY	2 MARCH
	a.m.	1 2	5 6 14	10	11	12	23
	p.m.	—	5 6 14	10	11	12	13 21
TUESDAY		28 JANUARY	4 FEBRUARY	11 FEBRUARY	18 FEBRUARY	25 FEBRUARY	3 MARCH
	a.m.	3 4	5 6 14	10	12 C	12	13 21
	p.m.	4	7 8 15 16	10	12 C	12	Voting 12
WEDNESDAY		29 JANUARY	5 FEBRUARY	12 FEBRUARY	19 FEBRUARY	26 FEBRUARY	4 MARCH
	a.m.	9	7 8 15 16	10	12	12	Voting 22 19 / 13 21
	p.m.	9	7 8 15 16	10	12	22	Voting on remaining items
THURSDAY		30 JANUARY	6 FEBRUARY	13 FEBRUARY	20 FEBRUARY	27 FEBRUARY	5 MARCH
	a.m.	9	7 8 15 16	17	12	22 19	—
	p.m.	9	18	24	12	19	—
FRIDAY		31 JANUARY	7 FEBRUARY	14 FEBRUARY	21 FEBRUARY	28 FEBRUARY	6 MARCH
	a.m.	5 6 14	18 20	Voting 4 9 / 5 6 14	Voting 7 8 15 16 / 18 20	Voting 10 17 11 / 24	25 26
	p.m.	5 6 14	20	Voting 4 9 / 5 6 14	Voting 7 8 15 16 / 18 20	Voting 10 17 11 / 24	25 26

발 신 전 보

WGV-0155   920128 1405   WH

번 호 :   종별 :

수 신 : 주   제네바   대사. ◆◆◆◆

발 신 : 장 관 (연이)

제 목 : 제48차 유엔 인권위 대표단

1. 표제회의 아국 옵서버 대표단을 아래와 같이 임명하였으니

    회의사무국에 통보바람.

    - 수석대표 : ~~박수길~~ 주제네바 대사

    - 대 표 : 이성주 참사관

              정달호 국제연합2과장 (2.18-2.29간 참석)

              위성락 서기관

              정기용 (Chung Ki-Yong) 법무부 인권과 검사

              (2.16-2.27간 참석)

2. 회의 기본대책은 별첨과 같으며, 참고자료는 추후 송부예정임.

3. 본부대표 귀지 도착일정은 추후 통보예정이니 숙소로 싱글 2실

    예약바람.

    첨부 : 회의 기본대책. 끝.

(국제기구국장 김재섭)

0074

제48차 유엔인권위원회 대책

1. 기본대책

o 세계인권상황에 대한 각국의 입장 및 국제적 동향파악

o 아국인권상황 거론시 적극 대응

o 정신대문제 제기시 토의내용 파악 및 필요시 발언

o 아국의 인권위원국 입후보 지지기반 확충을 위하여 회의참가 정부 대표와의 긴밀한 접촉

2. 세부대책

가. 아국인권상황 거론시 대응

1) 민간단체 거론시

o 다수국의 인권상황을 거론하는 가운데 아국인권상황이 포함될 경우 답변권 불행사

o 아국인권문제를 집중거론할 경우, 답변권을 행사하여 오류 지적 및 아국정부 인권보장 노력 설명

2) 북한대표 거론시

o 90.2월이래 북한대표가 아국인권문제를 직접 거론한바가 없이 금차 회의에서 직접 발언할 가능성은 희박함.

o 다만 이인모 사건등 북한 관심사항을 거론할 경우에는 동 내용에 대하여 구체적으로 반박하고, 북한인권문제를 적극 제기함.

0075

다. 인권위원국 입후보 지지기반 확충

　　ㅇ 주요의제 토의참여 및 각국대표와의 긴밀한 접촉을 통하여 아국의
　　　 인권위원국 입후보에 대한 지지기반 확충 노력 전개.　　끝.

0076

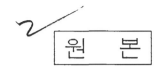

종 별 :

번 호 : GVW-0199   일 시 : 92 0128 1430

수 신 : 장 관(연이,법무부)

발 신 : 주 제네바 대사

제 목 : 48차 인권위(1)

1. 표제회의가 1.27(월) 11:00 BALLESTEROS (페루) 제 47차 회의 의장 사회로 개회되어, 동의장 개회사, MARTENSEN 유엔 인권담당 사무차장의 연설에이어 의장단을 선출하고 의제를 채택하였음.

2. 의장단구성은 아래와 같음.

0 의장: PAR SOLT 헝가리의 대법관 겸 부다페스트대학 법학교수 .

0 부의장:

- RONALD WALKER 당지 호주 대사(서구)

- MOHAMAD NASSER 당지 뷔니지 대사(아프리카)

- SIROUS NASSERI 당지 이란대사(아시아)

0 라포터: LIGIA GALVIS 당지 콜롬비아 대표부참상관(중남미)

3. BALLESTEROS 전의장 및 MARTENSEN 사무차장언급중 특기사항은 다음과 같음.

0 BALLESTEROS 전의장

- 1991년이 동.서 이념 대립을 중식시키고 국제협력 가능성을 증대시킨 분기점

. 민주주의, 자유, 복지의 보편적 추구 계기

. 각종 지역 분쟁해결에 진전

- 그러나 91년에 편협한 민족주의의 대두로 인권이 악화된 사례도 다수

- 민주주의, 평화없이는 인권의 보장이 어려우며, 인권과 민주주의는 상호 보완적인 개념

- 민주주의와 자유는 완성된 개념이 아니라 계속 만들어져가는 대상

- 질병, 마약, 공해, 용병문제등의 과제에 대하여도 각국의 적극적 협력 중요

- 인권 보장을 위한 인권위의 활동찬양

0 MARTENSEN 사무차장

국기국   1차보   법무부

- 인권문제관련, 근래의 국제적 환경에 심대한 변화 진행중인바, 이는 민주주의와 경제, 사회적 발전을 향한 열망의 결과
. 독재체제가 사라지고 반대세력이 용인되는 인권의 혁명이 여러곳에서 나타남.
- 이는 인권과 민주, 발전이 밀접히 연결되어있음을 반영
- 유엔의 평화 유지기능 또한 인권 신장에 기여
. 엘살바도르, 과테말라, 캄보디아 등
- 그러나 고문, 실종, 즉결처분, 소수민족, 기아, 빈곤등 문제에 있어 향후 과제 상존
- 금차 회의부터 53개 회원국으로 진행되는 인권위 역할 기대
. 동.서 대립 종식 이후 남.북 대립 현상이 나타나지 않기를 바람
- 향후 인권문제 대응 방향 설정을 위한 세계인권회의의 의의 언급
- 기타, 유엔 인권활동중 훈련, 자문기능 HUMANRIGHT CENTER 의 과도한 업무 부담등도 언급

4. 신임 SOLT 의장은 인사말을 통하여, 인권의 보편성을 강조하고 정치안정과 발전이 인권과 상호 보완 관계에 있음을 언급하였으며, 고문, 실종등 전통적 인권문제와 함께 차별, 인종적 INTOLERENCE 문제를 향후 주요 문제로 지적하였음. (유고 상황 인용)

5. 한편 북한 대표단은 이철대사, 박덕훈 참사관, 김철수 등 모두 당지 주재 북한 대표부 직원을 회의에 참가시키고 있는것으로 파악되었음. 끝

(대사 박수길-국장)

외 무 부

종 별 :

번 호 : FUW-0041   일 시 : 92 0128 1600

수 신 : 장관(아일,국연)(사본:주제네바대사:중계필)

발 신 : 주 후쿠오카 총영사

제 목 : 재일한국인 인권문제

연:FUW-0331

대:WFU-0188

1. 연호와 관련 최창화목사는 유엔 인권위원회가 1.27-3.6 제네바에서 개최됨을 알려오면서 상기회의 상세일정과 대호 유엔진정서 비밀심의 절차인 1503 과관련 동인이 제출한 재일한국인 인권문제 진정서의 토의 확정여부및 일본대표회의 참석 통보여부및 기타참고사항을 확인해 줄것을 요청해 왔는바 회시바람

2. 동인은 또한 상기 문제에 관계하고 있는 주제네바 대표부 직원성명도 알려주기를 요망함 끝.

(총영사-국장)

예고: 92.6.30 일반

아주국   국기국   중계

외 무 부

종 별 :

번 호 : GVW-0200   일 시 : 92 0128 1800

수 신 : 장 관(연이,법무부,기정)

발 신 : 주 제네바 대사

제 목 : 제 48차 유엔 인권위(2)

연: GVW-0186

1. 1.28 표제 회의는 연호 의제별 토의 일정을 채택하고 의제 4항 (피점령 아랍지역에서의 인권위반) 토의를 시작함.

2. 금일 의제 4항 토의시에는 예년과는 달리 이스라엘이 선두발언에 나서, 마드리드, 워싱턴 및 현재 진행중인 모스코 중동평화 회담을 77년 이집트, 이스라엘 관계 정상화 과정과 같이 동지역 역사의 새로운 지평을 여는 획기적과정이라고 평가하고 동 평화 수립 과정에 유리한 분위기 조성을 위해 인권위 토의에서도 불필요한 비난 및 적대적 태도는 지양해야 할 것이라고 언급한 반면, 모로코, PLO, 조르단 및 ARAB ORGFOR HUMAN RIGHTS 는 이스라엘의 유엔 결의 불준수, 정착사업 강행, 팔레스타인인에 대한 불법구금, 고문, 강제추방, 각종 파괴활동 및 학교 폐쇄등 조직적 인권 탄압 행위를 비난함.

3. 한편 금차 회의기간중 특별 연설예정인 주요 고위인사는 아래와 같음.

스위스 대통령, 소말리아수상, 미국 부통령, 영연방사무총장 (전 나이제리아 외상), 베네쥬엘라, 튜니시아, 페루, 코스타리카 외상, 불란서 인권담당장관, 폴투갈, 영국 외무차관. 끝

(대사 박수길-국장)

국기국   1차보   안기부   법무부

2

7/2

외 무 부

종   별 :

번   호 : GVW-0202   일   시 : 92 0128 2000

수   신 : 장관(아일,연이)사본; 주후쿠오카 총영사중계필

발   신 : 주 제네바 대사

제   목 : 재일 한국인 인권문제

대: WGV-0161(FUW)

연: GVW-2208(91.10.31)

표제관련 최창화목사의 문의사항에 관해 아래 보고하니 주후쿠오카 총영사관에 대한 회보에 참고 바람.

1. 진정서 채택여부

- 연호 전문 보고와 같이 인권소위실무 소위단계에서 기각된 것이 확실시(금차 회의 1503 절차 해당사항중 일본 관련 사항 없음을 확인)

2. 일본 대표단

- 세자끼 주 유엔(뉴욕)차석대사를 단장으로 5-6 명의 대표단 참석중

3. 기타사항

- 회의의제, 토의 일정 및 당관 관계관 성명등은 국제기구국(연이)에 기보고 사항 참조.끝

(대사 박수길-국장)

예고:92.6.30 까지

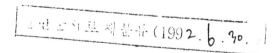

발 신 전 보

분류번호	보존기간

번 호 : WGV-0166　920129 1552　WG　종별 : 암호송신

수 신 : 주　　제네바　　대사. ♣♣♣♣♣

발 신 : 장 관 (연이)

제 목 : 인권위 대비 비상사태 보고서 시정

　　　　　대 ：GVW-0076

　　　　대호, 아국은 85년 이래 비상사태를 선포한 사례가 없으므로
이를 인권사무국에 통보, 비상사태 특별보고관 보고서가 시정되도록
조치바람. 끝.

　　　　　　　　　　　　　　　　　　　（국제기구국장　김재섭）

보 안 통 제	

앙고재	92년 1월 29일	유인 2과	기안자 성명	김종률	과 장	심의관	국 장	차 관	장 관	외신과통제

0082

발 신 전 보

WFU-OO19   920129 1552 WG

번 · 호 :   종별 :

수   신 : 주   후쿠오카   ♣♣♣ 총영사
                    (연이)

발   신 : 장 관

제   목 : 재일한국인 인권문제

대 : FUW-OO41

대호, 유엔 인권위 관련사항을 아래 통보함.

1. 금차 인권위 일정에 따르면 의제 12(세계인권상황)는
2.18-2.26간 토의 예정임.

2. 재일한국인 인권문제 진정서 심의결과는 1503 절차의 성격상
인권사무국으로부터의 공식적인 회답을 얻기는 어려움. 다만 주제네바
대표부에서 비공식적으로 파악한바에 의하면 동 진정서는 91년도 인권
소위원회 산하 진정서 실무위에서 기각된 것으로 보임.

일본은 세계기 주한인 차석대사로 수석대통로 5-6인의 대표가 참석함.

~~3. 일본은 인권위원국이므로 금차 인권위에 참석할 것임.~~

4. 금차회의 아국 대표단으로 참가하는 주제네바대표부 직원은
이성주 참사관 및 위성락 서기관임. 끝.

일반문서로 재분류 (1992. 6. 30.)

(국제기구국장   김재섭)

보안통제	ろ

앙고재	92년 1월 29일	유인 2과	기안자 성명	가영실	과장	집의관	국장	차관	장관	외신과통제

0083

2
김
copy 대검
(회사과자회)

법 무 부

인권 20314-3ㄴ   503-7045   1992. 1. 29

수신 외무부장관

참조 국제기구조약국장

제목 제48차 유엔 인권위 회의 대비자료 송부

　　1. 연어 20314-90 ('92.1.17)과 관련입니다.

　　2. 귀부에서 요청한 제48차 유엔 인권위 회의 대비자료를 별첨과
같이 송부합니다.

첨부 : 제48차 유엔 인권위 회의 대비자료 1부.   끝.

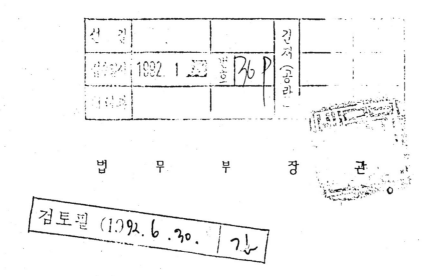

법 무 부 장 관

검토필 (1992. 6. 30.   김)

0084

제 48 차 유엔 인권위회의 대비자료

우리의 전반적 인권상황

우리 정부는 '88년 제6공화국 출범 이후 민주화. 자율화 정책을 과감히 추진하여 나가면서, 특히 민주주의를 지향함에 있어 가장 중요한 가치 척도인 인권의 완벽한 보장에 주력하고 있으며, 이러한 의지하에 인권 신장의 기반을 구축하기 위해서 기본권 조항이 대폭 강화된 제6공화국 헌법정신을 적극 반영, 형사사법 절차와 관련된 각종 법령 및 제도와 수사관행을 개선하고, 행형제도를 획기적으로 개선하는 한편, 나아가 나아가 법률구조사업을 적극 전개하고 출입국관리제도를 개선하는 등 실질적 인권보호에 최선의 노력을 경주하고 있음

○ 인권관련법령 등 합리적 법령 정비

- '88.2. 구속적부심청구에 대한 제한규정을 삭제하여 모든 범죄에 대해 구속적부심청구를 할 수 있게 하는 등 개정된 형사소송법을 시행하고, 개정된 형사보상법을 시행하여 무죄판결을 받은 사람 뿐 아니라 불기소처분된 구속피의자의 형사보상청구권을 인정하였으며,

- '89.3. 사회보호법을 개정하여 필요적 보호감호제도를 삭제하였고,

- '89.6. 사회안전법을 발전적으로 폐지하고 대신 보안관찰법을 제정하여 보안감호, 주거지 제한규정 등을 폐지하였으며,

0086

- '88.7.부터는 범죄피해자구조법을 시행하여 범죄피해자에 대한 피해구조를 실시하고, '91.6. 이를 개정하여 구조범위를 확대함과 아울러 구조금도 유족구조금은 1,000만원, 장해구조금은 600만원으로 대폭 인상하였으며,

- '91.5.에는 국민의 기본적 인권을 보다 광범위하게 보장하기 위해 국가보안법을 개정하는 등 전향적 조치를 취하였음

O 인권침해수사사례 근절을 위한 감찰강화

- 검사가 매월 1회 실시하고 있는 경찰서 등 수사기관의 구속장소 감찰을 더욱 강화하고, 사법경찰관리에게 고문금지에 관한 직무 교육과 수사지휘를 철저히 하고

- 수사방식을 과감히 개선해 나감으로써 비과학적인 자백위주의 수사방식에서 비롯되는 가혹행위의 발생소지를 근절시키고자 노력하고 있으며

- 정부는 보다 합리적인 인신구속제도의 도입 등 제도적 개선방안을 꾸준히 연구하는 한편, 과학적 수사장비를 확충하고 피의자를 체포하기 전에 충분한 증거를 수집하여 이것을 근거로 미리 구속 영장을 발부받거나 또는 형사소송법상 긴급구속제도 등을 활용함으로써 적법절차가 준수될 수 있도록 최선의 노력을 경주하고 하고 있음

0087

o 영세서민을 위한 법률복지의 증진

- 무주택 서민을 보호하기 위하여 '89.12. 주택임대차보호법을
  개정하여 최우선 변제를 받을 수 있는 소액보증금을 인상하고

- '87.9.부터는 법을 몰라 피해를 입은 무자력 국민들을 보호하기
  위해 대한법률구조공단을 설립, 각종 법률상담과 소송대행을
  실시하고 있으며, 또한 한국가정법률상담소도 적극 지원하여
  가정문제, 여성문제등 전문분야까지 법률구조사업을 펼치고 있음

o 행형제도의 개선

- '88.11. 행형제도를 획기적으로 개선하여 이를 계기로 재소자의
  접견, 서신발송, 도서열독 및 신문구독, 방송청취 등 재소자 처우
  에 대한 기존의 제한과 금지를 대폭 완화하거나 전면 허용하였
  으며, 재소자 급식의 질을 높이는 등 재소자의 권익과 처우를
  크게 향상시켰고,

- 천안개방교도소를 신설하여 모범수형자들에게 교도관의 계호없이
  자율적으로 수용생활을 할 수 있게 하고, 기업체와 연계하여 외부
  통근작업을 실시함으로써 사회복귀를 앞둔 수형자들이 민주시민
  으로서의 능력과 자질을 배양해 나가도록 하였으며

- 재소자에 대한 보건관리와 환자진찰을 위해 각 교정시설마다
  의사, 간호사를 배치하고 의료장비 등을 확보, 의료시혜에
  진력하고 있고

0088

- 앞으로도 재소자의 인권신장을 위한 개선대책을 적극 연구.
  검토할 것임

O 출입국규제제도 개선에 따른 출입국자 권익보호

- 내국인에 대한 출국금지업무의 적정을 기하기 위해서 '88.12.
  출국금지업무처리규칙을 제정하여, 출국금지는 필요한 최소한
  범위내로 하고, 출국금지기준도 수사대상자 (검사지휘서 첨부),
  금융부실거래자 (10억원 이상 손실초래), 국세.관세 미납자
  (2천만원 이상) 등 명백히 규정하여 출국금지자 수를 대폭 축소
  하였고

- 외국인에 대한 출국정지제도도 '92.1.20 업무처리규칙(법무부령)
  을 제정하여 정지제도의 남용방지 및 불복장치보장 등을 명문화
  함으로써 보다 신중한 출국정지처분을 할 수 있도록 보장함

O 국제적 인권보호노력에의 동참

- 정부는 '90.7. 국제인권규약에 가입하여 인권의 보편적 존중이
  라는 국제적 노력에 호응하고, 국내적으로도 기본적 인권문제에
  대한 인식을 제고하였으며, 그 후속조치로 '91.7. 시민적 및
  정치적 권리에 관한 최초보고서를 UN 인권국에 제출하였고,
  현재 경제적.사회적 및 문화적 권리에 관한 보고서를 작성중에
  있으며

0089

- 인권보장을 위한 국제적 노력에 적극 동참한다는 취지에서 고문
  방지협약에의 가입문제도 전향적으로 검토하고 있음

O 정치범, 양심수 논쟁의 종식

- 급속한 민주화 과정에서 사회 각 분야의 다양한 욕구가 한꺼번
  에 분출되고, 집단.지역 이기주의 분위기가 팽배하여 집단적인
  힘이나 폭력으로 문제를 해결하려는 사람들이 많아지자, 이에
  편승하여 자유민주주의체제를 근본적으로 파괴하려는 좌익폭력
  세력들의 활동이 격증함에 따라 정부는 체제수호차원에서 엄정
  한 법집행을 하지 않을 수 없었는데,

- 이에 대해 일부 재야.인권단체는 편향된 시각하에서 정부가
  정치범.양심수를 양산하여 인권상황이 악화되었다고 비판하고
  있으나, 정치범 또는 양심수로 거론되고 있는 자들은 모두 계급
  혁명을 주도하거나 폭력시위.불법노사분규를 조장하는 등 구체
  적인 범법행위를 자행함으로써 실정법을 위반한 범법자들임

- 다만, '88.6.29 이전에 과거 민주화 요구와 관련되어 구속된
  사람들을 시국사범이라고 부른 적은 있으나, '88.12.21 이들에
  대해 전면적인 사면을 실시하여 소위 정치범.양심수 논쟁을
  종식시킨 것은 주지의 사실임

0090

O 법치주의의 확립

앞으로도 정부는 민주발전에 역행하는 불법과 폭력을 뿌리뽑아
사회안정을 이룩해야 한다는 국민적 공감대에 바탕을 두고 법치
주의를 확립하기 위하여 모든 노력을 경주할 것이며, 아울러
국민의 인권신장을 위하여 인권관련제도 개선 등 지속적인 노력
을 할 것임

0091

간첩 및 국가보안법 위반 장기수 현황 및 고령 장기 수형자 석방을
요청하는 민간 인권단체 주장에 대한 정부입장

o 간첩 및 국가보안법 위반사건으로 수용중인 장기수는 '91.12.31
  현재 80명 이내임
  (우리나라는 재소자 인원을 외부에 대하여 밝히지 않고 있음)

o 대한민국은 제6공화국 출범이후 간첩죄 및 국가보안법 위반사건의
  고령 및 장기 수형자 중에서 자신의 잘못을 반성하고 재범의 우려가
  없다고 판단되는 자 215명을 인도적인 차원에서 12회에 걸쳐
  가석방 조치한 바 있음

o 앞으로도 고령 및 장기 수형자 중에서 자신의 잘못을 반성하고
  재범의 우려가 없는 자는 계속 가석방 등 인도적인 조치를 적극
  추진하여 나갈 계획임

0092

남북합의서 서명이후 국가보안법의 개정 또는 운용문제

1. 합의서중 국가보안법과 관련될 수 있는 내용

   o 상호체제를 인정하고 존중

   o 상호 파괴전복행위 및 무력사용 침략금지

   o 상호 자유로운 왕래접촉, 이산가족간의 서신거래, 왕래, 상봉, 방문실시 및 자유의사에 의한 재결합 실현

   o 출판보도둥 여러분야에서 교류협력 실시둥

2. 국가보안법의 합의서 저촉 여부

   (1) 상호체제인정, 존중, 불가침조항

   o 북한이 정부를 참칭하는 반국가단체인지, 국가변란목적의 반국가 단체인지 (법 제2조) 여부와 관련될 수 있는 내용임

   o 북한은 화해와 교류협력을 통해 통일문제를 함께 풀어나가야 할 민족공동체인 동시에 우리의 자유민주체제를 전복하기 위해 대남적화혁명노선을 견지하는 2중적 성격을 지니고 있음

0093

○ 우리가 북한을 화해와 협력의 대상으로 실체를 인정하는 것과
  북한이 혁명노선을 견지하고 대한민국에 대한 변란을 꾀하는데
  대하여 반국가단체성을 인정하는 것과는 별개의 문제임

○ 북한이 합의서 채택과 함께 대남혁명노선을 포기하고 우리국가의
  변란 전복행위를 즉각 완전히 중단했다고 볼 현실적 변화가
  없으며 북한은 대한민국정부를 오로지 타도되어야 할 대상으로
  규정하고 있는 노동당규약과 헌법 및 그 하위규범인 형법을 여전히
  유지하고 대한민국과 관련된 행위에 대하여 가혹하게 처벌하고
  있음

○ 앞으로 합의서 채택을 계기로 북한이 대남적화혁명노선을 명백히
  포기하고 우리국가를 전복 변란하려는 행위를 영원히 종식시켜
  평화공존체제가 완전히 구축된다면 그때는 반국가단체성 논의가
  자연히 해결될 것임

0094

(2) 상호 교류왕래 접촉 조항

　　o　금품수수, 잠입탈출, 회합통신 (법 제5,6,8조)등과 관련될 수 있는

　　　　내용임

　　o　지난해 남북교류 협력을 적극 지원하기 위하여 남북교류협력에관한

　　　　법률을 제정 시행하고 있으며 동법 소정의 절차만 거치면 남북한

　　　　주민간에 언제든지 접촉 왕래 협력사업등을 할 수 있으며 이러한

　　　　남북교류협력행위에 대하여는 국가보안법이 적용되지 않음

　　　　(남북교류협력에관한법률 제3조)

　　o　또한 현행 국가보안법은 과거와는 달리 "이적행위"를 넘어서

　　　　"국가의 존립안전이나 자유민주적기본질서를 침해하는 정을 알고

　　　　한 행위"만을 처벌하고 있어 이러한 행위가 아닌 순수한 교류행위는

　　　　국가보안법과 무관하다 할 것임

(3) 출판 보도의 교류협력 조항

　　o　이적표현물 제작 · 반포 소지등 (법제7조)과 관련될 수 있는 내용임

0095

○ 현재도 단순히 북한관련 출판물을 제작·반포·소지하였다는 행위 만으로 처벌하는 것은 아니며 그것이 국가의 존립안전이나 자유민주적기본질서를 침해하는 경우에만 제한적으로 처벌하고 있음

○ 따라서 상호 이해증진을 위해 남북간의 출판물과 언론이 상호 개방 교류된다 하더라도 국가보안법과 상충되지 않음

3. 결론

○ 합의서의 내용과 국가보안법이 서로 저촉되는 것은 아님

○ 또한 합의서 채택만으로 북한이 대남적화혁명노선을 명백히 포기하였다고 단정할 수 없고 더우기 평화공존체제가 완전히 구축되었다고 보기도 어려움

0096

o 국가보안법은 대한민국의 존립안전 및 자유민주적기본질서를 위태롭게

　하는 반국가단체의 활동을 규제함으로써 국민의 생존 및 자유를

　확보하고 우리의 자유민주체제를 수호하려는 방어적이고 자위적인

　법률임

o 따라서 현재로서는 국가보안법을 개폐하거나 운용을 달리할

　단계가 아니며, 앞으로 남북관계의 실질적 변화등을 감안하여

　추후 종합적으로 고려할 문제임

0097

발 신 전 보

	분류번호	보존기간

번   호 : WTN-0026   920131 1804 FL   종별 : 암호송신

수   신 : 주   튀니지   대사. 총영사
(연이)

발   신 : 장 관

제   목 : 제48차 유엔 인권위원회

   대 : 튀니지(정) 20352-27

   대호, 아국은 유엔 인권위원국이 아니므로 표제회의에서 실시되는

차별방지 및 소수민보호 소위원회(인권소위) 위원 선거에 참가할수 없음을

참고바람. 끝.

(국제기구국장   김재섭)

보안통제	
외신과통제	

앙고재	92년 1월 31일	유엔 2과	기안자 성명 강용훈	과장	심의관	국장	차관	장관

0098

원 본

외 무 부

종 별 :

번 호 : GVW-0251   일 시 : 92 0131 1930

수 신 : 장관(연이, 법무부, 기정동문)

발 신 : 주 제네바 대사

제 목 : 제48차 유엔 인권위(3)

연: GVW-0232

1. 표제회의는 금 1.31 의제 4항(이스라엘 점령지 인권) 및 9항(자결권) 토의를 종결하고, 의제 5항(남아프리카 인권 위반), 6항(남아공 지원의 부정적효과) 및 14항(인종차별 철폐 행동 계획) 토의에 들어갔음.

2. 1.30 의제 9항 토의시 미국대표는 자결권은 기본적으로 피치자의 동의에 의한 통치를 의미하므로 참된 민주주의의 실현이 자결권의 요체라고 전제한후최근 범세계적으로 민주화로의 많은 진전이 있었음을 환영한다고 하면서 여사한 시대적 추세에 역행하는 국가로 쿠바, 북한 및 버마를 구체적으로 거명, 앞으로 유엔의 인권 활동은 이들 국가의 인권 위반 억제에 역점을 두어져야 한다고 발언함.

3. 상기 미국대표 발언에 대해 북한은 답변권 행사(박덕훈 참사관)를 통해 남한을 군사적으로 점령하고, 살인, 강간, 학살, 마약, 테러, 약소국(그라나다등) 무력침공등 인권 유린의 표본이 되는 미국이 민주주의의 모범이 되고 있는 북한의 체제를 비판하는 것은 부당하다고 반박함.

4. 북한의 이철대사는 1.31 의제 9항 발언에서 미국이 한국에 군대를 주둔시킴으로써 한국민의 자결권을 침해하고 있다고 하면서 미국에 대해 주한 미군의철수를 촉구하는 내용의 발언을 행함(91.12. 남북합의서 합의, 핵무기 철수, 비핵화 합의, 팀스피리트 훈련 중지등 긍정적 요소도 함께 평가)

5. 아측은 상기 1.30 북한의 대미 답변권 행사에서 군사적 점령이라는 표현을 사용한점 및 의제 9항 발언에서 주한 미군 철수요구를 한데 대해 답변권을 신청해 두었으나, 북한의 이철대사가 개막식 당일 본직이 제의한 오찬 초청을 수락한다고 통보해 옴에 따라 연호 보고내용 및 남북관계 현황, 또한 북한의 발언이 미국과의 관계에서 연유되었다는 점등에서 비추어 답변권 신청을 철회하였음.

국기국 법무부	장관	차관	1차보	2차보	외정실	분석관	청와대	안기부

6. 한편 금 1.31 이철대사 발언후 미국 대표는 아대표단을 찾아와 1.30 북한의 답변권 행사후에는 대응 발언을 행할 것을 검토했으나 금일 북한의 발언은 신중한 표현 (CAREFULLY WORDED)을 사용하는등 종전의 북한의 행동 양태와는 다른점이 느껴진다고 평가하면서 답변권을 행사치 않겠다는 뜻을 알려왔음.

7. 1.29-31 간 기타 토의 내용은 별전 보고함. 끝
(대사 박수길-외정실장)
예고 92.6.30 일반

끝

일반문서로 재분류(1992. 6. 30.)

외 무 부

종 별 :

번 호 : GVW-0252

일 시 : 92 0131 1950

수 신 : 장 관(연이,법무부)

발 신 : 주 제네바 대사

제 목 : 제 48차 유엔인권위(4)

표제회의 의제4항 및 9항관련 1.29-31간 토의내용 아래 보고함.

1. 의제 4항(이스라엘 점령지인권)

- 28개 회원국 및 8개 옵저버 국가로 부터의 발언이 있었는바, 대부분의 국가가 중동평화 회담을 고무적 현상으로 평가하면서도 고문, 가옥파괴, 강제추방등 이스라엘의 각종 인권위반 사례를 규탄하면서 49년 전시 민간인 대우에 관한 제네바 협약의 준수 및 중동문제가 유엔안보리결의 242 및 338호에 입각 해결되어야 할것이라는 입장 표명

- 미국, EC, 호주, 카나다등 선진국대표부는 여러대표보다 중동평화 협상의 의의를 점더 부각시키고, 팔레스탄인의 자결권과 함께 이스라엘의 생존권도 인정되어야한다는 점을 주장한점에서 다소의 입장차이를 보임.

- AF, UNION OF ARAB LAYWERS 등 7-8개 NGO 가 이스라엘의 점령지 정책의 잔혹성을 열거, 비판함. 특히 AI 는 고문 및 행정구금 문제를 집중 추궁함.

2. 의제 9항(자결권)

- BALLESTEROS 용병문제 특별보고관의 보고 청취후 토의에 들어간바, 18개 회원국, 8개 옵서버국 및 13개 NGO 가 발언한바, 전반적으로 KUWAIT해방, 캄보디아 평화합의, 발틱 3국등 전소련 연방의 독립등을 긍정적 요소로 평가하고, 남아프리캄문제, 서부사하라문제, 유고문제 (코로아티나및 슬로베니아독립), 티벳, 터어키내 KURD 족, 동더몰 문제등이 비판의 대상이 됨.

- 러시아연방 대표는 구소련 체제당시 다수국이 소련내 인권문제에 대한 관심표명과 지원을 해준데 사의를 표하고 인권은 더이상 국내 문제가 아니라는 반응을 함.

- 중국대표는 자결권과 영토적 일체성간의 구분을 요한다 하면서 티벳은 중국의 국내문제임을 강조

국가국   법무부

PAGE 1

- 기타 카태리르 문제를 둘러싸고 인도, 파키스탄간 논쟁이 있었음.

쿠바대표는 열극체제 (UNIPOLALAS WORLD) 하에서 약소국의 자결권 (정부 및 사회.경제제도 선택권) 침해 위험등 경고

3. 특별 연사 발언

- 영국의 BOYD 외무담당 국무상은 인권문제에 대한 정부 및 국제사회의 책임추궁 (ACCOUNTABILITY)의 중요성을 강조하면서, 이락의 인권상황을 특별히 비판.

- GHALIT소 말리아 수상은 자국 전정권의 만행을 규탄하면서, 동정권 축출 노력에 대한 미국등 국제사회의 지원에 사의를 표명하고, 인도적 간섭권의 필요성은 인정하나 선별적으로 적용되어서는 안될것이라고 언급.끝

(대사 박수길-국장)

주 제 네 바 대 표 부

제네(정) 2031-118

1992. 1. 31.

수신 : 장관

참조 : 국제기구국장

제목 : 48차 유엔인권위

표제 회의시 주요 연설문을 별첨 송부합니다.

첨부 : 1. Martensen 사무차장 연설문

2. Solt 신임의장 연설문

3. 기타 미국, 일본, EC등 각국 대표 발언문 등. 끝.

주 제 네 바 대

0103

주 제 네 바 대 표 부

번 호 : GVW(F) - 0070   년월일 : 2 0/3/   시간 : 2000

수 신 : 장   관 (연이)

발 신 : 주 제네바대사

제 목 : 북한 대표 연설문

총 6 매 (표지포함)

보 안 통 제	토

| 외신과 통 제 | |

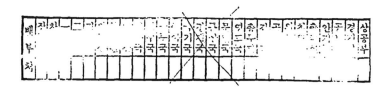

배부처	자치		과				경기국	무	어	총	지	고		처	축	인	주	경	상공부

배부처	장신	차신	일 차보	이 차보	기획실	정보 건국	분석관	의전장	아주국	미주국	구주국	중아국	국제국	경제국	통상국	문협국	영교국	총무과	감사관	공보관	외연원	청와대	총리실	인기부	공보처	경기인	상공부

10-6-1

0104

INTERVENTION

PRONONCEE PAR S.E. M. RI TCHEUL

AMBASSADEUR, REPRESENTANT PERMANENT DE LA

REPUBLIQUE POPULAIRE DEMOCRATIQUE DE COREE

A LA 48E SESSION DE LA

COMMISSION DES DROITS DE L'HOMME

GENEVE, LE 31 JANVIER 1992

7 0-6-2

0105

M. le Président,

Permettez-moi tout d'abord de vous féliciter d'être élu à la Présidence de la présente session.

Je me réjouis de pouvoir prendre la parole à la présente session, pour la première fois depuis l'adhésion l'an passé à l'ONU de la République Populaire Démocratique de Corée.

M. le Président,

Le respect du droit à l'autodétermination est une condition préalable à la jouissance de toute la gamme des droits fondamentaux.

Depuis la fondation de l'ONU, un grand nombre de pays ont accédé à l'indépendance nationale, tout en exerçant leur droit à l'autodétermination.

Cependant, dans certaines régions, ce droit est impitoyablement bafoué par l'occupation militaire étrangère; dans des pays d'un nombre non négligeable, ce même droit qui a été acquis à travers une lutte de longue haleine se voit menacé à cause de la domination, de l'ingérence et des forces armées extérieures.

Il y a dans le monde des pays grands et petits, des nations plus ou moins développées, mais on ne peut jamais parler de pays supérieurs ou inférieurs ni de nations prédestinées à dominer ou à être dominées.

Je pense que les propos, aussi bruyants que soient-ils, sur le droit à l'autodétermination nationale seraient vides de sens, si de tels idéaux et morale étaient méprisés dans la communauté internationale.

M. le Président,

Des progrès spectaculaires ont été enregistrés ces dernières années pour ce qui concerne de la jouissance du droit à l'autodétermination.

A la suite de l'indépendance du peuple de Namibie, le Cambodge est parvenu l'an dernier à une concorde nationale après des années de guerre, et 12 années de guerre civile ont pris fin tout récemment au Salvador.

Cela prouve que la voie principale que suit notre époque, aussi bien en temps de confrontation qu'à l'heure actuelle, est celle conduisant toujours à la souveraineté, à l'indépendance et à la paix.

M. le Président,

Par droits de l'homme, nous entendons dire ceux dont devra jouir l'être humain en tant que maître de la société. Pour que les droits humains authentiques soient assurés, les masses populaires, qui sont créatrices des biens et de la culture, devront, à notre avis, pleinement bénéficier de leurs droits en tant que maître du pouvoir d'Etat, des ressources matérielles, des biens sociaux et culturels.

Grâce aux efforts sincères de la communauté internationale de ces dernières 4 décennies, se sont produits en Afrique du Sud des

- 1 -

0106

changements notoires, tels que autorisations des activités d'organisations politiques, libération des prisonniers politiques, etc.

La communauté internationale devrait redoubler de vigilance à l'égard de l'Afrique du Sud, jusqu'à ce que tous les éléments racistes y soient éliminés.

M. le Président,

La Commission devrait rechercher les moyens beaucoup plus efficaces en faveur du droit du peuple palestinien à disposer de lui-même.

Ma délégation se sent d'autant plus préoccupée du fait qu'aujourd'hui encore où une Conférence sur la paix au Proche-Orient et une série d'autres réunions ont lieu à la suite de celle à Madrid, les négociations directes entre l'Israël et les représentants de l'Etat de Palestine ne sont toujours pas entamées.

Je crois que les contacts et consultations entre les parties intéressées sont déjà un pas en avant vers la solution du problème.

Ma délégation espère que les débats dans la présente session de la Commission aideront à la prise de contacts directs entre la Palestine et l'Israël.

La condamnation, la calomnie et les allégations contradictoires ne dresseront que l'obstacle à la solution du problème.

M. le Président,

La nation coréenne n'est actuellement pas en état de jouir de son droit à l'autodétermination.

Le Nord et le Sud de la Corée ont adopté en décembre dernier un "Accord sur la réconciliation, la non-agression, la collaboration et les échanges entre le Nord et le Sud" et sont également convenus de la "Déclaration conjointe sur la dénucléarisation de la péninsule coréenne.", ce qui a jeté les bases pour la réunification, voire la jouissance du droit de tout le peuple coréen à l'autodétermination.

Il faudra que cet Accord historique ne demeure pas lettre morte.

En vue de stimuler l'évolution d'une telle situation et de résoudre dans la paix la question coréenne, il faudra créer un climat propice.

Il conviendra, à cet effet, de bénéficier de l'appui de la communauté internationale et des pays concernés notamment et, en même temps, de mettre fin à l'ingérence des forces étrangères.

Dans ce sens, la présence des troupes américaines en Corée du Sud depuis 47 ans constitue un obstacle à l'exercice du droit à l'autodétermination de la nation coréenne et une source de tension et de menace permanentes pour la paix dans la péninsule coréenne.

M. le Président,

- 2 -

Les Etats-Unis ont préconisé depuis des années, au cours des travaux de différentes sessions de notre Commission, que, je cite, le "reniement le plus flagrant du droit à l'autodétermination est impliqué dans les régions occupées par les troupes étrangères".

Nous partageons entièrement cette idée. Il importe que la parole coïncide avec la pratique.

Je me demande si les troupes américaines stationnées en Corée du Sud ne sont pas une armée étrangère et si leur présence en Corée du Sud n'est pas une violation du droit à l'autodétermination de la nation coréenne.

Pourquoi les Etats-Unis ne veulent-ils pas retirer leurs forces armées de Corée du Sud, alors qu'ils insistent énergiquement sur le retrait des troupes étrangères d'autres pays?

Pour quelle raison cherchent-ils à procéder à l'intervention militaire, à l'exercice de pressions politiques et de blocus économique vis-à-vis des pays petits et indépendants?

Si nous avions renoncé à notre esprit d'indépendance et si nous nous étions laissés aller à plaire aux Etats-Unis, nous aurions pu échapper à la sphère de leur critique permente et délibérée.

Mais, hélas, l'indépendance et le droit à l'autodétermination sont pour nous plus précieux que notre survie.

M. le Président,

Récemment, les Etats-Unis ont retiré leurs armes nucléaires de Corée du Sud et les négociations coréo-américaines de haut niveau ont eu lieu pour la première fois dans l'histoire de nos deux pays.

La réalité montre qu'il est impossible de régler le problème en recourant à la menace et à la pression et que seuls les contacts et les négociations faisant preuve de la volonté politique mèneront à la solution du problème sur la base du principe de respect mutuel de l'indépendance et conformément aux intérêts réciproques.

Ils devront, pour cela, contribuer à la réunification coréenne en retirant leurs troupes, tout comme ils ont apporté leur contribution à la réconciliation entre le Nord et le Sud en retirant leurs armes nucléaires de Corée du Sud et en y cessant les manoeuvres militaires "Team Spirit" qui se poursuivaient durant 16 ans.

Nous espérons que les Etats-Unis qui contribuent au règlement des problèmes au sein de la communauté internationale s'efforceront d'aider à la solution de la question coréenne.

Aujourd'hui où la structure de confrontation en temps de guerre froide a disparu, le droit à l'autodétermination et la souveraineté sont une tendance puissante de notre époque.

Personne n'a le droit d'empiéter sur le droit à l'autodétermination et la souveraineté des autres pays.

- 3 -

0108

Tous les pays sont égaux; plus un pays est grand, plus lourde est son obligation de rester fidèle au principe internationale de justice et de l'égalité.

Lorsqu'ils s'acquittent de cette obligation, les relations internationales, stables et équitables, seront établies et l'authentique droit à l'autodétermination parfaitement assuré.

Je vous remercie.

- 4 -

공 란

공   란

공   란

공   란

공   란

공   란

외 무 부

원 본

종 별 :

번 호 : GVW-0262

일 시 : 92 0203 1700

수 신 : 장관(연이)

발 신 : 주제네바대사

제 목 : 비상사태 보고서 지정

대: WGV-166

대호 표제 특별보고관 사무실의 LEBAKIN담당관을 면담, 보고서 시정 요청
공한을 전달하고 후속조치를 당부한바, 동인은 조치하겠다고 하였음을 보고함. 끝

(차석대사 김삼훈-국장)

국기국

공   란

공   란

공   란

공 란

외 무 부

종   별 :

번   호 : GVW-0279   일   시 : 92 0205 1000

수   신 : 장 관(연이)

발   신 : 주 제네바대사

제   목 : 48차 인권위(5)

표제회의는 2.4 현재 남아공의 APARTHEID 와 기타인종차별 관련의제(ITEM 5,6,14)에관한토의를 종료한바, 특기사항은 다음과 같음.

　1. 남아공의 APARTHEID 관련

　O 미국,EC,일본등 서구제국

　- 최근 남아공에서의 사태 진전을 평가하고 민주정부 수립을 위한 모든 정파의 노력을 찬양하였으며 APARTHEID 의 완전한 철폐를위하여 보다 전진적 조치가 취해져야 함을 강조함.

　- 또한 UNHCR 이 남아공 정부와 함께 추진하고있는 난민 정착 사업을 평가함.

　- EC 는 특히 현재의 NATIONAL RECONCILIATION협의에 참석하고 있지 않은 그룹의참석을 촉구하였으며, 상황을 계속 모니터할 것임을 언급함.

　- 한편 일본은 유엔인권기구의 현장 조사를 허용하지 않고 있는 남아공 당국조치를 비판함.

　O 개도국

　- 인도, 인도네시아, 아프리카 제국들은 부분적으로 최근의 진전을 평가하면서도 극우 테러단체의 준동이 남아공 경찰, 군부의 공공연한 묵인아래이루어지고 있느등우려할 상황이 상존하고 있다고하고 지속적인 국제적 압력을 강조함.

　- 유고등 일부 국가는 APARTHEID 의 사회 경제적영향이 심각함을 지적, 남아공 흑인의 경제상태개선 필요성을 언급함.

　O NGO

　- INT'L MOVEMENT FOR FRATERNAL UNION AMONG RACES AND PEOPLE는 남아공에서 아직도 인권침해가 심각하며 민주적 정부,의회, 군대, 경찰등 무엇하나 구체적으로 이룩 된 것이 없다고 하며 가장 강한톤으로 비판적인 발언을 함.

국기국   구주국

PAGE 1   92.02.05   23:39 FL

외신 1과 통제관

0121

- 상기 기구는 특히 남아공 경찰이 극우 테러단체를 배후에서 지원하고, 용병들을 이용하고 있다고비난함.

2. 기타 인종차별 관련

O 호주는 자국내 원주민 문제해결을 위한정책을 소개하였음.

O INT'L TREATY COUNCIL 은 미국의 인디안 차별을 비판함.O INT'L COMMISSION OFJURISTS 는 동티몰, 미얀마문제를 간략히 지적하고 유럽등에서 일고 있는외국인 배척 운동에 우려를 표함.

O INT'L ASSOCIATION AGAINST TORTURE 북미 지부는 미국내 흑인에 대한 은밀한 차별, 남아공정부에대한 서구의 2중적 태도를 비판함.끝

(대사 박수길-국장)

PAGE 2

0122

공　　　란

공　　　란

공 란

원 본

종 별 :

번 호 : GVW-0299

일 시 : 92 0207 1000

수 신 : 장관(연이)

발 신 : 주제네바대사대리

제 목 : 48차 인권위(6)

표제회의는 2.6 현재 의제 7,8,15 및(RIGHT TODEVELOPMENT)에 대한 토의를 종료한바, 특기 사항을 아래 보고함.

1. 선진국 입장

0 미국은 정치적, 시민적 권리가 보장되어 자유롭고 민주적인 여건이 조성될때경제,사회 발전이 가능하다고 하고, 정부의 인권보장이 궁극적으로 개발을 극대화한다고 주장함.

- 이러한 시각에서 미국은 경제적 권리 보장등 개발권의 문제를 정부로 하여금보장케 할 경우,오히려 정부가 개발을 기본권 제약의 구실로 이용하며 이는, 개인 ' 창의력 말살로 이어져 궁극적으로 개발을 저해케 된다고함. (공산권몰락 사례 제시)

- 결국 미국은 개발의 문제는 인권 차원에서가아니라 유엔 총회 제2위 또는 UNDP에서 다루어야할 주제라고 함.

0 불란서, 카나다등은 다소 타협적인 입장에서 개발과 기본권 신장이 상호 연관되어 있음을 인정하면서도, 기본적 인권보장 없이는 경제사회적 발전 잠재력이 제약된다고 함.

- 특히 카나다는 개발문제에 대한 자국의 지원은기본적 인권 신장에 긴밀히 연계되어 있음을강조함.

2. 개도국 입장

0 중국,인도,멕시코,유고등은 개발권이 개인적자유를 제약하는 구실이 된다는 주장을 비판하고,경험적으로 경제 발전이 기본권 보장에 기여하였음을 언급함.

- 이들은 개발권이 인권의 일부라는 입장에서,개발권의 부인은 기본적 인권과개발을 모두부인하는 결과로 이어진다고 주장하고 개발권 보장을위한 국내경제

국기국   1차보   2차보   외정실   청와대   안기부

PAGE 1

92.02.07   21:11 BU

외신 1과 통제관

0126

정책수립, 정책조정, 국제적지원등 협력을 강조함.

0 쿠바는 개발권의 문제가 강대국 중심의 부당한 국제경제 질서, 과중한 외채,국제적 기술이전 장벽등으로 제대로 추진되지 못하고 있으며,걸프전이후 미국중심의 UNIPOLAR 상황으로저개발 약속국들은 독립,자주도 지키기 어렵게되었다고 하는등,개발 권의 문제를 신국제정치 질서와 연계, 미국을 비판함.

3. NGO 입장

0 다수의 남미,아프리카,중동문제 관련 NGO 들은사례를 들어가며 동지역의 빈곤,질병,노동,아동,여성등의 문제를 제기하고 개발권 신장을 통한 인권보호를 위해국제적 연대를 강조함.

4. 기타

0 일부 NGO 들은 중국의 티베트인 탄압, PNG의 부겐빌섬 원주민 탄압, 동티몰 문제등을 제기한바, 중국은 답변권을 행사, 티베트인탄압 주장을 부인함.끝

   (차석대사 김삼훈-국장)

외 무 부

종 별 : 긴 급

번 호 : GVW-0314   일 시 : 92 0207 1840

수 신 : 장관(정특)

발 신 : 주 제네바 대사대리

제 목 : 북한대사 면담 보도에 대한 반응

　　남북대사 면담 사실 및 내용 일부가 금 2.7(금) 자 서울발 연합통신 보도로당지에 입전되었는바, 동건 관련 하기사항에 대한 본부지침 지급 회시바람.

　　가. 당지 언론(특히 일본 특파원)으로 부터 동사실관계 확인 또는 코멘트 요구시 답변 방향

　　나. 당지 북한대표부로 부터 경위 설명 요구 및 금후 상호 언론대응 방향 문의시 대책.끝

　　(차석대사 김삼훈-차관)

　　예고:92.12.31. 일반지

검토필 (1992. 6 . 30.)

외정실　　장관　　차관　　상황실

발 신 전 보

분류번호	보존기간

번 호 : WUN-0303 920208 1024 DQ   종별 : 암호송신

수 신 : 주 (유엔) 대사. ♣♣♣♣♣

발 신 : 장 관 (연이)

제 목 : 제48차 유엔 인권위 대표단

표제회의에 참가하는 본부대표 귀지 도착일정을 아래 통보함.

- 정달호 유엔 2과장 : 2.18(화) 21:30 BA-732편
- 정기용 법무부 검사 : 2.17(월) 21:45 SR-729편. 끝.

(국제기구국장 김재섭)

보 안 통 제	

앙고재	92년 2월 8일	유엔 2과	기안자 성명 26광	과 장	심의관	국 장 7022	차 관	장 관	외신과통제

0129

분류번호	보존기간

발 신 전 보

WGV-0220   920208 1425 FL

번   호 : _____   종별 : _____

수   신 : 주   제네바   대사. ~~총영사~~

발   신 : 장 관   (연이)

제   목 : 제48차 유엔 인권위 회의 대비자료

표제회의에서의 아국 인권문제 토의에 대비한 아래 참고자료를 2.10. 정파편 송부함. 예정임.

- 전반적 인권상황

- 장기수 문제

- 남북합의서 서명이후 국가보안법 운용

- 이인모 문제 대책

- 정신대 문제 대책

- 91년도 미국무부 인권보고서(남.북한). 끝.

(국제기구국장   김재섭)

일반문서로 재분류(1992. 6. 30.)

		보 안	으
		통 제	

앙고재	92년 2월 8일	유인 2과	기안자 성명		과 장	심의관	국 장		차 관	장 관		외신과통제
			16긍글		은ζ	고간				겂		

0130

외 무 부

110-760 서울 종로구 세종로 77번지 / (02) 723-8934 / (02) 723-3505

문서번호 연이 20314-261

시행일자 1992.2.8.

(경유)

수신 주제네바대사

참조

취급		장 관	
보존			
국 장	전결		
심의관			
과 장			
기안	김종훈		협조

제목 제48차 유엔 인권위 회의 대비자료

표제회의에서의 아국 인권문제 토의에 대비한 아래 참고자료를 별첨
송부합니다.

- 아 래 -

1. 우리의 전반적 인권상황

2. 장기수 문제

3. 남북합의서 서명이후 국가보안법 운용문제

4. 이인모 문제 대책

5. 정신대 문제 대책 참고자료

6. 91년도 미국무부 인권보고서(남.북한) 및 참고자료

첨부 : 상기자료 각 1부.

일반문서로 재분류(1992. 6. 30.)

0131

공   란

외 무 부

종 별 :

번 호 : GVW-0337

일 시 : 92 0212 1030

수 신 : 장관(연이)

발 신 : 주제네바대사대리

제 목 : 48차 인권위(7)

금 2.10 회의시 DAN QUAYLE 미국부통령과 THOMASKLESTIL 오지리 외무차관이 연설한바, 특기사항 아래보고함.

1. QUAYLE 부통령 연설

가. 연설요지

0 80년대말과 90년대 초에 벌어진 소련 동구등지의 민주화 혁명은 미국 건국 과정과 불란서 혁명에 비견할 만한 변화임.

- 이는 미국과 우방들이 확고한 원칙을 견지하였기 때문에 가능하였음.

0 이제 세계적으로 인권, 민주를 실현하는데 가장 좋은 시기가 도래하였음.

- 과거처럼 냉전에 대처하기 위해 독재정부와 타협할 필요없음.

0 이락의 쿠웨이트 침공 응징은 자유,민주,인권을위한 국제사회의 협력을 과시한사례임.

0 인권위 위원국중 중대한 인권침해를 하는나라는 위원국 취급을 하지 말아야 함.

- 이락, 이란, 쿠바를 지명

0 새로운 세계질서는 인권존중의 바탕위에 세워져야 하며 미국은 이를 위해 소임을 다할것임.

나. 상기 연설에 대한 답변권 행사

0 이란,이락,쿠바, PLO 가 QUAYLE 부통령 연설을비난

- 이란은 QUAYLE 부통령이 인권위 회의를 미국선거에 이용하려는 의도를 드러냈으며 선별적으로 이란을 거명, 사실과 다른 언급을 하였다고 하고,미국이 독재와 인권탄압으로 악명높은 팔레비정권을 지지해온 사실을 상기

- PLO는 QUAYLE 부통령이 이스라엘이 점령지 인권침해를 언급하지 않고 여타 인권 문제만 거론한 것을 비난

국기국   차관   1차보   청와대   안기부

PAGE 1

2. KLESTIL 차관 연설

0 중대한 인권침해 사례에 즉각 대응할수 있는 'EMERGENCY PROCEDURE' 창설제안

 - 금번 인권위에서 채택하여 줄것을 요망(동제안은 91.9 MOCK 오지리 외상이 UN총회연설에서 기제안한 내용)

 0 상기 PROCEDURE 설명

 - UN 사무총장이 분야별 개인 전문가 명단을 유지

 - 유엔 회원국의 서면 요청이 있을시, UN사무총장은 인권위 위원국 다수의 동의를얻어 동 PROCEDURE 발동

 . 5인의 전문가 그룹 구성

 . 동그룹이 비밀 보고서 작성

 . 동보고서를 해당국에 송부, 의견 요청

 - 인권위 위원국 다수의 동의가 있을경우 상기보고서와 해당국 의견을 인권위특별회의(EXTRAORDINARY MEETING) 에 회부

 . 다수의 동의가 없을 경우, UN 총회 또는 인권위 정기 회의중 먼저 개최되는 회의에 회부.끝

 (차석대사 김삼훈-국장)

외 무 부

종 별 :

번 호 : GVW-0338   일 시 : 92 0212 1030

수 신 : 장관(연이)

발 신 : 주 제네바 대사대리

제 목 : 48차 인권위(8)   [91V

1. 인권위에 참가중인 아주지역 국가간 회의가 지역 COORDINATOR 인 인니측 사회로 금 2.11(화) 개최된바, 주요 내용은 아래와 같음.
  가. 인권위 의장단의 설명
   0 동의장단에 아주지역을 대표하고 있는 이란이 의장단 동향을 언급한바, PLO 아라파트의장의 연설 허용여부를 두고 일부 회원국의 반발이있었으나 SOLT 의장이 허용키로 결정하였음을 알림.
   - 연설 예정일자: 2.13(목)
  나. 아주지역국가 관심사항
   0 미얀마와 인니가 자국의 인권문제가 제기될시 아주지역 국가들의 지원을 요망한다는 발언을 한바, 여타국으로 부터 특기할 반응이 없었음.
  다. 오지리 KLESTIL 차관의 제안
   0 오지리의 EMERGENCY PROCEDURE 에 대한 아주그룹차원의 대응 방안이 논의되었으나 중국, 인도,파키스탄등이 중요한 제안이라고 하면서도 다음문제등이 불분명하므로 성급히 논의할수 없다고 하여 추후 지역 그룹회의에서 재론키로 함.
   - 어떠한 인권침해에 적용할지 여부
   - 현존 메카니즘과의 기능 중복 문제
   - 최종적으로 심할 유엔 BODY 가 일정치 않은문제
  2. 상기 오지리 제안에 대한 추후 논의에 대비, 아측입장을 정리해 두는 것이 좋을 것으로 사료되는바, 지침 하시바람.(오지리 차관 연설은 파편송부함)끝
   (차석대사 김삼훈-국장)

국기국   차관   1차보   청와대   안기부

외 무 부

관리 92
번호 -122

종 별 :

번 호 : GUW-0052   일 시 : 92 0212 2400

수 신 : 장 관(미중,국연,경일,정보,사본:주제네바대사-중계필,상공부)

발 신 : 주 과테말라 대사

제 목 : 유엔 인권실태 조사단 아국업체 방문

1. 금 2.12(수) 12:30 경주재국 인권실태 조사차 당지 방문(2.12-16)중인 유엔인권 조사단 (단장:CHRISTIAN TOMUSCHAT 유엔사무차장 인권자문관, 독일인)은 주재국 RAMIRO DE LEON CARPION 인권위원장과 EDUARDO COROMAC 형사지법 판사를 대동하고 아국업체 PRENDAS ESTRELLA(삼성, 대정 공동투자)를 불시방문, 1 시간에 걸쳐 동 업체에 근무하는 현지근로자의 인권실태를 조사한바 있음.

2. 당관이 언론기관등을 통하여 탐문한바에 의하면 동 조사단은 현지인 구타, 환기시설 부족, 화장실 불결, 식당시설 불량, 장기간 야간작업 강요, 노동시간에 비해 임금 저렴등의 사례를 지적하였다 하며 동 조사현장에는 현지언론 이외에도 UPI 및 REUTER 등 외신기자도 취재에 참여한바 있어 상기 내용이 외신에 보도될 가능성이 큰것으로 보임.

3. 소직은 동 조사단 방문결과가 보도될 경우에 대비하여 김옥주 참사관을 대동하고 주재국 4 대일간지를 방문, 동 기사 삭제, 불연일 경우 기사축소를 협조 요청한데 이어 AGUILERA 노동차관을 방문, 상기조사단의 아국업체 조사배경을 문의하고 동 사건이 확대되지 않도록 협조를 요청함.

4. 동 차관은 노동부를 비롯한 행정부가 금번 조사를 주선하거나 관여한바 없으며 주재국 정부로서도 이같은 조사에 깊은 우려를 가지고 있다고 언급하면서 동 조사단이 명일에도 아국업체를 포함한 외국진출업체를 방문한후 SOLORZANO 노동장관에게 현지노동 인권실태에 관한 조사결과를 브리핑할 예정이라고 하였음.

5. 금번 유엔조사단의 주재국 방문 목적은 CHRISTIAN 자문관이 현재 제네바에서 개최되고 있는 제 48 차 유엔인권위의 과테말라 인권실태 보고서 작성자료로 활용(당지 독일대사에 의하면 동 자문관이 인권위에서 일단 구두보고 예정이라고 함)하기 위한 것이라 함.

미주국	장관	차관	1차보	2차보	국기국	경제국	외정실	분석관
정와대	안기부	상공부	중계					

6. 한편, 아국업체 방문배경에는 지난 91.3-6 월 사이에 PRENDAS ESTRELLA 를 비롯한 4 개 아국업체가 법원에 제소되는등 아국업체의 인권침해 사례가 국내외에 대대적으로 보도된바 있어 이중 고발된 동업체를 선정 1 차 방문 한것으로 추측됨.

7. 당관은 당지 전아국업체에게 상기 조사단 방문시에 대비, 철저한 준비와 주의를 환기시키는 한편 CHRISTAN 조사단장과의 면담을 추진하고 있으나 동단장의 TIGHT 한 일정(일면 소직과의 면담을 기피하는 인상도 보임.)으로 실현가능성은 희박한 것으로 감지되고 있음.

8. 상기 진전사항 추보 하겠음. 끝.

(대사 강응식 - 국장)

예고: 92.12.31. 일반.

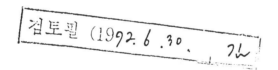

2 乃

주 과 테 말 라 대 사 관

GUW(F): 0001-1-1   년월일 : 1992.2.13.   시간 : 1855

수 신 : 장   판 (미중, 국언, 경입, 정보, 사본 : 상공부)

발 신 : 주 과테말라 대사

제 목 : 한국업체 관련기사 송부

보 안	
봉 제	如

(출처 :   )

26 PRENSA LIBRE (92.2.11)

Thomuschat inicia visitas a fábricas maquiladoras

VISITA. El experto en derechos humanos de la ONU, Christian Thomuschat, (2o. por la derecha) conversa con uno de los trabajadores de una fábrica de la zona 2. Le acompañan el Juez Eduardo Antonio Cornmac y el Procurador de los Derechos Humanos, Ramiro de León Carpio. (Roche)

EL PROFESOR Christian Thomuschat, experto en Derechos Humanos de ONU, inició ayer una serie de visitas a empresas maquiladoras de diversas nacionalidades para investigar la situación de centenares de trabajadores guatemaltecos.

El experto de la ONU arribó ayer mismo al país, para evaluar la situación de los derechos humanos, y su primera actividad fue acudir a una fábrica situada en la zona 2, para verificar denuncias formuladas por trabajadores, en el sentido de no recibir buen trato ni pago del salario mínimo.

El profesor Thomuschat llegó acompañado del Procurador de los Derechos Humanos, Ramiro de León Carpio, así como de otros funcionarios de esa institución, el Juez 2o. de 1a. Instancia Penal de Instrucción, Eduardo Antonio Coromac Ambrosio, y de Carlos Villán Durán, del Centro de Derechos Humanos de la ONU.

Los trabajadores de dicha empresa maquiladora expresaron a Thomuschat su descontento por el mal trato de que son víctimas por parte de los supervisores, a quienes acusaron de no pagarles el salario mínimo y obligarlos a trabajar hasta diez horas, sin cancelarles horas extras.

Indicaron, además, que en otra fábrica laboran más de 600 trabajadores, y en su mayoría devengan un salario diario de entre Q5.50 y Q8.50. Asimismo, explicaron que si faltan a sus labores un día, se los descuentan y también pierden el derecho al séptimo día.

Hicieron ver también los trabajadores que las instalaciones de la empresa no son [...] nas, les causa deshidratación cotidiana, y llevaron al visitante a los sanitarios, que están en malas condiciones, así como al comedor.

El visitante de la ONU condenó la situación y dijo que la empresa incumple las leyes del país. El Juez Coromac dijo que su presencia en el lugar con el profesor Thomuschat obedecía a la comprobación de violación a los derechos humanos de los trabajadores en ese lugar.

Esas anomalías ya fueron denunciadas al tribunal a su cargo, y recientemente decretó la reinstalación de 70 trabajadores que habían sido destituidos, así como otras medidas cautelares.

Afirmó que los empresarios afectados con tal medida presentaron un recurso de amparo, el cual conoce la Corte de Constitucionalidad.

En tanto, el Procurador de los Derechos Humanos, Ramiro de León Carpio, explicó al profesor Thomuschat que la institución a su cargo ha intervenido en base a la denuncia presentada por los afectados.

Por que en su oportunidad emitió una condena en la violación de que son víctimas los trabajadores, y señaló a las autoridades del Ministerio de Trabajo y Previsión Social, de avalar esos abusos en perjuicio de los intereses de los trabajadores.

Los representantes de la empresa mencionada declinaron hacer ningún comentario sobre la presencia del profesor Thomuschat y del licenciado de León Carpio.

외신 1 과	
봉 제	

배부처	장관	차관	一차보	二차보	기획실	의전실	실건	이주국	대주국	구주국	중아국	국기국	경제국	통상국	문교부	영교국	총무과	감사관	공보관	의연원	청와대	총리실	안기부	공보처	경기기원	상공부
	/	/	/	/	/				O			/	/						/		/		/	/	

0138

외 무 부

종 별 :

번 호 : GUW-0053

일 시 : 92 0213 1830

수 신 : 장관(미중,국연,경일,영사,사본:주제네바대사-중계필,상공부)

발 신 : 주 과테말라 대사

제 목 : 유엔 인권조사단의 아국업체 방문

연: GUW-0052

1. 소직은 금 2.13 12:00 당지 UNDP 대표의 주선으로 연호 조사단장인 CHRISTIAN THOMUSCHAT 사무총장 인권자문관을 방문,40 분간 단독 요담하였음. 동 자문관은 작일 한국업체(대정-삼성) 방문시 자신이 목격 및 청취한 인권침해 사례를 열거한후 이에 심한 우려를 표하면서 한국의 대표적 기업인 삼성이 여사한 위법 및 비도덕적 행위를 한데 대하여 유감으로 생각한다는 의견을 피력 하였음.

2. 소직은 에에 대하여 외국기업이라는 불리한 입장, 양국민간의 생활관습 및 사고방식의 차이와 언어불통에서 연유되는 오해와 마찰이 있을수 있고 대부분중소규모인 한국기업의 당지진출이 일천한 관계로 시설에 미흡한점이 있으나 향후 공관의 계도로 이를 시정해 나갈 것임을 밝히고 유엔 인권위 제출 보고서에는 아국관계 부분을 삭제해 줄것을 요망하였음. 이어 소직은 삼성이 상기사의 일부지분을 소유하고 있는것은 사실이나 경영에는 일체 참여치 않고 있음도 부언 설명하였음.

3. 이에 대하여 상기 자문관은 신규회원국으로 유엔에 가입한 한국의 향후 역활 및 한. 독 간의 우호관계등을 고려하여 가급적 한국 이미지에 부정적인 영향을 미치지 않도록 하겠다고 답변하였는바, 주제네바 대표부에서도 동인과의 접촉을 건의함.

4. 한편 당관 김옥주 참사관은 금일 오전 상기조사단과 함께 아국업체를 방문한 EDUARDO COROMAC 판사(지난해 4 개업체 고발사건 담당)를 면담, 아국업체 방문 동기 및 사법당국의 향후 조치에 관해 문의한바 동 판사는 THOMUSCHAT 조사단장의 방문시점인 지난주 주재국 인권위로부터 동 업체의 현지인 구타사건(2.7)이 고발된 것이 직접적인 동기이며, 구타자(이창근,35 세)는 유엔 인권위 및 주재국 인권위등 국내외 여론을 감안 사법조치(구속등)하여 그 조치결과를 언론에 보도할수 밖에 없는 입장이라고 하였음.

미주국 분석관	장관 정와대	차관 안기부	1차보 상공부	2차보 중계	국기국	경제국	영교국	외정실

PAGE 1

5. 당관으로로서는 구타사건과 관련한 주재국 여론악화 및전아국업체에 미치는 악영향을 최소화 하기 위하여 적절하다고 판단되는 시기에 아래내용의 보도자료를 주재국 언론매체에 배포코자 하는바 이에 대한 본부입장 을 지급회시 바람.

- 아 래 -

LA EMBAJADA DE LA REPUBLICA DE COREA INFORMA A TODO EL PUEBLO DE GUATEMALA A TRAVES DE SU MEDIO DE COMUNICACION QUE EL DIA 12 DE FEBRERO DEL PRESENTE ANO SE HA ENTERADO DEL INCIDENTE SOBRE DE QUE UN TECNICO COREANO COMETIO UN ACTO RUDO EN CONTRA DE UNA TRABAJADORA GUATEMALTECA EN EL CURSO DEL TRABAJO DIARIO EN UNA MAQUILADORA COREANA.

ESTA MISION DIPLOMATICA NO PUEDE TOLERAR ESTE TIPO DE INCIDENTE EN CUALQUIER SITUACION, MIENTRAS ESTA MISION ESTA EDUCANDO A LAS MAQUILADORAS A ACATAR LAS LEYES Y RESPETAR LAS COSTUMBRES DE GUATEMALA. POR LO TANTO, LA EMBAJADA DE LA REPUBLICA DE COREA LAMENTA LO OCURRIDO Y TIENE SENTIMIENTO DE RESPONSABILIDAD POR NO EVITAR ESTE INCIDENTE.

A ESTE RESPECTO, NO EXISTE NINGUNA OBJECION DE QUE LAS AUTORIDADES CORRESPONDIENTES TOMEN LAS MEDIDAS PERTINENTES SOBRE LA PERSONA CULPABLE. APARTE DE LA SANCION EMITIDA POR PARTE DE LAS AUTORIDADES GUATEMALTECAS, LA EMBAJADA DE LA REPUBLICA DE COREA TIENE TODA LA VOLUNTAD DE DEPORTAR A ESTESENOR QUE HA PUESTO EN MAL LA IMAGEN DE COREA Y DE LAS MAQUILADORAS COREANAS, ESPECIALMENTE HA CAUSADO DANO ENTRE LA RELACION LABORAL Y AMISTOSA ENTRE AMBOS PUEBLOS.

SINCERAMENTE, LA EMBAJADA DE LA REPUBLICA DE COREA OTRA VEZ LAMENTA ESTE HECHO E INFORMA QUE SEGUIRA HACIENDO TODO EL ESFUERZO PARA QUE NO VUELVA A OCURRIR ESTE TIPO DE VIOLACION A LOS DERECHOS HUMANOS, A LA VEZ, RUEGAAL PUEBLO Y A LAS AUTORIDADES DE GUATEMALA TODA SU COMPRENSION Y COLABORACION ANTE NUESTRA POSICION.

6. 또한 금 2.13 자 주재국 4 대 일간지중 3 대일간지는 동 보도 삭제, 최대일간지인 PRENSA LIBRE 지는 한국 및 문제업체명을 거명하지 않고 축소보도 하였는바, 동 관련기사 FAX 편 송부함.

7. 당관은 이번사건의 원만한 수습을 위하여 노동 장관 및

PAGE 2

0140

인권위원장(2.19.예정)등 주재국 주요인사를 접촉 예정임. 동 진전사항 추보
예정임.끝.

　　(대사 강웅식 - 국장)

　　예고: 92.12.31. 일반.

검토필 (1992. 6 .30 .) 　진

주 제 네 바 대 표 부

제네(정) 281-165   1992. 2. 14

수신 : 장 관

참조 : 국제기구국장

제목 : 48차 인권위 주요발언문

92 2. 14

　　　표제회의시 주요발언문(퀘일 미부통령 연설, Klestil 오지리 차관
연설 포함)을 별첨 송부합니다.

　　　첨부 : 1.　퀘일 미부통령 연설

　　　　　　 2.　Klestil 오지리 차관 연설

　　　　　　 3.　Kozyrev 러시아 외상연설

　　　　　　 4.　기타 각종 발언문.　끝.

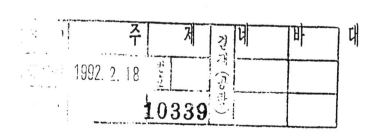

0142

주 제 네 바 대 표 부

제네(정) 2031-166   1992. 2. 14

수신 : 장 관

참조 : 국제기구국장

제목 : 48차 인권위 아국관련 사항   92. 2. 14

연 : GVW-0360

연호 표제 아국관련 사항 언급이 포함된 문건을 별첨 송부합니다.

첨부 : 1. Habitat Int'l 문서

　　　2. Int'l Confederation of Free Trade Union 문서. 끝.

주   제   네   바   대

0143

UNITED
NATIONS

Economic and Social Council

Distr.
GENERAL

E/CN.4/1992/NGO/2
16 January 1992

Original: ENGLISH

COMMISSION ON HUMAN RIGHTS
Forty-eighth session
Item 12 of the provisional agenda

QUESTION OF THE VIOLATION OF HUMAN RIGHTS AND FUNDAMENTAL FREEDOMS
IN ANY PART OF THE WORLD, WITH PARTICULAR REFERENCE TO COLONIAL
AND OTHER DEPENDENT COUNTRIES AND TERRITORIES

<u>Written statement submitted by Habitat International Coalition, a
non-governmental organization on the Roster</u>

The Secretary-General has received the following communication, which is
circulated in accordance with Economic and Social Council
resolution 1296 (XLIV).

[16 December 1991]

1.   Under international human rights law, violations of social and cultural
rights are equally serious as violations of civil and political rights,
although this fact is commonly ignored or even denied in practice and in
national legislation. A specific violation of these rights concerns the
practice of forced eviction - the involuntary and illegal removal of a person,
household or community from their home(s). Evictions continue to be carried
out in a majority of Member States of the United Nations, despite the view of
various United Nations human rights bodies that evictions constitute a gross
violation of a range of human rights, in particular the right to adequate
housing. This view has been formalized by both the Committee on Economic,
Social and Cultural Rights and the Sub-Commission on Prevention of
Discrimination and Protection of Minorities. If, as is consistently
reaffirmed, all human rights are indeed interdependent and indivisible, action
by the Commission on Human Rights is long overdue.

GE.92-10226/8418a

0144

2.   The Committee on Economic, Social and Cultural Rights took the
unprecedented step during its fifth session (1990) of concluding that the
Government of the Dominican Republic had violated the right to adequate
housing as contained in article 11(1) of the Covenant. The forced and violent
eviction of over 120,000 persons from the cities of Santo Domingo and Santiago
by the Government, in an attempt to "beautify" these cities for the
preparation of celebrations surrounding the 500th anniversary of Columbus's
landing there in 1992, led to this forward-looking and constructive
contribution to international human rights jurisprudence.

3.   More recently, in December 1991, the Committee in its
General Comment No. 4 on the right to adequate housing, stated, _inter alia_,
that "the Committee considers that instances of forced evictions are
prima facie incompatible with the requirements of the Covenant and can only be
justified in the most exceptional circumstances, and in accordance with the
relevant principles of international law".

4.   The Sub-Commission on Prevention of Discrimination and Protection of
Minorities adopted by consensus on 26 August 1991 resolution 1991/12, entitled
"Forced evictions". The first paragraph explicitly draws the attention of the
Commission on Human Rights to both the fact that the practice of forced
evictions constitutes a gross violation of human rights, in particular the
right to housing, and to the need for immediate measures to be undertaken at
all levels aimed at eliminating the practice of forced eviction.

5.   Resolution 1991/12 continues by recommending that the Commission
encourage Governments to undertake policy and legislative measures aimed at
curtailing the practice of forced eviction, including the conferral of legal
security of tenure to those currently threatened with forced eviction.
Additional emphasis is placed on the importance of the provision of
compensation and/or alternative accommodation, consistent with the wishes and
needs of persons and communities forcibly or arbitrarily evicted, following
negotiations with the affected persons or groups.

6.   Habitat International Coalition encourages the Commission to act upon the
recommendations found in resolution 1991/12 with a view to considering all
possible activities that could be undertaken towards eliminating the rapidly
growing global practice of forced evictions. Giving concrete substance to the
range of economic, social and cultural rights, including the right to adequate
housing, will require resolute and determined action by the Commission. To
attain these aims, Habitat International Coalition respectfully suggests two
specific, practical and attainable activities which could be carried out by
the Commission on the issue of forced evictions: 1. The adoption of
United Nations guidelines on the planning of international events;
and 2. The appointment of a United Nations special rapporteur on evictions.

United Nations guidelines on the planning of international events

7.   Through monitoring the practice of forced evictions throughout the world,
Habitat International Coalition has noted a disturbing, although almost
invariably ignored, tendency that forced evictions precede virtually all major
international events. Olympic games, world's fairs (Expos), international
conferences, Miss Universe contests, anniversaries, celebrations and other

0145

events, while perhaps positive events in promoting international cooperation, have damaging impact upon low-income groups and those groups not fully enjoying the human right to adequate housing. Governments and the international financial institutions often seek to hide or justify these human rights violations, in the name of "the public good", "public relations" and "in the name of progress for development". Sometimes evictions are carried out in an obvious fashion, accompanied often by bulldozers and demolitions. However, an equal if not greater number of people are effectively evicted by more subtle and hidden means, such as rent increases, the denial of basic services, urban renewal and other less easily seen processes.

8.   For example, the following selected international events, in chronological order, were preceded by various types of involuntary evictions in publicly justified attempts to "beautify" certain cities, to increase available luxury hotel accommodation and to "hide urban poverty and slums": (a) visit of Her Majesty the Queen of England (Harare, Zimbabwe, October 1991); (b) annual meeting of the World Bank and the IMF (Bangkok, Thailand, October 1991); (c) 1992 Summer Olympic Games (Barcelona, Spain, 1990-1991); (d) preparations for the celebrations of the 500th anniversary of Columbus's landing in the Americas (Santo Domingo and Santiago, Dominican Republic, 1989-1991); (e) 1988 Winter Olympic Games (Calgary, Canada, 1987-1988); (f) 1988 Summer Olympic Games (Seoul, South Korea, 1981-1988); (g) 1988 World's Fair (Brisbane, Australia, 1988); (h) 1986 World's Fair (Vancouver, Canda, 1985-1986); (i) 1982 World's Fair (Knoxville, USA, 1981-1982); (j) 1982 Asian Games (New Delhi, India, 1981-1982); (k) Miss Universe pageant/visit of the Pope (Manila, Philippines, 1982); (l) annual meeting of the World Bank and the IMF (Manila, Philippines, 1976); and (m) 1967 World's Fair (Montreal, Canada, 1967).

9.   Habitat International Coalition has also received reliable information concerning pending and planned evictions which are likely to be carried out in the near future prior to several international events. These include: further evictions in the community of La Cienega in the Dominican Republic, addressed in presidential decree 358-91 and set to evict up to 12,000 families, the 1992 Miss Universe Pageant (Bangkok, Thailand) and the 1996 Summer Olympic Games (Atlanta, USA).

10. The adoption and promotion by the Commission on Human Rights of a set of guidelines for the planning of international events could assist in creating practical policies upon which States could base plans prior to convening such events. Evictions during the planning stage of these activities need by no means be inevitable and international guidelines can go a long way towards promoting international understanding and cooperation, while simultaneously protecting the rights of vulnerable groups.

The appointment of a United Nations special rapporteur on evictions

11. The appointment of a thematic special rapporteur on evictions by the Commission could assist greatly in limiting a form of human rights violation which year after year denies some of the most fundamental rights to millions of persons throughout the world. As a wide variety of distinct yet interrelated developments indicate that evictions are a growing global

0146

phenomenon, the importance of concrete United Nations action on preventing evictions and finding viable and suitable alternatives to this practice is indisputable.

12. A special rapporteur on evictions could carry out several central functions. Firstly, the potential and actual victims of evictions - a group with virtually no access to international legal remedies or redress - would, like victims of other human rights violations, finally have direct access to United Nations human rights and legal protection. If requested, the rapporteur should be mandated to carry out on-site fact-finding missions aimed at evaluating the human rights implications of a planned or actual eviction. The huge group of victims of illegal abuse resulting from eviction requires enhanced consideration from the international community.

13. Secondly, a rapporteur on this issue could play an infinitely important role in searching for and advocating alternatives to forced eviction, placing due emphasis upon the fundamental right of all women and men to a secure place to live in peace and dignity. The United Nations special rapporteur on eviction, once aware of a planned mass eviction, could be requested to intervene as an independent intermediary between the evictors and the evicted, aiming most importantly at preserving and protecting the housing rights and housing freedoms of the world's citizens.

14. Thirdly, a rapporteur on this issue could attempt to document national legislation which impinges in any way on the right to housing through the eviction process, with a view to suggesting amendments such that the relevant legislation can be adapted so as to guarantee people's housing rights. Such a mandate could lead eventually to a compilation of legislative principles geared towards developing a United Nations human rights instrument aimed at halting evictions.

15. Fourthly, the annual preparation, distribution and compilation of reports outlining the details of evictions in a global sense and wherever they occur, will provide the Commission on Human Rights with a unique and comprehensive overview of this practice - something at present which is totally lacking.

16. Fifth, and finally, the special rapporteur on evictions could also explore the development of a set of reliable and accurate "eviction indicators", geared towards assessing the human rights impact of policies and practices promoted by international and bilateral development and financial agencies, which result in forced evictions.

17. Habitat International Coalition respectfully requests the Commission on Human Rights to consider the advantages for the advancement of legal and human rights inherent in adopting United Nations guidelines on the planning of international events and of appointing a United Nations special rapporteur on evictions, as substantial and concrete steps towards enhancing global respect for economic, social and cultural rights, in particular the right to adequate housing - a right still denied to over one billion persons throughout the world. At an absolute minimum, the Commission should adopt its own resolution equating forced evictions with gross violations of human rights and affirming the work on housing rights currently under way in the Sub-Commission.

0147

SPEECH BY REPRESENTATIVE OF
THE INTERNATIONAL CONFEDERATION OF FREE TRADE UNIONS

Agenda item 10:   RIGHT OF FREEDOM OF OPINION AND EXPRESSION

Mr Chairman,

The International Confederation of Free Trade Unions, and its associated International Federation of Journalists bringing together more than 200.000 journalists belonging to 68 unions in 54 countries wishes to draw the Commission's attention to the widespread violation of the rights of journalists, and its implications for the right of freedom of opinion and expression.

While 1991 was a very good year for democratic change, it was a murderous year for journalists. The IFJ recorded a total of 84 killings of journalists in 23 countries. They died while on assignment or in circumstances directly related to their work.

The IFJ believes that fresh international action is needed to curb the growing wave of violence against working journalists.

Unless Governments show more respect for independent journalism and take steps to ensure media freedom and freedom of expression there will be strongly negative consequences for democratiic life.

It is for this reason that the IFJ actively supports the work of all United Nations agencies, and particularly Unesco in efforts to develop free and independent media systems around the world.

The IFJ played a leading role in the organisation of the Unesco Windhoek seminar almost a year ago. This meeting, organised to focus on the needs of Africa, in the development of democratic media structures, was a

0148

watershed event.

Noting that at least 17 journalists, editors and publishers were at that time in African prisons, and that 48 African journalists had been killed in the exercise of their profession between 1969 and 1990, the participants asked the general assembly of the United Nations to declare censorship a grave violation of human rights, justiciable in the Commission on Human Rights.

The declaration said that, as a sign of good faith, African Governments which had jailed journalists for their professional activities should free them immediately. Where journalists had to leave their countries, they should be free to return to resume their professional activities.

The seminar called for specialist research into a range of issues, and adopted a list of specific projects to foster the development in Africa of a free, independent and pluralistic press, and the establishment of independent trade unions of journalists, and associations of publishers.

One of the most significant and important developments at this meeting was the strong support from African publishers and journalists for the right of journalists in African countries to establish independent, representative trade unions.

The creation of such organisations for journalists - and for independent publishers - is a matter of priority not just in Africa, but in all parts of the world. This requires that media and labour relations laws in all societies should be drawn up in such a way as to ensure that such representative associations can exist to fulfil their important tasks in defence of press' freedom.

Freedom of opinion and expression requires a quality press and audiovisual media system, staffed by trained journalists working in decent moral and material conditions.

For the IFJ there is no conflict of interest between trades

0149

unionism and professional journalism. Far from it. There can be no genuinely free press when journalists or other mediaworkers work in conditions of poverty and technological deprivation.

The time is right to consider whether or not there is a need to create a new media culture, one that is democratic and one that gives practical and concrete meaning to international declarations and commitments to freedom of opinion and expression.

Such a media culture would need to identify the necessary conditions for the exercise of these freedoms including:

- a proper commitment to openness and free flow of information through freedom of information legislation,

- a recognition of the "people's right to know" and guarantees of citizen's rights of access to sources of information, both political and commercial, upon which they can properly debate questions before making democratic decisions,

- the establishment and maintenance of an independent, pluralistic and free press which is essential for economic and democratic development.

By independent, is meant media systems independent from direct governmental, political or economic control and also independent of indirect controls through management of supply of materials and infrastructure essential for the production and dissemination of newspapers, magazines and periodicals.

Such independence must also be extended to journalists and other media professionals to ensure that they are protected from internal pressures which often lead to "self-censorship", the most pervasive and corrosive of all forms of censorship.

By pluralism, we meant an end to monopolies of all kind, and the existence of the greatest possible number of newspapers, magazines and periodicals reflecting the widest possible range of opinion within the community. Of course, these concepts and principles apply equally to electronic, film and audiovisual media.

Regrettably these minimum conditions which can guarantee freedom of opinion and expression exist in very few countries of the world. Recently, the IFJ has sent factfinding missions to report on situations in South Africa, El Salvador, Peru, Guatemala, Korea, Fiji, Israel and the Occupied Territories. In each of these regions press freedom has been compromised and freedom of expression denied.

While we welcome political changes which lead to increasing support for nations of multi-party democracy and which provide the climate in which an independent and pluralistic press and a new democratic media culture can emerge, we are in no doubt that more progress has to be made.

Specifically, we believe - having endured a year of killings of journalists in wars in the Gulf and Yugoslavia - that existing international instruments governing the rights of people in wartime need to be strengthened to protect journalists.

During the civil war in Yugoslavia some 21 journalists have been killed. Others are missing. The IFJ is very concerned by suggestions that journalists have been particularly targeted during this conflict. Indeed, wherever in the past 12 months there has been social and political struggle journalists have been the victims of those who wish to control and manipulate information to suit their own interests.

We believe that specific study should be undertaken to analyse and define minimum conditions for the exercise of journalism in areas of conflict. It is not good enough, in our view, for protagonists, even those who claim to be raising the banner of democracy, to justify manipulation of media and pressure on working journalists.

But, of course, there are some areas where democratic values have no weight at all. An area of familiar concern to the IFJ remains the high death toll in Latin American where 22 journalists were killed in 1991 -

0151

eight of them murdered in Colombia and seven in Peru. In Latin America journalists are under attack from drug gangs, paramilitary forces and terrorists.

In response to escalating violence the IFJ has sought to apply pressure on governments to take responsibility for their international commitments to the physical welfare of journalists.

In respect of Peru, in addition to initiatives at the international level the IFJ is negotiating at this present time with the Government to try to come to an acceptable arrangement for the proper and independent investigation of all attacks on journalists and media within that tragically divided country.

Journalists and mediaworkers demand that all governments fulfil their obligations and responsibilities. But getting them to do so can be difficult.

It has to be said that the procedures to make denunciations and to take cases before the international courts are time consuming, are complex and allow unco-operative governments opportunities to evade their responsibilities by technical means.

This should not be acceptable in an accountable and democratic world. We believe that the time may be right for substantial reform of the United Nations Human Rights apparatus with a view to improving the overall effectiveness of the machinery and making the system as accessible and as transparent as possible.

We are in no doubt that sharpening the teeth of United Nations human rights jurisdiction would be an important step forwards in guaranteeing freedom of opinion and expression. Certainly, improvements are necessary if our aim to have censorship declared a violation of human rights is to be meaningful at all.

Finally, while we journalists make many demands on governments, media organisations and intergovernmental authorities, we know well that we

0152

have a collective responsibility to ensure the highest standards of professionalism and solidarity in these difficult times.

It is with that in mind that the IFJ launched, on January 1st this year, a worldwide Humanitarian Aid Project - the IFJ SAFETY FUND. This is the first international fund established by journalists for the relief of journalists in need anywhere in the world.

Violence against journalists is not only a political outrage, but also a deep personal tragedy. This safety fund will provide humanitarian aid to journalists and their families who are the victims of violence.

The IFJ regrets that it should have to establish such a fund, but the issue of freedom of opinion and expression is not some intellectualised concept for many journalists. It is a matter of life and death.

* * * * * * * *

0153

주 제 네 바 대 표 부

제네(정) 2071-167   1992. 2. 14

수신 : 장 관

참조 : 국제기구국장, 아주국장

제목 : 48차 인권위

연 : GUW-0360

        연호 표제회의시 동티몰문제에 관하여 제기된 발언문을 별첨송부
합니다.

        첨부 : 상기 관련 문서. 끝.

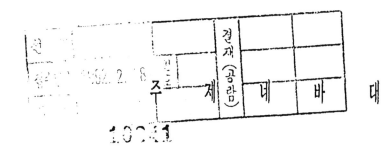

0154

Oral Intervention
of
Amy Goodman

Pax Christi International

Thank you, Mr. Chairman. My name is Amy Goodman. I'm a journalist with Pacifica radio, a public radio network in the United States. I want to thank Pax Christi International for inviting me to speak.

Several months ago, I survived a massacre in East Timor carried out by the Indonesian army.

On November 12, thousands of Timorese gathered for a mass commemorating the recent death of a young man killed when soldiers surrounded and shot into the Catholic Church.

After the mass, they marched to the cemetery. As the procession wove its way through the streets of Dili, more and more people joined – from their workplaces, schools and homes. The crowd was bold, but orderly, with junior high school boys trotting along, putting up the v sign and chanting "Viva", and older boys yelling, "Disciplina! Disciplina!" keeping them in line. And people carried banners, a forbidden act in East Timor. "Indonesia, why you shoot our church" and "Portugal, we are your responsibility" were among the slogans they carried. By the time the procession reached the cemetery, there were well over three thousand people. Like the funeral two weeks before, things were winding down and this seemed to be the time that everyone would go home. That is, until we saw hundreds of troops marching towards the crowd in formation, machine guns in hand.

At this point, journalist Allan Nairn and I moved to the front of the crowd, so that the soldiers would see us. As Westerners with head phones, tape recorder, microphone and camera in full view, we thought the soldiers would be less likely to attack. We were wrong. As the soldiers rounded the corner, without missing a beat, without warning or provocation, they began firing into the crowd, their automatic weapons spraying bullets from right to left and back again, mowing everyone down in front of them. The Timorese were trapped. With walled cemeteries on either side, they had nowhere to go. When they saw the soldiers coming, some people started to back up, others began to turn around and run.

A few seconds after the Indonesian soldiers began shooting, other soldiers surrounded me. One grabbed my microphone and shook it in my face, then pushed me onto the ground. Others ripped off my bag and equipment and began kicking me in the sides and stomach, punching me in the face and hitting me with their rifles. At that point, Allan, who was just behind me when the troops had opened fire, threw himself over me as I was being beaten, protecting me from further injury. We were then directly behind the line of fire and they just kept beating and kicking Allan in the head and chest and sides until his shirt was drenched in blood.

At one point, Allan's hands and legs went into spasm and he couldn't protect himself anymore. The soldiers continued to beat his head with rifle butts, until they fractured his skull. They then put the M-16s to our heads. We kept shouting "We are from America,

0155

America." After a few minutes, they decided not to execute us. Instead, they focussed their attention on an old Timorese man next to us who they beat into a sewer ditch. Every time he picked up his head, a soldier would mercilessly kick it or punch it down with his rifle butt. We kept our heads down and eyes averted, fearing that just our looking in his direction would enrage the soldiers further.

A truck drove by and we jumped into it, as the driver helped the old man in. No matter how brutally we had been treated, it was nothing compared to what had happened to the Timorese. Bodies were lying everywhere. The soldiers had now moved into the cemetery. As we drove off, we continued to hear gunfire. The jeep was soon flagged down by a young Timorese man and within minutes dozens of terrified people had climbed through the windows, were hanging off the sides and back of the jeep, as the soldiers sealed off the entire neighborhood around the cemetery, killing people as they went.

We drove to the hospital, where the wounded were crowding in. We saw a teenager shot in the back, another being operated on and a boy with his arm ripped open. People were lying in the hallways. We spoke with religious and medical people, all of whom said they had tried to get into the massacre area to help the wounded, but the soldiers wouldn't let them go. Kamal Bamadhaj, a New Zealand student studying in Australia had been in the crowd at the cemetery. He was standing behind us, holding a camera, minutes before the soldiers opened fire. He was shot. The Red Cross jeep that drove him to the hospital was stopped twice by the military and detained. The doctor who treated the young man told his family he could have lived through the bullet wounds, it was the loss of blood that killed him.

Hours later, when we fled the country, the army was moving from house to house, rounding people up. The Timorese Bishop estimated that more than 180 people were killed.

We had originally gone to East Timor to report on the human rights situation before, during and after the visit of the Portuguese delegation. Although their trip was cancelled, we still travelled throughout the countryside, speaking with dozens of Timorese. We heard the same story everywhere. The military had held meetings in each village, warning the people that if anyone spoke with the Portuguese, they would be killed as soon as the delegation left. In addition, the Timorese were told, mass graves had already been dug for their bodies. It was clear that a nationwide death threat had been issued. Before the massacre, East Timor Bishop Belo said the military had repeatedly told the Timorese if they spoke, their families would be killed "to the seventh generation."

We had also been in East Timor the summer of 1990. With this trip over a year later, we found the situation had deteriorated even further. Disappearances, imprisonment and torture had increased dramatically, further terrorizing the population. This was the context in which the massacre took place.

Recently, the Indonesian government officially banned the New Yorker correspondent and me from returning to the country. If Indonesia wants to cut down on negative publicity, the answer is not to beat and ban journalists, but to stop the killings, detentions and tortures that have continued even since the November 12 massacre. In addition they should abide by the two UN Security Council resolutions passed after the invasion calling on Indonesia to withdraw from East Timor without delay.

Thank you, Mr. Chairman.

0156

COMMISSION ON HUMAN RIGHTS
Forty-eighth session
Agenda item 10
February 1992

Oral Intervention
of
Allan Nairn

Pax Christi International

        Thank you Mr. Chairman. My name is Allan Nairn,
I'm a journalist from the United States and I've come to
speak at the request of Pax Christi International.
While in Dili last November 12 on assignment for the New
Yorker magazine, I witnessed and survived the massacre
outside the Santa Cruz Cemetery.

        Amy Goodman and I were standing between the soldiers
and the Timorese as the Indonesian troops advanced upon the
crowd. The Timorese were gathered peacefully outside the
cemetery gate as the uniformed soldiers marched up in massed
formation. They moved in a deliberate and disciplined
fashion -- many hundreds of troops, all wielding M-16s --
and as soon as they turned the corner and got close to the
Timorese they raised their rifles to their shoulders and
opened fire all at once.

        Timorese were backpedaling, gasping, trying to flee,
but in seconds they were cut down by the hail of fire.
People fell, stunned and shivering, bleeding in the road,
and the Indonesian soldiers kept on shooting. I saw the
soldiers aiming and shooting people in the back, leaping
bodies to hunt down those who were still standing. They
executed schoolgirls, young men, old Timorese. The street
was wet with blood, and the bodies were everywhere.

        As the soldiers were doing this they were beating me
and Amy; they took my camera and our tape recorders and
fractured my skull with their M-16s.

        It was clear that what we witnessed was a cold and
disciplined act of state. The crowd was utterly defenseless
and posed no threat of any kind. At the moment the soldiers
suddenly appeared, the crowd was standing still; the
procession from the church had ended ten minutes earlier.
When the Timorese spotted the long column of advancing
troops, many began trying to shrink away. But an army troop
truck had sealed one exit route and the crowd was hemmed in
by cemetery walls. It soon became quite evident from the
way the soldiers behaved that they had marched up with
orders to committ a massacre. They never issued a warning,
they did not even pause or break their stride, they simply
marched up and opened fire in unison. This was not a result

0157

of their interaction with the crowd: the Timorese were
simply standing there or trying to get away, and the
soldiers opened fire as soon as their column turned the
corner and got within a dozen yards of the Timorese.   There
was no provocation from the Timorese, there were no stones
or objects thrown; the crowd, in fact, was no longer even
chanting.

The reason these Timorese were killed was because they
had the courage to engage in public assembly and public
speech.   General Try Sutrisno, the chief of the Indonesian
armed forces, said in a speech on November 13 to graduates
of the national defense institute, that Timorese like those
who gathered outside the cemetery are "people who must be
crushed."   He said "delinquents like these agitators have to
be shot and we will shoot them." He added, "come what may,
let no one think they can ignore ABRI (the Indonesian armed
forces).   In the end they will have to be shot down."

After this, Indonesia responded to international
pressure by issuing a report saying that the Timorese had
behaved "savagely" and claiming that the massacre was a
spontaneous act that "clearly did not occur because of any
command or policy of the Government or the Armed Forces."

The Indonesian report is a very simple and damnable
lie, and no government that praises it can be taken
seriously. The only way that any government can put any
stock in this report is if they are willing to ignore the
testimony of every single known foreign and Timorese
eyewitness, as well as the policy statements of the
Indonesian armed forces chief.

General Sutrisno added on December 9, that as soon
as Indonesia's investigation of the massacre is completed
"we will wipe out all separatist elements who have
tainted the government's dignity."   Sutrisno has no legal
basis to say the Timorese are "separatist," since
Indonesia's occupation has been rejected by the
international community.   The Security Council has
affirmed that the East Timorese have the right to self-
determinatiion, and it carries on its books two
resolutions (from 1975 and 76) which call on Indonesia to
"withdraw without delay."

Since Indonesia invaded East Timor in 1975, its army
has massacred and killed through forced starvation about
a third of the East Timorese population.   This deliberate
murder of 200,000 people ranks as one of the major
genocides of this or any century, and is clearly the
continuing Jakarta policy.

President Suharto responded to the November 12
massacre by going out of his way to ridicule the
Timorese.   He said that when world leaders asked him
about the killings in Dili,"I showed them a map where
East Timor is located, the tiny island called East Timor.
That small thing caused everybody to make a fuss.   And,"

0158

he said, "they all laughed."   When later faced with
threats to cut off international aid, Suharto responded
with the phony report, and by transferring two mid-level
generals. He, for example, replaced the commander of
East Timor with a new general who promptly announced that
his predecessor has been "too soft" and too tolerant in
his response to the November 12 procession.

     Suharto also ordered the prosecution of East
Timorese who participated in the march to the cemetery
and were fortunate enough to survive the massacre. As
this was going on (with some of those prosecuted now
facing the death penalty), the army stepped up repression
still more, and East Timor has been terrorized, since
November 12, by a wave of abduction, torture, and
assassination of Timorese in Dili and the countryside.
The army has also been mounting a program of ruthless'
interrogation of clergy and people active in the Catholic
Church. In particular the army has been persecuting
Father Alberto Ricardo, the administrator of the Dili
diocese. There have also been several credible reports
of mass extrajudicial executions of Timorese who
witnessed the November 12 massacre or are thought to be
critics of Indonesia.

     It is hard to imagine a more simple or clear-cut
case of human rights crime than East Timor. The
government of Indonesia is engaged in mass murder of
unarmed, unprotected civilians. Many nations of the
world have a special responsibility to end their
complicity in this crime. The United States supplies the
weapons, along with England and other states, and Japan,
the Netherlands, Australia and others provide crucial   ⟵ add
financial support; without them Indonesia would not be
able to so openly defy law and the Security Council. But
there is also a responsibility for nations everywhere to
stand up for this persecuted people. If this Commission
is to be serious about complying with its mandate, it
will have to take decisive action on East Timor.

          2:00 rm 23.

          Under item 10
          Cuz do in p
          Torture, mentioned in
              R's inc

0159

PERMANENT MISSION OF THE REPUBLIC OF INDONESIA
TO THE UNITED NATIONS AND OTHER INTERNATIONAL ORGANIZATIONS

16, Rue de Saint-Jean · 1203 Geneva · Tel. (022) 45 33 50

STATEMENT

BY

THE INDONESIAN DELEGATION TO THE

48TH SESSION OF THE COMMISSION ON HUMAN RIGHTS

ON ITEM 10

<u>Please check against delivery</u>

0160

Mr. Chairman,

Speaking at this late stage of our debate on item 10, I shall confine my remarks mainly to the problem of torture, with regard particularly to the report of the Special Rapporteur as contained in document E/CN.4/1992/17 and its addenda. But, first, let me take this opportunity to express to Prof. P. Kooijmans the sincere appreciation of my delegation for the report and for his lucid introductory statement. I would also like to say at the outset that we share the concern of the Special Rapporteur to the effect that torture still is a disturbingly widespread phenomenon, and I even venture to say that often torture is practised by individuals belonging to government circles in an abuse of governmental power. However, we would definitely prefer to be much more cautious when it comes to identifying torture as a deliberate, let alone official, tool of government policy. As far as Indonesia is concerned, our state philosophy, constitution and national legislation all strictly prohibit the practice of torture as a means of extorting information or evidence.

The importance that we attach to the problem of torture has been concretely manifested in the decision of the Indonesian Government to invite the Special Rapporteur on the Question of Torture to visit Indonesia. It has been our sincere expectation to be able to learn and benefit from such a visit in order to eradicate the practice of torture that may exist in my country as in so many other countries in the world. The visit did take place, from 3 to 16 November of last year, and the report is now before us. My delegation has examined the report with keen interest and sincerely appreciates the Special Rapporteur's efforts to produce a critical analysis and to come up with recommendations. It should be taken as perfectly normal if in the course of such an exercise, apart from views on which we find ourselves in agreement and remarks which make us feel encouraged as well as recommendations which we find valuable, there are also points of honest disagreement. But we should be less than candid if we did not say that, regrettably, we also find points which are out of context and procedures which we find improper.

0161

Inasmuch as we take the report in a positive spirit, we do hope that the Special Rapporteur will also accept my observations with an equally open mind.

Mr. Chairman,

To begin with the happier notes, my delegation is encouraged by the findings and conclusions highlighted in the report, to the effect that basic human rights, including the right to physical and mental integrity, are indeed guaranteed by the Indonesian state philosophy, constitution and legislation. Furthermore it is gratifying to note the recognition that Indonesia is constantly improving the legal structure. We also see eye to eye with the Special rapporteur on the need for Indonesia to speed up the process of its ratification of, and accession to, a number of international instruments on human rights. Indeed we have established a working group to study all international instruments with a view to clearing the way for our ratification. We appreciatively noted Prof. Kooijmans' opinion on the necessity for a national commission on human rights since it is in line with the recommendation of our national seminar, held in cooperation with the UN Centre for Human Rights in January 1991.

While taking due note of the Special rapporteur's findings concerning loopholes in our administration of justice and weaknesses in our institutions which prevent us from combating torture more effectively, we detect some shortcomings in his conclusions due to his failure to see that there exist in Indonesia hundreds of legal aids institutions affiliated with universities or law schools as well as other social organisations. With regard to the identified weak point in our mechanism for complaint, although the report does mention several mechanisms for receiving complaints on the abuse of power such as the famous Post Office Box 5000, it does not give appropriate credit to the internal control mechanism within each respective body, nor does it take into account the level of prosecution and punishment of officials who abuse their power as well as the

0162

newly instituted Administrative Court which deals in particular
with the abuse of power by government officials. My delegation
accepts all those as honest differences which probably stem from
the lack of time available to the Special Rapporteur which has
prevented him from obtaining as much knowledge and information
as he might have wished.

On the other hand, there are aspects of the report that have
created problems which are unacceptable to my delegation. The
first problem concerns the strange manner in which the report has
been published. Although dated 8 January 1992, the report was
not actually made available to delegations until 28 January.
Strangely enough some items of the report have already been
quoted in the Dutch newspaper NRC Handelsblad of 25 and 27
January. We find this procedurally improper and it should be
corrected. The second problem which we consider out of context
is the alleged violation of the freedom of expression and
association contained in the report. It should be clear that the
question of the freedom of expression and association is a
separate thematic subject and outside the mandate of the Special
Rapporteur on the Question of Torture. Furthermore such
allegations are not substantiated and will only reduce the value
of the report.

Mr. Chairman,

The reference in the report that has created the most
serious problem for my delegation is the one related to the Dili
incident of 12 November 1991. Here I would like to make it clear
that in our view the difficulty was by no means created by the
Special rapporteur himself who, though he admittedly went beyond
his mandate, could not refrain from mentioning the incident in
his report because of his coincidental presence on the spot.
Rather the problem emerged because this particular reference has
been manipulated by a certain delegation to launch its usual
accusations against my country.

0163

4

It did not come as a surprise to my delegation that the representative of Portugal has dedicated almost his entire lengthy statement under this item to East Timor, trying desperately to convince this Commission of his outdated arguments linking allegations of human rights violations with what he calls "the denial of the right to self-determination". It is evident that the references made do not represent a genuine concern for human rights, but are loaded with political motivation, obviously attempting to cover-up Portugal's own infamous record as the former colonial master of East Timor for more than 400 years. Respecting mandate of this august Commission, I shall not dwell at length on the so-called issue of self-determination. Suffice it to recall a historical fact that Portugal irresponsibly abandoned the territory in mid-August 1975 on the verge of a civil war which it had itself instigated. It is against this unfortunate background that the overwhelming majority of the people of East Timor have long ago exercised their right to self-determination by choosing integration with Indonesia.

With regard to the Dili incident of 12 November 1991, from the beginning we have never denied that such an incident happened. Never have we considered ourselves free from errors. The Indonesian Government at the highest level has even formally and sincerely expressed its deepest regret over the incident and in particular the unfortunate loss of lives that the incident has caused. However, like any other responsible government, my government did immediately and seriously take the necessary measures to address the incident and to redress the situation. Swift and important actions were taken following the recommendation of our National Commission of Inquiry, including bringing to justice all those involved in the incident and suspected of having violated the laws. The process is still going on and will continue to be pursued. In this context the Indonesian Government is also cooperating with the United Nations by welcoming the Special Envoy of the Secretary General, Mr. Amos Wako, who is now in Indonesia to obtain clarifications on the incident. This important visit is now still in progress.

0164

Mr. Chairman,

Like any other tragic incidents, the Dili incident of 12 November 1991 has hurt us. We are now in the sensitive and delicate process of healing our wound. In this regard, what we think we can justifiably and legitimately expect from this august body is a measure of understanding and cooperation in this difficult period. What we precisely do not need in the process is an acrimonious statement like that of the Portuguese delegation, which amounts to, and is deliberately aimed at, perpetuating the wound. Such an act is clearly contrary to the very purpose of this august international forum of cooperation.

Thank you Mr. Chairman.

0165

주 제 내 바 대 표 부

김

2

제내(정) 2031- 168

수 신 : 장   관

참 조 : 국제기구국장

제 목 : 47차 인권위 자료

92. 2. 14

　　　　표제 회의기간중 입수한 UN 인권관련 각종 기본 자료를 별첨

송부하오니 참고 하시기 바랍니다.

　　　　첨부 : 상기 자료 각 1부.　끝.

제 　 내 　 바 　 대

결			결재 (공람)		
갈시 1992. 2. 8	10342				
과					

0166

외 무 부

종 별 :

번 호 : GVW-0360

일 시 : 92 0214 1200

수 신 : 장관(연이,아동)

발 신 : 주 제네바 대사대리

제 목 : 48차 인권위(9)

표제회의는 2.13 현재 의제 10 (피구금자 인권)에 대한 토의를 마친바, 주요 사항 아래 보고함.

1. 토의 개관

0 선.개도국을 망라하여 고문등 가혹행위가 상존되고 있는 현실을 개탄하고 유엔 관련협약의 철저한 이행 필요성을 강조하며, 고문방지협약에 다수국의 가입을 촉구함.

- 카나다는 피구금 상태에 있는 여성에 대한 가혹행위에 관심을 경주할 것을 강조함.

- 미국은 특정국에 대한 비난없이 과거 알젠틴의 군사 정권이 저지른 고문 살해사례를 의학적으로 규명하여 온 전문가의 경험을 소개함.

- 화란, 오지리는 각각 페루와 스리랑카의 인권침해 상황을 거론함.

0 NGO 들은 주로 페루, 과테말라, 알젠틴등 중남미 지역에서 우익세력의 테러행위와 터키의 쿠르드족 탄압, 스리랑카, 수단, 시리아, 이란, 쿠바,이락, 중국등의 인권 침해 사례를 거론함.

0 스리랑카, 인도등 개도국들은 민선정부를 전복시키려는 테러 구룹의 행위에대처하는 과정에서 문제가 과장되는 경우가 있다고 하고,경제적 빈곤이 인권 신장에저해가 되는 상황을 설명함.

2. 특이 쟁점(동티몰 문제)

0 폴투갈은 인니의 동티몰 주민 살해 사례를 집중거론 하여 인니정부 행위를 장시간에 걸쳐 비난하였으며, 책임자 처벌등 적절한 조치를 요구하였음.

0 이어 NGO 인 PAX CHRISTI INT'L 의 주선으로 발포현장을 목격한 2인의 미국 언론인이 발언,평화적 시위대에 무차별 사격과 구타를 행한 현장을 생생하게 증언하고 사건 발생이후에도 탄압이 계속되고 있다고 비난하였음.

국기국   1차보   아주국   외정실   분석관   안기부   청와대

92.02.15   06:28 DQ

외신 1과 통제관

0167

O 또한 폴투갈과 상기 미국언론인은 영국언론인이 촬영한 현장 비디오를 회의장인근에서 상영함.

O 이후에도 일부 GNO 와 국가들이 동티몰 문제를 언급한바, 인니측은 수차 답변권을 행사, 사건에 깊은 유감을 표하고 필요한 조치가 취해지고 있음을 강조하였으며,폴투갈이 사건을 치유하려 하기보다 정치적 목적에 이용하려 한다고 응수함.

O 금번 동티몰 문제는 상금 거론된 여하한 인권침해 사례보다 강도 높게 제기되고, 비교적 최근의 사건인 관계로 많은 관심을 모았는바, 인니측 입장이 다소 곤란하게 되는 결과를 가져옴.

3. 아국 관련 사항

O HABITAT INT'L 이 배포한 회의문서(E/CN.4/1992/NGO/2)상에 주민의 의사에반하는 이주 조치 사례중 하나로 88 올림픽 준비시 서울이 적시됨(예년과 동일한 내용)

O INT'L CONFEDERATION OF FREE TRADE UNION 은 2.12INT'L FEDERATION OF JOURNALISTS 의 활동을소개하면서, 최근 IFJ 가 한국등 수개국에 조사단을 보낸바, 그 결과 동국들에서 언론자유화가 타협(COMPROMISED)되고 있음이 밝혀졌다고 함. 끝

(차석대사 김삼훈-국장)

PAGE 2

0168

외 무 부

종 별 :

번 호 : GVW-0359   일 시 : 92 0214 1120

수 신 : 장 관(연이,동구일,중동일)

발 신 : 주 제네바 대사대리

제 목 : 48 차 유엔 인권위(10)

　　- 러시아 외상 및 PLO 의장연설 표제회의시 ANDREI KOZYREV 러시아 외상 (2.12)과
YASSER ARAFAT PLO 의장 (2.13)이 연설한바, 요지 아래보고함.

　　1. KOYREV 외상 연설

　　0 러시아는 소련의 과거사로부터 인권이 NATURAL하며, UNIVERSAL 함을 인식

　　- 인권은 이제문명의 척도

　　과거 소련에 대한 인권 관련 '간섭'이 우리를 전체주의에서 구해낸 결과

　　- 앰네스티, 헬싱키 연맹등 인권 단체의 기여를 평가

　　0 러시아에는 이제 인권의 타방위에서 새로운 체제건설중

　　- 공산주의 또는 파시즘의 대두 가능성을 막아야 함

　　- 잘못된 애국심, 외국인 배척, 반유태주의도 대두 가능성

　　0 러시아의 노력에 국제적 지원 여망

　　0 국제인권 체제의 효율성 강화 방안 연구 필요

　　- 유엔 산하에 MORAL LEADERS OF THE PLANET 의 모임을 설치, 인권 침해 사례를
심의케 하자는 사하로프의 제안 지지

　　- 인권 침해 사례 예방을 위한 국제 경찰 및 경제적 제재 구상도 방법

　　0 민주, 국제법, 인권위에 새로운 세계 질서를 형성하는데 러시아의 기여 다짐.

　　2. ARAFAT 의장 연설

　　0 이스라엘 점령지에서 팔레스타인인의 부쟁상상세 소개 및 지속적 부쟁 천명

　　- 이스라엘의 무력탄압, 정착촌 건설 맹비난

　　. 데모대에 국제적으로 금지된 화학탄을 최루탄으로 위장 사용

　　- 팔인의 피해 소개

　　0 이스라엘의 유엔 안보리 및 인권위 각종결의무시 사례 비난

국기국　　구주국　　중아국　　차관　1차보　2차보　의정실　분석관

PAGE 1   92.02.15   08:56 WG

- 국제사회가 이에 긴급히 대처할것을 촉구

0 미국 및 독일의 대 이스라엘 차관 공여 협의에 우려 표명

- 미국이 정착촌 건설에 반대하는 기존 입장을 견지할 것을 요망

0 중동 평화회담에서 이스라엘이 팔레스타인 대표단 구성에 간섭하는 점을 맹비난

- 이스라엘은 평화 협상에서 이탈하려는 구실을 찾고 있음.

0 팔인의 자결권이 회복될때 평화 도래

(ARAFAT 는 아랍국가등 개도국 대표의 높은 성원을 받으며, 등단, 장장 1시간 10분에 걸쳐 강도 높은 비난을 전개한바, 내용은 점령지에서 이스라엘 행위와 중동평화 회담등에 국한됨. 탐문한바에 의하면 미국등이 동인의 인권위 연설에 반대하였으나 아랍권이 과거 동인이 연설한 전례가 있음을 들어 관철 시켰다함).끝

(차석대사 김삼훈-국장)

PAGE 2

0170

관리 92
번호 ~127

외 무 부

종 별 :

번 호 : GVW-0362   일 시 : 92 0214 1630

수 신 : 장관(연이,미중) 사본:주과테말라대사(본부중계필)

발 신 : 주 제네바대사대리

제 목 : 유엔 인권실태 조사단

대: WGV-0251(GUW-0052), WGV-0257(GUW-0053)

1. 대호 인권조사단은 유엔인권 사무국의 기술자문(ADVISORY SERVICES)의 일환으로 주로 심각한 인권위반 사례가 발생하였거나 발생하고 있는 국가에 대해동 상황 개선을 지원하기 위한 목적으로 유엔 사무총장이 유엔인권 위원회의 요처에 따라 임명하는 개인자격의 전문가(INDEPENDENT EXPERT) 로서, 현재까지 볼리비아 적도기네, 하이티, 우간다, 중앙아프리카에 대하여 임명 활동케 한바 있음.

2. 대호 C.TOMUSCHAT 자문관은 87 년 과테말라 담당전문가로 임명되어 91 년 제 47 차 인권위에서 동 임기가 연장되었음.

3. 자문간의 활동결과는 매년 유엔인권위 회의에 보고(문서 및구두)되어 토의에 회부되는바, 작년 47 차 회의에서 동인이 행한 구두 보고는 자신의 2 회에 걸친 방문 결과를 토대로 대부분 불법구금, 납치, 실종등 정치적 권리에 관한 내용이 주가 되었음.(E/CN4/1991/SR 46 참조)

4. 현재 당지 개최중인 48 차 인권회의시에는 회의벽두 의장이 과테말라 보고서는 아직 준비가 되어 있지않아 당분간 토의를 연기한다고 발표한바 있으며, 2.13. 당관이 유엔인권 사무국에 알아본바, 동 보고서(E/CN4/1992/5)의 서반아본은 준비가 되어있으나 기타 공영어본은 내주경에나 준비 가능하며, 동 문제 토의는 작년과 같이 의제 19 항(ADVISORY SERVICES) 하에서 이루어질 것이라고 함.(2.27 예정)

5. 상기 자문관 보고서 서반아어본의 동건관련 언급내용(PARA 164)은 아래와 같음.(동 보고서 노동권 관련 부분은 FAX 송부)

0 인권담당 검찰관은 91.4.18 결의안에서 봉제업체들의 실태, 특히 안전 및위생 상태, 보수, 시간외 근무등에 관해 검토

0 동 검찰관은 특히 4 개 업체(CONFECCIONES OCEANO SA, PRENDAS ESTRELLA SA,

국기국   차관   1차보   2차보   미주국   영교국   정와대   안기부   중계

PAGE 1   92.02.15   07:37
                                                         외신 2과 통제관 BN
                                                              0171

MODAS DEL ESTE SA 및 SM MONDAS SA)가 노동자들의 인격, 자유, 노동과 신체의 존엄성등을 침해 하였다고 발표

0 상기업체의 작업장에는 노동자들의 생명과 건강을 보호할 수 있는 안전 위생시설이 결여되어 있고 실내온도가 지나치게 높음을 확인

0 또한 상기 업체들이 연소자를 고용 성인노동자와 같은 시간을 근무하도록강요하고 있으며 시간외 근무 보수를 지급하지 않는 사례가 많았다고 지적

0 또한 상기 업체에는 한국인이 노동부의 허가없이 불법취업하고 있는 것으로 확인

0 따라서 검찰관은 노동부가 상기 업체들의 노동자 인권침해를 묵인하고 있다고 공개적으로 비난하고 적법한 조치를 요구

0 또한 내무성에 대해서는 이민국이 동 업체에 취업하기 위해 입국하는 외국인들에 대해 효율적인 통제를 하도록 권고

6. 본건은 해당업체가 아국 투자진출 업체라 하더라도 유엔인권 차원에서는기본적으로 과테말라 국내인권과 관계되는 사항으로, 기작성된 상기 보고서에도 아국민의 불법취업 사실외에는 아국에 관한 언급이 없음.

7. TOMUSCHAT 자문관이 2.12-16 방문 결과를 토대로 현 보고서에 대한 ADDENDUM 형식의 추가 보고서를 제출할런지의 여부 및 구두 보고서 동건을 특별히 부각시킬 지의 여부는 불확실하나, 현재로서 동인의 구두보고는 과테말라 정치정세, 무력충돌과정에서의 인권문제, 정치적.시민적 권리 및 경제적, 사회적, 문화적 권리의 4 개 CHAPTER 를 포함하는 총 80 페이지에 달하는 보고서의 개요를 20 분내에 요약 소개하는 형식이 될것으로 전망됨.

8. 문제기업이 아국의 투자기업이라 하더라도 과테말라 국내법의 적용을 받는 현지법인이라면 아국 인권과는 무관한 사항일뿐만 아니라, 동 자문관이 구두보고에서 한국기업임을 밝힌다 하더라도 아국이 이에대해 해명 조치를 취하는 것은 불필요한 관심만 촉발시킬 것이라는 점에서 바람직하지 않다고 보나, 만일에 대비하여 제소된 4 개 업체 관련 현황자료(투자지분, 진출년도, 법인등록국, 제조품명, 종업원 규모, 아국인 취업현황) 및 과테말라내 아국기업 진출현황 자료 회시바람. 끝

(차석대사 김삼훈-국장)

예고:92.6.30 까지

2
7u

주 제 네 바 대 표 부

번 호 : GVR(F) - 0106   년월일 : 20214   시간 : 1630
수 신 : 장   관 (연미·口름)
발 신 : 주 제네바대사
제 목 : 과테말라 건享없세

풀세라료 별첨 송부함

총 6 매(표지포함)

보 안 통 제	도

외신관 통 제	·

배 부처	장관실	차관실	일차보	이차보	기획실	의전실	공보관	아주국	주국국	구주국	국제국	국기국	경제국	통상국	문화국	영교국	총무과	감사관	공보과	외연권	청화대	총리실	안기부	공보처	경기원	상공부
								1	0																	

대

106-6-1

0173

E/CN.4/1992/5
página 56

Santa Lucía; los vecinos se oponían a la tala de árboles de ese lugar. Hechas las averiguaciones oportunas, el Procurador declaró que se había comprobado la violación del derecho social al patrimonio natural, medio ambiente y reforestación, señalando como responsable de ello a la Dirección General de Bosques y Vida Silvestre, por no dictar las medidas necesarias en garantía de la utilización racional de la explotación de los recursos forestales situados en la finca denominada "Cumbre de Agua Zarca e Higueral". En definitiva, la citada Dirección General no había ejercido el debido control y vigilancia sobre la licencia de explotación forestal que se había concedido.

B. Los derechos sindicales

160. El Experto ha seguido con atención varios casos presentados ante el Comité de Libertad Sindical del Consejo de Administración de la Organización Internacional del Trabajo contra Guatemala. El primero de ellos es el caso N° 1512 que se originó en una queja interpuesta por la Confederación Internacional de Organizaciones Sindicales Libres (CIOSL) y que se refiere a amenazas de muerte, desapariciones forzadas, torturas y muertes violentas de que fueron víctimas varios sindicalistas, además de una constante represión contra el ejercicio del derecho de huelga, así como la negativa a conceder personalidad jurídica a nuevos sindicatos. Todas estas alegaciones constituyen graves obstáculos al ejercicio de los derechos sindicales (ver los antecedentes en E/CN.4/1991/5, párrs. 71 y 72). En 1991, el Comité de Libertad Sindical volvió a estudiar este caso, constatando una vez más que no se había facilitado información respecto a los alegatos formulados por la Confederación querellante, por lo que instó de nuevo al Gobierno a realizar investigaciones judiciales independientes respecto de los alegatos de asesinato el 2 de julio de 1989 de un miembro del Sindicato de Trabajadores de la Empresa Embotelladora Central S.A., "STECSA" (Coca-Cola), José Orlando Pantaleón, cuyo cadáver fue encontrado acribillado a balas y desfigurado por la tortura. También solicitó el Comité que se investigara el asesinato de nueve campesinos en Alta Verapaz, ocurrido el 22 de agosto de 1989, así como la muerte del dirigente de la huelga de maestros Carlos Humberto Ribera, que había sido secuestrado el 9 de septiembre de 1989; también el asesinato de Estanislao García y García, miembro del Sindicato Agrícola Independiente, ocurrido el 17 de septiembre de 1989; el asesinato de José León Segura de la Cruz, secretario general del Sindicato de Trabajadores del Instituto Nacional de Electrificación, ocurrido el 27 de septiembre de 1989 en el departamento de Chiquimula; en fin, la muerte de campesinos en San Marcos y en el departamento de El Progreso los días 14 y 15 de septiembre de 1989, así como la muerte de campesinos en el departamento de Quetzaltenango. En cuanto a la lentitud de las autoridades en la concesión de personalidad jurídica a los sindicatos, el Comité invitó al gobierno a garantizar a los trabajadores el derecho de constituir sus organizaciones sin autorización previa, y a las organizaciones de trabajadores el de redactar sus estatutos y sus reglamentos administrativos sin intervención de las autoridades públicas que limite este derecho (278° informe del Comité de Libertad Sindical, doc. GB.250/8/13, 250a. reunión del Consejo de Administración de la OIT, Ginebra, mayo-junio de 1991, caso N° 1512, párr. 399). En su siguiente reunión, el Comité recordó, ante el argumento del Gobierno de que los alegatos planteados no podían imputársele por haber tomado posesión el 15 de enero de 1991, que un gobierno que sucede a otro en el mismo Estado no puede por el solo hecho de ese cambio escapar a la responsabilidad contraída por los hechos sobrevenidos bajo el Gobierno

0174

precedente. En cuanto a los asesinatos denunciados, el Comité tomó nota de
los procesos incoados, lamentando que el tribunal militar competente en el
caso de los asesinatos de campesinos de Alta Verapaz haya ordenado la
suspensión del proceso por falta de pruebas (279° informe del Comité de
Libertad Sindical, doc. GB.251/8/11, Ginebra, 11-15 de noviembre de 1991,
párrs. 657 y 664).

161. El Comité de Libertad Sindical también estudio en 1991 el caso N° 1539,
originado por la queja presentada por la Confederación Mundial de
Organizaciones de Profesionales de la Enseñanza (CMOPE) contra el Gobierno de
Guatemala. Se refería a alegaciones de serios actos de represión e
intimidación, incluyendo el asesinato y desaparición de sindicalistas
pertenecientes al sector de los docentes y a otras organizaciones, a amenazas
de muerte contra dirigentes sindicales, a represalias contra el Sindicato de
Trabajadores de la Enseñanza de Guatemala (STEG) y otras organizaciones
sindicales por haber convocado una huelga el 29 de agosto de 1989 en favor de
sus reivindicaciones salariales y profesionales. El Comité deploró que el
Gobierno no hubiera respondido a esta queja y le instó a emprender las
investigaciones oportunas. Respecto a las amenazas de muerte contra
dirigentes del STEG, entre ellos su secretario general Werner Miranda
Calderón, el Comité deploró estas prácticas e instó al Gobierno a adoptar las
medidas que impidan toda suerte de amenazas e intimidación psicológica contra
los dirigentes y afiliados sindicales. Sobre la detención de sindicalistas
docentes que habían participado en la huelga de mayo a agosto de 1989, el
Comité recordó que el derecho de huelga de los trabajadores y sus
organizaciones constituye uno de los medios esenciales de que disponen para
promover y defender sus intereses profesionales. También solicitó al Gobierno
sus observaciones sobre prácticas de discriminación antisindical en contra de
los huelguistas, tales como la destitución de profesores y las sanciones
económicas que se les impusieron (278° informe del Comité de Libertad
Sindical, doc. GB.250/8/13, Ginebra, mayo-junio de 1991, párr. 421). En su
siguiente reunión, el Comité advirtió que el Gobierno no había respondido a
las denuncias de amenazas de muerte contra los dirigentes del STEG por lo que
le invitó a adoptar las medidas adecuadas que eviten amenazas de muerte u
otras formas de intimidación psicológica contra dirigentes y miembros
sindicalistas. Sobre la detención de docentes sindicalistas que habían
participado en la huelga de maestros de mayo a agosto de 1989, el Comité
consideró el argumento del Gobierno en el sentido de que habían sido detenidos
por razones de orden público, pero concluyó que se trataba de motivos
justificados por la ley como faltas, por lo que espera que el Gobierno
renunciará a las medidas de detención en caso de realización de una huelga
pacífica o de participación en la misma. Por último, sobre las medidas de
discriminación antisindical contra huelguistas tales como la destitución de
docentes y la aplicación de sanciones financieras, el Comité desea saber si
los profesores destituidos tuvieron la posibilidad de reintegrarse a sus
puestos de trabajo (279° informe del Comité de Libertad Sindical,
doc. GB.251/8/11, Ginebra, 11-15 de noviembre de 1991, párr. 664).

162. En lo que se refiere a hechos ocurridos en 1991, el Experto ya ha hecho
mención a la resolución de 16 de diciembre de 1991 del Procurador de los
Derechos Humanos, en la que se abordó la cuestión del derecho de huelga de los
médicos residentes de los hospitales nacionales. En este sentido, el
Procurador recordó que el artículo 116 de la Constitución de 1985 reconoce el

106 - 6 - 3

0175

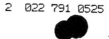

E/CN.4/1992/5
página 58

derecho de huelga de los trabajadores del Estado, pero lo limita en su ejercicio a "...la forma que preceptúe la ley de la materia y en ningún caso deberá afectar la atención de los servicios públicos esenciales" (art. 116, párr. 2). Pues bien, el Decreto 71-86 del Congreso dispone en su artículo 4 c) que no podrá realizarse huelga alguna cuando con ella se pretenda afectar los servicios esenciales a que se refiere el artículo 243 del Código de Trabajo. Entre esos servicios esenciales se comprende el de los trabajadores de clínicas y hospitales, higiene y aseo públicos, mientras no proporcionen el personal necesario para evitar que se suspendan tales servicios sin causar un daño grave e inmediato a la salud. Habiendo constatado que este requisito fue incumplido por los médicos residentes de los hospitales nacionales Roosevelt y San Juan de Dios, el Procurador declaró a los citados médicos como responsables de haber negado el derecho a la salud de la población guatemalteca, en especial la de escasos recursos económicos.

163. En otra ocasión, el Procurador de los Derechos Humanos abordó el derecho a constituir organizaciones profesionales libremente. En efecto, en su resolución de 23 de julio de 1991, el Procurador se pronunció sobre la denuncia que había recibido de Edgar Ovidio Duarte Gómez y otros siete trabajadores municipales que habían sido objeto de una serie de vejámenes por parte del alcalde municipal de San Pedro Carchá (departamento de Alta Verapaz), así como de varios familiares y amigos del alcalde, con el objeto de obligarles a renunciar a formar parte del sindicato de trabajadores que habían constituido. El alcalde y sus amigos incluso agredieron moral y físicamente al juez de paz de la localidad, así como al secretario del juzgado y al auxiliar del Procurador de los Derechos Humanos, a un periodista y al asesor de los sindicalistas. En consecuencia, el Procurador declaró que el alcalde de San Pedro Carchá, Otto Erwin Gutiérrez González, había sido responsable de la violación de los derechos a la dignidad, integridad y seguridad de las personas y libre sindicación, entre otros, ordenándole la cesación de la violación y la reinstalación de los ocho trabajadores municipales en sus puestos de trabajo.

164. Por otro lado, en la resolución de 18 de abril de 1991, el Procurador de los Derechos Humanos estudió la situación de las fábricas de maquila, sobre todo en lo que se refiere a las condiciones de seguridad e higiene, salarios y horas extraordinarias. En particular, el Procurador declaró que las empresas Confecciones Océano S.A., Prendas Estrella S.A., Modas del Este S.A. y SM Modas S.A., incurrieron en violación a los derechos a la dignidad, libertad, integridad física y trabajo de sus trabajadores. En efecto, el Procurador comprobó que las áreas de trabajo de esas empresas no reunían las condiciones de seguridad e higiene para proteger la vida y salud de los trabajadores, pues existía una acumulación excesiva de calor. También observó que en esas empresas trabajan muchos menores de edad, a quienes se les obliga a hacer jornadas iguales que los trabajadores adultos, incluidas horas extraordinarias que en muchos casos no se les remuneran. También constató que en esas empresas trabajaba personal coreano de manera no reglamentaria, pues no disponía de los permisos pertinentes del Ministerio de Trabajo y Previsión Social. Por ello el Procurador censuró públicamente a ese Ministerio, al tolerar la violación a los derechos humanos de los trabajadores de esas empresas, instando al Ministerio a ejecutar las medidas legales pertinentes.

106-6-4

0176

Por último, el Procurador recomendó al Ministerio de Gobernación que, a través de la Dirección General de Migración, ejerciera un control eficiente de la situación migratoria de los extranjeros que ingresan al país para trabajar en esas empresas.

165. En 1991, se han denunciado casos de despidos masivos e injustificados que según se alega constituyen un medio de represión e intimidación contra el ejercicio de derechos sindicales. Así, los despidos en la empresa "Inmobiliaria Los Estanques", donde a raíz de la constitución de un sindicato el 4 de septiembre de 1991 se obligó a los trabajadores a firmar su renuncia; trabajadores de esa empresa se quejan de ser presionados por parte del Tribunal de Antigua Guatemala a fin de que desistan del juicio que han entablado contra la empresa. Se denunciaron asimismo intimidaciones y amenazas de muerte a su secretario general, Héctor Oswaldo Hernández López. En la empresa "Camisas Modernas" se han producido despidos de mujeres maquiladoras, inclusive con uso de la fuerza; los directivos de esa empresa en forma expresa se pronunciaron en contra de la formación del sindicato. Una de sus trabajadoras, Ana Máxima Rodríguez de Ortega, habría sido recientemente asesinada y los directivos lo atribuyeron a la violencia callejera. Asimismo, han señalado despidos en el sector público: en el Ministerio del Trabajo se despidió al personal de un departamento donde laboraban diversos miembros del Comité Ejecutivo Sindical.

166. Asimismo, la Confederación de Trabajadores de Guatemala (CGTG) ha denunciado en carta abierta al Presidente de la República de fecha 19 de agosto de 1991 el intento de secuestro y asesinato de Yolanda Figueroa, Secretaria General del Sindicato Nacional de Aduanas y amenazas a José Pinzón y otros dirigentes; el caso de Rosendo de León, Secretario General del Sindicato de Tipografía Nacional; de Mauricio Roxcajo, miembro del Consejo Consultivo del FENASTEG, quien en abril de 1991 denunció casos de corrupción oficial, por lo que fue objeto de agresiones físicas en junio de 1991 y se vio obligado a salir del país. Hasta la fecha se estima que más de 20 sindicalistas han tenido que salir del país en 1991; algunos de ellos han obtenido asilo político en Canadá y los Estados Unidos. Todo ello, pese al Pacto Social, instancia política creada mediante acuerdo gubernativo emitido en Consejo de Ministros el 1° de marzo de 1991 con el objeto de estudiar, negociar y formalizar el citado Pacto como instrumento dinámico que aúne las voluntades de los sectores productivos representados en torno a la búsqueda de situaciones a la problemática social del país, como medio para lograr la estabilidad económica y social.

167. La Comisión de Expertos en Aplicación de Convenios y Recomendaciones de la OIT ha señalado su preocupación al encontrar algunas divergencias entre la legislación laboral de Guatemala, el Código de Trabajo y los convenios internacionales del trabajo de los que Guatemala es Parte. Así, la Comisión señaló que existen diversas disposiciones del Código de Trabajo que no se ajustan a lo dispuesto en el Convenio N° 87 sobre libertad sindical y protección del derecho de sindicación y son las siguientes: artículo 207 (prohibición a los sindicatos de intervenir en política); art. 211 a) y b) (estricta supervisión de las actividades sindicales); art. 22 f) y m) (requisito de contar con dos tercios de los miembros del sindicato para ir o no a la huelga); art. 223 b) (establece que sólo los naturales de Guatemala tendrán acceso a cargos sindicales directivos); art. 226 a), (disolución del sindicato que intervenga en asuntos de política electoral o de partidos);

106 — 6 — 5

E/CN.4/1992/5
página 60

art. 241 c) (requerimiento de dos terceras partes de los trabajadores para la declaración de huelga); art. 243 a) y 249 (prohibición de la huelga o suspensión de trabajo por parte de los trabajadores agrícolas durante el tiempo de cosecha); arts. 243 d) y 249 (prohiben la huelga o suspensión de trabajo a aquellos trabajadores de empresas o servicios que, a juicio del Gobierno, afecten gravemente la economía nacional); art. 255 (posibilidad por parte de las autoridades de trabajo de recurrir a la Policía Nacional para garantizar la continuación del trabajo en casos de huelga ilegal); art. 257 (prevé la detención y juicio a personas que inciten o participen en una huelga que contravenga las disposiciones del capítulo concerniente a la huelga y al paro en el Código de Trabajo); y art. 390, párr. 2 (penas de uno a cinco años de prisión para quienes saboteen o destruyan, paralicen o perturben el funcionamiento de las empresas, con el propósito de causar perjuicio a la producción nacional) (Conferencia Internacional del Trabajo, 78a. reunión, 1991, Informe II (Parte 4A), pág. 192).

168.	La Comisión señaló también que las legislaciones nacionales deben ser flexibles en el sentido de permitir el acceso a los trabajadores extranjeros a cargos directivos sindicales, al menos tras un período razonable de residencia. Asimismo, se debería permitir a los sindicatos intervenir ante las instituciones públicas a fin de buscar una mejora cultural, económica y social de los trabajadores. En lo que se refiere a las huelgas, las restricciones o prohibiciones a su ejercicio deben ser compatibles con el Convenio N° 87 en relación con los servicios esenciales, los cuales se deben entender en el sentido de que la interrupción de actividades provocada por la huelga puede poner en peligro la vida, seguridad o salud de la persona en toda o parte de la población, o en casos de crisis nacional aguda (ibid., págs. 192 y 193).

169.	Sobre las demoras excesivas en la inscripción de los sindicatos, el Gobierno respondió que existe una iniciativa de ley de reformas al Código de Trabajo que recoge todas las observaciones de la Comisión, por lo que ésta espera que el texto final del Código de Trabajo armonice plenamente la legislación y la práctica nacionales con las disposiciones del Convenio N° 87 (ibid., pág. 193).

170.	En cuanto a la compatibilidad del Código de Trabajo con el Convenio N° 98 sobre el derecho de sindicación y negociación colectiva, la Comisión de Expertos ha pedido al Gobierno la revisión del artículo 272 a), que impone una multa de 100 a 1000 quetzales al empleador que pretenda obligar al trabajador a afiliarse o desafiliarse a un sindicato. Señala la Comisión que debe revisarse el monto con la finalidad de que la sanción conserve su carácter coercitivo. Por último, la Comisión también expresó su esperanza de que el nuevo Código de Trabajo prevea sanciones suficientemente eficaces y disuasivas para todos los casos de discriminación antisindical (ibid., pág. 282).

C. El disfrute de la tierra

171.	El Experto ya señaló en su informe anterior que la vida en el campo guatemalteco está profundamente condicionada por una desigual distribución de la tierra entre minifundios y latifundios. Según el censo realizado en 1979, los minifundios (microfincas o fincas subfamiliares) eran el 88% de las fincas del país, abarcando solamente un 16% de la tierra cultivable. Estos minifundios son demasiado pequeños para proporcionar empleo a tiempo completo

0178

106-6-6

분류번호	보존기간

발 신 전 보

번 호 : WGU-0044   920214 1748 ED   종별 : _____

수 신 : 주   과테말라 대사. ♧♧♧♧

발 신 : 장 관   (연이)

제 목 : 유엔 인권조사단 아국업체 방문

대 : GUW-0052, 0053

대호, Tomuschat 유엔 인권위 과테말라문제 전문가(independent expert)의 아국업체 방문에 따른 대응활동과 관련, 아래사항을 참고바람.

1. 동 전문가 활동의 성격

O 동 전문가는 유엔 인권위 활동의 일환으로 특정국가 인권상황을 조사, 인권위에 보고하는 11명의 특별보고관(전문가)의 1인이며, 동인의 보고서는 91년도에 이어 금년도에도 인권위에 보고될 예정임.

O 과테말라 인권상황에 대하여 인권위에서는 불법처형, 납치, 고문등 심각한 성격의 인권위반상황이 주로 보고되고 있으며, 많은 민간 인권단체들이 동국의 인권상황을 강력히 비판하고 있는바, 대호 아국업체 방문은 국제로비 전반적 인권상황에 대한 조사의 일부임.

/ 계속 /

| | 보 안 통 제 | ⟨서명⟩ |

| 앙고재 | 92년 2월 14일 | 유엔 2과 | 기안자 성명 26흥흥 | | 과 장 ⟨서명⟩ | 심의관 ⟨서명⟩ | 국 장 기결 | | 차 관 | 장 관 ⟨서명⟩ | 외신과통제 |

0179

2. 보고서 처리 경위

　　○ 동 보고서는 금차 인권위에 제출될 것인바, 동내용은 ~~주재국의~~ 상기한
　　　 심각한 인권상황을 전반적으로 다룰 것으로 예상되며, 동 제출시
　　　 Tomuschat 위원의 구두설명이 있을 것임.

　　○ 금차 인권위에서는 동 보고서등에 기초하여 주재국 관련 결의안이
　　　 채택될 것으로 예상됨.　끝.

　　　　　　　　　　　　　　　　　　　　　　(국제기구국장　김재섭)

0180

발 신 전 보

분류번호	보존기간

번   호 : WGV-0269   920215 1459 FE   종별 : 암호송신

수   신 : 주   제네바   대사. ♣♣♣♣♣

발   신 : 장 관   (연이)

제   목 : 제48차 유엔 인권위 대표단

표제회의 본부대표 귀지 도착일정을 아래 통보함.

- 정달호 유엔 2과장 : 2.19(수) 21:45 SR-729편

- 정기용 법무부 검사 : 2.17(월) 21:45 SR-729편. 끝.

(국제기구국장   김재섭)

보안통제	

앙고재	92년2월15일	유엔2과	기안자성명	과장	심의관	국장	차관	장관	외신과통제

0181

분류번호	보존기간

발 신 전 보

번   호 : WGV-0272   920217 1127   DO 종별 : _____

수   신 : 주   제네바   대사. ~~총영사~~ (사본 : 주과테말라대사)   WGU -0047

발   신 : 장   관   (연이)

제   목 : 유엔 인권위 조사단 과테말라 방문

연 : GVW-0052, 0053

연호, Tomuschat 유엔 인권위 과테말라 문제 전문가(independent expert)의 아국업체 조사활동과 관련, 귀관에서는 아래와 같이 대처바람.

1. 동 전문가를 다시 접촉할 경우 ~~동인 보고서에서~~ 실질적인 효과를 기대하기 어려울뿐 아니라 오히려 아국업체 관련 문제가 ~~오히려~~ 부각되거나 불필요한 오해의 우려도 있으므로 동인에 대한 를 초래할 접촉은 추진하지 말기바람.

2. 동인의 보고서 및 인권위 회의에서의 발언등에서 아국업체 관련 내용이 언급되는지를 파악, 보고바람. 끝.

(국제기구국장 김재섭)

인반문서로 재분 : 1992 6. 30.

비각과장.

보 안 통 제	성

앙고재	92년 2월 15일	유민 2과	기안자 성명 김종훈	과 장	심의관	국 장	차 관	장 관

외신과통제

0182

관리 번호	92 — 133

외 무 부

종   별 :

번   호 : GUW-0058   일   시 : 92 0217 1800

수   신 : 장관(연이,미중,사본:주제네바대사-중계필,상공부장관)

발   신 : 주 과테말라대사

제   목 : 유엔조사단 주재국 방문

대:WGU-48

연:GUW-53

1. 연호 유엔 인권위 TOMUSCHT 전문가는 2.16(일) 기출국, 멕시코 향발하였으며 본 경유 제네바에 귀임 예정(일자 미정)이라함.

2. 한편 지난 2.14 밤 ESPINA 부통령이 소직에 전언한 바에 의하면 동인은 당지 체재중 부통령 및 SOLORZANO 노동장관을 방문하고 아국업체의 인권침해 사례를 지적하면서 이의 시정을 위한 적절한 조치가 요망된다는 의견을 피력하였다함을 참고로 보고함. 끝.

(대사 강웅식 - 국장)

예고: 92.12.31. 일반.

검토필 (1992.6.30.   간

국기국	차관	1차보	2차보	미주국	영교국	분석관	정와대	안기부
상공부	중계							

외 무 부

종 별 :

번 호 : GVW-0381

일 시 : 92 0218 1100

수 신 : 장 관(연이)

발 신 : 주제네바대사대리

제 목 : 48차 인권위(11)

1. 표제회의는 2.14 팔레스타인 문제 관련 다음 4개결의안을 표결, 채택하였음.

가. HUMAN RIGHTS IN THE OCCUPIED SYRIANGOLAN(E/CN.4/1992/L.2)

O 찬성 31, 반대 1, 기권 17로 채택된바, 미국이 반대하였으며, 서구, 일본, 러시아는 기권함.

나. QUSTION OF THE VIOLATION OF HUMAN RIGHTS IN THEOCCUPIED ARAB TERRITORIES. INCLUDINGPALESTINE(E/CN.4/1992/L.3)

O PART 4

- 찬성 30, 반대 16, 기권 3으로 채택된바, 미국, 서구, 일본, 러시아는 반대하였으며 오지리, 알젠틴, 칠레가 기권함.

- 다수의 서구국가들은 동 PART A 이 종래보다 강한표현과(KILLING 표현 사용, INTIFADA 를LEGITIMATE RESISTANCE 로 규정) SPECIAL RAPPORTEUR인 WAKO 의 보고서 인용(동 보고서에는입증되지 않은 인권침해 사례가 다수 포함)이 포함되었다는 이유로 반대함.

O PART B

- 찬성 31, 반대 1, 기권 17로 채택된바, 미국이반대하였으며, 서구, 일본, 러시아는 기권함.

다. ISRAELI SETTLEMENTS IN THE OCCUPIED ARABTERRITORIES(E/CN.4/1992/L 5)

O 찬성 45 , 기권 1으로 채택된바, 미국이 기권함.

라. SITUATION IN OCCUPIED PALESTINE(E/CN.4/1992/L.4)

O 찬성 31, 반대 2, 기권 17로 채택된바 미국, 우루과이가 반대하고, 서구, 일본, 러시아등은 기권함.

O 서구국가들은 동 결의안 전문 마지막 PARA'자국내 유태인의 이스라엘 이민을

국기국 외정실 청와대 안기부

조직적으로 추진함은 이스라엘의 점령지내 정착 정책을 지원하고 팔인의 자결권 행사를 저해하는 결과가된다'는 내용의 이민의 권리를 제약한다는 이유로 강한 반대를표명함.

2. 상기 결의 파편 송부함.끝.

(차석대사 김삼훈-국장)

공   란

공 란

주 제 네 바 대 표 부

번 호 : GVE(F) - 0113   년월일 : 2028   시간 : 1800
수 신 : 장   관 (인이, 아일)
발 신 : 주 제네바대사
제 목 :

GVW - 382 관련

총 5 매(표지포함)

보안 통재	机

외신과 통재	

TERNATIONAL EDUCATIⅡAL DEVELOPMENT, INC

8124 West 3rd Street
Los Angeles, California 90048
Phone: (213) 658-7156
Fax: (213) 658-8349

UNITED NATIONS
COMMISSION ON HUMAN RIGHTS
Forty-eighth session
Agenda item 11

PROMOTION OF HUMAN RIGHTS

Statement of International Educational Development,
a non-governmental organization on the Roster
(Secretary-General's list)

HUMAN RIGHTS AND ARMED GROUPS —THE SUDANESE PEOPLE'S LIBERATION ARMY AND UGANDAN HOSTAGES

In its resolution 1991/29 the Commission requested all rapporteurs and working groups to pay attention to acts committed by armed groups adversly effecting human rights, and asked the Secretary-General to collect relevant information on this topic.

International Educational Development brings to the attention of the Commission the situation of hostages being held by the Sudanese People's Liberation Movement (the SPLM) and its Army (the SPLA). A number of soldiers from the Ugandan Army had fled Uganda seeking refuge in Sudan. Unfortuately, the SPLA abducted them and has either forcibly conscripted them or holds them in detention.

One of these prisoner/hostages is Lt. Solomon Onyango Mariki, whose brother, a refugee in Norway, reports that in 1988, SPLM leader John Garang gave captured Ugandans the choice of joining his army or fending for themselves. Those who chose to fend for themselves, including Lt. Onyango Mariki, were recaptured, tried in "tribunals" and imprisoned. Since that time, they have been subjected to extremely harsh treatment and remain hostages.

This situation is not unique. IED proposes that in

1

0189

/13 — (-2

addition to attention being made to these situations by
rapporteurs and working groups, the Commission should prepare an
annual list of persons known to be hostages, including the state
or entity suspected of holding them. The holding powers should
also be asked to respond to inquiries by the Commission.
Governments with contacts with suspected holding powers should be
asked to carry out inquiries and report on the outcomes of them.
Particular situations, such as that now involving the SPLA,
should be addressed by resolution.

2

0190

공   란

공 란

외 무 부

종   별 :

번   호 : COW-0058   일   시 : 92 0218 1700

수   신 : 장관(미중,연이)

발   신 : 주 코스타리카 대사

제   목 : 주재국 외상 국제회의 참석

대:WCO-0010

연:COW-0023

1. NIEHAUS 외상은 제네바 개최 유엔 인권위 연례회의 참석(2.17-23) 및 포루투갈 리스본 개최 SAN JOSE VIII 회의 참석(2.24-26)차 출국하였음(3.2. 귀국예정)

2. 동 외상은 유엔 인권위 회의에서 연호 주재국이 아국 지지를 요청한 고문방지협약 선택의정서 초안 채택 지원, 과테말라 JORGE SERRANO ELIAS 대통령의 평화계획 지지와 하이티, 쿠바등 국가의 인권침해관련 인권존중 연설등 활동을 할 것으로 알려짐.

상기 리스본 회의에서는 중미제국과 EEC 국가간 제반 협력관계를 규정하고 있는 룩셈불그 합의서 유효기간 연장문제가 취급됨. 끝.

(대사 김창근-국장)

미주국	1차보	2차보	국기국	외정실		안기부

2

주 제 네 바 대 표 부

제네(정) 2031-174   1992. 2. 19

수신 : 장   관

참조 : 국제기구국장

제목 : 48차 인권위 결의

         연 : GVW - 0381

   연호 팔레스타인 문제. 관련 결의를 별첨 송부합니다.

   첨부 : 상기 결의 4건.   끝.

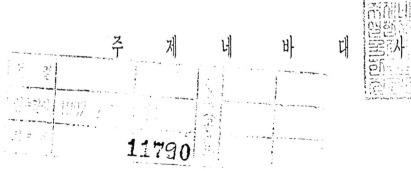

11790

0194

Economic and Social Council

Distr.
LIMITED

E/CN.4/1992/L.2
10 February 1992

Original: ARABIC/ENGLISH

COMMISSION ON HUMAN RIGHTS
Forty-eighth session
Agenda item 4

QUESTION OF THE VIOLATION OF HUMAN RIGHTS IN THE OCCUPIED ARAB TERRITORIES, INCLUDING PALESTINE

Algeria*, Bahrain*, Bangladesh, Cuba, Egypt*, India, Indonesia, Iraq, Iran (Islamic Republic of), Jordan*, Kuwait*, Lebanon*, Libyan Arab Jamahiriya, Madagascar, Mauritania, Morocco*, Oman*, Pakistan, Qatar*, Saudi Arabia*, Senegal, Somalia*, Sudan*, Syrian Arab Republic, Tunisia United Arab Emirates*, Yemen*, Yugoslavia and Zimbabwe*: draft resolution

Human Rights in the occupied Syrian Golan

The Commission on Human Rights,

Deeply concerned at the suffering of the population of the Syrian and other Arab territories occupied by Israel since 1967 and the continued Israeli military occupation, and that the human rights of the population continue to be violated,

Recalling Security Council resolution 497 (1981) of 17 December 1981, in which the Council, inter alia, decided that the Israeli decision to impose its laws, jurisdiction and administration in the occupied Syrian Golan was null and void and without international legal effect, and demanded that Israel should rescind forthwith its decision,

---

* In accordance with rule 69, paragraph 3, of the rules of procedure of the functional commissions of the Economic and Social Council.

GE.92-10474/2962H

0195

Recalling General Assembly resolutions 36/226 B of 17 December 1981, ES-9/1 of 5 February 1982, 37/88 E of 10 December 1982, 38/79 F of 15 December 1983, 39/95 F of 14 December 1984, 40/161 F of 16 December 1985, 41/63 F of 3 December 1986, 42/160 F of 8 December 1987, 43/21 of 3 November 1988, 43/58 F of 6 December 1988, 44/2 of 6 October 1989, 45/74 F of 11 December 1990 and 46/47 F of 9 December 1991.

Recalling General Assembly resolution 3414 (XXX) of 5 December 1975 and other relevant resolutions in which the General Assembly, inter alia, demanded the immediate, unconditional and total withdrawal of Israel from the Arab territories occupied since 1967,

Recalling General Assembly resolution 3314 (XXIX) of 14 December 1974, in which it defined an act of aggression,

Reaffirming once more the illegality of Israel's decision of 14 December 1981 to impose its laws, jurisdiction and administration on the occupied Syrian Golan, which has resulted in the effective annexation of that territory,

Reaffirming that the acquisition of territories by force is inadmissible under the principles of international law and under the Charter of the United Nations and the relevant resolutions of the Security Council and the General Assembly, and that all territories thus occupied by Israel must be returned,

Taking note with deep concern of the report of the Special Committee to Investigate Israeli Practices Affecting the Human Rights of the Palestinian People and Other Arabs of the Occupied Territories (A/46/522) of 18 October 1991 and, in this connection, deploring Israel's constant refusal to cooperate with and to receive the Special Committee,

Expressing its grave alarm, after considering the above-mentioned report of the Special Committee, over Israel's flagrant and persistent violations of human rights in the Syrian and other Arab territories occupied since 1967, despite the resolutions of the Security Council and the General Assembly which repeatedly called upon Israel to put an end to such occupation,

Reaffirming its previous relevant resolutions, the most recent being resolution 1991/2 of 15 February 1991,

Guided by the relevant provisions of the Charter of the United Nations and the Universal Declaration of Human Rights, and with particular reference

0196

to the Fourth Geneva Convention relative to the Protection of Civilian Persons in Time of War, of 12 August 1949, and the relevant provisions of The Hague Conventions of 1899 and 1907,

1.   Strongly condemns Israel, the occupying Power, for its refusal to comply with the relevant resolutions of the General Assembly and the Security Council, particularly resolution 497 (1981), in which the Council, inter alia, decided that the Israeli decision to impose its laws, jurisdiction and administration in the occupied Syrian Golan was null and void and without international legal effect, and demanded that Israel, the occupying Power, should rescind forthwith its decision;

2.   Condemns the persistence of Israel in changing the physical character, demographic composition, institutional structure and legal status of the occupied Syrian Golan and emphasizes that the displaced persons of the population of the occupied Syrian Golan must be allowed to return to their homes and to recover their property;

3.   Determines that all legislative and administrative measures and actions taken or to be taken by Israel, the occupying Power, that purport to alter the character and legal status of the Syrian Golan are null and void, constitute a flagrant violation of international law and of the Geneva Convention relative to the Protection of Civilian Persons in Time of War, of 12 August 1949, and have no legal effect;

4.   Strongly condemns Israel for its attempt to impose forcibly Israeli citizenship and Israeli identity cards on the Syrian citizens in the occupied Syrian Golan and for its practices of annexation, establishment of settlements, confiscation of lands and diversion of water resources, and imposing a boycott on their agricultural products; and calls upon Israel to desist from its settlement designs and policies aimed against academic institutions with the goal of distorting the historical facts and serving the objectives of occupation, and to desist from its repressive measures against the population of the occupied Syrian Golan;

5.   Calls once again upon Member States not to recognize any of the legislative or administrative measures and actions referred to above;

6.   Requests the Secretary-General to bring the present resolution to the attention of all Governments, the competent United Nations organs, the

0197

E/CN.4/1992/L.2
page 4

specialized agencies, the regional intergovernmental organizations and
international humanitarian organizations and to give it the widest possible
publicity, and to report to the Commission on Human Rights at its forty-ninth
session;

7.   Decides to include in the provisional agenda of its forty-ninth
session, as a matter of high priority, the item entitled "Question of the
violation of human rights in the occupied Arab territories, including
Palestine".

0198

UNITED
NATIONS

Economic and Social Council

Distr.
LIMITED

E/CN.4/1992/L.3
11 February 1992

Original: ENGLISH

COMMISSION ON HUMAN RIGHTS
Forty-eighth session
Agenda item 4

QUESTION OF THE VIOLATION OF HUMAN RIGHTS IN THE OCCUPIED
ARAB TERRITORIES, INCLUDING PALESTINE

Algeria*, Bangladesh, Burundi, China, Cuba, Ghana, India,
Indonesia, Iraq, Jordan*, Madagascar, Mauritania, Oman*,
Pakistan, Saudi Arabia*, Senegal, Somalia, Sudan*,
Syrian Arab Republic, Tunisia and United Arab Emirates*:
draft resolution

Question of the violation of human rights in the occupied Arab
territories, including Palestine

A.

The Commission on Human Rights,

Guided by the purposes and principles of the Charter of the
United Nations, as well as by the provisions of the Universal Declaration of
Human Rights,

Guided also by the provisions of the International Covenant on Economic,
Social and Cultural Rights and the International Covenant on Civil and
Political Rights,

---

* In accordance with rule 69, paragraph 3, of the rules of procedure of
the functional commissions of the Economic and Social Council.

GE.92-10531/8569a

0199

Taking into consideration the provisions of the Fourth Geneva Convention relative to the Protection of Civilian Persons in Time of War, of 12 August 1949, and the provisions of Additional Protocol I thereto, and the Hague Convention No. IV of 1907, as well as the principles of international law affirmed by the General Assembly in its resolutions 3 (I) of 13 February 1946, 95 (I) of 11 December 1946, 260 (III) A of 9 December 1948 and 2391 (XXIII) of 26 November 1968,

Recalling the relevant Security Council resolutions, in particular resolutions 252 (1968) of 25 May 1968, 267 (1969) of 3 July 1969, 298 (1971) of 25 September 1971, 446 (1979) of 22 March 1979, 465 (1980) of 1 March 1980, 471 (1980) of 5 June 1980, 476 (1980) of 30 June 1980, 478 (1980) of 20 August 1980, 605 (1987) of 22 December 1987, 607 (1988) of 5 January 1988, 608 (1988) of 14 January 1988, 636 (1989) of 6 July 1989, 641 (1989) of 30 August 1989, 672 (1990) of 12 October 1990, 694 (1991) of 24 May 1991, and 726 (1992) of 6 January 1992,

Recalling the General Assembly resolutions on Israeli violations of human rights in occupied Palestine, since 1967 and until now,

Taking note of the reports of the Special Committee to Investigate Israeli Practices Affecting the Human Rights of the Palestinian People and Other Arabs of the Arab Occupied Territories submitted to the General Assembly since 1968, in particular its report of 1 February 1991 (A/46/65),

Expressing its deep concern at the contents of the report by the Special Rapporteur, Mr. S. Amos Wako, (E/CN.4/1991/36) regarding summary or arbitrary executions and the acts committed by Israel in this respect referred to in the report, in particular in paragraphs 290 to 296,

Recalling all its previous resolutions on the subject,

1.   Condemns the policies and practices of Israel, which violate the human rights of the Palestinian people in the Palestinian territory occupied by Israel with military force, including Jerusalem, and, in particular, such acts as the opening of fire by the Israeli army and settlers on Palestinian civilians that results in killing and wounding them, as has happened continuously since the eruption of the Palestinian people's intifada against Israeli military occupation; the imposition of restrictive economic measures; the demolition of houses; the expropriation of houses as happened recently in Silwan village; the ransacking of property belonging individually or collectively to private persons; collective punishment; arbitrary and administrative detention of thousands of Palestinians; the confiscation of the

property of Palestinians, including their bank accounts, the expropriation of land, the prevention of travel, the closure of universities and schools, the perpetration of crimes of torture in Israeli prisons and detention centres, and the establishment of Jewish settlements in the occupied Palestinian territory;

2.   Affirms the right of the Palestinian people to resist the Israeli occupation by all means, in accordance with the relevant United Nations resolutions, consistent with the purposes and principles of the Charter of the United Nations, as has been expressed by the Palestinian people in their brave intifada since December 1987, in legitimate resistance against the Israeli military occupation;

3.   Calls once more upon Israel, the occupying Power, to desist from all forms of violation of human rights in the Palestinian and other occupied Arab territories and to respect the bases of international law, the principles of international humanitarian law, and its commitments to the provisions of the Charter and resolutions of the United Nations;

4.   Calls upon Israel to withdraw from the Palestinian territory, including Jerusalem, and other occupied Arab territories in accordance with the resolutions of the United Nations and the Commission on Human Rights in this regard;

5.   Requests the Secretary-General to bring the present resolution to the attention of the Government of Israel and of all other Governments, the competent United Nations organs, the specialized agencies, regional intergovernmental organizations and international humanitarian organizations, to disseminate it on the widest possible scale, and to report on its implementation by the Government of Israel to the Commission on Human Rights at its forty-ninth session;

6.   Also requests the Secretary-General to provide the Commission on Human Rights with all United Nations reports issued between sessions of the Commission that deal with the conditions in which the citizens of the Palestinian and other occupied Arab territories are living under the Israeli occupation;

7.   Decides to consider this question at its forty-ninth session as a matter of priority.

B.

The Commission on Human Rights,

Recalling Security Council resolutions related to the applicability of the four Geneva Conventions of 1949 to the Palestinian and other Arab occupied territories and the condemnation by the Security Council of Israel for its refusal to abide by these Conventions, particulaly resolutions 446 (1979) of 22 March 1979, 465 (1980) of 1 March 1980, 497 (1981) of 17 December 1981, 592 (1986) of 8 December 1986, 605 (1987) of 22 December 1987, 607 (1988) of 5 January 1988, 608 (1988) of 14 January 1988, 636 (1989) of 6 July 1989, 641 (1989) of 30 August 1989, 672 (1990) of 12 October 1990, 694 (1991) of 24 May 1991 and 726 (1992) of 6 January 1992,

Recalling all relevant General Assembly resolutions on the applicability of the Fourth Geneva Convention relative to the Protection of Civilian Persons in Time of War, of 12 August 1949, to the occupied Palestinian territory, which urge Israel's commitment to and respect of their provisions,

Recalling the decisions of the International Conference of the Red Cross in respect of the application of the Fourth Geneva Convention in all circumstances,

Recalling its previous resolutions on this question,

Recalling the different appeals and statements of the International Committee of the Red Cross which point to the continuing violations by the Israeli occupation authorities of the provisions of the Fourth Geneva Convention, particularly article 49 thereof, and which call upon those authorities to respect the provisions of the Convention and abide by them,

Taking into account that the States parties to the Fourth Geneva Convention undertake, in accordance with article 1 thereof, to respect, and ensure respect for, the Convention in all circumstances,

1.   Reaffirms that the Fourth Geneva Convention relative to the Protection of Civilian Persons in Time of War, of 12 August 1949, is applicable to Palestinian and all other Arab territories occupied by Israel since 1967, including Jerusalem, and that Israel's longstanding refusal to apply the Convention to those territories has led to the perpetration, by the Israeli authorities, of grave violations of human rights against Palstinian citizens, and calls upon Israel to comply with its international commitments, to respect the Fourth Geneva Convention and to apply it in the occupied Palestinian territory, including Jerusalem;

0202

2.   Urges once more all States parties to the Fourth Geneva Convention
to make every effort to ensure that the Israeli occupation authorities'
respect for, and compliance with, the provisions of that Convention in the
Palestinian and all other Arab territories occupied by Israel since 1967,
including Jerusalem, and to undertake the necessary practical measures to
ensure the provision of international protection for the Palestinian people
under occupation, in accordance with the provisions of article 1 and other
relevant articles of the Fourth Geneva Convention of 12 August 1949, as well
as article 89 of the First Protocol additional to the four Geneva Conventions;
it also urges the States Parties to the Fourth Geneva Convention to act in
accordance with article 90 of Additional Protocol I by requesting the
fact-finding mission referred to therein to investigate the grave violations
of international humanitarian law in the Palestinian occupied territory
mentioned in this resolution;

3.   Strongly condemns once more the refusal of Israel to apply the
Fourth Geneva Convention to Palestine and the Arab territories occupied since
1967 and to their inhabitants, Israel's policies of perpetrating crimes of
torture against Palestinian detainees and prisoners in Israeli prisons and
concentration camps, and its continued deliberate disregard for the provisions
of the Fourth Geneva Convention, in contravention of resolutions of the
Security Council, the General Assembly and the Commission on Human Rights;

4.   Strongly condemns Israel for its grave violations of article 49 of
the Fourth Geneva Convention, for continuing its policy of deporting
Palestinian citizens and of expelling them from their homeland, as recently
happened to the Palestinian citizens Ihab Mohammad Ali Al-Ashkar,
Sami Attiya Zayed Abu Samhadana, Ahmad Hassan Abdullah Youssef,
Marwan Hassan Mohammad Afana, Ra'fat Osman Ali El-Najjar,
El-Sheikh Ahmad Mohammad Ali El-Nimer Hawdan, Khader Attiya Khader Mohrez,
Iyad Elhami Abdelraouf Gouda, Ghassan Mohammad Soleiman Jarrar,
Hassan Abdullah Hassan Sha'ban, Ali Fares Hassan El-Khatib and
Omar Nimer Abdelrahman Safi, and calls upon Israel to comply with the
resolutions of the Security Council, particularly resolution 726 (1992) of
6 January 1992, of the General Assembly and the Commission on Human Rights on
this question;

5.   Calls upon Israel to refrain immediately from deporting Palestinian
citizens from their homeland, and to allow all those who have been deported
since 1967 to return to their homeland without any obstacle or delay;

0203

6.   <u>Requests</u> the Secretary-General to bring the present resolution to the attention of the Government of Israel and all other Governments, the competent United Nations organs, the specialized agencies, regional intergovernmental organizations, international humanitarian organizations and non-governmental organizations, and to submit a report on progress in its implementation by the Government of Israel to the Commission on Human Rights at its forty-ninth session;

7.   <u>Decides</u> to consider this question at its forty-ninth session as a matter of high priority.

0204

Economic and Social Council

Distr.
LIMITED

E/CN.4/1992/L.5
10 February 1992

Original: ENGLISH

COMMISSION ON HUMAN RIGHTS
Forty-eighth session
Agenda item 4

QUESTION OF THE VIOLATION OF HUMAN RIGHTS IN THE OCCUPIED ARAB TERRITORIES, INCLUDING PALESTINE

Australia, Austria, Bangladesh, Belgium*, Colombia, Cyprus, Czech and Slovak Federal Republic, Denmark*, Egypt*, Finland*, France, Germany, Greece*, Hungary, Iceland*, Ireland*, Italy, Japan, Lebanon*, Luxembourg*, Morocco*, Netherlands, New Zealand*, Norway*, Portugal, Russian Federation, Spain*, Sweden*, Switzerland*, Turkey*, United Kingdom of Great Britain and Northern Ireland and Yugoslavia: draft resolution

Israeli settlements in the occupied Arab territories

The Commission on Human Rights,

Recalling that, in accordance with article 13, paragraph 2, of the Universal Declaration of Human Rights, everyone has the right to leave any country including his own and to return to his country,

Reaffirming that the Fourth Geneva Convention relative to the Protection of Civilian Persons in Time of War, of 12 August 1949, is applicable to Palestinian and all Arab territories occupied by Israel since 1967, including Jerusalem,

Recalling its resolutions 1990/1 of 16 February 1990, and 1991/3 of 15 February 1991,

---

*   In accordance with rule 69, paragraph 3, of the rules of procedure of the functional commissions of the Economic and Social Council.

GE.92-10486/8560a

Gravely concerned at the large-scale establishment, by the Israeli Government, of settlers, including immigrants, in the occupied territories, which may change the physical character and demographic composition of the occupied territories,

Taking into account the need to create the stable environment required for progress in the negotiation process following the Middle East Peace Conference in Madrid,

Convinced that the halting by Israel of its policy of settlement would constitute a meaningful contribution to the creation of that environment,

1. *Reaffirms* that the installation of Israeli civilians in the occupied territories is illegal and constitutes a violation of the relevant provisions of the Fourth Geneva Convention relative to the Protection of Civilian Persons in Time of War, of 12 August 1949;

2. *Regrets* that the Government of Israel has not complied with the provisions of Commission on Human Rights resolutions 1990/1 and 1991/3;

3. *Urges* the Government of Israel to abstain from installing settlers, including immigrants, in the occupied territories.

0206

UNITED
NATIONS

Economic and Social Council

Distr.
LIMITED

E/CN.4/1992/L.4
10 February 1992

Original: ENGLISH

COMMISSION ON HUMAN RIGHTS
Forty-eighth session
Agenda item 9

THE RIGHT OF PEOPLES TO SELF-DETERMINATION AND ITS
APPLICATION TO PEOPLES UNDER COLONIAL RULE OR
ALIEN DOMINATION OR FOREIGN OCCUPATION

Algeria*, Burundi, China, Cuba, Ghana, Indonesia, Jordan*, Madagascar,
Mauritania, Pakistan, Saudi Arabia*, Senegal, Somalia, Sudan*, Tunisia,
United Arab Emirates*, Yemen* and Yugoslavia: draft resolution

Situation in occupied Palestine

The Commission on Human Rights,

Guided by the principles and purposes of the Charter of the
United Nations, in particular the provisions of Article 1 and Article 55
thereof, which affirm the right of peoples to self-determination,

Guided also by the provisions of article 1 of the International Covenant
on Economic, Social and Cultural Rights and article 1 of the International
Covenant on Civil and Political Rights, which affirm that all peoples have the
right of self-determination,

Taking into consideration the provisions of the Declaration on the
Granting of Independence to Colonial Countries and Peoples adopted by the
General Assembly in its resolution 1514 (XV) of 14 December 1960,

---

* In accordance with rule 69, paragraph 3, of the rules of procedure of
the functional commissions of the Economic and Social Council.

GE.92-10480/2961H

0207

Noting Security Council resolutions 183 (1963) of 11 December 1963
and 218 (1965) of 23 November 1965, which affirmed the interpretation of the
principle of self-determination as laid down in General Assembly
resolution 1514 (XV),

Recalling General Assembly resolutions 181 A and B (II) of
29 November 1947 and 194 (III) of 11 December 1948, as well as all other
resolutions which confirm and define the inalienable rights of the Palestinian
people, particularly their right to self-determination without external
interference and to the establishment of their independent State on their
national soil, especially resolutions ES-7/2 of 29 July 1980 and 37/86 E of
20 December 1982,

Reaffirming its previous resolutions in this regard,

Bearing in mind the reports and recommendations of the Committee on the
Exercise of the Inalienable Rights of the Palestinian People which from 1976
to 1991, have been submitted to the Security Council through the
General Assembly,

Reaffirming the right of the Palestinian people to self-determination in
accordance with the Charter of the United Nations, the relevant United Nations
resolutions and the provisions of the international covenants and instruments
relating to the right to self-determination as an international principle and
as a right of all peoples in the world,

Expressing its grave concern at the persistence of Israel in preventing
by force the Palestinian people from enjoying their inalienable rights, in
particular their right to self-determination, in defiance of the principles of
international law, United Nations resolutions and the will of the
international community, which has affirmed and recognized those rights,

Recalling that the military occupation by the armed forces of a State of
the territory of another State constitutes an act of aggression and a crime
against the peace and security of mankind, according to General Assembly
resolution 3314 (XXIX) of 14 December 1974,

Expressing its grave concern that no just solution has been achieved to
the problem of Palestine, which has constituted the core of the Arab-Israeli
conflict since 1948,

Reiterating its grave concern at the military, economic and political support given by some States to Israel, which encourages and supports Israel in its aggressive and expansionist policies, its continued occupation of Palestinian and other Arab territories and the Judaizing of Palestine by establishing Jewish settlements and settling Jewish immigrants therein,

Affirming that the directing of the immigration of Jews in an organized manner to Israel constitutes support to Israel's settlement policy in the occupied Palestinian territories and an obstacle to the exercise by the Palestinian people of their right to self-determination,

1.   Reaffirms that the Israeli occupation of Palestine constitutes a gross violation of human rights and an act of aggression against the peace and security of mankind;

2.   Reaffirms the inalienable right of the Palestinian people to self-determination without external interference and to the establishment of their independent sovereign State on their national soil, in accordance with the Charter of the United Nations and resolutions adopted by the General Assembly since 1947;

3.   Reaffirms the inalienable right of the Palestinians to return to their homeland, Palestine, in accordance with General Assembly resolution 194 (III) and subsequent relevant resolutions;

4.   Reaffirms the right of the Palestinian people to recover their rights by all means in accordance with the purposes and principles of the Charter of the United Nations and with relevant United Nations resolutions, and affirms that the intifada of the Palestinian people against the Israeli occupation since 8 December 1987 is a form of legitimate resistance against the military occupation of Palestine and an expression of the Palestinian people's rejection of the occupation and an affirmation of their unshakeable desire for liberation and for the exercise of their inalienable national rights on their national soil;

5.   Reaffirms its support for the call to convene an effective international peace conference on the Middle East, with the participation of the permanent members of the Security Council and the parties to the Arab-Israeli conflict, including the Palestine Liberation Organization, under

the auspices of the United Nations, in accordance with the relevant
resolutions of the General Assembly and the Security Council, and to guarantee
the inalienable national rights of the Palestinian people, in particular their
right to self-determination without external interference;

6. <u>Expresses its great interest</u> in the current process of negotiations,
which began in Madrid, between the parties to the conflict to resolve the
problem of Palestine and of the Middle East; affirms the necessity of this
process being based on international legitimacy, on the principles of
international law and on the United Nations resolutions concerning the
inalienable rights of the Palestinian people, at the forefront of which is
their right to self-determination, so that the process results in a just
solution leading to a just and permanent peace in the Middle East; also
affirms that any attempt to achieve a peaceful solution in the region which is
not based on the principles of international law and the United Nations
resolutions regarding the Israeli occupation of Palestine and other Arab
occupied territories and the right of the Palestinian people to
self-determination free from external interference will not ensure the
achievement of a just, permanent and comprehensive peace in the Middle East;

7. <u>Strongly condemns</u> Israel for its continued occupation of the
Palestinian territory, which constitutes the main obstacle to the exercise by
the Palestinian people of their national rights, the foremost of which is
their right to free self-determination on their national soil;

8. <u>Calls upon</u> Israel to comply with its obligations under the Charter
of the United Nations and the principles of international law and to withdraw
from the Palestinian and other Arab territories which it has occupied since
1967 by military force, including Jerusalem, in accordance with the relevant
United Nations resolutions;

9. <u>Urges</u> all States, United Nations organs, the specialized agencies
and other international organizations to extend their support and assistance
to the Palestinian people through their sole legitimate representative, the
Palestine Liberation Organization, in their struggle to recover their rights
and to liberate their land from Israeli occupation, in accordance with the
Charter of the United Nations and with the relevant United Nations resolutions;

0210

10. <u>Requests</u> the Secretary-General to transmit the present resolution to the Government of Israel and to all other Governments, to distribute it on the widest possible scale and to make available to the Commission on Human Rights, prior to the convening of its forty-ninth session, all information pertaining to the implementation of the present resolution by the Government of Israel;

11. <u>Decides</u> to include in the provisional agenda of its forty-ninth session the item entitled "The right of peoples to self-determination and its application to peoples under colonial or alien domination or foreign occupation" and to consider the situation in occupied Palestine under that item, as a matter of high priority.

- - - - -

0211

외 무 부

종 별 :

번 호 : GUW-0067   일 시 : 92 0219 1900

수 신 : 장관(미중,경일,국연,사본:상공부)

발 신 : 주 과테말라 대사

제 목 : 아국업체 문제

   대: WGU-52

   연: GUW-53

1. 연호 소직은 금 2.19(수),15:00 주재국 RAMIRO DE LEON CARPIO 인권위원장을
면담한바(김옥주 참사관), 동 면담 주요내용을 아래 보고함.

   가. 소직은 TOMUSCHAT 인권자문관이 방문한 아국업체의 문제점이 발견된데 대해
유감표명과 아울러 동인 및 ESPINA 부통령, MENDEZ 외상과의 면담을 통하여문제내용과
입장을 알고 있다고 전제한후 아국업체도 현재 자발적으로 문제점을 개선 또는
시정하고 있음에도 불구하고 귀 위원회나 유관기관등은 이를 인식하지 못하고 있을 뿐
아니라 3 만여명의 현지인을 고용하고 있는 아국업체를 비판 할려고 만하는 경향을
설명하면서 주재국 인권위의 이해와 협조를 요청함.

   나. 이에 RAMIRO 위원장은 동 위원회가 TOMUSCHAT 자문관으로 하여금 동업체를
방문토록 주선한바 없다고 하면서 동 업체의 작업환경등을 독일인인 자문관의
시각에서 보면 불량하였을 것으로 본다며, 주재국 인권위는 개별업체의 문제점
지적보다는 주재국 전분야의 인권개선과 복리 향상면을 항상 염두에 두고 있으며
아국업체의 기여도는 잘알고 있다고 하였음.

   다. 소직은 당관도 아국업체를 계속 계도 하겠으니 인권위의 많은 이해와 아울러
아국업체 비난 또는 진정사건이 입수될시 사전에 당관에 통지 해주면 문제점을
시정조치할 예정인바 주재국 인권위의 협조를 요청함.

   라. 동 위원장은 아국업체의 문제점을 언론에 유포하지 않고 문제점 시정과개선을
대사관과 긴밀히 협조 하겠다고 약속함.

2. 한편 소직은 작 2.14(금)전업체를, 작 2.17(월)에는 봉제협회 이사진을 당관에
소집하고 제네바 인권위 보고서중 아국업체 비난부분을 발췌, 설명 배포하고 전업체가

| 미주국 | 차관 | 1차보 | 2차보 | 국기국 | 경제국 | 분석관 | 정와대 | 안기부 |
| 상공부 | | | | | | | | |

자체적으로 문제점을 시정 개선토록 지시하고, 이를 위반시에는 행정제재조치를 취할 방침임을 주지시킨바, 봉제협회는 솔선시정토록 하겠으며, 현사태수습을 위한 PRESS RELEASE 배포등 향후 대책은 대사관과 긴밀히 협의하면서 사건 추이에 따라 취하겠다고 하였음을 보고함. 끝.

(대사 강웅식 - 국장)

예고: 92.12.31. 일반.

감도필 1992. 6. 30.)

공　　　란

공   란

외 무 부

종 별 :

번 호 : GUW-0069

일 시 : 92 0220 1830

수 신 : 장관(미중,경일,국연,영사,사본: 상공부)

발 신 : 주 과테말라 대사

제 목 : 아국업체 문제

연: GUW-67

1. 연호 소직은 금.2.20(목) 13:00 PRENDAS ESTRELLA 아국업체 사건담당 COROMAC 판사를 면담한바(김옥주 참사관 배석), 동 면담 주요내용을 아래 보고함.

가. 소직은 동 사건관련 TOMUSCHAT 인권자문관 및 금일 현재까지 주재국 요로 인사와의 면담내용과, 아국업체의 주재국에서의 현실 및 향후 당관 대책등을 설명한후 사법부의 선처를 요청함.

이에 동 판사는 전년도 고발된 4 개 업체중 PRENDAS ESTRELLA 는 작업환경등을 개선한 실적이 보이지 않고 또한 국내외적으로 이미 알려진 사건이라 사법부는 국내외 시선 때문에 동 사건을 법에 따라 처리할수 밖에 없는 입장이라고 하였음.

다. 소직은 PRENDAS ESTRELLA 가 작업환경을 개선한 실적내용을 수교하면서, 기존 양국간 우호관계 및 관계증진을 위해서는 동 사건을 법률측면과 정치측면도 고려되어야 하며, 특히 동사건을 언론에 여론화 하여 아국업체 및 아국이미지 손상과 양국간 관계를 저해하지 않도록 바라며 아울러 동 사건의 조속하고 원만한 처리를 위해 각별한 협조를 요청함.

라. 동 판사는 양국간 우호관계를 고려하여 가능한 내주중으로 동 사건을호의적으로 종결할수 있도록 최대한 노력하겠다고 하였음.

2. 소직은 동 면담에 이어 금일 15:30 PAIZ NOVALES 이민청장을 면담(동면담에는 금일 부임한 문호준 참사관도 배석)한바, 동 내용 아래보고함.

가. 소직은 먼저 아국기술자의 체류비자 발급협조에 사의를 표한후, 현재 교섭중인 사증면제 협정안에 이민청의 호의적인 검토의견을 요청함.

나. 동 청장은 현재 아국기술자 60 여명에게 1 년 임시거주 비자를 발급하였고 앞으로도 아국업체 관련 문제 해결에 최대한 협조 하겠으며, 상기 협정안에도

미주국	차관	1차보	2차보	국기국	경제국	영고국	정와대	안기부
상공부								

PAGE 1

92.02.21 10:08

외신 2과 통제관 BX

0216

이민청은 호의적인 검토의견을 제시 하겠다고 하면서, 4 월 중순경 방한을 희망한다는
의견을 부연하였음. 끝.

    (대사 강웅식 - 국장)

    예고: 92.12.31. 일반.

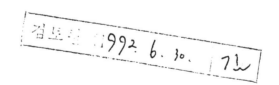

외 무 부

종 별 : 지급

번 호 : GVW-0405

일 시 : 92 0221 1000

수 신 : 장관(연이,법무부,기정동문)

발 신 : 주제네바대사

제 목 : 제 48차 인권위(14)- 미국의 북한비판

1. 표제회의는 금 2.19 현재 의제 12항(세계각지에서의 인권침해) 토의를 시작한바,미국(BLACKWELL 대사)은 토의 초기에 발언, 국별인권 침해양태를 거론하는 가운데 북한을'근본적으로 억압적인 사회'로 분류하고 다음과같이 언급함.(연설문은 파견 송부함)

IN THE DEMOCRATIC PEOPLE'S REPUBLIC OF KORA THE SECURITYAPPARATUS IS ARBITRARY AND HARSH, AND THE GOVERNMENT EXERTSCOMPREHENSIVE AND PERVASIVE CONTROL OVER ALL ASPECTS OFHUMAN BEHAVIOR. ROUTINE AND SYSTEMATIC SUPPRESSION OF THERIGHTSTO FREEDOM OF SPPECH, PRESS, ASSOCIATION ANDRELIGION, AS WELL AS THE DENIAL OFYET OTHER HUMAN RIGHTS,HAS EARNED NORTH KOREAN AUTHORITIES A PROMINENT PLACE AMONGTHE WORLD'S MOST OPPRESSIVE DESPOTS.

2. 동 미국 발언은 근래 수년간 세계 각지에서이룩된 인권 신장을 평가하고, 상금 문제가있는 나라를 다음과 같은 그룹으로 구분하여 비판하는 내용으로 되어있음.

0 '계속 우려(CONCERN)되는 상황'

-   아랍점령지,남아공,하이티,수단,아프칸,자이레,인니,유고를열거하고   1   PARA 씩할애, 문제점 지적

0   '근본적으로   억압적인(FUNDAMENTALLY   REPRESSIVE)사회'..-   쿠바, 이락,이란,북한,중국,미얀마를 열거하고 1-3 PARA 씩 할애, 문제점 지적

3. 상기 발언에 대한 북한의 대응은 상금없는바, 의제 12항이 내주 중반까지 계속되므로, 관심을 갖고 주시 위계임.끝

(대사 박수길-국장)

국기국	1차보	분석관	안기부	법무부	외정실

92.02.22   06:41 FE

외신 1과 통제관

0218

외 무 부

종 별 : 지급

번 호 : GVW-0412

수 신 : 장관(연이),법무부,기정동문)

발 신 : 주 제네바 대사

제 목 : 48차 인권위(15)

연: GVW-1691(1), 0325(2)

대: WGV-0300

1. 금 2.20 NGO 인 INT'L ASSOCIATION OF DEMOCRATIC LAWYERS 가 동기구 산하 "남한 민주.인권을 위한 법률가 위원회"와 공동 명의로 아국의 인권을 거론한바, 관련 사항 아래 보고함.

가. 발언 요지(발언문 불어 TEXT 및 주요 부분 영어 번역 별첨 FAX 송부)

0 한국에는 상당수의 장기수를 포함한 1500-3800 의 정치범이 있음.

- 다수가 각종 질병으로 고생

- 정치범중 임수경, 문익환 거명

0 데모진압시 군.경에 의한 폭력사용, 구금시 고문이 빈번함.

- 강경대, 박종철 거명

0 남. 북 긴장완화에도 불구 국가 보안법 민방위법, 집시법, 노동조합법, 노동쟁의 조정법, 일부 형법 조항등 인권 침해 법규가 상존함.

0 요구사항

- 정치범 석방

- 고문 종식

- 인권 관련법 개정

나. 관찰

0 동 NGO 는 인권위시 빈번하게 아국문제를 왜곡 거론해온 친북 성향 단체로서, 금번 발언 내용, 임수경, 박종철등의 영문 표기등에서 북한과의 관계를 감지할수 있다고 사료됨.

0 동 발언은 저녁 8 시경 넘어 다수 대표가 이석하는등 산만한 상태에서 이루어져

국기국 장관 차관 1차보 2차보 분석관 정와대 안기부 법무부

92.02.22   05:26

외신 2과 통제관 FK

0219

별 주의를 끌지 못하였음.

　　다. 대처 방향

　　0 다음과 같이 대처코자 하는바 별도 지시 사항 있으면 하시 바람.

　　(본 의제는 적어도 2.25 까지 토의됨)

　　- 91.8 월 인권소위시 연호(2) 로 건의한바와 같이 일부 NGO 의 왜곡된 언급에 일일이 대응함은 불필요한 관심을 증폭시키는 측면이 있으므로 <u>일단 무시하는 입장을 취함.</u>

　　- 대표단은 의제 12 항에서 발언할 경우에는 간단히 아국의 인권보장 노력과 성과를 언급함으로써 간접 대응함.

　　2. 정달호 국제연합 2 과장은 예정대로 도착, 회의 참석중임. 끝

　　첨부: GVW(F)-126

　　(대사 박수길-국장)

　　예고 92.6.30 까지

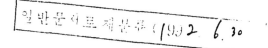
일반문서로 재분류 (1992. 6. 30)

주 제 네 바 대 표 부

번 호 : GVW(F) - 0126   년월일 : 2022/   시간 : 1800

수 신 : 장   관 (연이, 법무부, 기략성)

발 신 : 주 제네바대사

제 목 .   현복.

총 7 매 (표지포함)

보 안 품 재	親

외신과 품 재	

0221

126-7-1

L'Assoc. Int. des Juristes Démocrates
et son comité de juristes pour la
Démocratie et les Droits de l'Homme en
Corée du Sud

voudraient signaler ce qui suit:

Un "Accord sur la réconciliation, la non agression, la collaboration et les échanges entre le Nord et le Sud" a été conclu entre la Corée du Sud et la Corée du Nord le 13 décembre 1991. Ce premier accord entre les deux parties a ouvert la voie à un accord sur la dénucléarisation de la péninsule coréenne (31.12.91) (qui doit être formellement signé en février 1992).

Les premiers contacts directs entre la Corée du Nord et les Etats-Unis ont lieu. Le Président Bush a proposé de renoncer aux manoeuvres militaires américano-sud-coréennes "Team Spirit", qui ont lieu chaque année et qui provoquent une très vive tension entre les deux parties, tout en proclamant que "le jour viendra où cette dernière blessure de la guerre froide guérira : la Corée sera réunifiée" (6.1.92).

Les médias dans le monde entier ont répercuté cette nouvelle situation, comme si la question coréenne était en voie de règlement définitif ; l'opinion internationale peut (doit?) se désintéresser de la Corée, puisque tous les problèmes y sont "presque" résolus. Ainsi, le dialogue entamé par les autorités de Corée du Sud et de Corée du Nord et les premiers accords occultent la répression qui se poursuit en Corée du Sud et les violations des droits de l'homme et des libertés qui se prolongent à l'encontre de toutes les oppositions (étudiantes, paysannes, ouvrières), bien que cette violence systématique ait de moins et moins de prétextes. Au contraire, la réaffirmation de l'engagement des Etats-Unis à assurer la sécurité de la Corée du Sud et le soutien du Président Bush au but de la réunification pacifique de la péninsule coréenne conduit l'opinion à croire que les seules questions à résoudre se situent au Nord et que le Sud est le "champion du droit" !

La réalité est toute autre. La Commission des Droits de l'Homme doit être informée de la situation des droits de l'homme et des libertés en Corée du Sud, dissimulée ou minimisée [1] en permanence par la plupart des grands médias du monde inspirés par la stratégie et la tactique des Etats-Unis [2].

---

[1]. Le grand quotidien français "Le Monde", par exemple, du 19.9.91 consacre 7 lignes et 23 mots à la mort (inopportune sans doute) d'un étudiant tué par balles le 17 septembre à Séoul lors d'une manifestation ; celui du 12.11.91 accorde 13 lignes à une manifestation qui selon les agences de presse occidentales a réuni 30 à 40.000 personnes à Séoul, réclamant la démission du gouvernement sud-coréen, alors que le numéro du 9.10.91 consacrait presque 1/4 de page à l'intervention de Pékin pour "convaincre la Corée du Nord de s'ouvrir aux capitaux étrangers".

[2]. Le gouvernement des Etats Unis ne se fait pourtant aucune illusion : le rapport du Département d'Etat sur la situation des droits de l'homme pour l'année 90 confirme (bien qu'avec une certaine prudence) les pratiques répressives attentatoires aux droits de l'homme du régime Roh Tae Woo : "des éléments d'autoritarisme demeurent...".

0222

126 - 7-2

1° - Les détenus politiques pour délit d'opinion demeurent nombreux. Il sont au nombre, selon les évaluations de 1.500 à 3.800. 143 sont incarcérés depuis de très nombreuses années (entre 20 et 40 ans). La prison de Daidjeun, par exemple, accueille 57 détenus politiques dont 51 purgent des peines très lourdes (20 pour plus de 30 ans, 3 pour plus de 40 ans, alors que 25 d'entre eux ont entre 60 et 70 ans et 10 ont plus de 70 ans). Nombreux parmi ces prisonniers politiques sont atteints de maladies graves consécutives aux mauvais traitements : tuberculose, hypertension, cancer, etc...Le Ministre de la Justice en Corée du Sud a pu informer le Parlement sud-coréen qu'une trentaine de prisonniers mouraient chaque année dans les prisons sud-coréennes. La libération éventuelle des prisonniers politiques dépend de la signature d'une "déclaration de conversion" sorte de rétractation rejetant leurs convictions. Les libérés restent sous surveillance administrative.

Parmi les détenus d'opinion, certains cas sont particulièrement significatifs : l'étudiante Rim Sou Kyeung, condamnée en vertu de la Loi sur la "Sécurité Nationale" (30.12.80) sanctionnant les activités "perturbatrices" "anti-étatiques", dont tous les termes sont tellement imprécis qu'ils permettent de poursuivre toute opposition. Rim Sou Kyeung, en tant que représentante du mouvement de jeunesse ["Djeundaihyeup"] a participé au Festival Mondial de la Jeunesse qui se tenait à Pyong Yang durant l'été 89. Pendant toute la durée des festivités, la jeune étudiante sud-coréenne s'est astreinte (tous les enregistrements et publications en font foi) à ne jamais prendre une position politique. Elle s'est uniquement affirmée en partisane sans réserve de la réunification pacifique de son pays. Arrêtée lors de son franchissement public de la ligne de démarcation à Panmoudjeum, assimilée à une "espionne" coupable d'un "acte de trahison" (comme le prêtre catholique Moun Kyou Hyeun qui l'avait accompagné), elle a été condamnée à une lourde peine de prison ferme qu'elle purge encore actuellement. Il en a été de même pour le Pasteur Moon Ik-hwan (en avril 89) au retour d'une visite du Nord.

Ainsi, les simples citoyens, qui n'ont fait que précéder les autorités sud-coréennes elles-mêmes et qui continuent à le faire, sont poursuivis en justice et condamnés pénalement, alors que le gouvernement de Séoul se proclame, ainsi que toute la communauté internationale, favorable à la réunification. A la condition que le peuple ne s'en mêle pas !

2°. - Les violences policières et militaires à l'encontre des manifestations ainsi que la torture dans les lieux de détention sont la règle. En avril, mai et juin 91, par exemple, de très importantes manifestations étudiantes ont été réprimées, comme par le passé, avec la plus extrême violence provoquant morts et blessés graves. Le meurtre, par exemple, de l'étudiant Kang-Kyang Dae à coups de barre de fer par les sections de police "anti-émeutes" atteste de la stabilité des méthodes répressives.

0223

12-1 - 7 - 3

Les tortures les plus archaïques (comme celles subies par l'étudiant Pak Djeung Tcheul décédé en 87 ou l'étudiant Lee décédé en 89) tendent à céder la place à la "torture blanche" ne laissant pas de traces apparentes. A cette fin, la Corée du Sud importe des Etats-Unis et du Japon divers produits et du matériel sophistiqué.

Ainsi, la Déclaration contre la Torture, adoptée à l'unanimité des Nations Unies, le 9.12.75, est systématiquement violée. Les nombreux suicides par le feu de jeunes sud-coréens, témoignages de protestation, attestent du caractère insupportable des pratiques du régime Roh Tae Woo. La revue "Chronique d'Amnesty International" (avril 90 n° 41) le confirme.

3°. - L'ensemble des dispositions juridiques attentatoires aux droits de l'homme, malgré la détente officielle avec le Nord, dont sont victimes les étudiants, les hommes d'Eglise, les syndicalistes ouvriers, les dirigeants de l'opposition parlementaire eux-mêmes, demeure en vigueur. Peuvent être citées : en premier lieu, la loi sur la Sécurité Nationale, sanctionnant en fait tout contact avec le Nord, alors que la loi sur "les échanges et la coopération Sud-Nord" d'août 90 proclame le contraire ; la loi sur le "contrôle de la sécurité" ; la loi sur la défense civile ; la loi sur les réunions et les manifestations ; la loi sur les syndicats ; la loi sur l'arbitrage des conflits du travail, etc... et nombre d'articles du Code Pénal, constituant un arsenal répressif sans faille. implacable.

Nous demandons par conséquent
Sont donc nécessaires, en dépit de l'action médiatique internationale visant à occulter les pratiques du régime Roh Tae Woo :

   - la libération des détenus politiques, expression concrète de la volonté de détente et de coopération avec le Nord ;

   - la cessation de la torture et des violences attentatoires à la dignité de l'homme et aux libertés publiques ;

   - la révision du système juridique sud-coréen en matière de droits de l'homme et libertés publiques.

(Cf. le "Sixième Livre Blanc sur les Droits de l'Homme en Corée du Sud").

0224

126 - 7 - 4

J'ajouterai quelques mots sur le Sahara Occidental où la situation continue à nous préoccuper car les informations qui nous parviennent de ce territoire au sujet des violations des droits de l'homme sont alarmantes. A peine quelques jours avant la date prévue initialement pour l'organisation du referendum devant déterminer le statut du territoire, les autorités marocaines ont procédé à l'arrestation de plus de 400 civils sahraouis dont on ignore encore le sort.

Ces arrestations massives qui, paraît-il, se poursuivent encore, s'effectuent malgré la présence du contingent des N.U. présent sur place et chargé de superviser le referendum au Sahara Occidental. Sa présence devrait être une garantie supplémentaire de la sécurité de la population.

Les N.U. ne disposent-elles pas de moyens pour dissuader le Maroc de poursuivre ces arrestations? Comment justifier cette situation alors qu'il y a une année, à l'occasion de la guerre du Golfe, on promettait un nouvel ordre international s'inspirant des seules résolutions des Nations Unies fondé sur l'indivisibilité du droit ? Comment admettre aussi alors que la date et les étapes du referendum du peuple sahraoui ont été décidées par le Conseil de Sécurité, que le Maroc pose comme condition la certitude de gagner le referendum?

Les récents témoignages qui nous parviennent de sources autorisées nous confirment que le Maroc surveille et contrôle tous les mouvements des agents de la Paix des N.U. auxquels il interdit tout contact avec la population. On est en face d'un état de siège instauré au Sahara Occidental: les représentants de l'ONU sont confinés dans des endroits où tout déplacement à l'insu de la sécurité marocaine est interdit et la population sarahouie est réduite au silence.

Le Maroc refuse depuis 1975 la libre détermination du peuple sarahoui comme l'avait exigé l'ONU dans le plan de paix contenu dans la résolution 658 votée en juin 1990 à l'unanimité des membres du Conseil de Sécurité. La Commission des dts de l'Homme doit aider à enlever cette chape de plomb qui pèse sur le peuple sarahoui et oeuvrer pour que l'ONU puisse organiser cette année le referendum tant attendu dans des conditions de liberté et de justice définies par le Conseil de Sécurité. Un nouveau retard signifierait de nouvelles arrestations et même des disparitions parmi une population sans défense. Notre appel est pressant afin de rétablir le droit et la légalité internationaux, véritables gages de la crédibilité des Nations Unies.

- - - - - - - - - - - -

0225

126-7-5

In reality, this is not so. The Commission for Human Rights should be informed of the situation of human rights and liberties in South Korea, constantly dissimulated or minimalized by most media of the world inspired by the strategy and tactics of the United States.

1° - Political detainees held due to their opinions remain numerous. They number between 1,500 to 3,800 according to estimates. 143 have been in prison for many years (between 20 and 40 years). Daidjeun prison, for example, holds 57 political detainees, of whom 57 are serving very long sentences (20 for more than 30 years, 3 for more than 40 years, while 25 of them are between 60 and 70 years old and 10 are over the age of 70). Many among these prisoners are suffering serious illnesses following poor treatment: tuberculosis, hypertension, cancer, etc... The Minister of Justice of South Korea was able to inform the South Korean Parliament that about thirty prisoners died every year in South Korean prisons. The eventual liberation of political prisoners depends on the signature of a "declaration of conversion" sort of retraction rejecting their convictions. The freed prisoners remain under administrative surveillance.

Among those detained due to their opinions, certain cases are particularly significant: student Rim Sou Kyeung, convicted under the "National Security" Law (30.12.80) condemning "anti-state" and "disturbing" activities, for which all the terms are so vague that they allow the pursuance of any opposition. Rim Sou Kyeung, in the capacity of representative of the youth movement "Djeundaihyeup", participated in the World Festival of Youth held in Pyon Yang in the summer of 1989. Throughout the festivities, the South Korean young student refrained from taking a political position (all recordings and publications prove this). She only confirmed that she was a partisan of the peaceful reunification of her country. Arrested during her public crossing of the demarcation line at Panmoujeum, compared to a "spy" guilty of an "act of treason" (like the Catholic priest Moun Kyou Hyeun who accompanied her), she was sentenced to a long prison term which she is still serving. The same happened to Rev. Moon Ik-hwan (in April 1989) upon his return from a visit to the North.

As such, simple citizens who preceded the South Korean authorities themselves and continue to do so, are pursued in court and sentenced to prison, while the government in Seoul claims, as does the international community, to be in favor of reunification, but on condition of no interference from the people!

2° - Police and military violence in face of demonstrations as well as torture in detention areas is the rule. In April, May and June 1991, for example, very large student demonstrations were oppressed, as in the past, with extreme violence causing death and injuries. The murder, for example, of student Kang-Kyang Dae by blows with an iron bar inflicted by sections of the "anti-riot" police bears witness to the stability of repressive methods.

The most archaic torture (such as that suffered by student Pak Djeung Tcheul, who died in 1987, or student Lee, who died in

0226

126-7-6

1989) is yielding to "white torture", leaving no apparent marks. To this end, South Korea imports sophisticated products and material from the United States and Japan.

As such, the Declaration against Torture, adopted unanimously by the United Nations on 9.12.75, is systematically violated. The numerous suicides of young South Koreans setting themselves on fire in protest brings to light the insufferable character of the practices of the regime of Roh Tae Woo. The "Amnesty International Chronicle" (April 1990 n° 40) confirms this.

3° - In spite of the official détente with the North, most of the legal provisions offending human rights, whose victims are students, clergymen, union workers, organizers of the parliamentary opposition themselves, remain in force. First, the National Security Law, condemning all contact with the North while the August 1990 law on "South-North exchanges and cooperation" proclaims the opposite; the law on "security control"; the law on civil defence; the law on meetings and demonstrations; the law on unions; the law on arbitration of labour conflicts, etc... and many articles of the Penal Code, constituting an implacable repressive arsenal.

Consequently, in spite of the international mediatory action masking the practises of the regime of Roh Tae Woo, we request:

    - the liberation of political detainees, a firm expression of will for détente and cooperation with the North;

    - the end of torture and violence offending human dignity and public liberties;

    - the revision of the South Korean legal system with regard to human rights and public liberties.

0227

외 무 부

종 별 :

번 호 : GVW-0417

일 시 : 92 0221 2000

수 신 : 장관(연이,법무부)

발 신 : 주 제네바대사

제 목 : 제 48차 인권위(16)

1. 금 2.21. 지금까지 제출된 결의안 표결이 있었는바, 결과 아래와 같음.

가. 의제 8항

0 자결권 행사의 침해방법으로서 용병사용(L.8)

- 표결없이 채택

- 단, 미국은 사후 발언을 통해 남하공에서의 정치형상 진전 및 자결권이 인권문제가 아니라는점등을 들어 동 결의에 불참하였음을 밝힘.

나. 의제 6항

0 대 남아공지원이 인권향유에 비치는역효과(인권소위 결의)

- 33 : 14 : 5 로 채택(반대 : 서방,일본,동구,기권 :알젠틴, 코스타리카, 마다가스칼,러시아,우루과이)

다. 의제 14항

0 인종주의 및 인종차별주의 척결 제 2차 10년대 행동계획의 이행(L.22)

- 표결없이 채택

- 미국은 사후 발언을 통해, 제 46차 총회시 '시온주의는 인종차별주의' 결의 폐기 결의가 채택됨으로서 미국이 금번 동결의안의 콘센서스 채택에도 참여할 수있게되었다고 언급

라. 의제 7항

0 외채로 인한 경제조정정책이 발전의 권리에 관한 선언의 이행등 인권 향유에 미치는 영향(L.13) : 43 : 2 :7 로 채택(반대:미국,일본, 기권: 서구,러시아)

- 미국은 동결의안이 정치적.시민적 권리보장을 회피하는 구실로 이용될수 있기때문에 반대

- 일본은 경제 조정문제는 인권위에서 다룰사항이 아니기 때문에 반대한다고

국기국   법무부

92.02.22   08:02 WH

외신 1과 통제관
0228

각각표결후 발언을 통한 입장 표명

0 모든국가에서 인권선언과 A규약에 보장된 권리의 실현문제(L.14) : 투표없이 채택

0 인권과 극빈(L.17) : 투표없이 채택

- 불란서는 제안설명시 선진국의 HOMELESS문제에 대해서도 언급

- 미국은 표결후 발언을 통해 빈곤문제는 다른기관에서 다룰 문제 임을 언급

0 노동조합권리의 문제(L.20) : 투표없이 채택

- 미국과 일본은 각각 표결후 발언을 통해 노동조합의 권리문제는 인권위 보다 ILO 가 다룰 문제임을 언급

0 경제적.사회적.문화적 권리의 실현(인권소위결의) 및 기타 결의안(L.21, L.19, L.18, L.16, L.15, L.6, L.7) 은 투표없이 채택

마. 의제 4항 하 '팔레스타인과 기타 이스라엘 점령지 MFH제' 결의안(D.R.10)과의제 7항 하 '경제적.사회적.문화적 권리의 실현문제' (L.12) 결의안은 표결 연기

2. 금일 오후 중국은 2.21.오후 미국(RICHARD SHIFTER 인권차관보)이 중국의 인권 백서 내용을 비판한데 대한 답변권 행사를 통해 미국내 인권상황 비판을 하여 양국간 강한 설전이 있었음.

(대사 박수길-국장)

분류번호	보존기간

발 신 전 보

번 호 : WGV-0305   920222 1352 FL   종별 : 지 급

수 신 : 주   제네바   대사. 총영사

발 신 : 장 관   (연이)

제 목 : 제48차 인권위

대 : GVW-0412

1. 대호 Int'l Association of Democratic Lawyers의 발언에 대하여는
   아래와 같이 대처바람.

   O 일부 NGO의 발언에 일일이 대응할 경우 문제점도 있으나, 상기 단체의
      경우와 같이 집중적으로 아국 상황을 왜곡 비난한 경우에는, 인권위
      회의 ~~관행~~ 및 인권문제에 대한 국내적 관심이 점차 고조되고 있음을
      고려, 아국 입장을 적절히 밝히는 것이 바람직하다고 봄.

   O 따라서 이번 경우에는 의제 12항 관련 아국대표의 일반발언을 통해
      아국 인권상황을 개략적으로 설명하면서 대호 발언의 주요내용을
      반박함으로써 대응하는 것이 적절할것임.

   O 상기 우리대표 발언에는 아래내용이 반영되도록 하기 바람.

      - 한반도 분단의 특수한 상황에 따라 발생된 모든 사건관련자를
         무조건 양심수로 규정하는 일부 NGO의 무책임한 주장을 받아들일수
         없음.(별첨 법무부 국회답변자료 참조)

/ 계속 /

보 안 통 제	

앙고재	92년 2월 22일	유인 2과	기안자 성명		과 장	심의관	국 장		차 관	장 관	외신과통제
			김출림			12l2					

0230

- 정부는 법집행 과정에서 발생하는 불상사에 대하여는 즉각적인 조사를 통해 관련자 처벌, 재발방지대책 마련등의 노력을 기울여 왔으며, 이러한 노력은 평가되어야 함.(강경대 사건)

- 모호하고 주관적인 논거만으로 우리 인권상황을 비난하는 것은 동 NGO의 발언의도 및 NGO 배경을 의심케 함.

2. 지금까지 특정 NGO의 아국비난 발언에는 대부분 북한측이 직.간접으로 관련되어 있는 것으로 추정되며, 또한 인권위 회의등에서 한반도 인권 상황에 대한 균형된 토의가 필요한 점등을 고려할때, 과거의 예와 같이 NGO를 통해 북한 인권문제를 거론하는 방안도 검토할 필요가 있을 것으로 판단됨. 이와관련 최근의 한반도 상황에 비추어 동문제에 대한 귀견 및 필요시 구체적 추진방안을 보고바람.

첨부 : 상기 자료. 끝.

(국제기구국장   김재섭)

예고 : 92.12.31. 일반

검토필 (1992. 6. 30.) 김

제48차 인권위 자료

1. 원래 정치범 또는 양심수의 개념은 학문상 확립되어 있지 아니할뿐 아니라
    법령상의 용어도 정부가 사용하는 용어도 아니며, 이를 거론하는 사람들도
    그 개념과 범위를 명확하게 특정해서 사용하고 있는 것으로는 보이지 않고
    있음.

    O   다만 대표적인 국제인권단체라 할수있는 국제사면위원회는 정치범을
        "정치적 요소, 내지는 동기에 의한 행위가 실정법에 위반하는 경우"
        라고 하면서 범죄로서의 형사처벌을 인정하고 있는 반면, 양심수는
        "폭력을 사용하거나 옹호하지 않음에도 정치.종교등 신념이나 인종.
        성별등을 이유로 구금된 자"라고 해석하여 이들에 대하여는 석방을
        요구하고 있음.

    O   그러나 국내 일부 재야단체에서는, 정치범, 양심수에 대한 뚜렷한 개념
        구별없이 양개념을 혼용하여 정치사의적인 용어로서 사용하고 있는데,
        이는 개인이나 단체의 자의적인 개념으로서 우리의 법집행 기준이 될수
        없으며, 세계 어느나라도 이를 구속이나 석방등 법집행의 기준으로 삼고
        있는 예는 없음.

2. 그럼에도 불구하고 국내외 일부 인권단체나 정치권 일각에서 근거가 희박한
    정치범이나 양심수 숫자를 그때 그때 발표하면서, 우리의 인권상황을 비판하는
    경우가 있음.

    O   제6공화국 들어 과거에 제정된 집회 및 시위에 관한 법률, 국가보안법등
        논란이 많았던 법률에 대하여는 여.야 합의로 손질을 가하여 법집행
        요건을 더욱 엄격히 함으로써 인권침해의 소지를 불식하는 법적.제도적
        장치를 강구하였음에도, 일부 인권단체들은 집시법, 국가보안법,

0232

화염병법, 노동법등을 악법으로 매도하여 그 위반자는 무조건 양심수로 분류하고 신분이 대학생 또는 근로자이기만 하면 이들이 스승에게 폭력을 휘두르고, 근로현장을 불지르는등 반인륜적, 폭력적 범행을 하였다 하더라도 무조건 정치범, 양심수라고 하면서 석방을 요구하고 있음.

O 그러나 그들이 제시하는 정치범, 양심수 관련 구속자 통계는 발표자 마다 또는 발표하는 시점에 따라 분류기준이 상이할뿐 아니라, 그 대상자도 적게는 국제사면위가 91.10.1에 발표한 30명에서부터 많게는 한국 기독교 교회 협의회가 91.7.13에 발표한 1,600명에까지 일관성이 없으며, 신원 불특정자, 기히 석방된자, 이중 등재자, 불구속 입건자등이 상당수 포함 되어 있는등 내용자체가 부실하고, 구속의 원인이 되는 구체적 범죄사실은 전혀 언급함이 없이, 화염병으로 파출소를 방화한 대학생은 물론, 사이비 공갈기자나 동료학우를 때려 숨지게 한 폭력 대학생도 정치범, 양심수로 분류하는등 전혀 객관적 검증절차를 밟지 아니한채 정치선전적인 측면에서 발표되는 경우가 적지 않은 것으로 알고 있음.

O 근래 화염병을 던지며 시위를 하는 곳은 우리나라밖에 없는 것으로 알고 있으며, 또한 세계 어느나라에서도 파출소등 공공기관을 무단 점거하고 방화하는 시위대를 정치범이니 양심수니 하면서 관용을 요구하는 나라도 없는 것으로 알고 있습니다. 소위 인권선진국인 영국, 독일, 프랑스, 일본등에서도 이러한 공공건물 방화범죄를 중형으로 다스리고 있으며, 또 국가보안사범의 경우, 독일은 통일이 된 지금도 과거의 범행에 대하여 엄정히 법집행을 하고 있습니다.

3. 정부는 현행법을 위반하지 않고 단순히 내심에 특정한 사상을 가지고 있다거나 어떠한 정치적 신념을 가지고 있다는 이유만으로는 처벌하거나 구금한 사람은 단 한사람도 없음.

0233

o 현재 국가보안법, 화염병법, 집시법, 노동법 위반등 공안사범은
기결수 339명이 법무부 산하 교정시설에 수용, 복역하고 있을뿐 양심수,
정치범은 한사람도 없음.

4. 우리나라는 작년 7월 국제인권규약에 가입한데 이어 금년에는 UN에 가입함
으로써 국제사회의 일원으로 인권선진국을 지향하고 있을뿐 아니라 인권에
대한 국민의 관심도 매우 높아 예컨대 사회의 이목이 집중되는 사건의 경우
수십명에서 백수십명의 변호사가 선임계를 내고 활발하게 변론을 수행하고
있으며, 이를 언론이 자유롭게 보도하고 있음.   이러한 상황에서 실정법에
위반하지 않고 폭력을 휘두르지 않았음에도 불구하고 종교적, 정치적 신념
때문에 무고한 사람을 구속한다는 것은 있을수 없음.

o 그동안 법무부는 이러한 편향적인 인권시비에 대하여 국내외 관계자를
면담하거나 반박논평등을 통하여 그때마다 적극적인으로 진상을 설명해옴.

o 그 결과 국제인권단체의 시각도 많이 교정되어 객관적 시각으로 변화되어
가고 있고, 또한 최근 대한변협이 전국 변호사를 상대로 실시한 변호사
의식 설문조사 결과도 제6공화국 이후 인권상황이 대폭 개선되었다고
하는등 우리나라의 인권상황이 개선되고 있다는 객관적인 근거도 많이
있음.

0234

외 무 부

종 별 : 긴 급

번 호 : GVW-0422   일 시 : 92 0224 2330

수 신 : 장관(연이, 법무부, 기정동문)

발 신 : 주 제네바 대사

제 목 : 제 48차 유엔인권위(16)

    연: GVW-0412

    대: WGV-0315

1. 본직은 명 2.25. 오후 별전 TEXT 내용으로 표제회의 의제 12 항(세계각국의 인권위반) 관련 발언 예정임.

2. 한편 금 2.24. NGO 인 WORLD ORG. AGAINST TORTURE 는 중국, 수단, 마다가스칼, 인니, 자이레 및 일부 중남미 국가의 인권문제를 거론하는 가운데 아국인권 상황에 대해서도 언급(6 월 이후 인권 상황개선 불구 1300 여명의 정치범 수감, 반인권법, 고문행위등을 촉구) 한바 있으며, WORLD CONFEDERATION OF LABOUR는 역시 다수국의 노동권 문제를 거론하면서 한국에서의 노조활동이 제약받고 있다는 언급이 있었는바, 연호 INTERNATIONAL ASSOC OF DEMOCRATIC LAWYERS 포함상기 NGO 언급내용에 대한 대응은 GVW-1691(91.9.6)로 보고한 바와 같이 이에 일일이 응대할 필요가 없다고 보고는 있으나, 대호 감안 마지막에 일괄적으로 간단히 언급하는 것으로 대응코자 함.(법무부장관의 소위 대국회 보고(매년 30 명의 수형자 사망) 관련 IADL 언급내용의 허위는 당지 출장중인 정기용검사에 의하여서도 확인됨)

3. 한편 정신대문제도 국내여론과 국민감정등에 비추어 일본 변호사의 발언을 인도주의의 기본에 부합하는 것으로 평가, 이를 격려하는 방향으로 역시 말미에 간단히 언급코자 하니 양지 바람. 끝

    (대사 박수길-국장)

    예고:92.6.30 일반

    일반문서로 재분류(1.992. 6. 30.)

국기국   장관   차관   1차보   2차보   외정실   분석관   정와대   안기부
법무부

PAGE 1   92.02.25   07:39
                                        외신 2과 통제관 BN
                                                0235

유엔 인권위원회, 제48차. Geneva, 1992.1.27-3.6. 전2권 (V.1 1월-2.24) 501

주 제 네 바 대 표 부

번 호 : GVW(F) - 0/30   년월일 : 2022년   시간 : 2340

수 신 : 장   관 (언이)

발 신 : 주 제네바대사

제 목 :   회의라도

총 7 미 (표지포함)

보 안	
통 제	

외신과	
통 재	

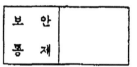

배부처	진건실	차보	一차보	二차보	기조실	감사관	의전장	정문국	아주국	미주국	구주국	중아국	국제기구국	경제국	통상국	문화국	영교국	총무과	감사관	공보관	여권과	청외대	총리실	안기부	공보처	경기원	상공부
												0														

0/30 - 7 -1

0236

48th Session of the U.N. Commission on Human Rights

Statement

By

Ambassador Soo Gil Park

Head of the Delegation of the
Republic of Korea
to the United Nations Commission on Human Rights

on

Item 12
Question of the Violation of Human Rights
and
Fundamental Freedoms in Any Part of the World

February 25, 1992

<u>Check against delivery</u>

0237

6/30 - 7-2

Mr. Chairman,

The drastic changes that have taken place around the globe in the past few years offer an unprecedented opportunity for the international community to promote conditions of well-being for all peoples, particularly their fundamental human rights.

Indeed, the deepening of the current trend toward democratization, and the increasing globalization of human rights issues, could contribute greatly to the realization of the fundamental principles of respect for human dignity, the rule of law, justice, equality, and non-discrimination.

The victory of the peoples' will in the former Soviet Union and Eastern and Central Europe, together with democratic changes in Latin America, Asia and Africa, reaffirm our conviction that human history is a manifestation of human reason, a record of progress toward freedom.

The time-old enmities, embittered by ideological confrontation, power struggles, territorial disputes and religious conflicts are giving way to peaceful dialogues. In Northeast Asia, Southeast Asia, Central America, Southern Africa, even in the Middle East, we see signs of peaceful evolution, though the signs range from symptoms of hope to implemented solutions.

Thanks to these momentous changes, we now have before us a world more devoted to peace and justice, and far less tolerant of human rights violations.

Efforts to improve the protection of human rights in the

1

0130-7-3

0238

Republic of Korea have been vigorously pursued, particularly since the inauguration of the popularly elected current Government in 1988. Now, Koreans are much more conscious of their rights, thus providing further impetus to enhance and promote human rights.

Confidence in its human rights accomplishments has led to increased Korean participation in international human rights activities. The Republic of Korea acceded to the International Covenant on Economic, Social and Cultural Rights, the International Covenant on Civil and Political Rights, and its Optional Protocol in April 1990. In December of last year, Korea became a party to the Convention on the Rights of Children. In addition, the Government is considering accession to several other human rights instruments, including the Convention and Protocol on the Status of Refugees.

Mr. Chairman,

While appreciating the positive impact that the recent political changes in the world have had on human rights, I am not turning my back on the daunting task before us. There are problems that persist and that are newly emerging. As a result, numerous human rights abuses are still occurring throughout the world.

First, let me talk about a persisting problem. There still remain totalitarian regimes that have yet to respond to the inexorable march of history. These are the last bastions of old ideologies, and they are the primary sources of human rights violations. Today the attention of the world is focused on these regimes to see if they can peacefully become more open and pluralistic societies.

Turning to emerging difficulties, I would like to point out the existing conflicts in the countries that underwent democratic

2

0239

0/30-7-4

revolutions. The disappearance of oppressive central control when
it is replaced by a democratic regime based on the free will of
the majority is likely to guarantee a better human rights
situation. However, it could lead to the fragmentation of a
nation, if the majority does not protect the fundamental rights
of minorities. In some countries, abuses are related to ethnic,
religious, or political issues, in other countries to power
struggles. No matter what causes these conflicts, the result is
always human rights violations.

Intolerance and injustice perpetrated on the basis of
political, racial, social, cultural and religious grounds should
never be condoned under any circumstances. Currently, we are
witnessing many cases where human rights are being violated on
these grounds. These abuses will grow if they are left unchecked.

Meeting the new challenge posed by these problems will be
our task in the post-cold war era. It is a task that should be
pursued vigorously by the international community.

It is from this perspective that I would like to make some
suggestions.

First, now is the time for the international community to
redouble its efforts in order to improve human right conditions
throughout the world. The members of the world community should
direct their attention to the remaining oppressive regimes, and
channel the worldwide tide of change toward these countries.
Effective application of U.N. Human Rights instruments by human
rights bodies, including this Commission, will be one of the
answers.

Second, the international community should spare no effort
in offering a helping hand to nations facing political and
economic chaos in the course of democratization. Linkage between
aid and human rights could also be a useful approach to assure
that the protection of human rights becomes irreversible.

3

0/3○-7-5

Third, economic development assistance to the developing
world may prove important to prevent future human rights abuses.
I have no inclination to open a debate on whether the development
issue is a human rights issue, but I believe no one would deny
that the two issues are closely related. To some extent, the
abuse of human rights may be linked to the frustration of
economic hardship, in both the developed and developing world.

Finally, the Western liberal democracies must also keep
their watchful eyes open to the potential for human rights abuses
in their own societies, due to the narrow-minded attitudes of
some of their citizens. If the soil of free society is used to
nurture the root of intolerance and bigotry, democracy's victory
over totalitarianism will be rendered nugatory.

Mr. Chairman,

As we are all aware, the U.N. has been the catalyst of an
impressive expansion of human rights since the adoption of the
Universal Declaration of Human Rights in 1948.

In this connection, this Commission should be commended for
its endeavour to make the U.N. system more effective in advancing
the cause of human rights. The fact that the Commission, in its
47th Session alone, adopted 82 resolutions and 10 decisions, of
which 66 resolutions and 9 decisions were approved by consensus,
attests to the outstanding contribution it is making to the
promotion of human rights throughout the world.

Mr. Chairman, before concluding, I would like to make a few
brief points concerning certain remarks about my country. It was
on the 14th of February when a distinguished Japanese lawyer,
representing International Education Development Inc., made a
valuable statement regarding the issue of "comfort women" drafted
by the Japanese military authorities during the Second World War.
My delegation believes that the statement has awakened the basic
conscience of humanity to the unprecedented cruelty caused by

4

0130-7-6

0241

human rights violations. It is our earnest desire that such voices of conscience further serve to enhance the cause of human rights and humanitarianism in the future work of this Commission.

Secondly, I would like to comment on a statement made by a representative of an NGO who alleged the death of 30 Korean prisoners per year, and who wrongly and maliciously attributed Korea's Justice Minister as the source of that statement, stating that the Minister had reported the alleged "abuses" to our National Assembly. The statement is wholly false, and this malicious fabrication of a ministerial statement should be enough to discredit what the NGO representative had to say.

In conclusion, Mr. Chairman, the world has seen great achievements in the field of human rights, however, new challenges do not allow time to be fascinated by our accomplishments. Now is the moment for the World Community to reach out and seize the opportunity to fashion a world free from human rights violations.

Thank you.

5

0130-7-7

0242

정 리 보 존 문 서 목 록

기록물종류	일반공문서철	등록번호	2021030660	등록일자	2021-03-31
분류번호	734.21	국가코드		보존기간	영구
명 칭	유엔 인권위원회 특별회의. Geneva, 1992.8.13-14				
생 산 과	국제연합2과	생산년도	1992~1992	담당그룹	
내용목차	* 유고슬라비아 사태 관련 특별회의 - 보스니아-헤르체고비나 및 세르비아 내 수용소에서의 인권유린문제 토의를 위해 8.5 미국이 개최 요청 - 미국 주도 결의안 만장일치 채택, 우리나라 옵서버 자격 공동제안국 참여 * 특별회의 제도는 1990년 경제사회이사회 결의(1990/48)에 따라 신설 - 유고사태 관련 특별회의는 긴급사태(인권침해상황)를 다루기 위한 최초의 특별회의				

0001

발 신 전 보

번 호 : WGV-1168   920806 1507 FP   종별 :

수 신 : 주   제네바   대사. ♣♣♣♣

발 신 : 장 관   (연이)

제 목 : 유고사태 관련 유엔 인권위 긴급회의 개최

　　　　1. 미 국무부는 8.5. 유고사태 관련 성명을 통하여, 보스니아-
헤르체코비나 및 세르비아내의 수용소에서의 인권유린문제를 토의하기
위하여 유엔 인권위 긴급회의 개최를 요청하였다고 밝힘.

　　　　2. 금번 긴급회의가 인권위원국 27개국의 동의에 따라 개최될 경우
인권위 최초의 긴급회의가 될 것인바, 동건 관련 귀지 동향 수시 보고바람.

　　　첨부 : 미국무성 성명. 끝.

　　　　　　WGV㈜- 315

　　　　　　　　　　　　　　　　　　　(국제기구국장 김재섭)

보 안
통 제

앙고재	유엔2과	기안자성명		과장	심의관	국장		차관	장관
92년8월6일		김종훈		代이	乙	김결			

외신과통제

0002

92- 8- 5 ; 18:14 ;   :# 1

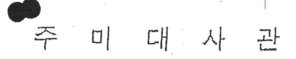

주 미 대 사 관

USW(F) : 5107   년월일 : 92.8.5   시간 : 18:15

수 신 : 장 관 (미일, 동자이, 연일)

발 신 : 주미대사

제 목 : 유고사태관련 국무부 성명   (출처 : CNS)

STATE DEPARTMENT REGULAR BRIEFING   BRIEFER: RICHARD BOUCHER
WEDNESDAY, AUGUST 5, 1992

MR. BOUCHER: Good afternoon ladies and gentlemen, I am sorry
to keep you and sorry to ruin your afternoon. I have a statement on
various things in Bosnia-Hercegovina and adjacent areas. This is a
statement by the Acting Secretary Lawrence S. Eagleburger, which I
will read to you, which I have been entrusted to read to you on his
behalf, and then afterwards I will be glad to take your questions
about it.

Over the past week we have seen an increasing number of
reports about detention centers in Bosnia-Hercegovina and Serbia,
including reports that indicate the possibility of executions,
torture, and other gross human rights abuses. These reports have
included press interviews, charges and counter charges by the
parties, and reports from others in the area. The International
Committee of the Red Cross has visited nine facilities where they
registered 4,300 prisoners. At this point the Red Cross has
reported on very difficult conditions of detention but they have not
found any evidence of death camps. Nonetheless, there are reports
of many other detention centers which the Red Cross has not been
able to visit and it is at some of these that atrocities have been
reported.

These reports, although unconfirmed, are profoundly
disturbing. It is vital that any and all prisons and detention
centers be open to the Red Cross and other neutral parties. Urgent
action is required to reveal the truth and to prevent any abuses
which may be occurring.

Yesterday morning we began a series of steps to support such
access. We instructed our diplomatic personnel immediately to
contact senior Serbian, Bosnian and Croatian officials to insist
that the International Committee of the Red Cross be granted
immediate, unimpeded and continuing access to any places of
detention. We have asked the United Kingdom, the presidency country
of the European Community, and through them, the other members of
the EC to make similar approaches. We have asked the Russians to

(5107 - 3 -/)   외신 1과
                   팀 제

배부	장관실	차관실	一차보	二차보	외정실	분석관	아주국	미주국	구주국	중아국	국기국	정재국	통상국	문협국	외연원	칙화대	안기부	공보처	경기원	상공무부	재무부	농수부	동자부	한정처	파기처
	/	/	/	/	/		/	/	0	/	/		/	/											

0003

유엔 인권위원회 특별회의. Geneva, 1992.8.13-14   511

use their influence with the Serbs to this same end. We proposed
and we obtained a statement by the Security Council yesterday
evening which endorsed this demand and reminded those involved in
any abuses that they can be held individually responsible for
breaches of the Geneva conventions.

Today we have called for an emergency extraordinary of the
United Nations Human Rights Commission in Geneva to examine this
situation in more detail, to discuss gross human rights violations,
and to press for full access to detention camps. We look to the
Human Rights Commission to forcefully exercise its mandate in this
regard by appointing a special representative who should be granted
access to investigate these charges and report back to the members

of the United Nations with his recommendations. This will be the
first-ever such meeting by the United Nations Human Rights
Commission. We have been urging governments throughout the world to
support this call immediately, even before the formal proposal was
circulated, so that the meeting could take place as soon as
possible.

Our proposal has now been circulated in Geneva, asking the 53
members for their views by 1;00 p.m. Eastern Daylight Time on
Monday, August 10th. We hope to see the necessary endorsement from
at least 27 members even before that, if possible.

In addition, we are undertaking other steps immediately. We
are calling on the CSCE to invoke the appropriate measure of the
CSCE human dimension mechanism in order to telescope the process of
choosing a rapporteur to look into the allegations. We are
undertaking renewed efforts to tighten sanctions enforcement in
addition to the efforts that we made earlier this month, which have
met with some success. We will facilitate the deployment of
monitors to Romania to ensure that the effect of the UN sanctions on
the Serbian economy is as devastating as possible. And we are
developing a Security Council resolution which would call on states
and organizations to collect substantiated information concerning
war crimes, and to make that information available to the Security
Council.

There are today some indications that our urgings are being
heard. In Belgrade, Mr. Panic promised our charge to invite
international observers to sites of alleged camps in Serbia and
Montenegro. Mr. Panic also pledged to support the UN presidency's
statement demanding the opening of camps run by Serbians in Bosnia.
Press reports today indicate leaders of the so-called Serbian
Republic of Bosnia have said that they are ready to open all
facilities to international inspection. Bosnian President
Izetbegovic told our charge in Belgrade that he has offered access
to international observers to all facilities within Bosnia.
President Tudjman told our consul general in Zagreb yesterday that
he would contact Croatian leaders in Bosnia to request their
complete cooperation with the ICRC.

5/ 07 - 3 - 2

These promises are welcome, but what is important is real action. We cannot allow excuses such as those used in the past -- that the safety of the ICRC delegates could not be ensured -- to block their important mission. We will press to see that real action is achieved.

Let me also add to that that we are intent upon seeing a UN Security Council resolution to ensure the humanitarian assistance is delivered through whatever means are necessary, and that we have been discussing with our key allies a draft of such resolution.

5/07-3-3

0005

외 무 부

종 별 :

번 호 : GVW-1518　　　　　　　　　　일 시 : 92 0806 1900

수 신 : 장관(연이) 사본: 주유엔,주미대사(본부중계필)

발 신 : 주 제네바대사

제 목 : 유고사태 관련 유엔인권위 긴급회의

　　대: WGV-1168

　　1. 금 8.6 인권위 아주그룹 회의후 참석자들간에 표제건에 관한 의견교환을 가졌는바, 각국이 아직 본부의 훈령 받지 못하여 사견임을 전제로 아래와 같은반응을 표명하였음.

　　가. 인도네시아는 미국의 긴급회의 소집 요청에 대해 아래 4 가지 문제점을지적하였는바, 사이프러스, 시리아, 인도, 중국등 다수국이 공감을 표시함.

　　1) 소말리아등 세계 곳곳에서 인권관련 긴급 상황이 발생하고 있는 가운데 특별히 유고사태에 대해서만 긴급 회의를 소집해야 할 필요성이 의문시됨

　　2) 과거 인권위 비동맹국가들간에 SPECIAL SESSION 은 가급적 열지 않기로 합의한바 있음.

　　3) 미국의 INITIATIVE 는 부시행정부가 이를 국내정치적 목적에 활용하려는 인상이 강함

　　4) 유고 사태에 대해 관련 국가간 별도의 CONFERENCE 가 추진되고 있는 상황에서, 인권위원회가 할수 있는 역할이 의문시됨.

　　나. 아울러 중국, 스리랑카, 파키스탄, 필리핀등은 인권위 긴급회의 MECHANISM 의 유용성에 의문을 표시하였으며, 일본만은 미국의 요청을 지지하게 될 것이라고 언급함.

　　2. 한편, 아랍권 국가들은 지난 6 월 팔레스탄인 점령지역 인권문제 관련 인권위 긴급회의 소집 요청이 미국등 서방국가들의 반대로 과반수 동의를 얻지 못한데 대해 강한 불만을 가지고 있는바, 진전 사항 파악되는 대로 보고 하겠음.

　　(차석대사 김삼훈-국장)

국기국　　차관　　1차보　　분석관　　청와대　　안기부　　중계

PAGE 1　　　　　　　　　　　　　　　　　　　92.08.07　　05:53

　　　　　　　　외신 2과　통제관 FM

0006

美, 유고에 軍事개입 시사

유엔 평화유지軍 철수 경고

【워싱턴·사라예보 AP·로이터=聯】 보스니아, 헤르체고비나 수도 사라예보에서 최근 두주일동안 가장 치열한 전투가 벌어지고 있는 가운데 美國은 5일 對유고 무력개입 가능성을 시사하는 한편 세르비아系 수용소내 「학살사태」를 다 루기 위한 유엔인권위원회 긴급회의 소집을 요구했으며, 보스니아 배치 유엔평화유지군은 사라예보에서 철수할 것을 고려하겠다고 경고했다.

조지 부시 美대통령은 이날 USA투데이紙와의 회견에서 유고 내전상황 결의안을 추진하면서 보스니아內 세르비아系 집단수용소에서 고문과 학살등 심각한 인권침해 사례가 벌어지고 있다는 보도와 관련, 유엔인권위원회 긴급회의 소집을 요청했다.

부시대통령은 인도적 목적을 위해 미군이 유용하게 활용될 수 있을 것이라고 말하고, 그러나 對유고 군사개입은 상황을 베트남式 게릴라전으로 비화시킬 가능성이 있다고 우려했다. 美대사는 유엔인권위에

호활동 강행을 위해 군사력 사용을 승인하는 유엔결의안을 추진하면서 보스니아內 세르비아系 집단수용소에서 고문과 학살등 인권상황을 다뤄야할 것으로 믿고 있다」고 말했다.

미국은 한편 유고내 구

보낸 긴급회의 요청서에서 「세르비아세력이 민간인 66개 수용소에만 크로아티아인과 회교도 12만여명이 단수용소에 모아놓고 처형 억류되어 있다고 주장했다. 보스니아는 지난달 29일 유엔 安保理측에 한 보고서에서의 학살자수만도 1만7천1백명에 이르며 만약카 규기지내 수용소 한곳에서만 8천여명이 집단처형됐다고 말했다. 세르비아측은 이와관련, 보스니아 몬테네그로에 1백5개 집단수용소를 인했다.

세르비아系가 민간인들을 마구 붙잡아들여 집단수용소에 모아놓고 처형을 자행하고 있다」면서 「美정부는 가능한 조속히 회의를 소집, 악화되고 있는 보스니아內 세르비아系 집단수용소 존재 자체를 부

외 무 부

종 별 : 지 급

번 호 : GVW-1541

일 시 : 92 0810 1930

수 신 : 장관(연이,동구이) 사본: 주미대사, 주유엔대사,주유고대사(중계필)

발 신 : 주 제네바 대사대리

제 목 : 유고사태 관련 긴급 유엔인권위

연: GVW-1518

1. 지난 8.5 미국이 요청한 표제 회의는 금 8.10(월) 인권위원국 과반수의 동의를 얻음에 따라 92.8.13-14 양일간 당지에서 개최키로 결정 되었음.

2. 금 8.10(월) 오후 현재 동 회의 소집에 동의한 위원국은 35 개국인바, 서구그룹(10 개국) 및 동구권 국가(유고제외), 알젠틴, 브라질, 콜롬비아, 코스타리카등 대다수의 중남미국가와 일본, 방글라데시등 다수 아주국가가 이에 참여한 것으로 파악되었음.

3. 한편 아랍권 국가들은 연호 미국의 INITIATIVE 에 불만을 가지고 있으나유고사태 피해자의 상당수 회교도들이 포함되어 있는점과 특별히 반대할 명분이 없는 점등을 고려 대세에 따르는 입장인 것으로 관측됨.

4. 금일 사무국에 확인한바에 따르면, 동 긴급 인권회의의 절차사항은 일반회의와 동일하며, 아국은 옵서버로 참가할 수 있는바, 동 회의 참가관련 지침 회시 바람.

(차석대사 김삼훈-국장)

예고:92.12.31. 까지

국기국 중계	장관	차관	1차보	구주국	외정실	분석관	청와대	안기부

PAGE 1

* 원본수령부서 승인없이 복사 금지

92.08.11   04:53

외신 2과 통제관 BZ

0008

	분류번호	보존기간

발 신 전 보

WGV-1185   920811 1044 WH

번 호 :＿＿＿＿＿＿＿＿   종별 : ＿＿＿＿

수 신 : 주   제네바   대사. ♣♣♣♣♣

발 신 : 장 관 (연이)

제 목 : 유고사태 관련 유엔 인권위 긴급회의

대 : GVW-1541

대호, 표제회의에는 귀관에서 적의 참석하고, 회의결과 및 동향을
보고바람. 끝.

(국제기구국장 김재섭)

	보 안 통 제	

앙 고 재	92 년 8 월 11 일	유 엔 2 과	기안자 성 명 기종순	과 장	심의관	국 장 지래	차 관	장 관

외신과통제

0009

^Eds: Recaps previous, meeting is scheduled to begin at 0800 GMT.<
^By ALEXANDER G. HIGGINS=
^Associated Press Writ

GENEVA (AP) _ The 53-nation U.N. Human Rights Commission on Thursday opens a two-day emergency session on atrocities in former Yugoslavia, with the United States stressing the urgent need for prompt action.

A draft resolution with the backing of most of the member countries calls for a special investigator to start compiling evidence that could be used in any future war crimes trials.

John Bolton, an assistant U.S. secretary of state, said Washington had received reports that Bosnian Serbs were trying to move prisoners to improve appearances before allowing the International Committee of the Red Cross to inspect.

``We want access to all of these supposed camps immediately and without impediment before these transfers of prisoners become more widespread,'' Bolton, head of the U.S. delegation, told reporters in Geneva.

The ICRC visited the Serb-held camp at Trnopolje, northeast of Banja Luka in northern Bosnia-Herzegovina, on Wednedsay, Red Cross spokesman Pierre Gauthier.

It was the first camp the Red Cross teams have been able to visit since Bosnian Serbs said last weekend they would open up all their camps to ICRC inspection.

Trnopolje brought to 11 the number of camps visited by the ICRC in former Yugoslavia. It was the fourth camp held by Serbs that the Red Cross has visited.

The United States called last week for the human rights session, the first emergency meeting ever held by the commission, because of what it said was ``the dangerous situation'' in former Yugoslavia, including reports of ``concentration camp-like'' conditions. The commission meets each winter for an annual review of human rights abuses around the world.

Bolton said the provision that the investigator report within two weeks was important for a prompt, balanced report on what is happening in former Yugoslavia.

The five-page draft also demands that ``all persons arbitratily arrested or detained'' be released and ``that the ICRC be granted immediate, unimpeded and continued access to all camps, prisons and other places of detention.''

Bolton said the resolution wouldn't place blame solely on one side.

``We are not interested in singling out anybody,'' he said. ``We want to eliminate the abuses of human rights that have been alleged in former Yugoslavia by anybody who commits them.''

He said the United States has its own independent information that Bosnian Serb forces have been moving prisoners ``to decrease crowding and improve the appearance of camps which may be visited by the ICRC and journalists.''

``As the ICRC found in World War II, it can be deceived,'' Bolton said, referring to the sanitized picture of concentration camps shown the ICRC by the Nazis. ``It's an organization that doesn't shoot its way in.''

It is ``particularly important'' that the investigations be as soon as possible, he said. ``We need to know what the facts are.''

The Bosnian Serbs' invitation the ICRC last weekend came after an widespread horror over photographs of emaciated prisoners that recalled Nazi concentration camps.

The ICRC keeps confidential its findings about the conditions in the camps and tries to pressure the captors into improving conditions, but the special U.N. investigator's report could be made public soon after it goes to the Security Concil, Bolton said.

Officials said that the Red Cross is in a better position now to unravel such deceptions than it was in World War II, partly because of Geneva conventions on the treatment of civilians and war prisoners.

Interviews with prisoners and record keeping quickly uncover any recent moves of inmates, a Red Cross official said.

10   0010

원 본

2

외 무 부

종 별 : 지 급

번 호 : GVW-1562

일 시 : 92 0813 1530

수 신 : 장 관 (연이, 동구이) 사본 : 주 유엔, 주 유고 대사 (본부중계필)

발 신 : 주 제네바 대사대리

제 목 : 유고사태 관련 유엔 특별인권위(결의안)

1. 금 8.13(목) 오전 개최된 표제회의에서 미국대표 (J.BOLTON 국무차관보)는 금번 특별 인권위 제안자로서 첫번째 발언권을 얻어 유고 사태에 관한 미국 입장을 밝히고 아래와 같은 요지의 결의안을 제안함. (발언문 및 결의안 별첨)

  O 자의적 (ARBITRARILY)으로 수용된 모든 사람들의 즉시 석방

  O 국제적십자사 (ICRC)의 구유고 지역내 모든 수용소, 형무소 접근 허용

  O 모든 분쟁 당사자들의 즉각적인 인권 침해 행위 중단

  O 구 유고지역 내 인권 침해 상황을 조사하기 위한 SPECIAL RAPPORTEUR 임명

  O SPECIAL RAPPORTEUR 는 조사후 8.28 까지 예비 (PRELIMINARY) 보고서 제출

  O 구 유고지역내 모든 분쟁 당사자들은 SPECIAL RAPPORTEUR 의 업무 수행을적극 협조

2. 동 결의안은 미국과 금번 회의 개최를 지지한 34 개국간의 사전협의를 거쳐 작성된 것으로 금일 오전 최종안이 작성되었으며 금일 오후 사무국에 제출 배포될 예정이며, 동 결의안에 대한 토의 및 표결은 명 8.14 일 예정인 바 문제없이 봉과될 것으로 관측됨.

3. 이와관련 위원국이 아닌 옵서버 국가들에게도 CO-SPONSOR 할 수 있는 기회가 열려 있으며 상당수 옵서버 국가들이 이에 참여할 것으로 파악되고 있는바 아국도 CO-SPONSOR 로 참여하는 것이 바람직할 것으로 사료되니 지침 지급 회시 바람.

4. 금일 회의는 야간회의로 계속 진행될 예정이며 동 회의 결과는 명일 회의 종료후 종합 보고 하겠음

  첨부 : 1. 미국 발언문

  2. 결의안 (GVW(F)-0490). 끝

  (차석대사 김삼훈-국장)

국기국	장관	차관	1차보	구주국	분석관	청와대	안기부	중계

92.08.14   07:52

외신 2과 통제관 FS

0011

예고 : 92.12.31. 까지

PAGE 2

0012

주 제 네 바 대 표 부

번호 : GVW(F) - *0410*
년월일 : *20813*   시간: *1530*

수신 : 장   관 **(영의.동구이)**

발신 : 주제네바대사

제목 : *침부*

총 *13* 매(프지프함)

브 관 통 제	*[서명]*
외신관 통 제	

410-13-1   0013

Office of Public Affairs
United States Mission

[illegible]
[illegible]
[illegible]

[illegible]
[illegible]

USIA

.STATEMENT BY

JOHN R. BOLTON

Assistant Secretary of State for

International Organization Affairs

to the Extraordinary Session of the United Nations

Human Rights Commission

on the Situation in Former Yugoslavia

Geneva, August 13, 1992

470-13-2

0014

SPEECH FOR EXTRAORDINARY UNHRC SESSION ON THE SITUATION IN
FORMER YUGOSLAVIA

The United States of America requested this
unprecedented extraordinary session of the United Nations Human
Rights Commission, because, along with many others, we are
appalled at the unspeakable, immoral savagery being unleashed
upon the citizens of what used to be Yugoslavia. Under the
United Nations Charter, this Commission has a critical moral
responsibility to turn the spotlight of international scrutiny
upon the darkness in that land. We are making use of a new
mechanism to convene the Commission on an emergency basis so
that it can address a human rights crisis as it unfolds.

That there are ongoing abuses of human rights in direct
violation of international law is not in doubt. The deliberate
targeting of civilians is a violation of one of the most basic
tenets governing the conduct of war, set forth in a host of
international treaties, covenants and declarations which
condemn, if not criminalize, these vicious acts. We have seen
the carnage being wreaked upon the innocent civilian population
of Bosnia as military forces vie for control in the name of
ethnic supremacy. The neighbors of former Yugoslavia, as well
as its several constituent Republics, know all too well the
campaign of expulsion being waged in wide swatches of
territory, which has created the largest refugee crisis in

- 2 -

Europe since the end of the Second World War.   The policy which
its perpetrators chillingly call "ethnic cleansing" is an
abhorrent breach of international human rights standards, as
we. is the norms of civilized behavior.

        In recent days, we have begun to receive yet even more
ominous, profoundly disturbing reports of camps where people
are being systematically abused, tortured and even executed.
Even worse, we now know that camp prisoners are being moved --
from Omarska, Banja Luka, and perhaps elsewhere -- in an effort
to hide the horrors inflicted upon them.   In the name of
humanity we must now exercise every effort to ensure that the
truth sets them free.

        Our objectives at this session are simple and direct:

    --   we want an investigation into human rights
         violations in the republics of the former
         Yugoslavia, particularly Bosnia-Herzegovina;

    --   we want a full airing of all charges relating to
         abuses of human rights and violations of
         international law;

    --   we want to know who is responsible for such
         abuses;

    --   we want to ensure that humanitarian organizations
         such as the ICRC have immediate, unimpeded and
         fully secure access to all victims of the
         conflict, including those held in detention.

    The United States believes that the most effective way
to accomplish this is to appoint a Special Rapporteur with the

4p.-13-4

0016

- 3 -

highest credentials for impartiality and thoroughness. This
Special Rapporteur, cloaked in the mandate of this Commission,
and acting under the authority of the United Nations, must be
granted immediate and unimpeded access by all the parties to
the conflict to all individuals in the former republics of
Yugoslavia -- wherever they may be located -- who can shed
light on what is happening. After conducting an urgent
first-hand investigation, he should immediately report so that
we can consider further, decisive action in the United Nations,
as well as by the Conference on Security and Cooperation in
Europe. I stress that we do not view such a United Nations
investigation as supplanting the efforts of other
organizations, particularly those of the International
Committee of the Red Cross or the Conference on Security and
Cooperation in Europe. A UN effort would complement and
reinforce such other efforts now being made. The more light
shed, the better.

     The United States has submitted a draft resolution to
the Human Rights Commission which we believe should be
overwhelmingly endorsed by its member governments. This
resolution is evidence of the uniform repulsion felt throughout
the world, and the joint determination that we cannot remain
idle. The speed with which this Commission was convened is
further proof of our deep concern and commitment.

- 4 -

I wish to make a direct appeal to the parties in the
conflict, and to those who control the weapons. Nothing can
come of this violence except more violence. Political gains
obtained through violence can only be maintained through
further violence and repression. Unquestionably such
political gains and violent territorial changes will never be
recognized or sanctified by civilized persons. Any state
enlarged through the bloodshed of innocent civilians is an
international pariah, an outlaw state. The international
community will never accept the redrawing of boundaries by
force in Yugoslavia; the sooner the parties accept this
fundamental fact, the sooner we can turn to peacefully
resolving this crisis.

To the perpetrators of the appalling acts now alleged,
I say that the international community took a vow when it
realized what had been committed by Nazism in Europe during the
Second World War: "Never again." The Nuremberg Tribunal
reaffirmed the principle of individual accountability for
crimes against humanity committed in the name of national or
ethnic groups. The United States is fully prepared to join
with others to see that individuals guilty of violations of
international law and human rights principles are held strictly
accountable. We have proposed in the UN a "war crimes"
resolution to ensure this accountability; we want to see it
adopted as soon as possible.

0018

＜PO-13-0

- 5 -

Our century has already borne witness to the most
ferocious and horrible violations of human rights. We do not
now wish to see this grievous record augmented as the century
draws to a close. We ask the people of Serbia-Montenegro this
simple question: Do they wish to go down in history as rulers
of the last fascist state in Europe?

We are human-beings. We recoil in horror and
revulsion at the tragedy of former Yugoslavia. We have a duty
to ourselves and to this United Nations Human Rights Commission
to act now to bring the weight of the international community
to bear against what is being done to the people of that
benighted place, whether Muslim, Croat, Serb or other ethnic,
national or religious group. The men of violence must be shown
that there is no real, lasting alternative to peaceful
negotiation to solve their differences. Nothing can excuse or
justify the slaughter and misery being heaped upon the innocent
people of the former Yugoslavia. The United States seeks your
support for the adoption of all measures, including a full and
immediate investigation, that will help protect the victims of
this tragic conflict, and bring it to a speedy end.

0019

1-90-13-9

August 13, 1992

The Situation of Human Rights
in the Territory of the Former Yugoslavia

The Commission on Human Rights,

Meeting in exceptional session,

Guided by the principles embodied in the Charter of the
United Nations, the Universal Declaration of Human Rights, the
International Covenants on Human Rights, the Convention on the
Elimination of All Forms of Racial Discrimination, and accepted
humanitarian rules, including those set out in the Geneva
Conventions of 12 August 1949 and the Additional Protocols thereto
of 1977,

Guided also by the need to implement the principles set out
in the aforementioned instruments,

Aware of its responsibility to promote and encourage respect
for human rights and fundamental freedoms for all and resolved to
remain vigilant with regard to violations of human rights wherever
they may occur, and to prevent such violations,

Appalled at the continuing reports of widespread, massive,
and grave violations of human rights occurring within the territory
of the former Yugoslavia and especially in Bosnia-Herzegovina,
including reports of summary and arbitrary executions, enforced
disappearances, torture and other cruel, inhuman, or degrading
treatment, arbitrary arrest and detention, hostage taking, lack of
due process and lack of respect for the rule of law, restrictions on
freedom of thought, expression and association, deliberate attacks
on noncombatants, hospitals, and ambulances, restrictions on access
to food and health care, wanton devastation and destruction of
property, and serious violations of human rights in places of
detention,

Expressing its particular abhorrence at the concept and
practice of "ethnic cleansing," in the former Yugoslavia, and
especially in Bosnia-Herzegovina, which at a minimum entails
deportations and forcible mass removal or expulsion of persons from
their homes in flagrant violation of their human rights, and which
is aimed at the dislocation or destruction of national, ethnic,
racial or religious groups,

· 0020

// ᵖ₀—/3— ^

- 2 -

<u>Deeply concerned</u> that the conflict in the former
Yugoslavia and deliberate violations of human rights have
resulted in the creation of more than two and a half million
refugees and internally displaced persons and that conditions
conducive to their return in safety and dignity have not been
achieved,

<u>Cognizant</u> of the acute danger that the current conflict
and its accompanying human rights abuses could spread to
additional areas of the former Yugoslavia, and the need to take
action to ensure this does not occur,

<u>Noting</u> the statement by the President of the Security
Council on 4 August 1992 concerning reports of the imprisonment
and abuse of civilians in camps, prisons, and detention centers
within the territory of the former Yugoslavia and especially in
Bosnia-Herzegovina, which demands that international
organizations, and in particular the ICRC, be granted
immediate, unimpeded, and continued access to all such places,
and which calls on all parties and organizations to make
available to the Council any further information they may
possess,

<u>Recalling</u> Security Council resolution 713 of 25
September 1991 and subsequent Security Council resolutions,

<u>Recalling</u> that the former Yugoslavia was a party to the
International Covenant on Civil and Political Rights, the
International Covenant on Economic and Social Rights, the
Convention Against Genocide, the Convention Against Torture,
and the Convention on the Elimination of All Forms of Racial
Discrimination,

<u>Welcoming</u> efforts by the Conference on Security and
Cooperation in Europe to investigate reports of serious
violations of fundamental human rights in the territory of the
former Yugoslavia, and welcoming also the interest of the
Organization of the Islamic Conference,

<u>Noting</u> the statements by parties in the former
Yugoslavia expressing their willingness to cooperate with
international observers,

0021

4Po -13- P

- 3 -

1. <u>Condemns in the strongest terms</u> all violations of human rights within the territory of the former Yugoslavia, and especially in Bosnia-Herzegovina, and calls upon all parties to cease these violations immediately and take all necessary steps to ensure full respect for human rights and fundamental freedoms and humanitarian law;

2. <u>Condemns absolutely</u> the concept and practice of "ethnic cleansing;"

3. <u>Expresses its alarm</u> at all repressive policies and practices directed against members of particular ethnic groups and also calls upon all the parties to ensure the protection of the rights of persons belonging to national or ethnic, religious, and linguistic minorities;

4. <u>Calls upon</u> all parties to release immediately all persons arbitrarily arrested or detained;

5. <u>Demands</u> that the ICRC be granted immediate, unimpeded and continued access to all camps, prisons, and other places of detention within the territory of the former Yugoslavia, and that all parties ensure complete safety and freedom of movement to the ICRC and otherwise facilitate such access;

6. <u>Demands also</u> that all parties in the former Yugoslavia extend full cooperation and protection to the United Nations High Commissioner for Refugees and her staff, and to other international humanitarian organizations and relief workers, in carrying out their efforts to assist refugees and displaced persons in the former Yugoslavia,

7. <u>Calls upon</u> all parties in the former Yugoslavia to cease immediately the human rights violations that have produced refugees and displaced persons and to promote and ensure conditions conducive to their return to their homes in safety and dignity,

8. <u>Affirms absolutely</u> the necessity of ensuring access for humanitarian assistance to those in need,

0022

- 4 -

9.   Reminds all parties they are bound to comply with
their obligations under international humanitarian law and in
particular the Third and Fourth Geneva Conventions and the
Additional Protocols thereto regarding the treatment of
combatants and noncombatants, and that persons who commit or
order the commission of grave breaches of the Conventions or
their Protocols are individually responsible in respect of such
breaches;

10.   Calls on all parties in the former Yugoslavia to
fulfill their obligations under the provisions of the
International Covenant on Civil and Political Rights, the
International Covenant on Economic and Social Rights, the
Convention Against Genocide, the Convention Against Torture,
and the Convention on the Elimination of All Forms of Racial
Discrimination,

11.   Affirms that states are to be held accountable for
violations of human rights which their agents commit upon the
territory of another state;

12.   Requests the Chairman of the Commission to appoint
a Special Rapporteur to investigate first-hand the human rights
situation in the territory of the former Yugoslavia, in
particular within Bosnia-Herzegovina, and to receive relevant,
credible information on the human rights situation there from
governments, individuals, intergovernmental and
non-governmental organizations, on a continuing basis, and to
avail himself or herself of the assistance of existing
mechanisms of the Commission on Human Rights;

13.   Requests the existing mechanisms of the Commission
on Human Rights, in particular the Special Rapporteur on
Torture, the Special Rapporteur on Summary and Arbitrary
Executions, the Expert on Internally Displaced Persons, and the
Working Group on Detention, to give urgent attention to the
situation in the former Yugoslavia and to provide on a
continuing basis their full cooperation, assistance, and
findings to the Special Rapporteur, and to accompany the
Special Rapporteur in visiting the former Yugoslavia if he or
she should so request;

0023

CPo -13-11

- 5 -

14.   Requests the Special Rapporteur to visit areas of
interest in the former Yugoslavia, and particularly
Bosnia-Herzegovina, forthwith and report on an urgent basis to
the members of the Commission on Human Rights, providing a
preliminary report no later than August 28, on the situation of
human rights in the former Yugoslavia including his or her
recommendations on bringing violations to an end and preventing
future violations, and requests the Secretary General to make
the Special Rapporteur's report available also to the Security
Council;

15.   Also requests the Special Rapporteur to report his
or her findings and recommendations periodically thereafter to
the members of the Commission on Human Rights until its next
regular session, and to report to the General Assembly at its
47th session, as well as to the Commission on Human Rights at
its next regular session under agenda item 12, and requests the
Secretary General to make the Special Rapporteur's reports
available also to the Security Council;

16.   Additionally requests the Special Rapporteur to
gather and compile systematically information on possible
violations of human rights in the territory of the former
Yugoslavia, including those which may constitute war crimes,
and to make this information available to the Secretary
General, and notes that such information could be of possible
future use in prosecuting violators of international
humanitarian law;

17.   Requests the Secretary General to provide all
necessary assistance to the Special Rapporteur to fulfill his
or her mandate;

18.   Requests all United Nations bodies and Specialized
Agencies, and invites informed governments, intergovernmental
and non-governmental organizations, to provide the Special
Rapporteur, through the Human Rights Center, on a continuing
basis, with all relevant and accurate information within their
possession on the situation of Human Rights in the former
Yugoslavia;

19.   Demands that all parties in the territory of the
former Yugoslavia cooperate fully with the Special Rapporteur
in the implementation of this resolution;

4P0 -13-12   0024

- 6 -

20. <u>Requests</u> that the Special Rapporteur take into account and seek to complement the efforts being undertaken by the Conferece on Security and Cooperation in Europe with respect to the crisis in the former Yugoslavia;

21. <u>Decides</u> to remain seized of the issue.

KPo—13-17

0025

	분류번호	보존기간
		·

발 신 전 보

번 호 : WGV-1206   920814 1743 FY   종별 : 긴급

수 신 : 주   제네바   대사. ♣♣♣♣♣

발 신 : 장 관 (연이)

제 목 : 유고사태 관련 유엔 인권위 특별회의

대 : GVW-1562

대호, 미국 결의안에 대한 공동제안국 참여 문제에 대하여는 아래 입장에
따라 대처바람.

1. 아국은 동 결의안 내용을 지지함

2. 공동제안국 참여 요청이 있을 경우에는 참여토록 함.

3. 참여 요청이 없는 상황에서는 아국이 옵서버이며, 본문 10항(고문방지
협약 준수의무) 등 일부 결의안 내용에 있어 검토가 필요한 점 등을 고려, 공동
제안에 참여치 않음. 끝.

(차관)

구주국장 :

| | | 기안자
성명 | 과 장 | 심의관 | 국 장 | 제1차관보 | 차 관 | 장 관 | |
|---|---|---|---|---|---|---|---|---|---|
| 앙
고
재 | 92
년
8
월
14
일 | 유엔2
과 | 강철 | | | | 전결 | | |

| 보 안
통 제	
외신과통제	

0026

7h

관리 번호	92 ~ 8-15

외 무 부

종 별 :

번 호 : GVW-1576   일 시 : 92 0815 1000

수 신 : 장관(연이,동구이) 사본: 주유엔,주미,주유고대사(본부중계필)

발 신 : 주 제네바 대사대리

제 목 : 유고사태관련 UN 인권위 특별회의

연: GVW-1562

대: WGV-1206

표제회의는 금 8.14(금) 연호 결의안을 표결없이 CONSENSUS 로 채택하고 폐막되었는바 요지 아래 보고함.

1. 결의안 채택

0 금일 오전 회의시 의장은 동결의안의 공동 제안국에 참여를 희망하는 국가는 조속히 서명하여 줄것을 요청하였는바, 아국대표단은 주요국가들이 대부분 참여하는 점과 93 년이후 인권위원국으로서의 아국의 위상등을 고려하여 옵서버국가로서는 17 번째로 공동제안국에 참여함.

0 ABRAM 미국대사는 오전회의 종료직전 공동제안국 대표들을 회의장 근처로초빙, 공동제안국으로 참여한데 대해 사의를 표명하고 동 결의안이 문구수정없이 CONSENSUS 로 봉과될수 있도록 협조를 당부함.(본 회의시 ABRAM 대사는 아국을 포함 공동제안국명을 낭독함)

0 한편 미국대표(EICHER 참사관)는 문봉주참사관에게 비유럽국가인 아국의 공동제안국 참여는 미국의 입장을 크게 도우는 것이 라고 개별적으로 사의를 표함.

0 동 결의안의 공동제안국 참여국가는 총 60 개국이며 이중 옵서버국가는 아국, 뉴질랜드, 파나마등 26 개국임.

0 동결의안은 사전협의 과정에서 문안내용중 회교권 국가들이 요청한 아래 3가지 문안수정을 공동제안국들이 수용함에 따라 별도 토의없이 CONSENSUS 로 채택됨.

- 전문 네번째 PARA 둘째줄 OCCURING 을 PERPETRATED 로 대체

- 전문 아홉번째 PARA UN 결의안 언급부분에 8.13 안보리 결의까지 관련 결의안 모두 포함.

국기국	장관	차관	1차보	구주국	분석관	정와대	안기부	중계

PAGE 1

- 전문 마지막부분에 8.13. 채택 인권소위 결의안 NOTE 문구삽입

0 한편 유고대표는 동결의안 채택직전 아래 요지로 자국입장을 표명함.

- 유고로서는 동 결의안을 받아들이기 어려운점이 많으나 CONSENSUS 를 거부할 의사는 없음

- SPECIAL RAPPORTEUR 의 방문을 허용할 것이나, 조사행위는 구유고연방내 모든지역, 모든당사자에게 대해 균등하게 이루어져야 어느 일방에 대해 특별히 불리한 방향으로 이행되어서는 않됨.

0 결의안 채택후 의장은 동결의안 12 항에 의거 폴란드의 TADEUS MAZOWIECKI (전수상)을 SPECIAL RAPPORTEUR 로 임명한다고 발표하였으며, 사무국은 동결의안 이행에 약 10 만불의 예산이 소요될것이라고 설명함.

2. 회의경과

동회의는 개회직후 의제안 채택시 리비아등 일부국가들이 일부 문구수정을 요청하여 장시간 논란이 있었으나 리비아의 제안 철회로 원안대로 채택되었으며, 미국, EC, 일본등 다수국가들이 유고연방(세르비아, 몬테네그론) 대표의 금번회의 참석이 구유고 사회주의연방의 지위 승계를 인정하는 것이 아니라는 입장 표명을 하였음., 0 대다수 국가가 일반발언을 통해 연호 미국대표의 발언 및 결의안을 지지하는 입장을 표명하였으며, 특히 SPECIAL RAPPORTEUR 임명조사, ICRC, UNHCR 등의 접근허용 및 구호사업 필요성을 강조하고 보스니아 헬체코비나 지역에서 벌어지고 있는 소위 "ETHNIC CLEANSING" 에 대해 강한 우려를 표명하였음.

0 유고대표는 보스니아 헬체코비나의 세르비아 점령지역내 집단수용소의 존재를 부인하면서 약 8000 명의 전쟁포로가 수용되엉 있을뿐이며, 이들은 제네바협약에 의거 공정한 대우를 받고있다고 밝히고, UN 인권위가 어느일방의 입장에 치우친 결정을 내려서는 않됄것임을 강조함.

(GVW-1577 로 계속됨) 약 8000 명의 전쟁포로가 수용되엉 있을뿐이며, 이들은 전

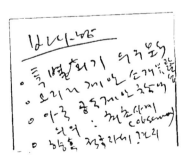

PAGE 2

0028

외   무   부

종   별 :

번   호 : GVW-1577   일   시 : 92 0815 1000

수   신 : 장관(연이,동구이) 사본:주유엔,주미,주유고대사(본부중계필)

발   신 : 주 제네바 대사대리

제   목 : GVW-1576 계속임.

3. 관찰 및 평가

O 금번 UN 인권위 특별회의는 최초의 특별회의 인바 미국의 긴급제의에 따라 소집되었으나 대부분 국가들이 금번회의를 소집한 미국의 노력을 평가하고 예외없이 구유고연방내에서 벌어지고 있는 소위 "ETHNIC CLEANSING" 을 강도높게 비난함으서 미국의 INITIATIVE 가 국제적인 지지를 확보한 것으로 평가됨.

O 대부분의 참석국가대표 및 NGO 들은 유고사태진상 조사를 위한 SPECIAL RAPPORTEUR 임명을 요청하는 미국의 입장에 지지를 표명하였는바, 결국 금번회의소집 목적 및 성과는 SPECIAL RAPPORTEUR 임명 및 진상조사를 골자로 하는 미국 주도의 결의안 채택이라 할수 있으며, 이에 많은 국가가 공동제안국으로 참여하고, 특히 결의안이 CONSENSUS 로 채택됨으로서 미국측의 특별회의 소집 의도가 달성된 것으로 평가됨.

4. 관련문서 차파편 송부하겠음. 끝

(차석대사 김삼훈-차관)

예고:92.12.31. 까지

국기국	장관	차관	1차보	구주국	분석관	정와대	안기부	중계

3. *Requests* the Secretary-General to submit a further report to the Council, at its first regular session of 1991, on the steps taken to implement the recommendations contained in its resolution 1983/30 by those Member States, United Nations organizations and other intergovernmental organizations that have not yet submitted such information and to make that report available to the Working Group on Contemporary Forms of Slavery of the Sub-Commission on Prevention of Discrimination and Protection of Minorities;

4. *Endorses* the request of the Commission on Human Rights, in its resolution 1990/63, that the staff member appointed to serve the Working Group and undertake other activities relating to contemporary forms of slavery in the post which has been included in the budget of the Centre for Human Rights of the Secretariat for questions relating to slavery and slavery-like practices be assigned on a full-time basis;

5. *Endorses* the request of the Commission on Human Rights, in its resolution 1989/35, which was reiterated in its resolution 1990/63, that the Secretary-General designate the Centre for Human Rights as the focal point for the co-ordination of activities in the United Nations for the suppression of contemporary forms of slavery;

6. *Decides* to consider the question of the suppression of traffic in persons at its first regular session of 1991 under the item entitled "Human rights".

14th plenary meeting
25 May 1990

1990/47. Developments relevant to the activities of the Centre for Human Rights

The Economic and Social Council,

Recalling General Assembly resolution 44/135 of 15 December 1989 and Commission on Human Rights resolution 1989/46 of 6 March 1989[94] and taking note of Commission resolution 1990/25 of 27 February 1990,[78]

Considering that the promotion of universal respect for and observance of human rights and fundamental freedoms is one of the basic aims of the United Nations according to the Charter and an issue of the utmost importance for the Organization,

Recognizing that the work-load of the Centre for Human Rights has increased rapidly in recent years,

1. *Takes note* of the report of the Secretary-General on the situation and developments regarding the logistical and human resources support for the activities of the Centre for Human Rights,[98] in particular the conclusion that the work-load of the Centre has increased, while resources have failed to keep pace with the increase in its responsibilities;[99]

2. *Requests* the Secretary-General to include in the proposed programme budget for the biennium 1992-1993, programme and resource proposals for long-term solutions of the problems posed by this situation, taking also into account the proposals contained in the report

of the Task Force on Computerization,[100] as well as in the study[101] carried out by an independent expert, concerning the effective implementation of international instruments on human rights;

3. *Also requests* the Secretary-General to submit to the General Assembly at its forty-fifth session a brief report on actions taken in 1990 and those planned for 1991, as interim solutions of these problems;

4. *Decides* to refer the report of the Secretary-General[98] to the General Assembly at its forty-fifth session, the Commission on Human Rights at its forty-seventh session and the persons chairing the human rights treaty bodies at their next meeting, for consideration.

14th plenary meeting
25 May 1990

1990/48. Enlargement of the Commission on Human Rights and the further promotion of human rights and fundamental freedoms

The Economic and Social Council,

Recalling General Assembly resolution 44/167 of 15 December 1989,

Bearing in mind the responsibilities of the Commission on Human Rights under the Charter of the United Nations,

Appreciating the contribution made by the Commission to the cause of human rights and recognizing the need to reinforce it,

Reaffirming that the Commission shall be guided by the standards in the field of human rights laid down in the various international instruments concerned with the protection and promotion of human rights,

Aware of the fact that the promotion, protection and full realization of all human rights and fundamental freedoms, as legitimate concerns of the world community, should be guided by the principles of non-selectivity, impartiality and objectivity and should not be used for political ends,

Emphasizing the importance of further improving the effective functioning of the Commission in the field of human rights,

Convinced that in order to achieve universally recognized objectives, improvements in the functioning of the Commission and measures of rationalization should be a matter for continuous consideration,

Taking note of the relevant section of the final documents of the Ninth Conference of Heads of State or Government of Non-Aligned Countries adopted at Belgrade on 7 September 1989[102] stating the need to strengthen the role and efficiency of the United Nations and to reinforce its mechanisms,

Stressing that the special rapporteurs and working groups of the Commission on Human Rights are some of the key elements for analysing, reporting on and monitoring human rights, which are essential for the

[98] E/1990/50.
[99] *Ibid.*, para. 59.
[100] See E/CN.4/1990/39, annex.
[101] See A/44/668, annex.
[102] See A/44/551-S/20870, annex.

37

0030

promotion and protection of human rights and fundamental freedoms in all countries,

Taking note of Commission on Human Rights decision 1990/115 of 9 March 1990,[103]

1. *Decides* to increase the membership of the Commission on Human Rights to fifty-three and to allocate the ten additional seats to the regional groups of Africa, Asia and Latin America and the Caribbean on the basis of the principle of equitable geographical distribution;

2. *Also decides* that the enlarged membership of the Commission on Human Rights shall be elected in 1991 and that the provisions contained in paragraphs 3 to 5 below shall take effect at the forty-eighth session of the Commission;

3. *Authorizes* the Commission on Human Rights to meet exceptionally between its regular sessions, provided that a majority of States members of the Commission so agree;

4. *Recommends* that the mandates of thematic rapporteurs and working groups established or to be established by the Commission shall, unless otherwise decided, be of three years' duration, requests the Secretary-General to provide the rapporteurs and working groups with all the assistance necessary to carry out their mandates in the best possible conditions, and calls on all Governments to co-operate fully with them and to support and promote their activities by ensuring unhampered access to all relevant sources of information;

5. *Decides* that, in the week following the session of the Commission on Human Rights, the Bureau shall meet to make suggestions about the organization of work of the Commission, including the effective use of conference time and facilities;

6. *Requests* the Secretary-General to prepare a report on the organizational implications of the present resolution for consideration by the Commission on Human Rights at its forty-seventh session, and requests the Commission to submit its observations to the Economic and Social Council at its first regular session of 1991.

14th plenary meeting
25 May 1990

1990/49. Implementation of the Programme of Action for the Second Decade to Combat Racism and Racial Discrimination

The Economic and Social Council,

Reaffirming the purpose set forth in the Charter of the United Nations of achieving international co-operation in solving international problems of an economic, social, cultural or humanitarian character and in promoting and encouraging respect for human rights and fundamental freedoms for all without distinction as to race, sex, language or religion,

Recalling the proclamation by the General Assembly, in its resolution 38/14 of 22 November 1983, of the Sec-

ond Decade to Combat Racism and Racial Discrimination,

Recalling also the Programme of Action for the Second Decade to Combat Racism and Racial Discrimination, approved by the General Assembly in its resolution 38/14 and contained in the annex thereto, to achieve the objectives of the Second Decade,

Reaffirming the plan of activities for the period 1990-1993, to be implemented by the Secretary-General in accordance with General Assembly resolution 42/47 of 30 November 1987, to which it is annexed, and recalling the activities which were proposed for the period 1985-1989,

Conscious of the responsibility conferred upon it by the General Assembly for co-ordinating and, in particular, evaluating the activities undertaken in the implementation of the Programme of Action for the Second Decade,

Bearing in mind, in particular, its mandate under General Assembly resolution 41/94 of 4 December 1986 to submit to the Assembly, during the period of the Second Decade, annual reports on the activities undertaken or contemplated to achieve the objectives of the Second Decade,

Having examined the report of the Secretary-General on the implementation of the Programme of Action for the Second Decade,[104]

Noting that despite the efforts of the international community, the principal objectives of the first Decade for Action to Combat Racism and Racial Discrimination and the first years of the Second Decade have not been attained, and that millions of human beings continue to be victims of varied forms of racism, racial discrimination and *apartheid,*

Welcoming the recent Declaration on *Apartheid* and its Destructive Consequences in Southern Africa,[105] unanimously adopted by the General Assembly at its sixteenth special session, which offers guidelines on how to end *apartheid* through genuine negotiations,

Noting with satisfaction the convening of a United Nations seminar on cultural dialogue between the countries of origin and the host countries of migrant workers, at Athens from 18 to 26 September 1989,

Noting with deep concern that the official invitations being extended to the President of South Africa by some countries could be construed to mean that pressure against the *apartheid* régime has been relaxed,

Stressing the need to continue the co-ordination of activities undertaken by various United Nations bodies and specialized agencies for the purpose of implementing the Programme of Action for the Second Decade,

1. *Reaffirms* the importance of achieving the objectives of the Second Decade to Combat Racism and Racial Discrimination;

2. *Takes note with appreciation* of the report of the Secretary-General on the implementation of the Programme of Action for the Second Decade to Combat

---

[103] See *Official Records of the Economic and Social Council, 1990, Supplement No. 2* and corrigendum (E/1990/22 and Corr.1), chap. II, sect. B.

[104] E/1990/20 and Add.1. (On 9 August 1990, two new addenda, E/1990/20/Add.2 and 3, were issued.)

[105] General Assembly resolution S-16/1, annex.

長 官 報 告 事 項

報 告 畢

1992. 8. 17.
國 際 機 構 局
國際聯合 2課 (46)

題 目 : 유고事態 관련 유엔 人權委 特別會議

8.13-14간 開催된 유고事態 관련 유엔 人權委 特別會議의 意義 等 關聯事項을 아래와 같이 報告드립니다.

1. 意 義

○ 緊急事態를 다루기 위한 人權委 最初의 特別會議
- 8.5. 美國, 各 委員國에 ~~유엔 人權委~~ 特別會議 開催 要請
- 8.10. 35個委員國의 會議召集 同意로 開催 決定
* 特別會議는 委員國 過半數의 同意로 開催
○ 향후 類似한 人權侵害狀況에 대한 先例가 됨.

2. 會議結果

○ 美國 提案 決議案이 60個國이 共同提案國 參與한 가운데 Consensus 採擇
- 우리나라도 옵서버로서 共同提案國 參與
○ 決議案 要旨
- 모든 紛爭 當事國들의 即刻的인 人權侵害 行爲 中斷
- 舊유고 地域內 人權侵害 狀況調査를 위해 Special Rapporteur 任命
(前 폴란드 首相 Tadeus Mazowiecki 旣任命)

3. 特記事項 : 우리나라의 옵서버 資格 共同提案國 參與 事例

○ 92.3. 女性地位委員會 (對女性暴力問題 決意)
○ 92.7. 經濟社會理事會 (社會開發頂上會議 開催 決意)

4. 言論對策

○ ~~報道資料 作成.~~ 別途. 끝
해당없음.

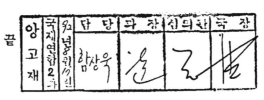

0032

長官報告事項

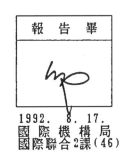

報 告 畢

1992. 8. 17.
國際機構局
國際聯合2課(46)

題 目 : 유고事態 관련 유엔 人權委 特別會議

> 8.13-14간 開催된 유고事態 관련 유엔 人權委 特別會議의 意義 等
> 關聯事項을 아래와 같이 報告드립니다.

1. 意 義

- 緊急事態를 다루기 위한 人權委 最初의 特別會議
  - 8.5. 美國, 各 委員國에 特別會議 開催 要請
  - 8.10. 35個委員國의 會議召集 同意로 開催 決定
  - * 特別會議는 委員國 過半數의 同意로 開催
- 향후 類似한 人權侵害狀況에 대한 先例가 됨.

2. 會議結果

- 美國 提案 決議案이 60個國이 共同提案國 參與한 가운데 Consensus 採擇
  - 우리나라도 옵서버로서 共同提案國 參與
- 決議案 要旨
  - 모든 紛爭 當事國들의 卽刻的인 人權侵害 行爲 中斷
  - 舊유고 地域内 人權侵害 狀況調査를 위해 Special Rapporteur 任命
    (前 폴란드 首相 Tadeus Mazowiecki 旣任命)

3. 特記事項 : 우리나라의 옵서버 資格 共同提案國 參與 事例

- 92.3. 女性地位委員會 (對女性暴力問題 決意)
- 92.7. 經濟社會理事會 (社會開發頂上會議 開催 決意)

4. 言論對策

- 해당사항 없음. 끝.

0033

유고사태 관련 유엔 인권위 특별회의 관련 설명자료

1992.8.18.
국제연합2과

1. 제네바에서 8.13-14간 개최된 유고사태 관련 유엔 인권위원회 특별회의가
   미국대표인 J.Bolton 국무차관보가 제안한 결의안을 60개국이 공동제안국으로
   참여, 콘센서스(Consensus)로 채택한 가운데 폐막되었음.

2. 동 특별회의는 8.5. 미국의 유엔 인권위원회 특별회의 개최 요청에 따라
   8.10. 35개 인권위원국의 회의소집 동의하에 8.13-14간 개최된 것으로,
   특별회의는 위원국 과반수의 동의로 개최될 수 있으며, 향후 인권관련 긴급
   사태시 선례가 될 수 있다는 점에 금번 특별회의의 의의가 있다고 할 것임.
   * 특별회의 제도는 1990년도 경사리 결의(1990/48)에 따라 신설

3. 동 결의의 요지는 (1) 자의적으로 수용된 모든 사람들의 즉시 석방, (2) 국제
   적십자사의 구 유고지역내 모든 수용소, 형무소의 접근 허용, (3) 모든 분쟁
   당사국들의 즉각적인 인권침해 행위중단, (4) 구 유고지역내 인권침해 상황
   조사를 위한 특별보고관(Special Rapporteur)의 임명 및 진상조사 등임.
   * 특별보고관으로는 전 폴란드 수상 Tadeus Mazowiecki가 임명되었음.

4. 금번 유엔 인권위원회 특별회의는 긴급 사태를 다루기 위한 인권위원회 최초의
   특별회의로서 대부분의 국가들이 금번 회의를 소집한 미국의 노력을 평가하고,
   구 유고연방내에서 벌어지고 있는 소위 "인종말살(Ethnic Cleansing)"을
   강도높게 비난하였음.

5. 금번 회의에서 우리나라는 유고사태의 심각성에 대한 공동인식 표명 및
   국제적 대처 노력에 적극 참여한다는 점과 93년 이후 인권위원국으로서의
   우리의 위상 등을 고려하여 옵서버로 참가하였을 뿐 아니라 결의안에도
   공동제안국(co-sponsor)으로 참여하였으며, 앞으로도 국제적인 인권문제에
   대하여 적극적인 참여 자세를 견지해 나아갈 것임.

1

0034

(1) 유엔가입후 우리나라가 옵서버로서 공동제안국에 참여한 사례

　　o　92.3.　여성지위위원회 (대여성 폭력문제 결의)

　　　　-　여성폭력에 대한 선언 초안 작성을 위한 실무위 개최 결정

　　　　-　모든 회원국에 대해 행정, 사회, 교육적 방법을 통한 여성보호

　　　　　강화 요청

　　o　92.7.　경제사회이사회 (사회개발 정상회의 개최 결의)

　　　　-　1995년초 사회개발 정상회의 개최를 유엔총회에 권고

　　o　92.8.　인권위원회 유고사태 관련 특별회의 (구 유고영역내 인권상황

　　　　　결의)

(2) 경제사회이사회에서 옵서버의 지위

　　o　경제사회이사회 및 그 산하기구 회의에서 옵서버 국가는 결의안

　　　표결에는 참여할수 없으나, 발언 및 결의안의 공동제안국(co-sponsor)

　　　참여가 가능함.

2

외 무 부

종 별 :

번 호 : UNW-2243   일   시 : 92 0818 1940

수 신 : 장관(연이,동구이)사본:제네바,미,유고대사(직송필)

발 신 : 주 유엔 대사

제 목 : 구 유고 인권 문제 토의(ECOSOC)

대:WUN - 2005

금 8.18 당지에서 92 경사리실질회기 속개회의가 개최되어 대호 인권위특별 회의가 권고한 표제관련 결정을 투표없이 채택하였는바 주요사항 아래 보고함.

1. 회의 경과

가. J. GUERRERO 부의장은 경사리 결의 1990/48에따라 인권위 특별회의가 8.13-8.14간 제네바에서개최되어 결의 1992/S-1/1의 채택을 ECOSOC에 권고하였다고 설명함.

(이어 사무국관계자가 금번 결의의 시행에 약10만의 예산이 소요될것임을 언급함)

나. 금일회의에서는 미국, 영국 (EC 대표),터키(이스람기구 대표), 카나다, 러시아, 모로코, 오지리,호주, 일본, 쿠바, 브라질, 유고, 말레이지아등13개국대표가 발언하였는바, 쿠바와 유고의 모든국가는 상기 인권위의 결의를 전폭 지지한다는입장이었으며 주요국 발언 요지는 아래와 같음.

ㅇ 미 국

- 인권위의 신속한 조치 평가

- 전 YUGO내 대규모 인권위반 사태에 심각한 우려표명

- 특별보고자의 임무수행에 협조 필요성언급

ㅇ 터 키

- 세르비아의 보스니아내 인종구성 변경기도 비난

- 모스렘 학대사태 규탄

ㅇ 유 고

- 보스니아 사태는 인종간 내란이며 유고와는 무관함.

- 억류 시설의 존재부인 및 유고에 대한 일방적 규탄행위 비난

국기국   구주국   중계

- 관계당사자간 평화적 해결촉구

ㅇ 쿠 바

- 인권위 특별회의 소집을 절차상 이유를 들어비판하고 결의안중 특별
보고자의임무에 이의 제기

다. 상기 결의안이 투표없이 채택된 이후 중국,멕시코, 콜롬비아대표는 결의안
14항, 15항이사무총장에게 특별 보고자의 보고를 안보리에제공하도록(MAKE AVAILABLE)
요청한것은잘못되었다고 발언하였음. (중국대표는 안보리가인권문제에 대하여 권능이
없으므로 자국입장을유보한다고 발언하였으며 콜롬비아, 멕시코도 유사한내용으로
이의를 제기하였음)

2. 관찰 및 평가

ㅇ 금번 미국의 주도로 보스니아 사태가인권침해측면에서도 부각되어
예외적인인권위 특별회의가 개최되고 즉시 ECOSOC 에서인권위의 권고사항을 승인 하게
된것은인권문제가 국제사회에서 정치적 이슈로 전화하는단적인 예를 보여준 것으로
평가됨.

ㅇ 또한 인권문제가 간접적으로나마 유엔 안보리와연계된것은 법률적으로는 논의의
여지가 있으나최근 안보리의 권한 확대 및 역할강화 추세와맥을 같이
하는것으로분석됨.

ㅇ 다만 금번 결의안이 특별 보고자 (MAZOWIECKI 전폴란드 수상)로 하여금
현지방문후 92.8.28까지 최초보고서를 제출토록 한것은 봉상 유엔활동에소요되는
시간으로 보나 그방법으로 보아 상당히이례적인 것으로 보임

(대사 유종하 - 국장)

유고사태 관련 유엔 인권위 특별회의 및 경사리 속개회의 관련 설명자료

1992. 8. 19.
국제연합2과

1. 유엔 인권위 특별회의 (92.8.13-8.14)

가. 제네바에서 8.13-14간 개최된 유고사태 관련 유엔 인권위원회 특별회의가
   미국대표인 J.Bolton 국무차관보가 제안한 결의안을 60개국이 공동제안국
   으로 참여, 콘센서스(Consensus)로 채택한 가운데 폐막되었음.

나. 특별회의는 8.5. 미국의 유엔 인권위원회 특별회의 개최 요청에 따라
   8.10. 35개 인권위원국의 회의소집 동의하에 8.13-14간 개최된 것으로,
   특별회의는 위원국 과반수의 동의로 개최될 수 있으며, 향후 인권관련 긴급
   사태시 선례가 될 수 있다는 점에 금번 특별회의의 의의가 있다고 할 것임.
   * 특별회의 제도는 1990년도 경사리 결의(1990/48)에 따라 신설

다. 결의의 요지는 (1) 자의적으로 수용된 모든 사람들의 즉시 석방, (2) 국제
   적십자사의 구 유고지역내 모든 수용소, 형무소의 접근 허용, (3) 모든 분쟁
   당사국들의 즉각적인 인권침해 행위중단, (4) 구 유고지역내 인권침해 상황
   조사를 위한 특별보고관(Special Rapporteur)의 임명 및 진상조사 등임.
   * 특별보고관으로는 전 폴란드 수상 Tadeus Mazowiecki가 임명되었음.

라. 금번 유엔 인권위원회 특별회의는 긴급 사태를 다루기 위한 인권위원회
   최초의 특별회의로서 대부분의 국가들이 금번 회의를 소집한 미국의 노력을
   평가하고, 구 유고연방내에서 벌어지고 있는 소위 "인종청소(Ethnic
   Cleansing)"을 강도높게 비난하였음.

1

0038

다. 금번 회의에서 우리나라는 유고사태의 심각성에 대한 공동인식 표명 및
   국제적 대처 노력에 적극 참여한다는 점과 93년 이후 인권위원국으로서의
   우리의 위상 등을 고려하여 옵서버로 참가하였을 뿐 아니라 결의안에도
   공동제안국(co-sponsor)으로 참여하였으며, 앞으로도 국제적인 인권문제에
   대하여 적극적인 참여 자세를 견지해 나아갈 것임.

2. 경사리 속개회의 (92.8.18)

가. 8.18. 뉴욕에서 개최된 92년도 경사리 속개회의는 인권위원회 특별회의가
   경사리에 권고한 유고사태 관련 결정을 표결없이 채택함.
   - Mazowiecki 특별보고관은 92.8.18까지 최초보고서를 제출

나. 동 회의에서는 미국, 영국(EC 대표), 터키(이슬람기구 대표), 유고, 쿠바,
   일본, 말레이지아 등 13개국 대표가 발언하였는 바, 쿠바와 유고를 제외한
   국가들은 인권위 결의를 적극 지지하는 입장을 표명함. 쿠바는 인권위
   특별회의 소집을 절차상 이유로 비판하고, 결의중 특별보고관의 임무에
   이의를 제기함.

다. 결의안 채택후 중국, 멕시코, 콜롬비아 대표는 결의 제14 ,제15항에서
   사무총장에 대해 특별보고관의 보고서를 안보리에 제공하도록 요청한 것은
   안보리가 인권문제에 대하여 권능이 없음으로 잘못되었다고 발언함.

2

0039

(1) 유엔가입후 우리나라가 옵서버로서 공동제안국에 참여한 사례

    o 92.3. 여성지위위원회 (대여성 폭력문제 결의)

    - 여성폭력에 대한 선언 초안 작성을 위한 실무위 개최 결정

    - 모든 회원국에 대해 행정, 사회, 교육적 방법을 통한 여성보호

       강화 요청

    o 92.7. 경제사회이사회 (사회개발 정상회의 개최 결의)

    - 1995년초 사회개발 정상회의 개최를 유엔총회에 권고

    o 92.8. 인권위원회 유고사태 관련 특별회의 (구 유고영역내 인권상황

       결의)

(2) 경제사회이사회에서 옵서버의 지위

    o 경제사회이사회 및 그 산하기구 회의에서 옵서버 국가는 결의안

       표결에는 참여할수 없으나, 발언 및 결의안의 공동제안국(co-sponsor)

       참여가 가능함.

(3) 오지리가 제안한 인권침해 관례 긴급절차

    o 오지리는 91.9월 제46차 유엔총회에 이어 92.2월 제48차 인권위 회의시

       아래 내용의 긴급절차 채택을 제안

    - 유엔 사무총장이 분야별 개인 전문가 명단을 유지

    - 회원국 서면요청이 있을 경우 사무총장은 인권위 위원국 다수의

       동의를 얻어 동 절차 발동

    - 5인의 전문가 그룹이 구성되어 비밀보고서를 작성, 동 보고서에

       대한 해당국 의견을 요청

    - 다수 위원국의 동의가 있을 경우, 보고서와 해당국 의견을 인권위

       특별회의에 회부. 단, 다수의 동의가 없을 경우 UN총회 또는 인권위

       정기 회의중 먼저 개최되는 회의에 회부

1

0040

주 제 네 바 대 표 부

20, Route de Pre-Bois, POB 566 / (022) 791-0111 / (022) 791-0525(FAX)

문서번호 제네(정) 2032 - 750

시행일자 1992. 8. 21

수신 장 관

참조 국제기구국장

선결			지시		
접수	일자시간		결재		
	번호		공람		
처리과					
담당자					

제목 유고사태 관련 유엔인권위 특별회의   48013

92.8.13-14간 개최된 표제회의 문서 별첨 송부합니다.

첨부 : 문서 1셋트 끝.

92. 8. 21

주 제 네 바 대

0041

＇Ｋ

주 국 련 대 표 부

주국련 203125- 1067   1992. 10. 1.

수신 장 관

참조 국제기구국장

제목 인권위 특별회기

            92.8.13-14 당지개최, 인권위원회 특별회기 보고서(최종문서)를 별첨

송부합니다.

     첨 부 : E/1992/22/Add.1/Rev.1. 끝.

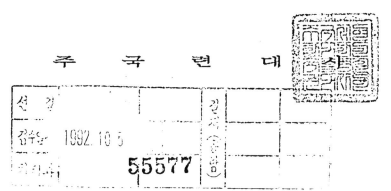

0042

발 신 전 보

WGV-1870   921202 1641 WG

분류번호	보존기간	

번   호 : _____   종별 : 암호송신

수   신 : 주   제네바   대사. 총영사♣♣♣♣♣

발   신 : 장 관 (연이)

제   목 : 보스니아 사태 관련 유엔 인권위 개최

    귀지발 외신보도에 따르면, 구유고 인권문제를 논의하기 위한 유엔

인권위원회가 11.30-12.1간 귀지에서 개최되었다는 바, 관련사항 파악

보고바람. 끝.

                                        (국제기구국장 김재섭)

보안통제	

앙고재	93년12월2일	유엔2과	기안자 성명 설경호	과장	심의관	국장 전결	차관	장관

외신과통제

0043

유엔인권위,보스니아 사태 논의

　　(제네바.베오그라드 AFP.UPI=聯合) 보스니아 헤르체고비나 내전은 이민족의 대량 학살과 중족 밀실을 목적으로 의도적으로 수행되고있으며 이같은 만행을 자행하고있는 주범은 세르비아계 민병대라고 유엔에 제출된 보스니아내전의 인권유린 문제 특별조사보고서가 밝혔다.

　　보스니아.헤르체고비나의 인권 문제에 관한 유엔특별조사위원인 타데우스 마조비에츠키 전 폴란드충리는 보스니아 내전에서의 이민족 대량학살문제 논의를 위해 지난달 30일 제네바에서 개막된 유엔인권위원회회의에서 보고를 통해 이른바 "인종청소"로 불리우는 이민족 말실 행위는 내전에서 비롯된 결과가 아니며 오히려 내전을 일으키게한 근본 동기라고 지적했다.

　　이 보고서는 유엔이 보스니아에서의 이민족 학살 행위를 전쟁범죄로 규정하고 이에대한 재판을 실시할 경우 기본적인 조사자료로 채택된다.

　　그는 현지 실사를 통해 작성한 이 보고서에서 보스니아 회고도와 크로아티아인도 부분적으로 이민족 말살행위의 책임이 있지만 이같은 만행의 주범은 세르비아계 민병대라고 지적했다.

　　1일까지 이틀간 개최되는 이번 유엔인권위원회 회의에서는 마조비에츠키 특별조사위원의 보고를 바탕으로 보스니아-헤르체고비나에서 자행되는 대량 학살 문제에대한 대책이 논의되며 미국과 터키가 궁동 제안한 결의안의 채택 여부가 결정된다.

　　이 결의안은 보스니아의 이민족 학살 참극과 관련 세르비아당국에 "1차적 책임이 있다"고 규탄하고 계획적인 인종말살 행위를 금지하고있는 유엔협약에 근거해 전세계 모든 국가들에게 보스니아의 이민족 학살 행위에 대한 적절한 판단과 대응을 촉구하고있다.

　　이번 회의에서 모리스 에이브람 미국 대표는 세르비아민병대의 만행이 유엔의 근본 원칙과 가치에 도전하고있다고 비판하고 학살 만행의 범죄자를 유엔이 뉘른베르크 전범재판과 같은 특별 법정을 통해 단죄해야한다고 촉구했다.

　　한편 신유고연방와 밀란 파니치 충리는 오는 20일 실시되는 세르비아의 대통령선거에 입후보,재차 대통령 선거에 나선 세르비아의 실력자 스로보단 밀로세비치 대통령과의 대결을 선언했다.

　　그러나 세르비아의 대통령선거관리위원회는 대통령 선거 입후보자는 선거 궁고일 이전 최소한 1년이상 세르비아에 거주한 국민이어야한다는 조항을 근거로 파니치 충리의 입후보 자격을 문재삼고있어 파니치 충리의 출마가 인정될 지는 아직 불투명하다.

27　　　　　　　　　　0044

신 유고연방 정부는 파니치 총리의 대통령 출마에 반발해 지난달 30일까지 친 밀로셰비치 각료 4명이 잇따라 사임하는등 진통을 겪고있다.

부투로스 부트로스-갈리 유엔사무총장은 크로아티아가 유엔평화유지군의 활동에 협력하지 않고있다고 비난하고 현 상황이 계속될 경우 유엔평화유지군은 크로아티아 를 떠나거나 아니면 영구히 주둔해야하는 사태에 이를 것이라고 경고했다.

보스니아의 세르비아계 민병대와 크로아티아군의 휴전 협정이 지난달 30일 새벽 0시(현지시간)부터 발효됐으나 보스니아와 크로아티아의 접경지대에서만 일부 휴전 이 이뤄지고 다른 지역에서는 전쟁이 계속됐다.(끝)

```
YUGOSLAV-BRITAIN 12-1
   BRITAIN TO ACCEPT 4,000 REFUGEES FROM FORMER YUGOSLAVIA
      BY JOANNE MERRIWEATHER
   LONDON (UPI) -- BRITAIN ANNOUNCED MONDAY IT WOULD ACCEPT A TOTAL
OF 4,000 REFUGEES AND THEIR FAMILIES FROM THE FORMER YUGOSLAVIA.
   FOREIGN OFFICE MINISTER CHARLES WARDLE SAID BRITAIN AGREED TO TAKE
IN A FURTHER 850 HIGH PRIORITY REFUGEES AND THEIR DEPENDENTS IN
ADDITION TO THE 150 ANNOUNCED BY HOME SECRETARY KENNETH CLARK ON NOV.
5, BRINGING THE TOTAL TO AROUND 4,000.
   +WE ARE READY TO RECEIVE THE FIRST 150 AND ARE WAITING FOR THEM TO
ARRIVE,+ WARDLE SAID.
   WARDLE SAID ARRANGEMENTS FOR THE TRANSFER OF THE REFUGEES WAS IN
THE HANDS OF THE UNITED NATIONS HIGH COMMISSION FOR REFUGEES AND THE
INTERNATIONAL RED CROSS.
   ONLY LAST MONTH BRITAIN REFUSED TO ACCEPT A GROUP OF REFUGEES
STRANDED ON THE BORDER WITH AUSTRIA, SAYING THEY WERE NOT HIGH
PRIORITY CASES.
   THE 4,000 REFUGEES WILL BE ADMITTED ON A TEMPORARY REFUGEE BASIS,
WHICH MEANS THEY WILL BE ALLOWED TO STAY FOR AN INITIAL 6 MONTHS AND
THEN A DECISION WILL BE TAKEN ON THEIR FUTURE AT THAT POINT, A
GOVERNMENT SPOKESMAN SAID.
   HE ADDED THAT THE REFUGEES WERE BEING TAKEN FROM
BOSNIA-HERZEGOVINA TO CAMPS IN KARLOVAC, CROATIA IN BATCHES OF
500-1,000, WHERE THEY WERE BEING PROCESSED BY THE RELIEF
ORGANISATIONS.
   BRITAIN WOULD TAKE BETWEEN 150-250 FROM EACH BATCH, WHICH WERE DUE
TO ARRIVE EVERY FOUR TO FIVE WEEKS, THE SPOKESMAN SAID. THE REFUGEES
FAMILIES WOULD FOLLOW LATER.
   TEMPORARY ACCOMMODATION HAS BEEN ARRANGED FOR THE INITIAL GROUP OF
REFUGEES IN LONDON, CAMBRIDGE AND SURREY AND THE REFUGEE COUNCIL WILL
ARRANGE PERMANENT ACCOMMODATION LATER, WARDLE SAID.
   THE BRITISH RED CROSS WILL THEN LIAISE WITH THE ICRC TO TRACE THE
DEPENDENTS OF THE DETAINEES AND ARRANGEMENTS WILL BE MADE IN
CONSULTATION WITH THE FOREIGN AND COMMONWEALTH OFFICE AND VOLUNTARY
ORGANISATIONS TO BRING THEM TO BRITAIN, WARDLE SAID.
   THE WAR IN BOSNIA-HERZEGOVINA ERUPTED IN LATE MARCH WHEN SERBIAN
FORCES IN THE REPUBLIC, WITH MILITARY AND POLITICAL ASSISTANCE FROM
THE COMMUNIST SERBIA, LAUNCHED A LAND-GRAB CAMPAIGN TO RIP OFF A
SELF-DECLARED SERBIAN STATE FROM THE REPUBLIC.
   BOSNIA-HERZEGOVINA IS MADE UP OF 1.9 MILLION MUSLIM SLAVS, 1.4
MILLION CHRISTIAN ORTHODOX SERBS AND 750,000 ROMAN CATHOLIC CROATS.
   SERBIAN FORCES NOW CONTROL ABOUT 70 PERCENT OF BOSNIA-HERZEGOVINA,
THE TERRITORY OF THE +SERBIAN STATE+ FOR THE SERBS WHO MAKE ONLY 31
PERCENT OF THE REPUBLIC'S 4.4 MILLION POPULATION.
   JAB-EKMI
UPI 00:10 GMT
```

28

0045

```
=12010024
NNNN
```

외　무　부

종　별 :

번　호 : GVW-2260　　　　　　　　　　일　시 : 92 1202 1940

수　신 : 장관(연이) 사본: 주유엔대사(본부중계필)

발　신 : 주 제네바 대사

제　목 : 구유고 인권문제 관련 유엔인권위 특별회의

　　대: WGV-1870

　　92.11.30-12.1 간 당지에서 개최된 표제회의 결과 아래 보고함.

　　1. 회의개최

　　0 11.16 터키가 유엔인권위 의장(헝가리, SOLT) 에게 지난 8 월 유고사태 특별인권위 결정에 따라 작성 유엔총회에 제출된 SPECIAL REPPORTEUR (폴란드 MAZOWLECKI) 의 구유고지역 인권상황보고서 (A/47/666) 검토를 위한 긴급인권위 소집을 요청하였으며 또한 11.18 미국이 BLANCA 사무차장에게 동건 관련 유엔인권위 특별 회의 소집을 요청, 위원국 대부분의 찬성을 얻어 개최됨.

　　2. 유고지위 문제

　　0 회의초반 미국, EC(영국), 일본, 카나다, 호주, 오지리등이 유고의 인권위원국 자격문제를 제기하였으나, 유고대표는 UN 내 유고지위에 관한 UN 사무차장 (LEGAL COUNSEL) 의 의견서(A/47/485)를 원용 유고의 위원국지위에 문제가 없음을 천명함.

　　3. 결의안 채택

　　0 미국은 아래 요지의 결의안을 제안하였으며, 서구 및 동구지역 17 개 옵서버국가 포함 총 52 개국이 공동 제안국으로 참여함

　　- 구유고지역내에서 벌어지고 있는 ETHNIC CLEANSING 에 대한 1 차적인 책임이 세르비아측에 있음을 인정하고 동 행위중단을 위한 영향력 행사 촉구

　　- 구유고지역내 모든 당사국에게 인권침해 행위 중단 촉구

　　- VUKOBAR 등 대량학살 행위 발생 보도지역에 대한 즉각적으로 조사 실시

　　- SPECIAL RAPPORTEUR 는 조사작업 계속 수행후 49 차 인권위에 보고서 제출

　　- 49 차 인권위에서 구유고지역 인권문제 검토(ITEM 12)

　　0 한편 상기 결의안에 대해 유고대표는 SPCIAL REPPROTEUR 의 보고서에 사실과

국기국	장관	차관	1차보	분석관	정와대	안기부	중계

다른 내용이 많이 포함되어 있음을 지적하고 이를 반박하는 내용을 공식문서로 제출하였으며, 따라서 이에 기초한 결의안 채택에 동의 할수 없음을 천명하고 표결을 요청하였음.

O 결국 상기 결의안은 표결(ROLL CALL) 로 채택되었는바, 부표결과는 찬성 45: 반대 1(유고) : 기권 1(쿠바)이며 소말리아등 6 개국은 불참함.

4. 상기 결의안 별첨 FAX 송부하며 기타 관련문서는 금파편 송부함.

첨부: 결의안(GVW(F)-0724). 끝

(대사 박수길-국장)

주 제 네 바 대 표 부

번 호 : GV제(F) - 0724   년월일 : 2/202   시간 : 1945

수 신 : 장   관 (연이)

발 신 : 주 제네바대사

제 목 : 첨부

총 6 매(표지포함)

브 안 등 제	✓

의신규 등 제	

0048

724-6-1

**UNITED
NATIONS**

E

Economic and Social Council

Distr.
LIMITED

E/CN.4/1992/S-2/L.2
30 November 1992

Original: ENGLISH

COMMISSION ON HUMAN RIGHTS
Second special session
November - December 1992
Agenda item 3

LETTER DATED 16 NOVEMBER 1992 FROM THE AMBASSADOR OF THE REPUBLIC OF
TURKEY TO THE REPUBLIC OF HUNGARY ADDRESSED TO THE CHAIRMAN OF THE
COMMISSION ON HUMAN RIGHTS AND LETTER DATED 18 NOVEMBER 1992
FROM THE CHARGE D'AFFAIRES A.I. OF THE PERMANENT MISSION OF THE
UNITED STATES OF AMERICA TO THE UNITED NATIONS OFFICE AT GENEVA
ADDRESSED TO THE UNDER-SECRETARY-GENERAL FOR HUMAN RIGHTS

Albania*, Argentina, Australia, Austria, Bangladesh, Bahrain*, Belgium*,
Bulgaria, Chile, Colombia, Costa Rica, Czech and Slovak Federal Republic,
Denmark*, Finland*, France, Germany, Greece*, Hungary, Iceland*, Ireland*,
Italy, Luxembourg*, Madagascar, Mexico, Netherlands, Norway*, Peru, Poland*,
Portugal, Romania*, Senegal, Slovenia*, Spain*, Sweden*, Switzerland*,
Tunisia, Turkey*, United Kingdom of Great Britain and Northern Ireland,
United States of America and Zambia: draft resolution

* In accordance with rule 69, paragraph 3, of the rules of procedure of
the functional commissions of the Economic and Social Council.

GE.92-14753 (E)

0049

724-6-2

E/CN.4/1992/S-2/L.2
page 2

<u>The situation of human rights in the
territory of the former Yugoslavia</u>

<u>The Commission on Human Rights</u>,

Meeting in special session,

<u>Guided</u> by the principles embodied in the Charter of the United Nations,
the Universal Declaration of Human Rights, the International Covenants on
Human Rights, the International Convention on the Elimination of All Forms of
Racial Discrimination, the Convention on the Prevention and Punishment of the
Crime of Genocide, the Convention Against Torture and Other Cruel, Inhuman or
Degrading Treatment or Punishment, and international humanitarian law,
including the Geneva Conventions of 12 August 1949 for the protection of war
victims and the Additional Protocols thereto of 1977,

<u>Aware</u> of its responsibility to promote and encourage respect for human
rights and fundamental freedoms for all, and to prevent violations of such
rights,

<u>Deeply concerned</u> at the human tragedy in the former Yugoslavia and at the
continuing grave, massive and systematic violations of human rights occurring
there, particularly in the areas of Bosnia and Herzegovina under Serbian
control,

<u>Recalling</u> its resolution 1992/S-1/1,

<u>Noting with appreciation</u> the efforts of the Special Rapporteur appointed
pursuant to resolution 1992/S-1/1, as well as <u>those</u> of the Chairman of the
Working Group on Arbitrary Detention, the Special Rapporteur on extrajudicial,
summary or arbitrary executions, the Special Rapporteur on the question of
torture and the Representative of the Secretary-General on internally
displaced persons, who accompanied the Special Rapporteur on one or both of
his missions,

<u>Noting with alarm</u> the three reports of the Special Rapporteur on the
situation of human rights in the former Yugoslavia (A/47/666 - S/24809,
E/CN.4/1992/S-1/9 and E/CN.4/1992/S-1/10),

<u>Gravely concerned</u> in particular at the continuing, <u>odious</u> [hateful,] practice of
<u>ethnic cleansing</u>, which is the direct cause of the vast majority of human
rights violations and whose principal victims are the Muslim population
virtually threatened with extermination, which the Special Rapporteur reports
has continued, and in some regions intensified, in an effort to create a <u>fait
accompli</u> in disregard of international commitments, in particular the
statement of principles and the programme of action of the London Conference,
entered into by those who carry out such ethnic cleansing, and recalling, as
noted in its resolution 1992/S-1/1, that ethnic cleansing is aimed at the
dislocation or destruction of national, ethnic, racial or religious groups,

<u>Alarmed</u> that although the conflict in Bosnia and Herzegovina is not a
religious conflict, it has been characterized by the systematic destruction

0050

profane: treat disrespectfully.

and profanation of mosques, Catholic churches and other places of worship, as
well as other sites of cultural heritage, in particular in areas currently or
previously under Serbian control,

Deeply concerned that the human rights situation in the former Yugoslavia
has resulted in more than two and a half million refugees and displaced
persons and at the catastrophic humanitarian situation now prevailing,

Recalling with appreciation the continuing efforts of the International
Conference on the Former Yugoslavia and the Co-Chairman of its Steering
Committee, including their proposals for the constitution for the Republic of
Bosnia and Herzegovina designed to protect human rights on the basis of
fundamental international human rights instruments,

1.   Commends the Special Rapporteur for his activities to date, and in
particular his two missions and his reports;

2.   Condemns in the strongest terms all violations of human rights in
the former Yugoslavia, including killings, torture, beatings, rape,
disappearances, destruction of houses and other acts or threats of violence
aimed at forcing individuals to leave their homes, as identified by the
Special Rapporteur;

3.   Categorically condemns the ethnic cleansing being carried out, in
particular in Bosnia and Herzegovina, recognizing that the Serbian leadership
in territories under their control in Bosnia and Herzegovina, the Yugoslav
army and the political leadership of the Republic of Serbia bear primary
responsibility for this reprehensible practice;

4.   Demands an immediate end to the practice of ethnic cleansing, and in
particular demands that the Republic of Serbia use its influence with the
self-proclaimed Serbian authorities in Bosnia and Herzegovina and Croatia to
bring the practice of ethnic cleansing to an immediate end and to reverse the
effects of that practice, re-emphasizing the rights of refugees, displaced
persons and other victims of ethnic cleansing to return to their homes and the
invalidity of acts made under duress;

5.   Affirms that States are to be held accountable for violations of
human rights which their agents commit upon the territory of another State;

6.   Condemns in particular the violations of human rights and
humanitarian law in connection with detention, including killings, torture and
the systematic practice of rape, and calls upon all parties in the former
Yugoslavia to close immediately all detention centres not authorized by and in
compliance with the Geneva Conventions of 12 August 1949 and to release
immediately in conditions of safety all persons arbitrarily or illegally
detained;

7.   Condemns also the indiscriminate shelling of cities and civilian
areas, the systematic terrorization and murder of non-combatants, the
destruction of vital services, the besieging of cities, and the use of
military force against civilian populations and relief operations by all
sides, recognizing that the main responsibility lies with Serbian forces;

724-6-ℂ

0051

E/CN.4/1992/S-2/L.2
page 4

8. Calls upon all parties in the former Yugoslavia, and especially those
most responsible, to cease violations of human rights and international
humanitarian law immediately and to take appropriate steps to apprehend and
punish those guilty of perpetrating or authorizing them; *take into police control*

9. Expresses deep concern at the number of disappearances and missing
persons in the former Yugoslavia and calls on all parties to make all possible
efforts to account for those missing;

10. Welcomes the establishment by the Security Council in its
resolution 780 (1992) of 6 October 1992 of a Commission of Experts to examine
and analyse information relating to violations of international humanitarian
law and encourages the closest possible cooperation between the Special
Rapporteur and the Commission of Experts, recommends that this Commission be
granted the staff and resources necessary to enable it to act effectively, and
requests the Commission of Experts to provide its conclusions to the
Secretary-General in order to allow the Security Council to consider further
appropriate steps towards bringing those accused to justice;

11. Reaffirms that all persons who perpetrate or authorize crimes
against humanity or other grave breaches of international humanitarian law are
individually responsible for those breaches and that the international
community will exert every effort to bring them to justice, and calls on all
parties to provide all pertinent information to the Commission of Experts in
accordance with Security Council resolution 780 (1992);

12. Calls upon all States to consider the extent to which the acts
committed in Bosnia and Herzegovina and in Croatia constitute genocide, in
accordance with the Convention on the Prevention and Punishment of the Crime
of Genocide;

13. Urges the Commission of Experts, with the assistance of the Centre
for Human Rights, to arrange for an immediate and urgent investigation by
qualified experts of a mass grave near Vukovar and other mass grave sites and
places where mass killings are reported to have taken place, and requests the
General Assembly to provide the resources necessary for this undertaking;

14. Expresses its grave concern at the information contained in the
third report of the Special Rapporteur (A/47/666 - S/24809) on the dangerous
situation in Kosovo, Sandzak and Vojvodina, and urges all parties in those
areas to engage in a meaningful dialogue under the auspices of the
International Conference on the Former Yugoslavia, to act with utmost
restraint and to settle disputes in full compliance with human rights and
freedoms, and calls on the Serbian authorities to refrain from the use of
force and immediately to stop the practice of ethnic cleansing, and to respect
fully the rights of persons belonging to ethnic communities or minorities in
order to prevent the extension of the conflict to other parts of the former
Yugoslavia;

15. Welcomes the call of the Special Rapporteur for the opening of
humanitarian relief corridors to prevent the imminent death of tens of
thousands of persons in besieged cities;

0052

72R-6-5

E/CN.4/1992/S-2/L.2
page 5

16. Welcomes Security Council resolution 787 (1992) of 16 November 1992 in which it invites the Secretary-General in consultation with the United Nations High Commissioner for Refugees and other relevant agencies, to study the possibility and the requirements for the promotion of safe areas for humanitarian purposes and the recommendation of the Special Rapporteur for the creation of such security zones for the protection of displaced persons, while keeping in mind that the international community must not acquiesce in demographic changes caused by ethnic cleansing;

17. Affirms that all the parties in the former Yugoslavia share the responsibility for finding peaceful solutions through negotiations under the auspices of the International Conference on the Former Yugoslavia, and welcomes the acceptance by the Government of Bosnia and Herzegovina of the constitutional proposals of the Co-Chairmen as a basis for negotiations;

18. Requests the Special Rapporteur to continue his efforts, especially by carrying out such further missions to the former Yugoslavia as he deems necessary, to call on other existing mechanisms of the Commission on Human Rights to assist him and to report his findings and recommendations at its forty-ninth session, and requests the Secretary-General to continue to make the reports of the Special Rapporteur available to the Security Council;

19. Urges the Secretary-General to take steps to ensure the full and effective cooperation of all United Nations bodies to implement the present resolution and calls upon those bodies entrusted with human rights monitoring in the former Yugoslavia to cooperate closely with the Special Rapporteur and the Commission of Experts.

20. Requests the General Assembly and the Secretary-General, within the overall budgetary framework of the United Nations, to make all necessary resources available for the Special Rapporteur to carry out his mandate and to comply with the request of the Special Rapporteur for staff based in the territory of the former Yugoslavia to enhance effective continuous monitoring of the human rights situation there;

21. Decides to examine the situation of human rights in the former Yugoslavia at its forty-ninth session under agenda item 12.

0053

주 제 네 바 대 표 부

20, Route de Pre-Bois, POB 566 / (022) 791-0111 / (022) 791-0525(FAX)

문서번호 : 제네(정) 2031 - 1066

시행일자 : 1992.12. 3.

수신 : 장   관

참조 : 국제기구국장

선결			지시		
접수	일자시간		결재공람	대 사	
	번호	68762		차석대사	
처 리 자				참 사 관	
담 당 자				서 기 관	

제목 : 구 유고지역 인권문제 관련 특별유엔인권위

연 : GVW-2260

92. 12. 4

92. 11.30-12. 1간 당지 개최된 표제회의 관련 문서 별첨 송부합니다.

첨부 : 상기 문서. 끝.

주   제   네   바   대   사

0054

외 무 부

종   별 :

번   호 : SZW-0692   일   시 : 92 1212 0030

수   신 : 장 관(구이, 연이, 정보)

발   신 : 주 스위스 대사

제   목 : 스위스 93 국제인권협약개최 제의(자료응신 61호)

　　1. 주재국 FELBER 대통령은 12.9. 상하원 합동회의에서 유고사태 관련 다음내용 발표함.

　　2. 스위스는 그간 유고 분쟁해결을 위한국제회의에 참여하여 왔으며, 피난민 접수 및 원조제공 등으로 나름대로의 책임을 다하여 왔음을 강조, 유고내 분쟁이 계속되고 있음과 잔인행위가 자행되고 있음을 개탄하면서 무력에 의한 분쟁 해결행위가 하루속히 종식되어야 함을 호소함.

　　3. 동 성명은 또한 유고 사태 종식을 위하여 스위스가 93년중 국제인권협약회의개최를 제의할 계획임을 밝히고 있음.

　　4. 동 국제회의에서는 유엔 사무총장이 임명하는 전문가 위원회에서 작성한 국제인권협약 위반사례 조사결과를 토대로 심의하고, 인도적 범법자에 대한 책임을 묻기위한 재판소 창설을 제의하고 있음.

　　5. 동 대통령 성명문 정파편 송부함. 끝.

　　(대사 강대완-국장)

구주국　　국기국　　외정실　　안기부

외교문서 비밀해제: 한국 인권문제 15

한국 인권문제 유엔 반응 및 동향 2

초판인쇄 2024년 03월 15일
초판발행 2024년 03월 15일

지은이 한국학술정보(주)
펴낸이 채종준
펴낸곳 한국학술정보(주)
주 소 경기도 파주시 회동길 230(문발동)
전 화 031-908-3181(대표)
팩 스 031-908-3189
홈페이지 http://ebook.kstudy.com
E-mail 출판사업부 publish@kstudy.com
등 록 제일산-115호(2000. 6. 19)

ISBN 979-11-7217-069-1 94340
      979-11-7217-054-7 94340 (set)